Index to

The Modern Theatre

THE MODERN THEATRE

A collection of plays

selected by

MRS. ELIZABETH INCHBALD

First published London, 1811

in ten volumes

Reissued in 1968
in five volumes
by Benjamin Blom, Inc.

Benjamin Blom, Inc.

New York

THE

MODERN THEATRE;

A COLLECTION OF

SUCCESSFUL MODERN PLAYS,

AS ACTED AT

THE THEATRES ROYAL, LONDON.

PRINTED FROM THE PROMPT BOOKS UNDER THE AU-
THORITY OF THE MANAGERS.

SELECTED BY

MRS INCHBALD.

———

IN TEN VOLUMES.

———

VOL. VII.

I'LL TELL YOU WHAT.   WISE MAN OF THE EAST.
NEXT DOOR NEIGHBOURS.   PERCY.
TRIP TO SCARBOROUGH.

———

LONDON:

PRINTED FOR LONGMAN, HURST, REES, ORME, AND BROWN,
PATERNOSTER-ROW.

1811.

First published London, 1811
Reissued 1968,
by Benjamin Blom, Inc. Bx 10452

Library of Congress Catalog Card No. 67-13004

I'LL TELL YOU WHAT;

A

COMEDY,

IN FIVE ACTS.

AS PERFORMED AT THE

THEATRE-ROYAL, HAYMARKET.

BY

Mrs. INCHBALD.

VOL. VII.

DRAMATIS PERSONÆ.

MAJOR CYPRUS,	*Mr Palmer.*
MR ANTHONY EUSTON,	*Mr Bensley.*
COLONEL DOWNRIGHT,	*Mr Aickin.*
CHARLES EUSTON,	*Mr Bannister, jun.*
SIR GEORGE EUSTON,	*Mr Williamson.*
SIR HARRY HARMLESS,	*Mr R. Palmer.*
SERVANTS, *Messrs Ledger, Gaudry, and Lyons.*	
MR EUSTON,	*Mr Parsons.*
LADY EUSTON,	*Mrs Bulkley.*
LADY HARRIET CYPRUS,	*Mrs Bates.*
BLOOM,	*Mrs Riley.*
A YOUNG LADY,	*Miss Farren.*

I'LL TELL YOU WHAT.

ACT THE FIRST.

SCENE I.

A Room at Sir George Euston's.

Enter Mr. Euston, *followed by* Sir George.

Sir Geo. But, my dear uncle, why in such a passion?

Mr Eus. I can't help it—I am out of all patience! Did not I leave you one of the happiest men in the world?

Sir Geo. Well, and so you find me, Sir.

Mr Eus. 'Tis false—you are not happy—you can't be happy; 'tis false—and you shan't be happy.

Sir Geo. If you are resolved to make me otherwise, Sir—

Mr Eus. No, I am not resolved—'tis yourself
that is resolved. Did not I leave you one of the
happiest of men?—married to one of the most beautiful women in the world? Did not I give you my
blessing and a large fortune, and did I not stay and
see you father of a fine boy?—Then only just stept
over to visit my estate in St. Kitt's, and now, I'm
come back, here I find you married to another woman, and your first wife still *living*—and, egad, she
is married to another man!

Sir Geo. Dear uncle, I should certainly have
asked your opinion and my uncle Anthony's on the
subject, but your absence put it out of my power;
and it was universally believed the ship in which you
sailed was lost.

Mr Eus. Well, you will hear what my brother
will say to it.

Sir Geo. I trust, Sir, when I have explained
every thing, you will not only think me worthy of
your pardon, but even of being pleaded for to my
uncle.

Mr Eus. Not I, indeed—Nay, were it in my
power to do you any good, I would not; I shan't forgive you myself; much less ask him. But you are right
in fixing on me for a mediator; my brother pays
much regard to me, truly. I have been of infinite
service, to be sure, in reconciling him to his own poor
boy. Nay, did he not even (for my brother Anthony
would always be master, although he was the youngest) when I went to him to persuade him to forgive
poor Charles, his son, did he not even (instead of
my gaining him over, and getting something for the
poor boy,) did he not even draw me into a promise
never to do any thing for him myself? My brother
does what he pleases with me—but nobody else shall
—No, what I want in resolution to him, I'll make
up in obstinacy, to other people.

Sir Geo. Sir, if you will but hear the just pleas I have to offer—

Mr Eus. I will hear no pleas—What do you think my brother will say? Why, you inconsiderate boy! He had designed you for his heir!

Sir Geo. I should be as sorry, Sir, to excite his displeasure as I am at incurring yours; yet, give me leave to add, I should derive very little enjoyment from the possession of a fortune which his son, my poor cousin, (but for a single act of imprudence) had a right to expect. And be assured, Sir, that if this seeming indiscretion of mine, when compared with that of his son's, shou'd be regarded so unfavourably as to make *his* offence appear lighter to my uncle, and move him to forgiveness, I will contentedly support the burthen of his resentment.

Mr Eus. Why now, that's well spoken. You silly young rogue, I am not angry with you for getting rid of your wife (for that, I dare say, is what every sensible man in the world wou'd do if he cou'd,) I am only angry with you for getting another. Could not you know when you were well off, you blockhead?

Sir Geo. Dear uncle, as you are a bachelor, and can only speak of wives from theory, suppose we drop the subject? Is my uncle Anthony come to his house? He knows nothing of the alteration that has taken place in my family, you tell me: Shou'd I wait on him, or do you think he will favour me with a visit first?

Mr Eus. Now, what a deal of ceremony! 'Tis a fine thing to *look* like a man of consequence. My brother Anthony has had more privileges from his looks than I ever had from being eldest son—even you, whom I love so well, and have given half my fortune to, (and 'tis not long you know that you have expected a sixpence from Anthony,) yet you

never meet *him* without a low bow. " How do you
do, Sir? I hope you are well, uncle! I am glad
to see you!" And you stumble over *me*, with " So
uncle, how is it? how is it, uncle?"—And when you
invite us both, " Uncle Anthony, I hope I shall
have the *honour* of your company:" While you give
me a nod, " Uncle, I shall see you."

Sir Geo. Dear Sir—

Mr Eus. Nay, with every other person 'tis the
same thing—If we are stuffed into a coach, with a
little chattering pert Miss, " Oh dear, Mr Anthony
Euston, you must not ride backwards, here is
room for *you* on this seat—and *Mr Euston,* I know,
will like one seat as well as another;"—and then am
I put with my back to the horses, though my head
is whirling all the time like one of the coach wheels.
Then if any thing be lost, or wanted, when no servant is by, " Mr *Anthony* Euston must not stir for
the world—but *Mr Euston,* they know, will be so
kind as to go for it." And this is all because I am
good natured. Egad! if this is my reward, no
wonder there are so few in the world of my temper.

Sir Geo. But, dear Sir, no jesting. Does my
uncle intend to call on me or not?

Mr Eus. Yes, I dare say he did intend it; and,
if he does not hear of what you have been doing,
before he gets to your house, he will.

Sir Geo. Why then, my dear uncle, will you
step home, and give orders that none of the servants
mention any thing to him this morning?

Mr Eus. There now!—" *I* step home and give
orders!" There 'tis, again!—Wou'd you ask my
brother to " step home, and give orders?" No, I
fancy not!—But I—poor I—will be so good as to do
it, you think—But, for once I won't. Besides, Anthony never asks questions of servants. We enquired of our house-keeper, indeed, how you did, last

night; she told us both you and your lady were well, and so we thought all safe. Anthony will ask no more questions; therefore, you may have the pleasure of explaining matters to him yourself, as you have to me.

Sir Geo. I shou'd be sorry if any imperfect account shou'd reach him; for, so sincere is my respect for him, I wou'd not even suffer for a moment in his esteem. I will be with him in half an hour, but I am afraid—

Mr Eus. No, no, he'll not be out, nor have had any company in that time; for my brother is no sailor, and he'll be too fond of the exchange of a bed for a hammock to be stirring so soon. However, I think I *will* step home, and give a caution to the servants that they don't mention your divorce to him. As for myself, I'll keep out of his way— I'll not go near him; for I will say this for my brother, although it was never in my power to persuade him to forgive an injury or an indiscretion in my life, yet I never said to him, " Brother Anthony, *don't* forgive a thing," that he did not take my advice.

Sir Geo. Come, uncle, walk into the parlour before you go; let me introduce you to Lady Euston— Do step in, and take your chocolate with her.

Mr Eus. And, by the time I have taken a turn in the Park, and eaten a mouthful of dinner, you'll, perhaps, have a new Lady Euston to introduce me to, and I may drink tea with *her*.

Sir Geo. Well, uncle, whether you stay or go, I must bid you a good morning; for I am obliged to attend a friend, who has a law-suit depending, and I fear I shall be waited for—my presence won't be required long, and I'll be with my uncle Anthony within half an hour.

Mr Eus. Very well, [*Going*] but you had better take an hour—Let me advise you to take an hour. Anthony is devilish sharp—he is not to be imposed

upon.   Take an hour, or an hour and half, before
you see him—Anthony is a deep man, he is not to
be deceived; for, I dare say, in his time, he has
been as idle as yourself—and I *will* go on your
errand.

    [*Exeunt Mr Euston and Sir George, separately.*

SCENE II.

A Room at MAJOR CYPRUS'.

LADY HARRIET CYPRUS, *and* BLOOM, *waiting.*

Lady Har. Married!
Bloom. Yes, my Lady, as sure as death.
Lady Har. Amazing! It cannot be.
Bloom. O yes, my Lady, I have known of it
these three months; but, as they kept out of town
till within this fortnight, and your ladyship has
been abroad most of that time, I thought I would
not tell your ladyship till we returned to London,
when your ladyship was sure to hear of it.   Why
they live but just by, madam; and my master, I
know, has been several times in company where they
have been visiting.

    Lady Har. Ay, she was your master's intended.
Bloom. O yes, my lady, I know that.
Lady Har. Insignificant girl! I triumphed, when
I snatched him from her, and now I suppose she
thinks to triumph equally.

    Bloom. No doubt, madam; but, if I was you,
I wou'd let her see I cared nothing about him.

Lady Har. And do you imagine I do care? No, indeed, Bloom; my exchange is for the better, I am certain; and (*sighing*) entirely to my satisfaction.

Bloom. Indeed I think so, Madam: you certainly have changed for the better—and, bless me, I think, of all the husbands I ever saw, my present master is sure the fondest.

Lady Har. As for that—no one cou'd be fonder than Sir George, at first.

Bloom. Ay, my lady, but Major Cyprus is not so flighty as Sir George.

Lady Har. Not so flighty—(*sighs.*) I have been envy'd Sir George's gaiety a thousand times.

Bloom. Yes, my lady, when your ladyship married first, I suppose; but, you know, in a few months, Sir George altered so much, and seemed so miserable, I protest, every single rap that came at the door made my blood run cold, for I took it for the report of a pistol.

Lady Har. You need not have feared him, Bloom —he is too fond of the pleasures of this life—Dear pleasures, which he wanted to retrench me in.

Bloom. More shame for him, madam. Now my present master is a soldier; and, what is more, I dare say will soon be call'd on to go abroad.

Lady Har. Ha!

Bloom. Nay, I beg your ladyship's pardon—I thought perhaps your ladyship wished to see the Major show himself a courageous gentleman in the field; and that that was the reason of your preferring him to Sir George.

Lady Har. I prefer! Did not my brother, from Sir George's humiliating suspicions and cruel treatment of me, compel us to a divorce; and then, as a defence for my weakness, forced me into the arms of the Major; being, I suppose, convinced that no-

thing less than a soldier, should undertake the guard
of a lady's honour!

Bloom. Very true, madam—and I heard the
Major say, this morning, as your ladyship left the
room, that " your ladyship's honour would require
the guard of a file of musketeers."

Lady Har. Ungenerous man—even worse to
me than Sir George; for poor Sir George, from
my indiscreet partiality to this ingrate, had some
pretence for his unkind apprehensions; but Mr Cyprus, who knows what proofs of affection I have
given him, even in preference to the man I had
sworn to love—

Bloom. Nay, I fancy, that is what frightens my
master; for I believe he is a little fearful lest your
ladyship shou'd chance to be forsworn again.

Lady Har. Insolent supposition! He knows the
delicacy of my sentiments—my honour to Sir George
—knows that, although his unwearied artifices conquered my too susceptible heart, and hurried me to
indiscretions, I merited not that severe contumely
I have endured.

Bloom. Bless my soul! Well now, I assure you,
you surprise me! And so, my lady, there was nothing at all in it, when Sir George found my master in the closet?

Lady Har. What did you suppose?

Bloom. Oh, my lady, nothing—I hope I did not
distress your ladyship by the mention of Sir George's
second marriage.

Lady Har. Ridiculous!

Bloom. Nay, indeed, I always thought, as your
ladyship wou'd not live with him yourself, your
ladyship did not wish to prevent them that wou'd.

Lady Har. Don't mention that insignificant woman!

Bloom. If I was your ladyship, I am sure, I

wou'd not care—especially as I got married before
him.

Lady Har. Leave me.

Bloom. (Aside.) She'll have another husband
within half a year—and so have three all alive at
once.—Well, I will say, 'tis very hard that, because
I am poor, I never can have above one at a time.

[*Exit* BLOOM.

Lady Har. And so, Sir George has been married
these three months to another, and entirely forgot
me. To be so soon forgotten!—I shall never
now forget him, I am certain. He has behaved
like a man of resolution and spirit, in casting me
from his heart, and I feel the irreparable loss. Why
were we divorced? I shou'd have disliked him still
had he been my husband; and yet how tender, how
patient to my failings to what Mr Cyprus is. His
cruel and unjust suspicions of me are not to be borne.
How provokingly did he treat me last night—I was
too tame; but the next time he insults me, with his
jealousy, I will endeavour to augment rather than
pacify it—I'll try a reverse of conduct—Though,
indeed, I *am* tolerably provoking in all our wrangles:
—Yes, thank heaven, I can say as cool, spiteful
things, as any woman in the world.   [*Exit.*

SCENE III.

Another apartment in Maior Cyprus' house.

Enter COLONEL DOWNRIGHT, *followed by the* MAJOR.

Col. Down. I assure you, Major, this is the first
visit I have made since I set my foot in London.—
Nay, and faith, no great compliment to you, neither;

for, as I parted with my fellow passengers at Portsmouth, I don't know that I have a friend or acquaintance in the whole town but yourself.

Major Cyp. I am happy in your want of friends, Colonel, if it gives you occasion to consider me as one.

Col. Down. As for that, I don't want friends, neither, I believe; only they are not here, at present. I have plenty of friends on the other side the Atlantic.—Zounds! I think it wou'd be hard for a man, who has been so long in the army, and borne a post like mine in it, not to have a *regiment* of friends, at least.

Major Cyp. Which is a great consolation to you, no doubt, Colonel.

Col. Down. The greatest in the world, Major. But what! you have changed your house since I was last in England: this is not the same, I think, tho' near the same spot.

Major Cyp. Yes, I have changed my house; and, what is more, changed my state too, Colonel.

Col. Down. Why, you are not married?

Major Cyp. What surprises you?

Col. Down. Nay, I am not surprised at your marrying; only at your appearing so easy about it!

Major Cyp. And why not, Colonel? A valuable woman—

Col. Down. Very true, very true—and so I wish you joy, with all my heart. *(Shaking hands.)* But, who is the Lady, pray? Do I know her, or any of her family?

Major Cyp. Did you know Sir George Euston?

Col. Down. I have heard of him.

Major Cyp. She was his lady.

Col. Down. A widow!

Major Cyp. No—she was no widow.

Col. Down. Did not you say she was Sir George Euston's wife?

Major Cyp. Very true; but Sir George is still living.

Col. Down. What, the devil! is the man living, and you married to his wife?

Major Cyp. It was a divorce, Colonel.

Col. Down. A divorce!—Whu! Now I understand you. Why, that's *mariage en militaire.* You might well appear so easy.

Major Cyp. Fye, Colonel ;—I assure you, Lady Harriet Cyprus and I are a most happy couple—and my having snatched her from " a dull, doating husband," gives superior pleasure and triumph to our bliss.

Col. Down. The husband is much obliged to you both.

Major Cyp. Why, poor fellow, that is the worst. In spite of the congratulations I receive from my friends, and my natural desire of fame, and propensity to conquest, I do feel, and cannot help it, a most deep sorrow and compassion for the thorns I have planted in his bosom.

Col. Down. But, I suppose, he used his lady very ill, before he provoked her to the divorce, and certainly preferred some other?

Major Cyp. Oh no, by no means! He doated on her, even to the day of their separation, notwithstanding it was he who sued for the divorce.

Col. Down. *He* who sued for the divorce—Oh ! that was it! I understood you, that you had planted *thorns*—but you said *horns,* I suppose.

Major Cyp. (*Smiles.*) Ha! Ha!

Col. Down. Oh ! I wish you much joy—

Major Cyp. Why ironically, Colonel? Depend upon it, I am the envy of all the men in town : Lady Harriet Cyprus is a perfect beauty.

Col. Down. a Im glad she is perfect in some respect.

Major Cyp. Oh! (*With some inquietude.*) ridiculous, Colonel—Divorces happen now every day; and
the favoured lover is the most admired and envied
of mortals, while the poor husband becomes an object
of general pity.

Col. Down. Ay, the husband?

Major Cyp. Yes, the husband.

Col. Down. Ay, and *you* are the husband now.¹

Major Cyp. Pshaw! the forsaken husband.

Col. Down. You pity him?

Major Cyp. Certainly.

Col. Down. And, if he is a tender hearted man, I
suppose, he pities you.

Major Cyp. Ha, ha, ha!—Let me describe a scene
to you, where poor Sir George's situation must affect
the most obdurate heart.   Lady Harriet Euston,
(now Lady Harriet Cyprus,) was, when I first became acquainted with her, a very loving wife: (We
are friends, Colonel, and I will venture to recount a
few anecdotes to you) a very loving wife, indeed;
and but for my insinuations—artful insinuations I
may call them—had continued her conjugal regard—
she had been to this hour an example to wives, if I
had not tempted her to stray.

Col. Down. Ay, you! or somebody else.

Major Cyp. (*Disturbed.*) Hear me out, Colonel.
She was long an example to wives—she was, I assure you.   But to describe to you Sir George's piti-
able situation, and what was chiefly the cause of the
divorce.—One evening, we had prolonged the *tête-a-
tête* rather beyond the usual time; when, unexpectedly, Sir George and a party of beaux and belles
were rushing up stairs,—" Dear Major," cried my
wife——

Col. Down. Your wife? Sir George's, you mean.

Major Cyp. Yes, Sir George's *then,* but my wife *now.*

Col. Down. Ay, ay, and I most sincerely give you joy! (*Ironically.*)

Major Cyp. Pshaw! you put me out.—" Dear Major," cried my wife; or Sir George's, if you will have it so—" What will become of us," (for Sir George had given us some little proofs of his jealousy,) " what will become of us!" exclaimed the then Lady Harriet Euston. " Put me into your thimble; into the eye of your needle, madam," said I—Instead of which, cramm'd I was into that closet.

Col. Down. That closet!

Major Cyp. That very identical closet, which you see there; for Sir George never loved the house after, and so settled it on her Ladyship.—Screwed up in that closet, I believe I remained ten minutes; when old Lady Downfall, who was of the party, called for drops; the door was opened,—and out dropt your humble servant.

Col. Down. Zounds! it was enough to make you wish yourself—

Major Cyp. Nay, it was Sir George's place to wish. Every beau in the room was round me in a moment; and, in a whisper, " Give you joy, Major,"—" The happiest man in the world,"—" An Alexander,"— " A conqueror every where." Even old Sir Samson Shrivel, shook his head, and wished to be in my place.

Col. Down. Zounds! I would have thrust him into the closet, and kept him there for a month. But what did the husband say all this time?

Major Cyp. That is what I was going to tell you. What did he say? Why, he said nothing. You may depend upon it, he heard and saw all the half-stifled laughs, and was wise enough to know to whom they were directed: So, poor fellow, he turned pale, bit his lips—looked at her ladyship—looked at me—looked at his sword—and then cried " Heigh ho !"

Col. Down. Heigh ho ! And what the deuce did you say ?

Major. What do you think I said ? Egad, I *was* a little confused.

Col. Down. Confused !

Major Cyp. And do you know I said—Faith, it was an odd speech, and has been laughed at since in a thousand fashionable circles—the conclusion of it has been particularly marked.—" Dear Sir George," said I.—He was standing where you may be (here, a little more this way,) and I just where I am at present—" Dear Sir George," said I, (half stifling a laugh, for by my soul I could not help it, though I pitied the poor devil, too,)—" Dear Sir George," said I, " I'll tell you what,"—you will find *nobody* to blame in this affair—I protest my being in that closet was entirely owing to—" I'll tell you what,"—in short, to an—an *undescribable something*——There I made a full stop.

Col. Down. " An undescribable something."

Major Cyp. 'Tis true, upon my soul ! those were the very words.

Col. Down. Owing to an " Undescribable something," and " I'll tell you what," that I got into this closet :—And so, I suppose, the next day Sir George left both his wife and the closet, and you have ever since held possession ?

Major Cyp. After some other explanations, and regular proceedings, I became the happy husband he was never formed to be.

Col. Down. But I hope you keep the key of the closet ?

Major Cyp. You will have your joke, Colonel.—Sir George, out of despair, is just married again ; and Lady Harriet's affection for me is such—yet faith, I must confess to you too, Colonel, that notwithstand-

ing I am so very happy in my marriage—my wife so
very beautiful and so affectionate, yet I am a sad
wicked fellow; I have not forgot my old ways—no,
I am going to-morrow evening to meet a lady of un-
tarnished reputation—a married lady. Faith, 'tis
wrong—I know it is; but I cannot withstand the
temptation—no, I cannot forget my old ways.

                           (*Yawning.*)

  Col. Down. And do you suppose her Ladyship can
forget *her* old ways either?   (*Yawning.*)

  Major Cyp. For shame, Colonel! but you are so
fond of a joke.   Egad, I have a great mind to make
you laugh most heartily at the business I have now
on my hands—you wou'd say it was the most impudent thing of me.   I'll tell you another time, on purpose to make you laugh; no other design whatever.
(*A bell rings.*) That is her ladyship's bell—Come,
I will introduce you to her directly; and, I flatter
myself, you will admire my choice.

  Col. Down. It does indeed excite my admiration,
most prodigiously!

                             [*Exeunt.*

ACT THE SECOND.

SCENE I.

Enter MR ANTHONY EUSTON, *and a* SERVANT.

  Ser. I'll let my master know immediately, Sir.

                             [*Exit.*

  Mr Ant. Sir George has changed all his servants,
I think, as well as his house, for I have not seen one

that I know; and not one of them seems to know their old friend Anthony Euston.

Enter SERVANT.

Ser. I beg your pardon, Sir; I thought my master had been at home; but he is not.

Mr Ant. Is not he?

Ser. No, Sir; he has been gone out this half-hour.

Mr. Ant. He is gone to my house then, I dare say. Is your lady at home?

Ser. Yes, Sir.

Mr Ant. Be so kind as to let her know I should be glad to see her.

Ser. What name, pray Sir?

Mr Ant. Only say a relation she will be glad to see. [*Exit Servant.*] Sir George may not be gone to my house, neither; for, perhaps, my brother has not yet called on him, and he may be ignorant of our arrival.—This house is a handsome one; yet, I wonder Sir George should leave his other; for I remember my niece was remarkably fond of its situation.— Poor girl—if she knew it was Anthony, Anthony Euston, I believe she wou'd not be so long in coming. (*Goes to the side of the scene, and calls.*) Come, come, my dear! 'tis an old friend that wants to see you. (*He walks to the opposite side, and, when he hears Lady Euston entering, he returns and calls.*) Come, come—sure you have kept me long enough!

Enter LADY EUSTON.

(*As Mr Anthony is going with great eagerness to salute her, he stops short, and she curtsies.*)

Mr Ant. I beg your pardon, madam! I thought I had been speaking to my niece.

Lady Eus. Your niece, Sir?

Mr Ant. The lady of the house, madam.

Lady Eus. I have the honour to be mistress of this house, Sir.

Mr Ant. Madam?

Lady Eus. My name is Euston, Sir.

Mr Ant. Good Heaven! Is then my niece, that beautiful young woman, dead?

Lady Eus. The lady that was Lady Harriet Ogle, Sir?

Mr Ant. Yes.

Lady Eus. No, Sir, she is still living, and very well: I saw her the other morning.

Mr Ant. Madam, you rejoice me.

Lady Eus. You are only mistaken in the house, Sir; that's all.

Mr Ant. Madam, you make me happier than I can express. But how cou'd the mistake happen? They told me my nephew lived here. Indeed, I named no names at the door, but only ask'd the man if his master was within; and your name being Euston, madam, I suppose, first caused the mistake.

Lady Eus. Very likely, Sir.

Mr Ant. I beg pardon for the trouble I have given you.

Lady Eus. No apologies, Sir. Permit me to let one of my servants shew you to Lady Harriet's.

Mr Ant. No, I am much obliged to you. If it is the same house that Sir George Euston lived in, about two years ago, I know it very well.

Lady Eus. It is, Sir.

Mr Ant. Madam, I thank you—and once more beg pardon for the trouble I have given you, through a mistake.

Lady Eus. Dear Sir, no apology. Permit the servant to shew you to Lady Harriet's.

Mr Ant. No, madam, I thank you; I have been often there, and know the house very well.—Madam, good morning to you—I beg your pardon—good morning, madam.   [*Exit* Mr ANTHONY.

Lady Eus. Good morning to you, Sir.—This is certainly an uncle of Lady Harriet's, who is unacquainted with her divorce—and I cou'd not inform him of it; 'twould have led to such disagreeable explanations, and such a long round-about story it must have caused—" Sir, I am *second wife* to your *present* niece's *first husband.*" Lud! Lud! how ashamed I shou'd have been. Lady Harriet had better explain it by far.   [*Exit* LADY EUSTON.

SCENE II.

A Room at MAJOR CYPRUS'.

Enter COLONEL DOWNRIGHT *and* SIR HARRY HARMLESS.

Sir Har. Now the Major is gone, Colonel—notwithstanding all he has been talking, of love, and his vast happiness, you will hardly believe it, perhaps—but he is not so very happy.

Col. Down. No!

Sir Har. No, poor man: you will hardly think it, but he is jealous.

Col. Down. What, already? And, for Heaven's sake, of whom?

Sir Har. Nay, I assure you he has no cause—Nor is he jealous of one alone alone—he is so of every body—and will be so of you; therefore, I tell you, that you may be on your guard. I am constantly with his lady and him, and, because the poor woman once shut him up in her closet, he now suspects a lover concealed in every part of the house; and I have known him, when the mad fit has been upon him, search for a supposed rival even in her drawers and band-boxes.

Col. Down. Pray, Sir, do you live in the house?

Sir Har. I have been on a visit here these six weeks.

Col. Down. And during that time—

Sir Har. I have seen such things! Enough to terrify me from marrying; for wives are sometimes so provoking, I am sure I cou'd not keep my temper. Now, here is Lady Harriet Cyprus, you cannot think how provoking she is—she sometimes says such terrible things to her husband, that, I am sure, if she was my wife—

Col. Down. Why you wou'd not beat her, would you, or lock her up?

Sir. Har. No—but perhaps I might kick her lapdog, or do some outrage to her dress.

Col. Down. You wou'd make an admirable soldier, Sir Harry.

Sir Har. I must own, Colonel, I shou'd have no objection to a commission, where the regimentals were becoming.

Col. Down. Really!

Sir Har. And indeed, Colonel, I am positive you wou'd be obliged to *press* commissioned officers, if it were not for the becomingness of some of their dresses.

Col. Down. Give me your hand, Sir Harry. I like you much; and could I see you master of a firelock, or a wife—

Sir Har. No. While my neighbours marry, I never shall.

Col. Down. Why so, Sir Harry?

Sir Har. Their wives will do for me.

Col. Down. I am amazed, Sir Harry, that the Major, jealous as you describe him, should suffer you to remain in his house!

Sir. Har. I have often been surprised at it myself.

Col. Down. You have!

Sir Har. But he never was jealous of *me*. Zounds! it piques me sometimes. The ladies are fond of me, and yet the gentlemen are not jealous of me. But, indeed, my amours have all been managed so secretly, that none of them have ever yet come to light.

Col. Down. But who has been to blame there, Sir Harry?

Sir Har. I have paid regard to the reputation of the ladies, and none to my own. I expect an assignation to-morrow evening; and I question whether I shall mention it to above three or four of my acquaintance, notwithstanding the lady is reputed a woman of honour, and is, besides, a married lady.

Col. Down. And would you divulge the appointment sooner on that account?

Sir Har. Certainly! Had I a wish to build a reputation.

Col. Down. Who have we here? (*Looking out.*)

Sir Har. The Major and her ladyship! He has been following her into the Park, and is now conducting her home. I assure you their company at present will not be very desirable; so step this way, dear Colonel, and I will indulge you with a few more particulars. Egad, I can surprise you!

[*Exeunt* COLONEL DOWNRIGHT *and* SIR HARRY.

Enter LADY HARRIET CYPRUS, *followed by* MAJOR CYPRUS.

Major Cyp. So, Madam, I have followed you home, and now shou'd be glad to know, what unusual whim brought you into the Park so early?

Lady Har. How can you be so teazing as to ask questions? Especially when you see I am too fatigued to answer.

Major Cyp. Fatigued, madam? How is it possible—

Lady Har. Don't speak so loud.—I'm thinking of something else.

Major Cyp. Zounds, madam, I say—

Lady Har. How can you, Major? Sir George Euston, with all his faults, never asked me such impertinent questions!

Major Cyp. Sir George, madam! How dare you mention his name to me, madam? How dare you mention to me that contemptible ——?

Lady Har. Dear Major, do not be severe—consider you are—a married man yourself now.

Major Cyp. Heavens! Madam, do not imagine—

Lady Har. And you know every gentleman is liable to—

Major Cyp. What, madam?

Lady Har. *Be* married. There is nothing certain in this world.

Major Cyp. Very well, madam! Very well—I believe I understand your insinuation; and I deserve it. I justly deserve it for venturing my happiness with a woman whose principles I *knew*.

Lady Har. How dare you, Major Cyprus, upbraid me, or think, because my unhappy partiality for you *once* betrayed me into indiscretions, I am not now an altered woman? I am sure I have most heartily repented of all my faults, and wished a thousand times I had never seen you.

Major Cyp. Exceedingly well, indeed, madam! Exceedingly well. Repent you ever saw me! What am I to expect after such a declaration? And why repent you ever saw me? What, you won't speak! I believe you are the only woman who cou'd call me her husband, and be insensible of her happiness. When you consider, too, your release from Sir George.—What makes you smile, madam? Surely, after all your seeming contempt for Sir George, you

wou'd not, even in *idea*, put him in competition
with *me*?   Though, by heaven, your continual
mention of him is enough—did I not know how
much you despise him.   I am amazed how you
cou'd ever consent to marry such a being, and so I
have told you a hundred times—Not one accomplishment.

Lady Har. Now you provoke me—he had a thousand !

Major Cyp. That I am destitute of?

Lady Har. (*Sighs.*) Oh !

Major Cyp. Zounds, madam, what do you mean
by that sigh?   And in what quality, pray, did your
first husband, your *first* husband, madam—in what
quality did he eclipse your humble servant?

Lady Har. (*After a pause.*) He danced better
than any man I ever saw.

Major Cyp. Dance better !

Lady Har. And his bow was exquisite.

Major Cyp. (*Bowing.*) O—your most obedient!

Lady Har. Then, sometimes, he was the most
entertaining—

Major Cyp. You would have a husband entertain
his wife then?

Lady Har. Certainly—and entertain himself, at
the same time.

Major Cyp. I wish to heaven you had kept him,
with all his accomplishments !

Lady Har. (*Sighs, and shakes her head.*) Oh !

Major Cyp. Damnation !—(*After a pause, comes
up to her with a softened tone of voice.*) Come hither.—Come, tell me,—wou'd you?—and so you
wou'd really prefer your old husband to me?

Lady Har. Old! He was the youngest.

Major Cyp. Madam, madam, I'll hear no more—
I'll suffer no more.   Since you can compare that

contemptible animal to me, I have done with you—
you are below even my resentment.

Lady Har. Dear Major, say what you will, Sir
George had his virtues—He seldom asked me where
I was going; or who visited me in his absence?
Where I had been walking? What made me so remarkably cheerful, or why I looked so very ill-natured? In short, he was truly and literally, in
every respect, a fashionable husband.

Major. Cyp. You are—

Enter SERVANT.

Ser. Sir, a gentleman below desires to see you;
I did not know whether you chose to be at home
or not, so I told him I believed you were gone out,
but that I wou'd come and see.

Major Cyp. I *am* gone out—go and tell him so.
[*Exit Servant.*] I am in too ill a humour to see any
body—my temper is spoiled. I am neither fit for
company, pleasure, business, nor any thing.

Lady Har. Nor I—I am spoil'd too.

Enter SERVANT.

Ser. The gentleman, madam, begs to see you.
Do you chuse I should show him up?

Lady Har. Yes, show him up—he may be of
service to my spirits. Who is he? What is his
name?

Serv. I ask'd him, madam, but he would not say.
He first asked me if my master was within; and
when I return'd, and told him no, he said, tell your
lady, Lady Harriet, I desire to see *her.*—He
spoke as if he was acquainted with your ladyship.

La. Har. Show him up.

Major Cyp. You will please to take him into another room.

La. Har. It is not my intention to leave this room till dinner.

Major Cyp. Nor mine.

La. Har. Then you'll have an opportunity of assuring the gentleman, *yourself*, you are not at home.

Serv. Shou'd I shew the gentleman into another room, madam?

Major Cyp. No!   [*Exit angrily.*

La. Har. Shew the gentleman up. (*Exit Servant.*) Who in the name of wonder can it be, that wants both the Major and me? I thought our acquaintance had been all separate visitors.

Enter the SERVANT, *with* MR ANTHONY EUSTON *following.*

La. Har. Mr Anthony Euston!—*(Mr Anthony salutes her.)*—Is it possible I shou'd have the honour of a visit from *you?*

Mr Ant. My dear lady, and why *not?* What, you heard, I suppose, I was lost;—but have not you heard again that I was found?

La. Har. No, upon my word, Sir; and the sight of you amazes me.

Mr Ant. Was not my brother here this morning?

La. Har. No, Sir.

Mr Ant. Nor did not your husband expect me?

La. Har. No, indeed, Sir!

Mr Ant. My brother not here to tell your husband of our safety, after all the perils of shipwreck, imprisonment, and a story fit for a romance!

Lady Har. Is Mr Euston too return'd safe?

Mr Ant. Certainly.—'Tis strange he has not been here before me! Where is your husband?

Lady Har. Did you ask for him when you came in?

Mr Ant. Yes, I asked the servant if his master was at home, but he returned and said, no;—so I

then asked him for his mistress—and here I find
you, my dear lady, as beautiful as ever! But where
is my nephew? I am all impatience till I see him.

Lady Har. (*Aside.*) He does not know what has
happened, I find.

Mr Ant. What is the matter, my dear?

Lady Har. You are just arrived from abroad, Sir?

Mr Ant. Only left the ship yesterday morning,
came to London late in the evening, and, not having
had a night's rest on shore for many months, went
to bed as soon as I arrived; and, as soon as I rose
this morning, came with my respects to you.

Lady Har. Then you have seen no acquaintance
since you came to town?

Mr Ant. You are the first. Can you suppose I
shou'd visit any one before I had seen you; or do
you think any of my friends wou'd find me out the
very night of my arrival.

Lady Har. And have you met with none of your
English aquaintance while you have been abroad—
nor read any of our English newspapers?

Mr Ant. I have seen neither since I left England.
—Indeed, when I am at a distance from my friends,
as I hate to be imposed on, I seldom ask a question
concerning them, and never read a paragraph where
their names are mention'd.

Enter COLONEL DOWNRIGHT.

Col. Down. I beg your Ladyship's pardon—I
thought the Major had been here;—he promised he
wou'd go with me into the city on some business—
He is not gone out, I hope?

Lady Har. Mr Euston, you will excuse me a
moment—I will send (*To the Colonel*) the Major to
you immediately, Sir. (*Aside.*) Let him explain to
Mr Euston—the task wou'd be too much for me.

Mr. Ant. My fellow traveller! Have you forgot
me?   (*Going up to the* COLONEL.)

Col. Down. My good friend! Is it you?—I am
heartily glad to see you—I thought it *was* you? and
then again—Where is my friend your brother? Why
you got to town before me—I am glad to meet you,
faith!—So unexpectedly too!

Enter MAJOR CYPRUS, *and bows to* MR ANTHONY.

Major Cyp. Colonel, I beg your pardon; I am
afraid I have tired your patience?

Col. Down Not at all—Sir Harry Harmless has
been an excellent companion, but he has just left me.
(*To Mr Anthony*) I shou'd have call'd on you in the
afternoon—Who wou'd have thought of meeting you
here?

Mr Ant. Why faith, Colonel, I do not know a more
likely place to find a man at, than a relation's house.

Col. Down. What, are the Major and you related?

Mr Ant. Sir!

Major Cyp. Have I the honour of being related
to you, Sir?   (*Bowing.*)

Mr Ant. Not that I know of, Sir.— (*Bowing.*)

Major Cyp. If Lady Harriet has that honour, Sir,
I presume to claim the same.

Mr Ant. You are related to Lady Harriet then,
Sir?

Major Cyp. By very close ties.—

Mr Anthony. Sir I shall be happy to be better acquainted.

Col. Down. (*Aside to the* MAJOR.) Tell him the
story of the closet—Egad 'twill make him laugh.

Major Cyp. (*Aside to the* COLONEL.) Fy, fy!
He is a relation of my wife's.

Col. Down. (*Aside.*) He wou'd not like a good
story the worse for that.—Would you, Mr Anthony,
have any dislike to a good story?

Mr Ant. A story, Sir ?—

Col. Down. Ay, a good story of a—a—zounds " I'll tell you what !" and " an undescribable something !"—

Major Cyp. For shame, for shame, Colonel !

Mr Ant. Why, my fellow traveller, you are at your jokes ; the same as ever, I find. What is all this ?

Major Cyp. Nothing, Sir ; nothing, I assure you.

Col. Down. As good a story as ever was told. Tell it, Major ; I wou'd, but I cannot *look* it as you do. Egad, you *look* it to the life.

Mr Ant. Well, gentlemen, I should be very happy to hear this story, but I am obliged to defer it till some other time. I have waited for Sir George as long as possible, and, as I find he does not come, I'm resolved to go in search of him—So, gentlemen, your humble servant. If I meet with Sir George, I shall return, I dare say, immediately ; and, if not, I shall certainly call in the afternoon. My compliments to her ladyship—Your servant, gentlemen.

Maj. Cyp. Pray, Sir, who did you expect to meet here ?

Mr Ant. Only Sir George, Sir.

Major Cyp. What Sir George, pray, Sir ?

Mr Ant. Sir George Euston, Sir.

Major Cyp. Sir George Euston, Sir ! Did you expect to meet Sir George Euston *here* ?

Mr Ant. Certainly I did, Sir.

Col. Down. That's all for want of hearing the story.—Do, my good friend, come back and hear the story of the " undescribable something,"—and of the closet—that little closet—and, " I'll tell you what !"

Major Cyp. Colonel, permit me to speak seriously to the gentleman.—Sir, (*to Mr Anthony*) you will never see Sir George Euston in this house, I am certain.

Mr Ant. How so, pray Sir?

Major Cyp. I am now master of this house, and—

Mr Ant. You are master of this house!

Major Cyp. Yes, Sir.

Col. Down. He took possession of the closet, some time ago.

Mr Ant. But pray, Sir, does not Lady Harriet Euston then live here?

Major Cyp. That lady is no longer Lady Harriet Euston, Sir, but Cyprus: she is my wife.

Col. Down. You have spoiled the whole story, by beginning at the wrong end.

Mr. Ant. You astonish me!—I beg your pardon: I came but last night from the West Indies, where I have been for some time, and where not the smallest intelligence from England has ever reached me; therefore you will excuse my ignorance. But I think her ladyship, knowing how great a stranger I was, ought to have dealt a little more openly with me.

Major Cyp. I dare say, Sir, her ladyship——

Mr Ant. Yes, I suppose her ladyship was unwilling to be the first to acquaint me with the death of Sir George.

Major Cyp. The death of Sir George, Sir.

Mr Ant. Yes, Sir; for, while I give you joy on your marriage, give me leave to say, that mine is all damped by the loss of him: And my grief is doubly poignant; because, till this moment, I was not only unacquainted with Lady Harriet's second marriage, but, till this moment, I did not even know Sir George was dead!

Major Cyp. Sir George is not dead, Sir.

Mr Ant. What do you mean? Did you not tell me you were married to his wife?

Major Cyp. Very true, Sir; but you know that is no reason, now-a-days, why the lady's first husband should be dead.

Col. Down. Why, my brother messmate, you are just like me—I had forgot that a man in England might marry his neighbour's wife, and his neighbour living in the next street. And 'tis not the wives of their neighbours, only, these generous gentlemen assail, but more especially the wives of their *friends.*

Mr Ant. Shame on such friendship! Shame on such neighbourhood! Let every tender husband and virtuous wife desert it! (*To the Major.*) Sir, I wish you joy; and, though I know not who are the parties to be censured in this business, I wish her ladyship joy—But more, in particular, I wish *myself* joy, with the sincerest congratulation, that, amidst the depravity of the times, I have followed a beloved wife to her peaceful grave, (mournful as the day was) without seeing her wrested from my arms by the insinuations of a villain: or being myself that villain to force her to seek a refuge from my perjuries, in the protection of another!

Major Cyp. Dear Sir, let me assure you that, however Lady Harriet's conduct may meet censure from the unfeeling prude, the woman of sensibility and taste must applaud her spirit, which could no longer submit to the tyranny of Sir George.

Mr Ant. Did her Ladyship then sue for the divorce?

Major Cyp. No—Sir George, on some frivolous suspicion, was pleased to sue for it.

Mr Ant. Is Sir George married again?

Major Cyp. Yes, Sir, he is married. He has won the lady, and he has won her fortune; but for her affection—there, I believe, we must excuse Sir George—that is a stake now playing for by many noblemen of fashion.

Mr Ant. I suspect Sir George is the dupe of a fashionable gallantry. I know his virtues, and am sorry to find a man of merit so betrayed.

Major Cyp. Dear Sir, think on Lady Harriet, your relation.

Mr Ant. Thank heaven, all ties between Lady Harriet and me were dissolved when she was divorced from Sir George: and so they should, Sir, had she been my own daughter, and Sir George, with the principles I know he possesses, an utter stranger to me.

Col. Down. Why then, I believe, my friend, you are *not* at a relation's house.

Mr Ant. Colonel, you will call on me shortly.—Sir, (Mr Cyprus, I think you call yourself,) I assure you, Sir, as a particular friend of my nephew's, and of the family in general, I am, Sir, your most obedient servant—your humble servant, Sir. (*With contempt.*)   [*Exit* MR ANTHONY.

Major Cyp. For heaven's sake! who is this man? I took him to be Lady Harriet's uncle! Explain to me who the brute is.

Col. Down. He came passenger from the West Indies in the same ship with me, and that was the first of our acquaintance. As he was no more reserved than I, we soon became intimate; and I learnt from him that his fortune, (a pretty good one) was designed for a nephew, whom I now recollect, (tho' the deuce take me if I thought of it before) to be this very Sir George Euston; and a son, an only child, by that wife he speaks so tenderly of, he disinherits.

Major Cyp. This is the very savage I heard Lady Harriet say the other day was drown'd. What, has his son been guilty of the criminality of a divorce?

Col. Down. No; his guilt is in being married—married to some poor girl, without friends or fortune. Thank heaven, I have neither child nor wife to offend me; but, if I had, I don't know which I would make the most obedient.

Major Cyp. And were you never a lover, Colonel? Never in the service of the ladies?

Col. Down. O yes—I have been in a closet before now—and under a bed, too ; but then I was never pull'd out by a *husband ;* and, on a discovery, I could always describe the something that brought me there.

Major Cyp. By heaven! you are so taken with that joke, I cannot reserve that which I before hinted at from you any longer : Rat me if I have not an appointment for to-morrow evening with Euston's *other* wife! Is it not the most impudent thing of me—

Col. Down. I'll be shot if I dont think so!

Major Cyp. The poor fellow thinks her as chaste as Diana ; and so she is at present, as far as I know. I was happy in her favour a few years ago ; but marriage not being then convenient, my passion was postponed. On her becoming Euston's wife, I renewed my addresses, and she has kindly allotted to-morrow evening for our first *tête-à-tête.*

Col. Down. Zounds, have a care, or you will be obliged to marry *her* too.

Major Cyp. No, no ; we shall be very circumspect in our conduct. But laugh! Why the devil don't you laugh!

Col. Down. No, I was thinking—

Major Cyp. On what?

Col. Down. Come, I must be gone, or I shall be too late for my business.

Major Cyp. I'll attend you immediately.   ut what were you thinking on?

Col. Down. I was thinking on the happiness—of a married man.

[*Exeunt* COLONEL DOWNRIGHT *and* MAJOR CYPRUS.

ACT THE THIRD

SCENE I.

A Rcom at SIR GEORGE EUSTON's.

Enter MR EUSTON *and* SIR GEORGE.

Mr Eus. Bless my soul! Bless my soul! Why, what did my brother Anthony say? Was not he in a dreadful passion? Only think of *his* being made such a fool of! It would not have signified had it been *me*. It had been a good joke if the mistake had happened to me; then you wou'd have had something to have laughed at.

Sir Geo. Dear Sir, let us think no more about it —my uncle has listened to reason, and approves my conduct in every circumstance.

Mr Eus. Ay, 'tis very well, George—'tis all very well—but I know, had you been his son, he wou'd not have forgiven you—he loved that boy so well, he wou'd never forgive him the smallest fault.

Sir Geo. A very cruel proof of his affection.

Mr Eus. 'Tis true, notwithstanding—you know it is. Poor Charles! George, you must do something for him—You know your uncle won't—and I am tied from it by a solemn promise. Many a letter and petition came from his wife to my brother and me, before we went abroad, but all in vain ; for I had but just then given Anthony my word, and wou'd not equivocate, by causing the poor boy or his family to be relieved, in any shape, through my means; and therefore I forebore to mention their distress to you. However, now, though I have not forgot my promise, I will not be so *particular* about it; and, when the deviation from my word disturbs my conscience, I'll hush it to rest with having relieved a destitute family.

Sir Geo. Say no more, Sir; I understand you—and to find out my cousin and his family shall immediately be my care.

Mr Eus. (Shaking hands with Sir George.) That's right, George—Poor Charles is a lieutenant in the East Indies. His wife must be the first object of your bounty. Just before I left England, she wrote me a letter from a village near York—where he left her, with two children, and she styles them, in her letter, " the offspring of want and wretchedness." I was a hard-hearted fellow, not to listen to her complaint; but, I think, since I have been at sea, I have been more compassionate. I never knew, before, what it was to be cold or hungry.

Sir Geo. Can you tell me the name of the village, Sir, where I am to seek her?

Mr Eus. Write to her at the post office, Selby. If she should have left the place, they may still know where to send her letters. I wish some friend, that had not made a promise, would speak to my brother Anthony about them at present; perhaps, going to sea has changed his heart too.

Sir Geo. No, Sir; I touched on that subject when I was with him this morning.

Mr Eus. Did you? Did you? And what did he say?

Sir Geo. Asked if I meant to make him forbid me his sight—and, on my apologising, commanded me never to mention my poor cousin in his hearing again.

Mr Eus. Ay, that is what I must never do—

Well, so much the better ; for now, George, nei-
you nor I can tell tales one of another.

Sir Geo. You are right, Sir.   Had my uncle Anthony an estate to bestow on each of his family, he
could not exact more obedience to his will than he
does at present.

Mr Eus. 'Tis very true, George.   But what keeps
him so long away ?   I expected he wou'd have been
with your lady before this time, acknowledging her
for his niece : though, they have had one meeting,
it seems.

Sir Geo. My uncle cannot be introduced to Lady
Euston till to-morrow, Sir.   Lord Layton, for whom
he settled some business when he was abroad, called
on him just as I came away, and, as his lordship
is going to Italy in a day or two, he entreated my
uncle to accompany him immediately to his country
house, (about ten miles from town) in order to look
over some papers he has there.

Mr Eus. Here comes your lady, so I'll leave
you.

Enter LADY EUSTON.

La. Eus. Dear Mr Euston, I hope I do not fright-
en you away—Sir George will be offended with me
if I do.

Mr Eus. No, madam—I am sure no man cou'd
be offended at being left in such charming company.
                                        [*Exit Mr Euston.*

Sir Geo. My uncle is grown a man of gallantry !

La. Eus. Yes, I inspire all the men.

Sir Geo. I believe you do.

La. Eus. Cou'd I only inspire you with reason to
listen to my arguments—

Sir Geo. 'Tis in vain—The Major shall now feel
my resentment.   Did he imagine, because I was indifferent to the conduct of an *undeserving* woman,

that I am not to be roused at such an injury as this? An attempt on the principles of a woman of virtue! 'Tis done on purpose to try me, and by Heaven he shall find—That wretch too, Sir Harry!

L. Eus. Oh, pray have pity on poor Sir Harry.

Sir Geo. No, madam. I only defer my resentment till I have had some conversation with my uncle Anthony.

L. Eus. Do, my dear Sir George, suffer me to revenge my own cause this once—and ever after—

Sir Geo. I positively must!

L. Eus. Nay, Sir George, 'in a year or two, may, perhaps, have no objection to your fighting a duel; but only three months married—I do wish to keep you a little longer.

Sir Geo. Depend upon it, Lady Euston, death had never half the terrors I have beheld it with since I called you mine; but that life you have endeared to me——

L. Eus. You wou'd throw away immediately in my service. No, no, Sir George, a fond wife will never suffer her husband to revenge her wrongs at so great a risk: Besides, the exertion of a little *thought* and *fancy*, will more powerfully vindicate innocence, than that brilliant piece of steel, I assure you.

Sir Geo. Perhaps you are right.

L. Eus. Certainly I am! Now, suppose a gentleman makes love to me—I divulge the affront to you; you call my insulter to an account—*Your* ball misses; he fires into the air; and, to the fame of having dared to wound your honour, he gains that of presenting you with your life.

Sir Geo. But, why must these circumstances take place?

L. Eus. Well, then, we will suppose he kills you ;
how do you like that ?

Sir Geo. (*Smiling.*) Hem !

L. Eus. Or, we will suppose, you kill him—even
how do you like *that* ?

Sir Geo. Well, I confess that, if a severe punishment could be thought of, for such insolence—

L. Eus. There is as severe a punishment to men
of gallantry, (as they call themselves,) as sword or
pistol : laugh at them ; that is a ball which cannot
miss ; and yet kills only their vanity.

Sir Geo. You are right.

L. Eus. Let me see ; we have been now only three
months married : and, in that short time, I have
had no less than five or six men of fashion to turn
into ridicule. The first who ventured to declare his
passion, was Lord William Bloomly; his rank, joined
to his uncommon beauty, had insured him success;
and wherever I went, I was certain to hear his distress
whispered in my ear ; at every opportunity he fell
even upon his knees; and, as a tender earnest of my
pity for him, begged, with all the eloquence of love,
for "a single lock of my hair, which he wou'd value
more than any other woman's person ; the wealth of
worlds ; or (he is a great patriot you know,) even
the welfare of his country."

Sir Geo. I am out of patience !

L. Eus. You will be more so—For I promised
him this single lock.

Sir Geo. You did not !

L. Eus. But I did; and added, with a blush, that
I must insist on a few hairs from one of his eye-
brows in return ; which he absolutely refused ;—and,
on my urging it, was obliged to confess, " he valued
that little brown arch more than the loc he had
been begging for ; consequently, more han any
woman's person ; the wealth of worlds ; or even the

welfare of his country." I immediately circulated
this anecdote, and exhibited the gentleman, both as
a gallant and a patriot ; and now his lordship's eye-
brow, which was once the admiration, is become
the ridicule of every drawing room.

Sir Geo. Your ladyship then wou'd not menace
your lover ?

L. Eus. Certainly not ; " You are the most beautiful woman I ever saw," said Lord *Bandy ;* " and
your lordship is positively the most lovely of mankind."—" What eyes," cried he ; " what hair," cried
I ; " what lips," continued he ;" " what teeth," added I ; " what a hand and arm," said he ; " and what
a *leg* and foot," said I ;—" Your ladyship is jesting,"
was his lordship's last reply ; and he has never since
even paid me one compliment. Prudes censure my
conduct ; I am too free—while their favourite, Lady
Strenuous, in another corner of the ball-room, cries
to *her* admirer—" Desist, my lord, or my dear Sir
Charles shall know that you dare thus to wound my
ears with your licentious passion ; if you ever presume to breathe it again, I will acquaint him with it—
depend upon it I will. *(Sighs and languishes.)*
Oh ! you have destroyed my peace of mind for
ever."

Sir Geo. There are too many such ladies, but
no such wou'd I hazard my life for—that I have
proved.

L. Eus. And, upon my word, Sir George, even
the virtuous wife, who wou'd not have some regard
to her husband's *life*, as well as his *honour*, if I
were a gentleman, I should not feel myself under
many obligations to.

Sir Geo. You wou'd protect both ?

L. Eus. And the guilty not escape. Now, (with
your consent,) what must be the confusion, shame,
and disappointment, of my two masked lovers to-

morrow evening; the brutal audacity of one, and
insignificance of the other; both beneath *your*
resentment, yet deserving objects of mine. And,
indeed, Si George, it is my fixed opinion, that,
the man who wou'd endeavour to wrong a virtuous
wife, shou'd be held too despicable for the resentment
of the husband, and only worthy the debasement in-
flicted by our sex. I have already sent a letter to
Sir Harry, with the appointment at the masquerade,
and the Major has my promise of a meeting at the
same time. Come, come, Sir George, it is the first
petition I ever presented; do not refuse me!

Sir Geo. Give me till the morning to consider of
it?

L. Eus. With all my heart; and in the mean time
reflect on this—that, in regard to your terrible sex,
whether as licentious lovers or valiant champions—
women, of *real honour*, are not in danger from the
one; and, therefore, like me, ought to forego the
assistance of the other.

[*Exeunt Lady Euston and Sir George.*

SCENE II.

A Room at COLONEL DOWNRIGHT'S.

Enter COLONEL DOWNRIGHT *and* MR ANTHONY
EUSTON.

Col. Down. My good friend, I was just going to
bed; but I am glad of your company, though I did
not expect it.

Mr Ant. Colonel, my errand at this time was
merely to ask a favour of you.

Col. Down. Command it, and you will make me proud.

Mr Ant. Why then, Colonel, with Lord Layton to-day, (at whose house I dined,) a circumstance happened, on which account I expect his lordship will call on me to-morrow for a fashionable satisfaction ; and though, depend upon it, I wish for no such rash means of ending a dispute ; yet, if his lordship *shou'd* call upon me, 'tis fit I be prepared with a second ; and I thank you for the friendly assurance you have now given me of your service.

Col. Down. You are as welcome to it—I was going to say, as my king ; but, zounds, if I shou'd be killed in a pitiful quarrel at home, I shou'd blush even in my grave ; for, when I die, I hope to have my knell rung by the groans of a score or two of our country's treacherous foes.

Mr Ant. The service I shall put you to, Colonel, will not prevent that hope.

Col. Down. But what, for Heaven's sake, has brought you into a quarrel ?

Mr Ant. The cause of our quarrel was—you will call it a very trivial one, I dare say—a woman !

Col. Down. Why, my old friend, you have not been quarrelling about a woman—Oh, if I shou'd be killed for a woman, I shou'd cut a noble figure, indeed ?

Mr Ant. Hear me, Colonel, hear me—and, as you may question my prudence, let me tell you the whole adventure.

Col. Down. Nay, nay, I did not mean to question your prudence, nor to speak against the women either. I like them as well as you do.

Mr Ant. I own I have a respect for their sex, which nites me to them as their father, their friend, and admirer. And I beg you will give me your sentiments upon the character of one whose behaviour, this day, has surprised me beyond measure; I will describe it to you, and you will then tell me whether you believe me imposed upon, or whether you think she really claims that extraordinary attention I have, some how, been compelled to give her.

Col. Down. Well, let me hear.

Mr Ant. Lord Layton and I had no sooner plac'd ourselves in his lordship's coach, than he exclaim'd, he had just seen the most beautiful girl his eyes ever beheld, to whom he had given a look of solicitation, and that she was returning her answer by making up to the coach. He begged a thousand pardons, but, with my permission, (as he expected no other company at his country house,) he wou'd take her down to dine with us. I, knowing his lordship well, (and the girl being now arrived at the coach door) reluctantly assented, and she was immediately handed in.

Col. Down. Zounds, he shou'd have taken a companion for you too!

Mr Ant. Don't interrupt me. When she had been seated about a minute, I cast my eyes upon her—

Col. Down. 'Sdeath, I shou'd not have staid half so long.

Mr Ant. I was struck with her beauty—

Col. Down. And wish'd his lordship out of the way, I suppose.

Mr Ant. No, no; there was a sensibility in her countenance that amazed me; blushes on her cheeks; tears in her eyes. When his lordship spoke to her, she answered him with a forced smile, and a tremor on her voice. She avoided all conversation; and, when we alighted, I handed her out of the coach.

Col. Down. Ay, ay, I thought how it was.

Mr Ant. You misunderstand me. I perceived her hand tremble——

Col. Down. And so, I suppose, did yours.

Mr Ant. If you interrupt me, sir, you shall hear no more.

Col. Down. And, I believe, it will be for your credit if I don't.

Mr Ant. Let me tell you all that passed.

Col. Down. With all my heart—if you don't blush at it, I shan't.

Mr Ant. I believe her to be a woman of virtue.

Col. Down. Then what the devil were my lord and you——

Mr Ant. I have rescued her from him.

Col. Down. Why then, the deuce take me if you are not more in love than I thought you were.

Mr Ant. Oh, had you seen her countenance, so expressive of anguish! The hope with which she lifted up her eyes to me, for deliverance! The horror painted in her face, when I left the room! Heard her piercing cries, that called me back to her protection? The despair and earnest supplication that hung upon her tongue, while she entreated him to view her, not as an object of *love,* but *charity!* The grief! the pathetic tenderness with which she declared herself, " a virtuous, though forsaken wife! A poor, indigent, forlorn mother; perishing, with her children,—for whose sake she had been tempted by the first lure that offered (prompted by more than common grief,) to add the sense of guilt to all her other miseries!"

Col. Down. 'Sdeath——

Mr Ant. Cou'd I? Ought I to have gone and left her?

Col. Down. Left her! No. But what did you do?

Mr Ant. Returned to the chamber, and insisted on his lordship resigning her to me.

Col. Down. And did he?

Mr Ant. She hung upon me; and, in spite of his menaces, I led her to my coach, (which was then come for me,) and brought her safe away.

Col. Down. I hope she got safe home too.

Mr Ant. Perfectly so. As her tears interrupted her, whenever she attempted to tell me where she lived, or explain any circumstance of her life to me, I asked no questions, but took her to my own house— desired my house-keeper to show her an apartment, and treat her with attention—and, promising to see and speak with her in the morning, left her to the repose which she must greatly want.

Col. Down. And now you think his lordship will send *you* to repose for all this.

Mr Ant. He may attempt it, for which I wish to be prepared.

Col. Down. Well then, here is my hand; and, though I must acknowledge that you have had too little of the man of the world about you in the business, yet, as I said before, command me.

Mr Ant. Come then, Colonel, my coach is waiting for me at the door; will you go with me to the next coffee-house? I have to meet a gentleman there on a little business; and afterwards we will enjoy half an hour's conversation together.

Col. Down. With all my heart.

[*Exeunt* MR ANTHONY *and* COLONEL.

ACT THE FOURTH.

SCENE I.

A Room at MR ANTHONY EUSTON's.

Enter MR EUSTON.

Mr Eus. Wonders will never cease! Who wou'd have thought it! Why surely it cannot be! My brother Anthony to bring home a girl!—What wou'd he have said to *me* if I had done such a thing? For my part, I never durst think of such a thing. Perhaps it is some neighbour's child! But if she is —the servant tells me she is very handsome, and Anthony wou'd not bring her home without some meaning. What wou'd my nephew George say to this? Why he would not believe it! He wou'd a great deal sooner believe it of me. And yet, I—I!—Lord bless me—how people may be mistaken! Here he comes.

Enter MR ANTHONY.

Mr Ant. Brother, good morning to you. Have you seen George this morning?
Mr Eus. No, brother.
Mr Ant. Are you going there?
Mr Eus. I believe I shall be presently, brother.

Mr Ant. (*Sitting down.*) Perhaps he may call here first.

Mr Eus. (*Sitting down.*) Perhaps he may, brother.

(*Mr Anthony appears thoughtful, and leans on the table.*)

Mr Eus. (*After a long pause, and with significant looks.*) It was a fine moon-shining night, last night.

Mr Ant. Yes, a fine night.

Mr Eus. (*After another pause.*) And 'tis a very fine day, to-day.

Mr Ant. Yes—it is.

Mr Eus. We have very fine weather, indeed.

Mr Ant. We have.—You have breakfasted, I suppose?

Mr Eus. Yes—and so, I suppose, have you?

Mr Ant. Yes, some time.—(*He begins writing.*)

Mr Eus. I interrupt you, brother—but I am going.—(*Rises.*)

Mr Ant. No, you do not. But tell Sir George, if you should see him, that I cannot call on him this morning, because I shall be busy.

Mr Eus. You shall be busy!

Mr Ant. Yes, I have got a little business to settle.

Mr Eus. To be sure, *business* must be minded.

Mr Ant. But be particular in delivering my apology, for I wou'd not have his lady affronted.

Mr Eus. One wou'd not affront a *lady* to be sure. No—no—no!

Mr Ant. I wou'd not have her think I slight her.

Mr Eus. No! I am sure you wou'd not slight a lady! (*He coughs.*) Good morning, brother!

Mr Ant. Good morning.

Mr Eus. We shall see you, perhaps, when your *business* is done! Good morning, brother.

[*Exit* MR EUSTON, *coughing.*

Mr Anthony pulls a letter out of his pocke

Mr Ant. Yes, here is the challenge; and, truly, something noble in it. He applauds my taking away the lady, but says my manner was too rough. I must retract some words. My lord, that cannot be. (*Puts up the letter.*) And now for a few bequests to my relations, in case his lordship should prove victorious. It is well my will is already made—for he has scarcely given me time to—(*He writes, then throws down the pen.*) What paternal weakness! (*Rises.*) How strange it is, altho' I *have* resisted, and *can*, with manly firmness, resist every innate pleading for that ungrateful boy I once called my son; that careless prodigal of a father's peace, and his own welfare—yet—when I consider myself as shortly to be an inhabitant of another world, and without the power to assist him—I wish—I wish— What?—Why, that heaven may then raise him up a friend to deal more gently with him than I have done. A friend, whose temper, whose *place* it better may become to forgive his faults than an offended father. (*He takes the paper.*) In vain are the strugglings of nature. Justice—example—and my word irrevocably past, silence its pretences. (*He seals the paper, directs it, and looks at his watch.*) The time is almost expired, and I must pay a short visit to my new lodger, and be gone.—John!

Enter SERVANT.

Mr Ant. Is not this the time that the lady gave me permission to wait on her?

Serv. The lady sent word she wou'd wait on you, sir. This is the time; and, sir, she is coming.

Mr Ant. Shew her in.   [*Exit Servant.*

(*Mr Anthony walks two or three turns, and then the lady is shewn in.*)

Mr Ant. I hope, madam, my message did not disturb you?

Lady. Not at all, sir. I had asked permission to see you before I received it. *(He draws chairs, and they sit.)*

Mr Ant. Well, madam—Unless you have enquired of the servants, you are yet a stranger to my name and connections.

Lady. I am a stranger to them, sir. But your humanity must ever be engraved on my heart.

Mr Ant. Then, madam, for the service you are pleased to acknowledge I have rendered you, all I request, in return, is your confidence. Explain clearly to me the circumstances, the temptations that brought you into the situation from whence I released you! Declare them with frankness, and tax my humanity yet further; it shall not forsake you. To encourage you to this confession, my name is——

Lady. Hold, Sir! That is an information I cannot return—therefore let us wave it; and as I can remain grateful for your goodness, without knowing to *whom* I am indebted, so pity still my weakness, and my miseries, without a further knowledge of the wretched sufferer.

Mr Ant. Madam, you have imposed on me a task too hard. 'Tis true you have won my pity; but 'tis fit you shou'd *secure* it too. And while explanations are reserved, *Doubt,* that hardener of the human heart, must be your enemy.

Lady. Alas! *(Rises.)*

Mr Ant. Come—I wish not to exact too much; but I am a *man,* madam, and with every frailty incident to the species: *suspicion* has its place.

Lady. I know I am an object of suspicion; but you are deceived in me—indeed you are. Guilt never *harboured* in my heart. Maternal tenderness, for two helpless infants, hurried me in a moment to do I know not what, rather than lose them : **A** deed ! the horror of which (altho' by the mercy of eternal Providence, I have escaped its direst consequences,) must ever cover me with blushes ; and, shou'd indulgent heaven reserve me for a meeting with my husband, must, with remorse, damp every joy the fond; fond interview would give !

Mr. Ant. Be comforted. (*Leading her to her seat.*) I mean not to increase, but soothe your grief. Tell me but *who* you are, and *why* thus abandoned by all your relations, friends, and husband ? I can excuse the feelings of a mother—the sudden starts, or rather madness of resolution, formed by the excessive anguish of the soul. Trust me, I can deal tenderly with human failings. No frivolous curiosity, but a desire to serve you, thus urges me to entreat you will *unfold* yourself.

Lady. Oh, Sir, I have a husband, *I think,* who loves me. Once I am sure he did. *My* heart has never stray'd from *him,* since our fatal union. What must that poor heart suffer, torn with remorse for the rash step my mad despair suggested to preserve my children ? Oh ! in my bosom let his name lie hid, that none may know his wretched fortune in a hapless wife.

Mr Ant. Your reasons have satisfied me. I do not ask your name. Tell me but the *circumstances* that drove you to the state from whence I released you : Be so far explicit, and I will ask no more.

Lady. Most willingly ! When first my husband saw me, I was friendless. Compassion caused his love for me—Gratitude mine for him. Forlorn and destitute, no kind relation, no tender benefactor taught my heart affection. Unused to all the little offices of kindness, could they but endear the object who bestowed them? Sense of obligation, never before excited, pressed on my thoughts, and soon was

changed to love. He scorned to violate the heart
that was his own, and we were married.

Mr Ant. I find no room for accusation here. Go
on—go on, madam. What has alienated your husband from you, and left you thus destitute at present? If you can resolve me that; if you still have
acted with equal propriety, I am your friend—I have
no censure for you.

Lady. But you will condemn my husband; even
I must own he was to blame. Born of wealthy parents,
the heir to large possessions, and I to none, when
he married, all were given up, and he changed his
state for mine. We had no friend, but in each other;
yet happy was that state to *me*, till poverty surprised
us ; and the fond hope (which once he cherished) of
paternal forgiveness, vanished from my husband.
Then all our days were bitter as they had before
been happy; tears were my only food, and sighs
were his; even *reproach* I have endured from him,
for making him the friendless wretch he call'd himself. Yet—yet, at our parting, oh! then he can-
cell'd all ; for when the regiment, in which he served, was ordered from the kingdom, he hung upon
me, clasped his poor children, begg'd our forgiveness for the thousand outrages distress at our misfortunes had caused him to commit; swore that affection for us, was the source of his impatience—prayed
heaven to bless *us*, whatever might be his fate—nay,
prayed that death might speedily be his doom, so
that it turned his father's heart to us.

Mr Ant. And have you never applied to his
father ?

Lady. Yes, but all in vain; and two months since,
hearing my husband was made prisoner, (and destitute of every relief and every hope while he remained so,) I left my children and came to London, resolved, in *pers n.* to supplicate his father's bounty :

when I learnt (dire news,) his father, visiting an estate abroad, was lost, and we left to despair.

Mr Ant. What do you say?

Lady. Nay, do not blame him; I pardon him from
my soul. And as my husband, spite of his disobedience, loved him tenderly, I will ever give a tear in
tribute to his memory.

Mr Ant. Without hesitation!—without the smallest reserve, tell me your husband's name! Is it
Euston?

Lady. It is!

Mr Ant. His father is not dead! He lives, and
pardons him this moment! (*Embracing her.*)

Mrs Eus. You are his father! I know it! I
see it in your looks! (*Kneeling.*)

Mr Ant. And you shall henceforth see it in my
actions! Rise, rise, and behold (*Taking the paper
from his pocket,*) where I this moment again disown'd
him for my son, while the poor of every kind (except
himself) I ever styled my children—Oh! charity,
partially dealt, never more receive that heavenly virtue's title. Here (*Pointing to the paper.*) I provide
for you as a poor stranger, who never asked, and
might not have deserved my bounty; while, as a
daughter, begging for an alms, I shut my heart, and
sent your supplications back. Where was the merit
of my thousands given, while one poor wretch, from
proud resentment, petitioned me in vain?

Mrs Eus. I dare not call myself your daughter!

Mr Ant. You *are* my daughter; and, when I have
supplicated heaven to pardon my neglect of you, I'll
ask your pardon, too. You *are* my daughter—and
let the infamy you have escaped serve only to make
you more amiable; make you compassionate—compassionate to your own weak sex, in *whatsoever* suffering state you see them—They all were virtuous
once, as well as you—and, had they met a father,

might have been saved like you. For me—(*Pulls out his watch.*) Bless me, how has the time flown!—My dear, I have an engagement I cannot postpone above half an hour ; and that time I must dedicate to——Now, methinks, I wou'd wish to live. (*Aside.*) Retire to your chamber. I will, if possible, be with you speedily.—Where your husband is, and in what poor place your children, I am impatient till I know ; but now I cannot wait. Retire, my child. May we meet again in safety. (*He leads her to the door, and she withdraws.*)

Mr Ant. Now where's the Colonel ? I have just time to draw up a writing for him to sign when he arrives ; and I'll about it instantly. Oh ! with what transport does the human heart dislodge the unnatural guests, malice, and resentment, to take to its warm recesses the mild inhabitant, peaceful Charity. Yet even more welcome is the returning virtue, when thus 'tis strengthened by parental fondness.

                                                    [*Exit.*

ACT THE FIFTH.

SCENE I.

An Apartment at MAJOR CYPRUS'.

Enter LADY HARRIET, *and* BLOOM, *meeting.*

La. Har. What success? Will Sir George come?
What a tedious time have you been gone!

Bloom. Dear madam, if you cou'd suppose how
obstinate Sir George was; and how I had to beg,
and to pray—

La. Har. But will he come?

Bloom. Yes, madam—at last he said he wou'd.

La. Har. Thank Heaven—Then I shall have the
unspeakable joy of giving him this! (*Pulling out a
letter.*)

Bloom. What, Sir George, madam? Well, I declare, I was at my wit's ends to know what you cou'd
want with Sir George.

La. Har. To give him this letter, Bloom, from
Lady Euston to the Major, which you so luckily
found, and to have the extreme pleasure of informing
him that I am not the only object deserving his resentment: but that even his wife of a few months—

F 3

she whom the world says he doats upon, and who has driven me from his remembrance, is indiscreet as I have been; to see with my own eyes his confusion—hear him reproach her conduct, and make him own—He promised he'd come?

Bloom. Yes, ma'am—but not till I knelt down and swore your ladyship was *dying*; suddenly taken ill; and cou'd not leave the world in peace till you had communicated something from your own lips to him.

La. Har. You did right; just as I ordered you— And what did he say to that?

Bloom. (*After a long pause.*) Why, he said,—" I will come to the poor unhappy wretch !"

La. Har. Wretch ! Are you sure he said so ?

Bloom. I am sure he said " Poor," and " unhappy," and then, you know, " wretch" follows of course.

La. Har. Who will be *most* wretched, in a few moments, he or I ?

Bloom. Very true, madam; I believe he'll find he has not changed for the better.

La. Har. (*Looking at the letter.*) Confusion! What have you made me do? You told me this letter was for the Major; it is directed to Sir Harry Harmless.

Bloom. Oh that I shou'd not look at the direction!

La. Har. No matter; this is even a greater dishonour to Sir George than were it to the Major, and will wound him deeper—But where is the Major then ? He will not be engaged as I supposed—and may return.

Bloom. Oh, no, my lady, that I dare say he won't —you need not fear; go into your chamber, madam, and make yourself easy till Sir George comes, and make yourself easy when he does come too; for, though the Major may not be with Lady Euston, I dare say he has his appointments in some corner or another, as well as your ladyship.   [*Exeunt.*

SCENE II.

MR ANTHONY EUSTON'S.

Enter MR ANTHONY EUSTON *and* COLONEL DOWN-
RIGHT.

Mr Ant. I have been waiting for you all day—
What meant the few words in your letter? Why is
my meeting with his lordship deferred?

Col. Down. I am just come from Lord Layton—a
friend of his lordship's, knowing I was acquainted
with you, called and took me there; and, to tell you
the truth, I think this business between you and his
lordship might be amicably and honourably settled—
However, if you don't fight with *him*, you must fight
with a mad-headed fellow I have left below—So
which do you choose?

Mr Ant. What do you mean?

Col Down. Nay, you will have a worse chance than
you wou'd have had with his lordship; for this man
is a soldier, one who has been fighting for these four
or five years past; besides, he's desperate—half mad;
and has sworn, he'll either kill or be killed by you,
instantly.

Mr Ant. Let him come—Who, and what is he?
What has he to demand of me?   (*Angrily.*)

Col. Down. Nay, don't be too violent neither—He's a poor unfortunate lad, I fancy ; and, notwithstanding all his blustering—he now and then looks so heart-wounded, I cannot help pitying him.

Mr Ant. But what's his business ?　What is his quarrel with me ?

Col. Down. Lord Layton is the innocent cause of it ; he told the young man, who came to his lordship's (somewhat sooner than I did) in search of the lady whom you took away, that the lady had confessed herself poor ; and even perishing for subsistence ; and that, consequently, she was willing to resign herself to the most liberal; which, you proving, in spite of his lordship's generosity, you carried off the prize ; and, egad, I owned it was what I had suspected, notwithstanding your grave countenance last night.

Mr Ant. You told him you thought so ?

Col. Down. Yes ; for I wished to turn the whole matter into a joke with his lordship ; I did not think, at the time, that the young fellow wou'd have been so violent ; for till this was explained he was as patient as a lamb ; and only inquired, with *trembling* and *sighs,* for the lady ; but, when he heard what I said, egad, he laid hold of me, and swore, till I brought him to my friend, the " unpitying, vile purchaser of innocence," (meaning you) he wou'd not quit me— So here he has followed me through the streets ; and, on condition that he wou'd be patient while I came and announced him to you, I have promised him you shall give him satisfaction.

Mr Ant. What is this gentleman's name ?　(*Anxiously.*)

Col. Down. He did not tell us.

Mr Ant. Does he know mine ?

Col. Down. No; I thought it most prudent not to

tell him ; for, he is such a madman, he might have bawled it as we came in the streets.

Mr Ant. (*Much embarrassed.*) What is he to the lady ? Her brother ?—her cousin ?

Col. Down. Why, faith, I've a notion, (though he did not say so,) I have a notion he is her husband.

Mr Ant. Indeed !—(*Starting.*)

Col. Down. Why you don't like the business the worse for that ? 'Tis *crim. con.* now, and you'll be quite in the fashion.

Mr Ant. Let the young man come up ; I'll withdraw for a moment ; but do not give him to suppose I have *not* injured him.

Col. Down. That you may depend upon ; I never tell a falsehood for myself, much less for another.

Mr Ant. Neither let him know my *name*. I'll first send the lady to him, and then return myself.

Col. Down. He's coming. [*Exit Mr Anthony.*

Charles. (*Without.*) Where is this gentleman ?

Col. Down. Walk in here, sir.

Enter CHARLES EUSTON.

Col. Down. The man you wish to see—and whom you say has injured you—will be here and give you satisfaction immediately.

Cha. I thank him—Then I shall die and never see her more. (*Aside.*) Oh, sir ! cooled with the restraint you have thus long imposed on me ! I wish to ask a favour ; I thought I was resolved never again to behold the wretch I have been deprived of ; but, my rage for a moment gone, I cannot think of dying, and she so near me, without once looking on her ; I have come far to see her—suffered much—crossed half the Eastern clime in poverty ; have endured more pain, more toil, to gain my freedom, but to starve with her—and, dying, comfort her, than, had a throne been my waiting reward, my spirits could

have struggled with. And, after all, I feel, I feel
I could be repaid with a mere look. Then, why
refuse me? If I scape my antagonist, I have resolved on death! Let me then see her! I will not
exchange a word with her—will they refuse her
coming?

Col. Down. No—for here she is—

Enter MRS EUSTON, *and stops* (*with emotion*) *as soon
as she enters.*

Mrs Eus. Oh! But I am commanded not to fly
to your arms—I must not run to you, and tell you
all I feel!

Cha. (*After a pause.*) I said—I thought—I
wou'd not speak to you—but pity for your crimes and
miseries compel me ; and, I tell you, to alleviate
your remorse, I *pardon you*—nay, perhaps, love you
better, even in this agony of affliction, than if we had
been blest with prosperous, virtuous days! I know
what you have suffered! Your guilt convinces me !
I want no other plea from a heart like yours. But
where's your vile purchaser? My rage returns !
I must die soon—but first in his breast! (*Draws
his sword.*)

Col. Down. He's here!

Enter MR ANTHONY.

Cha. Then to his heart—(*Going to stab him, sees
it is his father, and after a pause, falls on his knees.*)
My father!

Mr Ant. Yes—I am the man, whose life you seek.
And, as your father, you might pursue your purpose
—But, as your wife's friend and preserver, still kneel
to me ; and receive her, virtuous, from my hands.

Cha. (*Embracing her.*) Virtuous! Virtuous !—
O my father—Even groaning under your displeasure,

ever dear, and revered! What are you now, while heavenly consolation pours from your lips?

Col. Down. Father and son! Why, then there's to be no battle at last?

Mr. Ant. No—Hostilities are past—and may their future days know only peace! My son— (*Embracing him.*)

Cha. That tender name distracts me! Let me be more composed—prepared—before I experience such unexpected happiness. Maria, lead me from my father—Hereafter I will thank him; but now, I cannot.

Mrs Eus. Oh! Yes, my husband, kneel to him again!—Kneel for me! For your poor children! Saved from want and wretchedness! From being orphans! Kneel to him for us all!—preserved from infamy!

Cha. O spare the recollection—I feel too much! A poor, forsaken, desperate, dying man, restored to love, to life, to *him*, too—whose anger, (even while blest with thee,) plung'd me in constant sorrow. It is too much!

Mr Ant. I thought my heart had been—but— (*He faulters and wipes his eyes.*)

Col. Down. What? Do *you* weep?—Now, that affects me more than any thing that has been said or done yet. I don't like to see a woman cry, but I can't bear to see a man: a man's tears flow from so deep a source—they always appear to have come a long journey, and therefore I notice them as strangers, that have gone through fatigue, and trouble, on their way. While a woman's tears I consider as mere neighbours, that can call upon you when they like, and generally drop in on all occasions.   [*Exeunt.*

SCENE III.

Major Cyprus'.

Enter LADY HARRIET *and* BLOOM.

La. Har. (*A loud rap.*)   That is Sir George—
Heavens !—

Bloom. Yes, my Lady, that it is—

La. Har. Heavens ! What a sensation—How am
I agitated at his approach ! Cou'd I have thought,
a few hours ago, I shou'd ever see him again?—
Speak to him again ! Oh this shame—

Bloom. Shame ! Bless me ! One does feel a
little ashamed sometimes on seeing a stranger ; but,
my lady, Sir George is (as one may say) an *old
acquaintance.*

La. Har. I must retire for a moment—Do you
receive him—and, before I return, give him to understand that I am *not* dying ; but will come to him
immediately.   [*Exit.*

Bloom. Well, now I declare I begin to be ashamed
myself—Own all I swore to him on my knees was a
falsehood ? Why, what will he say ? Dear me,
I'm quite alarmed ! I must retire for a moment
too ! (*Goes to the back of the stage.   A servant
shows Sir George in, and retires.*)

Sir Geo. How strange does it seem to me to find
myself once more in this house, especially when I
consider who resides here—Who ? Perhaps, by this
time, poor Lady Harriet is no more—How amiably

did my dear Lady Euston enforce her dying request
—I doubted the *rectitude* of complying with it—but
she surmounted all my scruples, and her tenderness
and generosity have endeared her to me more than
ever.

BLOOM *comes down.*

Sir Geo. How does Lady Harriet?

Bloom. As well as can be expected, sir.

Sir Geo. How!

Bloom. I hope you won't be angry, sir—but she's
a *little* better.

Sir Geo. Angry! No; I am very glad to hear it!

Bloom. Are you indeed, sir? Why, then I believe she is a *great deal* better.

Sir Geo. Indeed! I am very glad; but then, if
my attendance can be dispensed with—I may as
well—

Major Cyp. (*Without.*) Let the chariot wait—
perhaps, I may go out again.

Bloom. Oh! Oh! Oh! Oh! Oh!—that's the
major—that's my master! my *other* master! Oh,
what will become of us all?

Sir Geo. How unlucky!

Bloom. Sir! Dear sir, hide yourself!

Sir Geo. Hide!

Bloom. On my knees I beg—Consider my poor
dying lady!

Major Cyp. (*On the stairs.*) Go with that note
immediately.

Bloom. Here! in here, sir, for Heaven's sake.
                    (*Opening the closet door.*)

Sir Geo. 'Sdeath! What shall I do? See *him?*
Damnation! And see him *here* too? No, I can't
bear it—I must avoid him.
                    (*Going towards the closet.*)

Bloom. Here, Sir—here quick! (*She puts Sir George into the closet, and shuts the door.*)

Bloom. There, there he is! thank Heaven! For, if my poor lady had lost the major, she might never have got a third husband. Lord bless me, I'm just as terrified as if I had never been used to these sort of things!   [*Exit to Lady Harriet.*

Enter MAJOR CYPRUS.

Major Cyp. Ridiculed, baffled—laughed at—disappointed! How Sir George will enjoy this! A fine figure I cut on my knees to Sir Harry, when the colonel and his friends were shown in! And then my ridiculous vanity in wishing him to be unmasked, confidently expecting it was Euston's wife! Oh, damn it! I'll think no more of it; but as I am deprived the satisfaction of revenge on the lady abroad, I'll e'en torment my lady at home! (*Calls*) Lady Harriet——Lady Harriet.

Enter LADY HARRIET *and* BLOOM.

Major Cyp. What's the matter? You tremble—you look pale!

La. Har. (*Trembling.*) Tremble! Bless me—I've been fast asleep—and such a dream! I thought I was falling—

Bloom. Ay, my lady, I always dream of falling too!

La. Har. (*Yawns and rubs her eyes.*) How long have you been come home? What's o'clock? How long do you think I have slept, Bloom?

Bloom. I dare say, pretty near an hour and half, my lady.

La. Har. A miserable dull book—fell out of my hand! and I dropp'd insensibly—

Bloom. And with the candles so near your lady-ship! I'm sure your ladyship was very lucky, you did not set yourself on fire!

Major Cyp. Aye; does your ladyship consider the danger with the lights so near you? You might have caught fire, and I shou'd have had all my va-luable pictures, and library, consumed in an instant!

La. Har. And I consumed too.

Major Cyp. Aye—and your ladyship.

La. Har. Very true—but I am fond of reading melancholy books; that set me to sleep.

Major Cyp. Then I desire, for the future, you wou'd *not* read.

La. Har. And don't you desire I wou'd not sleep too! I'm very sorry you disturbed me.— Bloom, come and dispose the sofa, and the lights— I'm resolved I'll finish my nap.

Major Cyp. But, Mrs Bloom, first order the French horns up—I'm out of spirits.   [*Exit Bloom.*

La. Har. And do you imagine your horns will disturb my repose? I shall like them of all things —they'll lull me to sleep.

Major Cyp. Like them or not—I will have them.

La. Har. You shall—you shall have them. (*Significantly.*)   [*Exit.*

Enter SERVANT.

Ser. Colonel Downright, Sir, with two gentlemen, strangers, desire to be admitted.

Major Cyp. (*Aside.*) What can bring them here? They dare not come to laugh at me! No matter—I'll see them. (*Aloud.*) Shew them up.

Enter COLONEL DOWNRIGHT, MR EUSTON, *and* MR ANTHONY EUSTON.

Col. Down. Major, these gentlemen, the Mr Euston's, have begged me to introduce them to you,

late as it is, on business in which they are ma-
terially—

Mr Ant. Sir—Major Cyprus, I beg your pardon
—but I have received intelligence that my nephew,
Sir George Euston, is in this house, and I am come
to conduct him safe out of it.

Major Cyp. Sir!

Mr. Ant. In short, Sir—Sir George Euston has
been, by some unwarrantable means, led to pay a
visit here, and I cannot leave the house until I see
him.   If I should, my niece, Lady Euston, will be
highly alarmed (knowing you are at home,) for her
husband's safety.

Major Cyp. Sir George in this house! Ridiculous
supposition!

Mr Eus. Call her ladyship's woman—She deliver'd the message of invitation—I shall know her
again, for I saw her—and I saw Sir George soon
after follow her.

Major Cyp. Bloom! Bloom! Where's Bloom?

Enter BLOOM.

Pray were you at Sir George Euston's to-day, or
this evening?

Bloom. I! At Sir George Euston's, sir!

Mr Eus. Yes: I saw you there.

Bloom. Oh! Oh! Oh! (*crying*) Oh dear! I
was not there indeed, sir!

Major Cyp. You see she denies it, and confirms
the truth with her tears.

Mr Ant. I distrust them both—Both her truth
and her tears.

Major Cyp. Come, come, Mr Anthony Euston,
confess you were not brought hither to seek Sir
George—Clear yourself, in your turn, from the
suspicions I entertain of you.   But, if you dare to

avow yourself the contriver, or even abettor of the
affront offered me at the masquerade—

Mr Eus. Major Cyprus! My brother Anthony
knew no more of the appointment at the masquerade,
than the child unborn. But, bless you, my niece
and we meant you no ill by it; we only meant to
have a joke at your and Sir Harry's expense—that
was all.

Major Cyp. Then give me leave to tell you, Mr
Euston, and you also Mr Anthony, that your present
visit—

Mr Ant. We understand you, Sir—only assure
us that Sir George Euston is safe, and we'll leave
your house immediately—

Major Cyp. *I!* assure you that Sir George
Euston is safe!

Mr Ant. You seem surprised—Let me then
speak a word with Lady Harriet, whom the servants
tell me is at home. Is she or not?

Major Cyp. (*To a servant without.*) Desire your
lady to come hither. But have a care, gentlemen,
how far you provoke me by your suspicions! For,
by Heaven—

Mr Ant. I have no fears but for Sir George—nor
will now your utmost rage induce me to quit the
house till I am assured of his safety.

Major Cyp. And pray, sir, *who* in this house is
to assure you of it?

Sir Geo. (*Bursting from the closet.*)—Himself!

Major Cyp. Confusion!

Mr Ant. You see, Sir, my intelligence was good.

Sir Geo. Strange as my concealment may appear,
the cause was such as I can with honour reveal.

Major Cyp. Then, pray sir, with " honour re-
" veal it."

Sir Geo. Why then I assure you, major—and I
assure you all—upon my honour—and on the word

G 3

of a gentleman—that my being here—was—entirely
—owing—to—to—

Major Cyp. (*Warmly.*)   To what?   To what,
sir?

Col. Down. " I'll tell you what"—to " an un-
" describable something"—to be sure!

Major Cyp. Damnation!

Col. Down. Did not I tell you to keep the *key* of
the closet?

Major Cyp. Colonel, I beg—this is not a time—

Enter BLOOM.

Bloom. (*To the Major.*)   The horns are ready,
sir—wou'd you choose to have them?

Major Cyp. No.   (*In a fury.*)   [*Exit* BLOOM.

Enter LADY EUSTON, *and* LADY HARRIET, *at opposite doors.*

La. Eus. Where is Sir George?

Mr Eus. Here, my dear—just stept out of the
closet.

La. Eus. What closet?

Col. Down. That—that very *identical* closet.

Major Cyp. Heigh ho!

Mr Eus. Indeed, Lady Euston, you have cause
to reproach him.

La. Eus. I fear he will rather reproach me for
this abrupt intrusion—but my apprehensions for his
safety (hearing no tidings from his uncles) have
alone impell'd me to it.

La. Har. Had your ladyship not written this
letter to the amiable Sir Harry Harmless, (which I
unfortunately supposed intended for Major Cyprus,)
your ladyship's alarming " apprehensions" might
have been spared, as I sent for Sir George but to
shew him this letter.

Mr Eus. And that letter was only a joke—a scheme to mortify the Major and Sir Harry.

La. Eus. It was so—I own it. And the confusion the scheme has occasioned, Sir George, needs all your forgiveness.

Sir Geo. I sincerely pardon it—and hope the whole company will do me the justice to believe that my sole motive, for entering this house, was a compliance with, what I then thought, the dying request of that lady. And I now believe, that her ladyship's sole motive for wishing to see me was merely to shew me the letter of which she speaks— a copy of which, not without my knowledge, but against my opinion, was written by Lady Euston to Major Cyprus, appointing a fictitious interview, in return for his having dared to offend her with the profession of a licentious passion!

Major Cyp. Sir George, I am perfectly satisfied with this explanation. But, after what has happened, the world may despise me for being so, and therefore, Lady Harriet, from this moment we separate—And we had been wiser, as well as happier, if we had never met.

La. Har. Most willingly separate—Your unkind treatment—and my own constant inquietude—have long since taught a woman of the world too feelingly to acknowledge, " No lasting friendship is form'd on " vice."

Mr Ant. Preach this, my dear lady, to all your fair countrywomen—enforce your words by your future conduct, and they shall draw a veil over the frailty of your past life.

La. Har. Oh! Mr Anthony, cou'd I but retrieve my innocence, my honour, for ever lost!

Mr Ant. Yet, do not despair. You can still possess *one* inestimable good—that inborn virtue which *never perishes*—which never leaves us but to return

For, when you think it extinguished, feel but due
remorse, and it rises again in the soul.

Mr Eus. That's right, brother Anthony—comfort
her—it is your duty.   And we are all *relations,* you
know—the whole company are related to one another.
Though it is in an odd kind of a jumbled way—I
wish some learned gentleman, of the law, would tell
us *what* relations we all are—and what relation the
child of a first husband is to his mother's second
husband, while his own father is living.

Mr Ant. Brother, you think too deeply.

Mr Eus. Not at all, brother Anthony !   And,
for fear the gentlemen of the long robe shou'd not be
able to find out the present company's *affinity,* let us
apply to the *kindred ties* of each other's passions,
weaknesses, and imperfections; and, thereupon, agree
to part, this evening, not only *near relations,* but
good friends.

NEXT DOOR NEIGHBOURS;

A

COMEDY,

IN THREE ACTS.

AS PERFORMED AT THE

THEATRE-ROYAL, HAYMARKET.

BY

Mrs. INCHBALD.

DRAMATIS PERSONÆ.

SIR GEORGE SPLENDORVILLE,	*Mr Palmer.*
MR MANLY,	*Mr Kemble.*
MR BLACKMAN,	*Mr Baddeley.*
MR LUCRE,	*Mr R. Palmer.*
LORD HAZARD,	*Mr Evatt.*
WILLFORD,	*Mr Aickin.*
HENRY,	*Mr Palmer, jun.*
BLUNTLY,	*Mr Bannister, jun.*
LADY CAROLINE SEYMOUR,	*Mrs Brooks.*
LADY BRIDGET SQUANDER,	*Miss Heard.*
EVANS,	*Mrs Edwards.*
ELEANOR,	*Mrs Kemble.*

Other Ladies, Gentlemen, Servants, &c.

SCENE,—London.

NEXT DOOR NEIGHBOURS.

ACT THE FIRST.

SCENE I.

An Antichamber at SIR GEORGE SPLENDORVILLE'S, *adjoining a Ball-room.*

Enter BLUNTLY, *meeting a Servant in Livery.*

Blun. Come, come, is not every thing ready ? Is not the ball-room prepared yet ? It is past ten o'clock.

Ser. We have only to fix up the new chandelier.

Blun. I'll have no new chandelier.

Ser. My master said the last ball he gave, the company were in the dark.

Blun. And if you blind them with too much light, they will be in the dark still.

Ser. The musicians, sir, wish for some wine.

Blun. What, before the ball begins? No, tell them if they are tipsy at the end of it, it will be quite soon enough.

Ser. You are always so cross, Mr Bluntly, when my master is going to have company.

Blun. Have not I a right to be cross? For while the whole house is in good humour, if there was not one person cross enough to take a little care, every thing would be wasted and ruined through extreme good temper. *A man crosses the stage.*) Here, you—Mister—Pray, are you the person who was sent with the chandelier?

Shop. Yes, sir.

Blun. Then please to take it back again—We don't want it.

Shop. What is your objection to it, sir?

Blun. It will cost too much.

Shop. Mr Bluntly, all the trades-people are more frightened at you than at your master. Sir George, Heaven bless him! never cares how much a thing costs.

Blun. That is, because he never cares whether he pays for it or not; but if he did, depend upon it he would be very particular. Tradesmen all wish to be paid for their ware, don't they?

Shop. Certainly, sir.

Blun. Then why will they force so many unnecessary things, and make so many extravagant charges, as to put all power of payment out of the question?

Enter EVANS.—*The Tradesman goes off at the opposite Door.*

Blun. How do you do, Mrs Evans?—(*Sullenly.*)

Ev. What makes you sigh, Mr Bluntly?

Blun. What makes you smile?

Ev. To see all the grand preparations for the ball this evening. I anticipate the joy my lady will take here, and I smile for *her*.

Blun. And I sigh for my master. I foresee all the bills that will be brought in, for this evening's expence, and I anticipate the sorrow it will one day be to *him*.

Ev. But consider, Mr Bluntly, your master has my lady's fortune to take.

Blun. Yes, but I consider, he has your lady to take along with it ; and I prophecy one will stick by him some time after the other is gone.

Ev. For shame. My lady, I have no doubt, will soon cure Sir George of his extravagance.

Blun. It will then be by taking away the means. Why, Lady Caroline is as extravagant as himself.

Ev. You are mistaken. She never gives routs, masquerades, balls, or entertainments of any kind.

Blun. But she constantly goes to them whenever she is invited.

Ev. That, I call but a slight imprudence. She has no wasteful indiscretion like Sir George. For instance, she never makes a lavish present.

Blun. No, but she *takes* a lavish present, as readily as if she did.

Ev. And surely you cannot call that imprudence?

Blun. No, I call it something worse.

Ev. Then, although she loves gaming to distraction, and plays deep, yet she never loses.

Blun. No, but she always wins—and *that* I call something worse.

(A loud rapping at the street-door.)

Ev. Here's the company. Will you permit me,
Mr Bluntly, to stand in one corner, and have a peep
at them ?

Blun. If you please. (*Rapping again.*) What
spirit there is in that, Rat, tat, tat, tat. And what
life, frolic, and joy, the whole house is going to experience, except myself. As for me, I am ready to
cry at the thoughts of it all. [*Exit.*

Enter LADY CAROLINE.

L. Car. Here, the first of the company. I am
sorry for it. (*Evans comes forward.*) Evans, what
has brought you hither ?

Ev. I came, my lady, to see the preparations making on *your* account—for it is upon your account
alone, that Sir George gives this grand *fête.*

L. Car. Why, I do flatter myself it is. But where
is he? What is it o'clock ?—It was impossible to
stay at the stupid opera.—How do I look? I once
did intend to wear those set of diamonds Sir George
presented me with the other morning—but then, I
reflected again, that if——

Ev. Ah, my lady, what a charming thing to have
such a lover ; Sir George prevents every wish ; he
must make the best of husbands.

L. Car. And yet my father wishes to break off the
marriage ; he talks of his prodigality ; and, certainly, Sir George lives above his income.

Ev. But then, madam, so does every body else.

L. Car. But Sir George ought undoubtedly to
change his conduct, and not be thus continually giving balls and entertainments ; and inviting to his table acquaintance, that not only come to devour his
dinners and suppers, but him.

Ev. And there are people malicious enough to call
your ladyship one of his devourers too.

L. Car. As a treaty of marriage is so nearly concluded between us, I think, Mrs Evans, I am at liberty to visit Sir George, or to receive his presents,
without having my character, or my delicacy called
in question. (*A loud rapping.*) The company are
coming: is it not strange he is not here to receive
them.   [*Exit* EVANS.

*Enter two ladies and a gentleman, who curts y ad
bow to* LADY CAROLINE.—SIR GEORGE *enters at
the opposite door, magnificently dressed.*

Sir Geo. Ladies, I entreat your pardon ; dear
Lady Caroline excuse me. I have been in the country all the morning, and have had scarce time to return to town and dress for your reception. (*Another
rapping.*)

Enter MR LUCRE, LORD HAZARD, LADY BRIDGET
SQUANDER, &c.

Sir Geo. Dear Lucre, I am glad to see you.

Mr Lu. My dear Sir George, I had above ten engagements this evening, but they all gave place to
your invitation.

Sir Geo. Thank you.—My dear Lady Bridget—

L. Brid. It is impossible to resist an in ation
from the most polished man alive.   (*Sir George
bows.*) What a superb dress ! (*in his hearing, as
he turns away,*) and what an elegant deportment !

Mr Lu. (*After speaking apart with Sir George.*)
No, I am not in a state to take any part at Pharo—
I am ruin'd. Would you believe it, Sir George, I
am not worth a farthing in the world.

Sir Geo. Yes, I believed it long ago.

Mr Lu. Now we are on that subject ; could you
lend me a hundred pounds ?

Sir Geo. (*Taking out his pocket-book.*) I have
about me only this bill for two hundred.

Mr Lu. That will do as well; I am not circumstantial. *Takes it.*) And my dear Sir George, command my purse at any time—all it contains, will ever
be at your service.

Sir Geo. I thank you.

Mr Lu. Nay, though I have no money of my own,
yet you know I can always raise friends; and by heaven! my dear Sir George, I often wish to see you
reduced to my circumstances, merely to prove how
much I could, and *would*, do to serve you.

Sir Geo. I sincerely thank you.

Mr Luc. And one can better ask a favour for one's
friend than for one's-self, you know: for when one
wants to borrow money on one's own account, there
are so many little delicacies to get the better of; such
as I felt just now. I was as pale as death, I dare
say, when I asked you for this money; did not you
perceive I was?

Sir Geo. I can't say I did.

Mr Lu. But you must have observed I hesitated,
and looked very foolish.

Sir Geo. I thought for my part, that I looked as
foolish. But I hope I did not hesitate.

Mr Lu. Nor ever will, when a friend applies to
you, I'll answer for it—Nor ever shall a friend hesitate when you apply.

L. Haz. (*Taking Sir George aside.*) The obligations I am under to you for extricating me from that
dangerous business—

Sir Geo. Never name it.

L. Haz. Not only name it, Sir George, but shortly
I hope to return the kindness; and, if I do but
live——

Sir Geo. (*To the company.*) Permit me to conduct
you to the next apartment.

L. Car. Most willingly, Sir George. I was the
first who arrived; which proves my eagerness to dance.

Sir Geo. (Aside to her.) But let me hope, passion for dancing was not the only one, that caused your impatience.

(As the company move towards the ball-room, Mr Lucre and Lord Hazard come forward.

Mr Lu. Oh! there never was such a man in the world as the master of this house; there never was such a friendly, generous, noble heart; he has the best heart in the world, and the best taste in dress.

[*The company Exeunt, and the music is heard to begin.*

SCENE II.

An apartment, which denotes the Poverty of the Inhabitants. Henry *and* Eleanor *discovered.*

Elea. It is very late and very cold too, brother; and yet we have neither of us heart to bid each other good night.

Hen. No—beds were made for rest.

Elea. And that noise of carriages and link-boys at Sir George Splendorville's, next door, would keep us awake, if our sorrows did not.

Hen. The poor have still more to complain of, when chance throws them thus near the rich,—it forces upon their minds a comparison might drive them to despair, if—

Elea. If they should not have good sense enough to reflect, that all this bustle and show of pleasure, may fall very short of happiness; as all the distress *we* feel, has not yet, thank Heaven, reached to misery.

Hen. What do you call it then?

Elea. A trial; sent to make us patient.

Hen. It may make you so, but cannot me. Good morning to you. (*Going.*)

Elea. Nay, it is night yet. Where are you going?

Hen. I don't know.—To take a walk. The streets are not more uncomfortable than this place, and scarcely colder.

Elea. Oh, my dear brother! I cannot express half the uneasiness I feel when you part from me, though but for the shortest space.

Hen. Why?

Elea. Because I know your temper; you are impatient under adversity; you rashly think Providence is unkind; and you would snatch those favours, which are only valuable when bestowed.

Hen. What do you mean?

Elea. Nay, do not be angry; but every time you go out into this tempting town, where superfluous riches continually meet the eye of the poor, I tremble lest you should forfeit your honesty for that, which Heaven decreed should not belong to you.

Hen. And if I did, you would despise and desert me?

Elea. No: not desert you; for I am convinced you would only take to bring to me; but this is to assure you, I do not want for any thing.

Hen. Not want?—Nor does my father?

Elea. Scarcely while we visit him. Every time he sees us we make him happy; but he would never behold us again if we behaved unworthy of him.

Hen. What! banish us from a prison?

Elea. And although it is a prison, you could not be happy under such a restriction.

Hen. Happy! When was I happy last?

Elea. Yesterday, when your father thanked you for your kindness to him. Did we not all three weep with affection for each other? and was not that happiness?

Hen. It was—nor will I give up such satisfaction, for any enticement that can offer. Be contented, Eleanor,—for your sake and my father's, I will be honest. Nay, more; I will be scrupulously proud; and that line of conduct which my own honour could not force me to follow, my love to *you* and *him*, shall compel me to. When, through necessity, I am tempted to plunder, your blushes and my father's anguish shall hold my hand. And when I am urged through impatience, to take away my own life, your lingering death and his, shall check the horrid suggestion, and I will live for you.

Elea. Then do not ever trust yourself away, at least from one of us.

Hen. Dear sister! do you imagine that your power is less when separated from me? Do you suppose I think less frequently on my father and his dismal prison, because we are not always together? Oh, no! he comes even more forcibly to my thoughts in his absence; and then, more bitterly do I feel his misery, than while the patient old man, before my eyes, talks to me of his consolations; his internal comforts from a conscience pure, a mind without malice, and a heart, where every virtue occupy a place. Therefore, do not fear that I shall forget either him or you, though I might possibly forget myself. [*Exit.*

Elea. If before him I am cheerful, yet to myself I must complain. (*Weeps.*) And that sound of festivity

at the house adjoining is insupportable! especially
when I reflect that a very small portion of what will
be wasted there only this one night, would be sufficient to give my dear father liberty.

> (*A rapping at the door of her chamber, on the
> opposite entrance.*)

Elea. Who's there?

Mr Blac. Open the door. (*Without.*)

Elea. The voice of our landlord. (*Goes to the
door.*) Is it you, Mr Blackman?

Blac. Yes, open the door. (*Rapping louder.*)

> (*She opens it.*—BLACKMAN *enters, followed by*
> BLUNTLY.)

Blac. What a time have you made me wait! And
in the name of wonder, why do you lock your door?
Have you any thing to lose? Have not you already
sold all the furniture you brought hither? And are
you afraid of being stolen yourself?·

> (ELEANOR *retires to the back of the Stage.*)

Blun. Is this the chamber?

Blac. Yes, sir, yes, Mr Bluntly, this is it.

> (BLACKMAN *assumes a very different tone of voice
> in speaking to* BLUNTLY *and* ELEANOR ; *to the
> one, he is all submissive humility, to the other,
> all harshness.*)

Blun. This! (*Contemptuously.*)

Blac. Why yes, sir ; this is the only place I have
left in my own house, since your master has been
pleased to occupy that next door, while his own magnificent one has been repairing. Lock yourself up,
indeed! (*Looking at Eleanor.*) You have been continually asking me for more rooms, Mr Bluntly, and
have not I made near half a dozen doors already from
one house to the other, on purpose to accommodate

your good family. Upon my honour, I have not
now a single chamber but what I have let to these
lodgers, and what I have absolute occasion for myself.

Blun. And if you do put yourself to a little incon-
venience, Mr Blackman, surely my master—

Blac. Your master, Mr Bluntly, is a very good
man ; a very generous man ; and I hope at least he
has found me a very lucky one ; for good luck is all
the recommendation which I, in my humble station,
aspire to ; and since I have been Sir George's attorney, I have gained him no less than two law-suits.

Blun. I know it. I know also that you have lost
him four.

Blac. We'll drop the subject. And in regard to
this room, sir, it does not suit, you say ?

Blun. No, for I feel the cold wind blow through
every crevice.

Blac. But suppose I was to have it put a little into
repair ?   That window, for instance, shall have a
pane or two of glass put in ; the cracks of the door
shall be stopt up ; and then every thing will have a
very different appearance.

Blun. And why has not this been done before ?

Blac. Would you have me be laying out my money,
while I only let the place at a paltry price, to people
who I am obliged to threaten to turn into the streets
every quarter, before I can get my rent from them ?

Blun. Is that the situation of your lodgers at present ?

Blac. Yes.—But they made a better appearance
when they first came, or I had not taken such persons to live thus near to your master.

Blun. That girl (*looking at Eleanor,*) seems very
pretty ; and I dare say my master would not care if
he was nearer to her.

Blac. Pshaw, pshaw ; she is a poor creature ; she is in great distress. She is misery itself.

Blun. I feel quite charmed with misery. Who belongs to her ?

Blac. A young man who says he is her brother : very likely he is not ; but that I should not enquire about, if they could pay my rent. If people will pay me, I don't care what they are. (*Addressing himself to Eleanor.*) I desire you will tell your brother when he comes in, that I have occasion for the money which will be due to me to-morrow ; and if I don't receive it before to-morrow night, he must seek some other habitation.

Blun. Hush, Mr Blackman ; if you speak so loud, you will have our company in the next house hear you.

Blac. And if they did, do you think it would spoil their dancing ? No, Mr Bluntly. And in that respect, I am a person of fashion : I never suffer any distress to interfere with my enjoyments.

Elea. (*Coming to him.*) Dear sir, have but patience a little while longer. Indeed, I hope you will lose nothing.

Blac. I *won't* lose any thing. (*Going.*)

Elea. (*Following him.*) Sir, I would speak a single word to you, if you will be so good as to hear me ?

Blun. Ay, stay and hear her.

Elea. (*Looking at Bluntly.*) But I wish to speak to him by ourselves.

Blun. Then I'll withdraw.

Blac. What have you to say ? (*In anger.*)

Blun. Hear her, Mr Blackman ; or may none of her sex ever listen to you.   [*Exit.*

Blac. If it is only to entreat me to let you continue here, I am going in an instant. Come, speak quickly, for I have no time to lose. Come, speak, speak.

Elea. But are you resolved to have no pity ? You know in what a helpless situation we are ; and the deplorable state of my poor father. (*Weeping.*)

Blac. Ay, I thought what you had to say ; farewell, farewell.

Elea. (*Laying hold of him.*) Oh ! do not plunge us into more distress than what we can bear ; but open your heart to compassion.

Blac. I can't—'tis a thing I never did in my life.
(*Going, he meets Bluntly, who stops him.*)

Blun. Well, have you granted her request?

Blac. I would do a great deal to oblige you, Mr Bluntly; and if you will only give your word for the trifle of rent owing, why, I am not so hard-hearted but I will suffer her to stay.

Blun. Well, well ; I will give my word.

Blac. But remember, it is not to be put down to your master's account, but to your own.   I am not to give credit.

Elea. Nor am I to lay my brother under an obligation of this nature.   (*To Bluntly.*)   I thank you for your offer, sir, but I cannot accept it.

Blac. (*In extreme anger.*) What do you mean by that ?

Blun. Perhaps she is right.

Elea. My brother would resent my acceptance of a favour from a stranger.

Blac. Your brother resent !   A poor man resent ! Did you ever hear of any body's regarding a poor man's resentment ?

Elea. No ; nor a poor woman's prayers.

Blac. Yes, I will regard your prayers, if you will suffer this gentleman to be your friend.

Elea. Any acquaintance of your's, Mr Blackman, I must distrust.

Blac. Do you hear with what contempt she treats us both ?

Blun. But perhaps she is right ; at least, in treating one of us so, I am sure she is ; and I will forgive her wronging the one, for the sake of her doing justice to the other.

Enter HENRY : *he starts at seeing* BLACKMAN *and* BLUNTLY.

Hen. Who are these ?

Blac. " Who are these ?" Did you ever hear such impertinence ?   (*Going up to him.*)   Pray who are you, sir ?

Hen. I am a man.

Blac. Yes ; but I am a lawyer.

Hen. Whatever you are, this apartment is mine, not your's—and I desire you to leave it.

Blac. But to-morrow it will be mine, and then I shall desire *you* to leave it, and force you to leave it.

Hen. Eleanor, retire to the other chamber ; I am sorry I left you.   (*Leads her off.*)

Blac. And I am sorry that I and my friend should come here to be affronted.

Blun. Mr Blackman, I won't be called names.

Blac. Names, sir !   What names did I call you ?

Blun. Did not you call me your friend ?   I assure you, sir, I am not used to be called names.   I am but a servant, whose character is every thing ; and I'll let you know that I am *not* your friend.

Blac. Why, you blockhead, does not your master call himself my friend ?

Blun. Yes, my master is a great man, and he can get a place without a character,—but if I lose mine, I am ruined ; therefore, take care how you miscal me for the future, for I assure you I won't bear it. I am not your friend, and you shall find I am not.

[*Exit* (*in great anger,*) BLACKMAN *following.*

ACT THE SECOND.

SCENE I.

An Apartment at SIR GEORGE SPLENDORVILLE'S.

Enter SIR GEORGE, *followed by* BLUNTLY.

Sir Geo. What's o'clock?   (*Rubbing his eyes.*)

Blun. Just noon, sir.

Sir Geo. Why was I waked so early?

Blun. You were not waked, sir—You rung.

Sir Geo. Then it was in my sleep—and could not you suppose so? After going to bed at five, to make me rise at noon!   *in a violent passion.*)   What am I to do with myself, sir, till it is time to go out for the evening?

Blun. You have company to dinner you know, sir.—

Sir Geo. No, it is to supper—and what am I to do with myself till that time?

Blun. Company again to supper, sir?

Sir Geo. Yes, and the self-same company I had last night; I invited them upon lady Caroline's account; to give her an opportunity of revenge, for

the money she lost here yesterday evening; and I
am all weariness; I am all lassitude and fretfulness
till the time arrives. But now I call to mind, I have
an affair that may engage my attention a few hours.
You were giving me an account, Bluntly, of that
beautiful girl I saw enter at Blackman's?

Blun. Yes, sir, I saw her late last night in Mr
Blackman's house; she lodges there.

Sir Geo. Indeed! In Blackman's house? I am
glad to hear it.

Blun. And he has assured me, sir, that she and
her family are in the greatest poverty imaginable.

Sir Geo. I am glad to hear it.

Blun. They have been it seems above a twelve-
month in London, in search of some rich relations;
but instead of meeting with them, the father was seen
and remembered by an old creditor, who has thrown
him into prison.

Sir Geo. I am very glad to hear it.

Blun. But the young woman, sir, has been so
short a time in town, she has, seemingly, a great
deal of modesty and virtue.

Sir Geo. And I am very glad to hear of that too—
I like her the better—you know I do—for I am weary
of that ready compliance I meet with from the sex.

Blun. But if I might presume to advise, sir—as
you are so soon to be married to her ladyship, whom
you love with sincere affection, you should give up
this pursuit.

Sir Geo. And I *shall* give it up, Bluntly, before
my marriage takes place; for, short as that time may
be, I expect this passion will be over and forgotten,
long before the interval has passed away. But that
brother you were mentioning——

Blun. I have some reason to think, that with all
his poverty, he has a notion of honour.

Sir Geo. (*Laughing.*) Oh! I have often tried the effect of a purse of gold with people of honour. Have you desired them to be sent for as I ordered?

Blun. I have, sir.

Sir Geo. See if they are come. (*Exit* BLUNTLY.) Ah! my dear Lady Caroline, it is you, and only you, whom I love with a sincere passion! but in waiting this long expected event of our marriage, permit me to indulge some less exalted wishes.

Enter BLUNTLY.

Sir Geo. Are they come?

Blun. The young man is in the anti-chamber, sir, but his sister is not with him. (*Speaking to Henry who is without.*) Please to walk this way—my master desires to see you.

Sir Geo. No, no, no—I do not desire to see him, if his sister is not there. Zounds, you scoundrel, what do you call him in for?

Enter HENRY, *and bows.*

(SIR GEORGE *looks at him with a careless familiarity*—BLUNTLY *leaves the room.*)

Sir Geo. Young man, I am told you are very poor: you may have heard that I am very rich; and I suppose you are acquainted with the extensive meaning of the word—generosity.

Hen. (*After an hesitation.*) Perhps not, sir.

Sir Geo. The meaning of it, as I comprehend, is, for the rich to give to the poor. Have you any thing to ask of me in which I can serve you?

Hen. Your proposal is so general, I am at a loss what to answer; but you are, no doubt, acquainted with the extensive meaning of the word, *pride*,—and that will apologize for the seeming indifference with which I receive your offer.

2

Sir Geo. Your pride seems extensive indeed. I heard your father was in prison, and I pitied him.

Hen. Did you, sir ? Did you pity my father :—I beg your pardon—if I have said any thing to offend you, pray forgive it ; nor let my rudeness turn your compassion away from him, to any other object.

Sir Geo. Would a small sum release him from confinement ? Would about a hundred pounds——

Hen. I have no doubt but it would.

Sir Geo. Then take that note.—Be not surprised ; I mean to dispose of a thousand guineas this way, instead of fitting up a theatre in my own house. That (*giving him the note,*) is a mere trifle ; my box at the opera, or my dinner ; I mean to dine alone to-morrow, instead of inviting company.

Hen. Sir George, I spoke so rudely to you at first, that I know no other way to shew my humility, than to accept your present without reluctance—I do therefore, as the gift of benevolence, not as the insult of better fortune.

Sir Geo. You have a brother, have not you ?

Hen. No, sir—and only one sister.

Sir Geo. A sister is it ? well, let me see your father and your brother—sister I mean—did not you say ? you said a sister, did not you ?

Hen. Yes, sir.

Sir Geo. Well, let me see your father and her ; they will rejoice at their good fortune—I imagine, and I wish to be a witness of their joy.

Hen. I will this moment go to our lawyer, extricate my father, and we will all return and make you the spectator of the happiness you have bestowed. Forgive my eagerness to disclose your bounty, sir, if, before I have said half I feel, I fly to reveal it to my father ; to whom I can more powerfully express my sensations—than in your presence.   [*Exit.*

Sir Geo. That bait has taken—and now, if the sister will only be as grateful.

Enter BLUNTLY.

Blun. Dear sir, what can you have said to the young man? I never saw a person so much affected!

Sir Geo. In what manner?

Blun. The tears ran down his cheeks as he passed along, and he held something in his hand which he pressed to his lips, and then to his heart, as if it was a treasure.

Sir Geo. It *is* a treasure, Bluntly—a hundred guineas.

Blun. But for which, I believe, you expect a greater treasure in return.

Sir Geo. Dost think so, Bluntly?—dost think the girl is worth a hundred pounds?

Blun. If she refuses, she is worth a thousand; but if she complies, you have thrown away your money.

Sir Geo. Just the reverse.

Blun. But I hope, sir, you do not mean to throw away any more thus; for although this sum, by way of charity, may be well applied, yet indeed, sir, I know some of your creditors as much in want as this poor family.

Sir Geo. How! You are in pay by some of my creditors, I suppose?

Blun. No, sir, you must pay them, before they can pay any body.

Sir Geo. You are impertinent; leave the room instantly, and go in search of this sister; now, while the son is gone to release his father. Tell her, her brother is here, and bring her hither immediately.

Blun. But, sir, if you will only give me leave to speak one word—

I 3

Sir Geo. Do, speak ; (*Goes to the chimney-piece and takes down a pistol.* Only speak a single syllable, and I'll send a ball instantly through your head.

Blun. I am dumb, sir ; I don't speak indeed, sir ; upon my life I don't. I wish I may die if I speak a word.

Sir Geo. Go on the errand I told you; and, if you dare to return without the girl, this is your fate.

(*Holding up the pistol.*)

Blun. Yes, sir.   [*Exit.*

Sir Geo. (*Laying the pistol on the table.*) Impertinent puppy ; to ruffle the temper of a man of. fashion with hints of prudence and morality, and paying his debts ! all this from a servant, too. The insolent, chattering——

Enter BLUNTLY.

Blun. May I speak now, sir ?
Sir Geo. What have you to say ?
Blun. Mr Blackman, sir.
Sir Geo. Bid him come in.

Enter BLACKMAN. *Exit* BLUNTLY.

Sir Geo. Good morning, Mr Blackman ; come, sit down.

Blac. (*Bowing respectfully.*) I am glad, Sir George, I have found you alone, for I come to speak to you on important business.

Sir Geo. Business ?—no ; not now if you please.

Blac. But I must, sir ; I have been here ten times before, and have been put off ; but now you must hear what I have to say.

Sir Geo. Don't be long then—don't be tedious, Mr Blackman ; for I expect a—a—in short, I expect a pretty woman.

Blac. When she comes, I will go.

Sir Geo. Very well, speak quickly then. What have you to say?

Blac. I come to speak upon the subject of your father's will; by which you know, you run the hazard of losing great part of what he left behind.

Sir Geo. But what am I to do?

Blac. There is no time to be lost. Consider, that Mr Manly, the lawyer, whom your father employed, is a man who pretends to a great deal of morality; and it was he who, when your father found himself dying, alarmed his conscience, and persuaded him to make this will in favour of a second person. Now, I think that you and I, both together, ought to have a meeting with this conscientious lawyer.

Sir Geo. But I should imagine, Mr Blackman, that if he is really a conscientious man, you and he will not be upon good terms.

Blac. Oh! people of our avocation differ in respect to conscience. Puzzle, confound, and abuse each other, and yet are upon good terms.

Sir Geo. But I fear——

Blac. Fear nothing. There are a vast number of resources in our art. It is so spacious, and yet so confined; so sublime, and yet so profound; so distinct, and yet so complicated; that if ever this person with whom your fortune is divided should be found, I know how to envelope her in a labyrinth, where she shall be lost again in a hurry. But your father's lawyer being a very honest—I mean a very particular man in his profession,—I have reason to fear we cannot gain him over to our purpose.—If, therefore,—

Enter BLUNTLY.

Sir Geo. My visitor is come, as I told you.

Blac. And I am gone, as I told you.

(*Rising.—Going.*)

Enter ELEANOR.

Blac. (*Aside.*) My lodger! ah! ah! (*To her in a whisper.*) You may stay another quarter.   [*Exit.*

Sir Geo. (*To Eleanor.*) I am glad to see you.— Bluntly—(*Makes a sign to him to leave the room.*)

Blun. Sir?

(SIR GEORGE *waves his hand and nods his head a second time.*)

Blun. Sir?——(*Still affecting not to understand him.*)

Sir Geo. I bid you go. (*Angrily.*)

Blun. You bid me go, sir?—Oh yes, sir. Very well, sir. But indeed, sir, I did not hear you before, sir. Indeed I did not.

[*Bows and exit with reluctance, which Eleanor observes.*

Elea. Pardon me, sir; I understood my brother was here, but I find he is not.

Sir Geo. He is but this instant gone, and will return immediately. Stay then with me till he comes. (*Takes her hand.*) Surely you cannot refuse to remain with me a few moments; especially as I have a great deal to say to you that may tend to your advantage.

Why do you cast your eyes with such impatience on that door? (*Goes and locks it.*) There, now you may look at it in vain.

Elea. For heaven's sake, why am I locked in?

Sir Geo. Because, you should not escape.

Elea. That makes me resolve I will—Open the door, sir. (*Going to it.*)

Sir Geo. Nay, listen to me. Your sentiments, I make no doubt, are formed from books.

Elea. No, from misfortunes,—yet more instructive.

Sir Geo. You shall never know misfortune more;

you, nor your relations. But this moment I presented your brother with a sum of money, and he left
me with professions of the deepest gratitude.

Elea. My brother ! Has he received money from
you ? Ah ! he promised me he'd not disgrace his
family.

Sir Geo. How ! Family, indeed !

Elea. I cannot remain here a moment longer.—
Open the door, sir—open it immediately.

(*Raising her voice.*)

Blun. (*Without.*) Sir, sir, sir ; open the door, if
you please; you are wanted, sir.

Sir Geo. S'death ! who can want me in such
haste ?   (*Opens the door, and appears confounded.*)

Enter BLUNTLY.

Sir Geo. Well, sir !

Blun. ——Did you call, sir ?

Sir Geo. It was *you* who called, sir.

Blun. Who, I, sir ?

Sir Geo. Yes, sir, you—Who wants me ?

Blun. (*Looking at Eleanor.*) Perhaps it was *you*
that called, ma'am ?

Elea. It *was* I that called: and pray be so kind as
to conduct me to my own lodgings.

(BLUNTLY *offers her his hand.*)

Sir Geo. Dare not to touch her ; or to stay another moment in the room.   Begone.

BLUNTLY *looks at* ELEANOR *aside, and points to the
pistol ; then bows humbly, and retires.*

Sir Geo. And now, my fair Lucretia—

*He is going to seize her—she takes up the pistol and
presents it.*

Elea. No, it's not *myself* I'll kill—'Tis you,

Sir Geo. (*Starting.*) Nay, nay, nay, lay it down. Lay that foolish thing down; I beg you will. (*Trembling.*) It is charged; it may go off.

Elea. I mean it to go off.

Sir Geo. But no jesting—I never liked jesting in my life.

Elea. Nor I—but am always serious. Dare not, therefore, insult me again, but let me go to my wretched apartments.

(*Passes by him, presenting the pistol.*)
Sir Geo. Go to the——

She turns short at the door, and presents it again.

Sir Geo. What would you do? Here Bluntly! Bluntly!

[*Exit* ELEANOR.

Enter BLUNTLY.

Blun. Did you call or no, sir?

Sir Geo. Yes, sir, I did call now. (*In a threatening accent.*) Don't you think you have behaved very well this morning?

Blun. Yes, sir, I think I have.

Sir Geo. I am not joking.

Blun. Nor am I, sir.

Sir Geo. And do not you think I should behave very well, if I was to discharge you my service?

Blun. As well as can be expected, sir.

Sir Geo. Why did you break in upon me just now? Did you think I was going to murder the girl?

Blun. No, sir, I suspected neither love nor murder.

Sir Geo. What then did you suspect?

Blun. Why, sir, if I may make bold to speak, I was afraid the poor girl might be robbed: and of all she is worth in the world.

Sir Geo. Blockhead ! I suppose you mean her virtue ? (*Smiling with contempt.*)

Blun. Why, to say the truth, sir, virtue is a currency that grows scarce in the world now-a-days—and some men are so much in need of it, that they think nothing of stopping a harmless female passenger in her road through life, and plundering her of it without remorse, though its loss embitters every hour she must afterwards pass in her journey.

Enter HENRY.

Hen. Sir George, my father, liberated from prison by your bounty, is come gratefully to offer——

Enter WILLFORD *and* ELEANOR.

Elea. (*Holding her father by the hand, to prevent his going forward.*) Oh, my father ! whither are you going ?   Turn back—turn back.

Hen. (*To his father.*) This is your benefactor ; the man whose benevolence has put an end to your sufferings.

(ELEANOR *bursts into tears and retires up the stage.*)

Wil. How, sir, can I ever repay what I owe to you?—or how describe those emotions, which your goodness at this moment makes me feel ?

Sir Geo. (*In confusion.*) Very well—very well—'tis all very well. (*Aside.*) I wish it was.—(*To him.*) I am glad I have been of service to you.

Wil. You have been like mercy to us all.   My daughter's gratitude overflows in tears.   But why, my child, do you keep apart from us ?   Can you be too timid to confess your obligation ?

Sir Geo. Let her alone ; let her indulge her humour.

Wil. Speak, Eleanor.

Sir Geo. No, I had rather she would be silent.

Wil. You offend me by this obstinacy.

Elea. (*Going to Willford and taking his hand.*)
Oh, my father !—Oh ! I cannot——I cannot speak.

Wil. Wherefore ? Explain this moment, what
agitates you thus.

Elea. You must return to confinement again.

Wil. How ?

Elea. The money that has set you free, was given
for the basest of purposes ; and by a man as far beneath you in principle, as you are beneath him in
fortune. Disdain the obligation; and come, my father,
return to prison.

Wil. Yes.—And with more joy than I left it. (*To
Sir George.*) Joy, in my daughter's virtuous contempt of thee. (*To his children.*) Leave the house
instantly.   [*Exit* HENRY *and* ELEANOR.

Wil. (*Addressing himself to Sir George.*) Your
present is but deposited in a lawyer's hands, whose
word gained me my liberty ; he shall immediately
return it to you, while I return to imprisonment.

Sir Geo. If the money is in a lawyer's hands, my
good friend, it may be some time before you get
it returned. (*Going.*)

Wil. Stay, Sir George—(*he returns.*) And look
me in the face while you insult me. *Sir George
looks on the floor.* You cannot. I therefore triumph, while you stand before me abashed like a cul-
prit. Yet, be assured, unthinking dissipated man,
that with all your insolence and cruelty towards me
and mine, I have still the charity to rejoice, even for
your sake, at seeing you thus confounded. This
shame is at least one trait in your favour ; and while
it revenges my wrongs, gives me joy to find, you
are not a *hardened* libertine.   [*Exeunt.*

ACT THE THIRD.

SCENE I.

The apartment at SIR GEORGE SPLENDORVILLE'S, *where the night has been passed at play—Several card-tables with company playing—*SIR GEORGE *and* LADY CAROLINE *at the same table.* SIR GEORGE *rises furiously.*

Sir Geo. Never was the whole train of misfortunes so united to undo a man, as this night to ruin me.   The most obstinate round of ill luck——

Mr Luc. (*Waking from a sleep.*) What is all that? You have lost a great deal of money, I suppose?

Sir Geo. Every guinea I had about me, and fifteen thousand besides, for which I have given my word.

Mr Luc. Fifteen thousand guineas! and I have not won one of them.   Oh, confusion upon every. thing that has prevented me.

Sir Geo. (*Taking Lady Caroline aside.*) Lady Caroline, you are the sole person who has profited by my loss.   Prove to me that your design was not to ruin me; to sink me into the abyss of misfortune; prove to me, you love me in return for all my tender love to you. And (*taking up the cards*) give me my revenge in one single cut.

L. Car. If this is the proof you require, I consent.

Sir Geo. Thank you. And it is for double or quit. Thank you. (*She shuffles and cuts.*

Sir Geo. Ay, it will be mine, thank you—I shall be the winner, thank you. (*He cuts, then tears the cards, and throws them on the floor.*) Distraction !— Furies of the blackest kind conspire against me, and all their serpents are in my heart. Cruel, yet beloved woman ! Could you thus abuse and take advantage of the madness of my situation ?

L. Car. Your misfortunes, my dear Sir George— make you blind.

Sir Geo. (*Taking her again aside.*) No, they have rather opened my eyes, and have shown me what you are. Still an object I adore ; but I now perceive you are one to my ruin devoted. If any other intention had directed you, would you have thus decoyed me to my folly ? You know my proneness to play, your own likelihood of success, and have palpably allured me to my destruction. Ungrateful woman, you never loved me, but taught me to believe so, in order to partake of my prodigality.— Do not be suspicious, madam ; the debt shall be discharged within a week.

L. Car. (*with the utmost indifference.*) That will do, sir, I depend upon your word ; and that will do.
                        [*Exit, curtsying.*

Sir Geo. Ungrateful, cruel—she is gone without giving me one hope. She even insults, despises me.

Mr Luc. (*coming forward.*) Indeed, my dear friend, I compassionate your ill luck most feelingly ; and yet I am nearly as great an object of compassion on this occasion as yourself ; for I have not won a single guinea of all your losses : if I had,

why I could have borne your misfortune with some
sort of patience.

L. Bri. My dear Sir George, your situation
affects me so extremely, I cannot stay a moment
longer in your presence. (*Goes to the door, and returns.*) But you may depend upon my prayers.

[*Exit.*

Lo. Haz. Sir George, if I had any consolation to
offer, it should be at your service—but, you know—
you are convinced—I have merely a sufficiency of
consolation—that is, of friends and of money to
support myself in the rank of life I hold in the world.
For without that—without that rank—I sincerely
wish you, good morning. [*Exit* LORD HAZARD.

Sir Geo. Good morning.

(*The company by degrees all steal out of the room,
except* MR LUCRE.)

Sir Geo. (*looking around.*) Where are all my
guests? the greatest part gone without a word in
condolence, and the rest torturing me with insulting
wishes. Here! behold! here is the sole reliance
which I have prepared for the hour of misfortune; and what is it? Words, compliments, desertion, and from those, whose ingratitude makes
their neglect still more poignant. (*Turns and perceives Mr Lucre.*) Lucre, my dear Lucre, are not
you amazed at what you see?

Mr Luc. No, not at all—'tis the way of the world,
we caress our acquaintances whilst they are happy and in power, but if they fall into misfortune,
we think we do enough if we have the good nature to pity them.

Sir Geo. And are you one of these friends?

Mr Luc. I am like the rest of the world. I was in
the number of your flatterers; but at present you

K 2

have none, for you may already perceive, we are grown sincere.

Sir Geo. But have not you a thousand times desired me, in any distress, to prove you?

Mr Luc. And you do prove me now, do you not? Heaven bless you. *Shaking hands with him.*) I shall always have a regard for you, but for any thing farther—I scorn professions which I do not mean to keep.   *(Going.)*

Sir Geo. Nay, but Lucre! consider the anguish in which you leave me! consider, that to be forsaken by my friends is more affecting than the loss of all my fortune. Though you have nothing else to give me, yet give me your company.

Mr Luc. My dear friend, I *cannot.* Reflect that I am under obligations to you; so many, indeed, that I am ashamed to see you. I am naturally bashful; and do not be surprised if I should never have the confidence to look you in the face again.   [*Exit.*

Sir Geo. This is the world, such as I have heard it described, but not such as I could ever believe it to be. But I forgive, I forget all the world except Lady Caroline: her ingratitude fastens to my heart, and drives me to despair. She, on whom I have squandered so much; she, whom I loved, and whom I still love, spite of her perfidy!

Enter BLUNTLY.

Well, Bluntly, behold the friendship of the friends I loved! This morning I was in prosperity, and had many; this night I am ruined, and I have not one.

Blun. Ruined, sir?

Sir Geo. Totally: and shall be forced to part with every thing I possess to pay the sums I owe. Of course I shall part with all my servants, and do you endeavour to find some other place.

Blun. But first, sir, permit me to ask a favour of you?

Sir Geo. A favour of me? I have no favours now to grant.

Blun. I beg your pardon, sir, you have one, and I intreat it on my knees.

Sir Geo. What would you ask of me?

Blun. To remain along with you still. I will never quit you; but serve you for nothing, to the last moment of my life.

Sir Geo. I have then one friend left. (*Embracing him.*) And never will I forget to acknowledge the obligation.

Enter BLACKMAN.

Black. Pardon me, sir; I beg ten thousand pardons; pray excuse me, (*In the most servile manner,*) for entering before I sent to know if you were at leisure; but your attendants are all fast asleep on the chairs of your antichamber. I could not wake a soul, and I imagined you yourself were not yet up.

Sir Geo. On the contrary, I have not yet been in bed. And when I do go there, I wish never to rise from it again.

Black. Has any thing unexpected happened?

Sir Geo. Yes. That I am ruined, inevitably ruined. Behold (*Shewing the cards,*) the only wreck of my fortune.

Black. (*Starting.*) Lost all your fortune?

Sir Geo. All I am worth, and as much more as I am worth.

(BLACKMAN *draws a chair, sits down with great familiarity, and stares* SIR GEORGE *rudely in the face.*)

Black. Lost all you are worth? He, he, he, he! (*Laughs maliciously.*) Pretty news, truly! Why then I suppose I have lost great part of what I am worth? all which you are indebted to me? However,

there is a way yet to retrieve you.   But—please
to desire your servant to leave the room.

Sir Geo. Bluntly, leave us a moment.

(*Exit* BLUNTLY.)

Well, Mr Blackman, what is this grand secret?

Black. Why, in the state to which you have reduced yourself, there is certainly no one hope for
you, but in that portion, that half of your fortune,
which the will of your father keeps you out of.

Sir Geo. But how am I to obtain it?   The lawyer in whose hands it is placed, will not give it up,
without being insured from any future demand by
some certain proofs.

Black. And suppose I should search and find
proofs?   Suppose I have them already by me?—But
upon this occasion, you must not only rely implicitly
on what I say, but it is necessary you should say the
same yourself.

Sir Geo. If you advance no falsehood, I cannot
have any objection.

Black. Falsehood!—Falsehood!—I   apprehend,
Sir George, you do not consider, that there is a particular construction put upon words and phrases in
the practice of the law, which the rest of the world,
out of that study, are not clearly acquainted with.
For instance, *falsehood* with *us,* is not *exactly* what
it is with other people.

Sir Geo. How!   Is truth, immutable truth, to
be corrupted and confounded by men of the law?

Black. I was not speaking of truth—that we have
nothing to do with.

Sir Geo. I must not say so, however, sir; and
in this crisis of my sufferings, it is the only comfort, the only consolotary reflection left me, that
truth and I will never separate.

Black. Stick to your truth, but confide in me as
usual.   You will go with me, then, to Mr Manly

your father's lawyer, and corroborate all that I shall say.

Sir Geo. Tell me but what you intend to say?

Black. I can't do that. In the practice of the law, we never know what we intend to say—and therefore our blunders, when we make them, are in some measure excuseable—and if I should chance to make a blunder or two, I mean any trivial mistake, when we come before this lawyer, you must promise not to interfere, or in any shape contradict me.

Sir Geo. A mere lapse of memory, I have nothing to do with.

Black. And my memory grows very bad, therefore you must not disconcert me.

Sir Geo. Come, let us begone—I am ready to go with you this moment.

Black. I must first go home, and prepare a few writings.

Sir Geo. But call to mind that I rely upon your honour.

Black. Do you think Bluntly, your servant, is an honest man?

Sir Geo. I am sure he is.

Black. Then, to quiet your fears, I will take him along with us; and you will depend on what he shall say, I make no doubt?

Sir Geo. I would stake my being upon his veracity.

Black. Call him in, then, and bid him do as I command him.

Sir Geo. Here, Bluntly. (*Enter* BLUNTLY.) Mr Blackman has some business with you—listen to him with attention, and follow his directions.   [*Exit.*

Black. You know, I suppose, the perilous situation of your master?

(BLUNTLY *shakes his head, and wipes his eyes.*)

Black. Good fellow! good fellow!—and you would,

I dare say, do any thing to rescue him from the misery with which he is surrounded !

Blun. I would lay down my life.

Black. You can do it for less. Only put on a black coat, and the business is done.

Blun. What, 's that all? Oh ! if I can save him by putting on a black coat, I'll go buy mourning, and wear it all my life.

Black. There's a good fellow. I sincerely thank you for this attachment to your master.

                    (*Shaking him by the hand.*)

Blun. My dear Blackman, I beg your pardon for what I am going to say ; but as you behave thus friendly on this unfortunate occasion, I must confess to you—that till now I always hated you—I could not bear the sight of you. For I thought you (I wish I may die if I did not) one of the greatest rogues in the world. I fancied you only waited on, and advised my master to make your market of him. But now, your attention to him in his distress, when all his friends have forsaken him, is so kind— Heaven bless you—Heaven bless you—I'll go buy a black coat.   [*Going.*

Black. I have something more to say to you. When you have put on this coat, you must meet your master and me at Mr Manly's, the lawyer ; and when we are all there, you must mind and say, exactly what I say.

Blun. And what will that be?

Black. Oh ! something.

Blun. I have no objection to say something—but I hope you won: t make me say any thing.

Black. You seem to doubt me once more, sir ?

Blun. No, I am doubting you now for the first time ; for I always thought I was *certain* before.

Black. And will you not venture to say yes, and no, to what I shall advance ?

Blun. Why, I think I may venture to say yes to your no, and no to your yes, with a safe conscience.

Black. If you do not instantly follow me and do all that I shall propose, your master is ruined.—Would you see him dragged to prison?

Blun. No, I would sooner go myself.

Black. Then why do you stand talking about a safe conscience. Half my clients would have been ruined if I had shewn my zeal as you do. Conscience, indeed! Why, this is a matter of law, to serve your master in his necessity.

Blun. I have heard necessity has no law—but if it has no conscience, it is a much worse thing than I took it for. No matter for that—come along. Oh my poor master! I would even tell a *lie* to save him.   [*Exeunt.*

SCENE II.

A Lawyer's study.

MR MANLY *discovered at his writing desk—a Servant attending.*

Man. Who do you say wants to speak with me?

Ser. Mr Lucre, sir.

Man. And who else?

Ser. A person who says his name is Willford; he looks as if he came from the country, and seems in mean circumstances.

Man. Shew him to me directly. And take Mr Lucre, or any other person of fashion that may call, to my clerks. (*Exit Servant.*) But for the poor, let them be under *my* protection.

Enter WILLFORD *and* ELEANOR.

Man. Come in—walk in, and let me know what I can do to serve you.

Will. I deposited, sir, in your clerk's hands, a sum of money to set me free from confinement for debt. On his word, I was discharged—he owns he has not yet paid away this money, still he refuses to restore it to me, though in return I again render up my person.

Man. And why would you do this?

Will. Because my honour, I mean my conscience —for that's the poor man's honour, is concerned.

Man. Explain yourself.

Will. A son of mine received this sum I speak of, and thought it *given* him; while it was only meant as a purchase—a purchase of what we had no right to sell—and therefore it must be restored to the owner.

Man. And who is he?

Will. Sir George Splendorville—I suppose you have heard of him?

Man. He, you mean, who, by the desire of his father's will, lately changed his name from Bland-ford?

Will. Sir!

Man. The name, which some part of the family, while reduced, had taken.

Will. Good Heaven! Is there such a circumstance in his story?

Man. Why do you ask with such emotion?

Will. Because he is the man, in search of whom I

left my habitation in the country, to present before him a destitute young woman, a near relation.

Man. What relation? Be particular in your answer.

Will. A sister.

Man. I thank you for your intelligence. You
have named a person, who, for these three years
past, I have in vain endeavoured to find.—But, did
you say she was in poverty?

Will. I did.

Man. I give you joy, then—for I have in my
possession a deed which conveys to a lost daughter
of Sir George's father, the other half of the fortune
he bequeathed his son—but, as yet, all my endea-
vours have been in vain to find where she, and
an uncle, to whose care she was entrusted in her
infancy, are retired.

Will. (*turning to Eleanor.*) Now, Eleanor, arm
yourself with fortitude—with fortitude to bear not
the frowns, but the smiles of fortune. Be humble,
collected, and the same you have ever been, while I
for the first time inform you—you are not my daughter.—And from this gentleman's intelligence add, you
are rich—you are the deceased Blandford's child, and
Splendorville's sister.

Elea. Oh! Heavens! Do I lose a father such as
you, to gain a brother such as he is?

Man. (*to Willford.*) There can be no mistake on
this occasion.—And you, if I am not deceived, are
the brother of the late Mr Blandford. Your looks,
your person, your very voice confirms it.

Will. I have writings in my care, shall prove
it beyond a doubt; with the whole narrative of our
separation, when he, with his son, then a youth,
embarked for India; where, I suppose, riches soon
succeeded poverty.

Enter SERVANT.

Ser. Lady Caroline Seymour, sir, is at the door in her carriage, and will not be denied admittance. She says she must see you upon some very urgent business.

Man. (to Willford and Eleanor.) Will you do me the favour to step for a moment into this room? Lady Caroline will not stay long. I'll not detain you.

[*Exit* WILLFORD *and* ELEANOR.

Enter LADY CAROLINE.

L. Car. Dear Mr Manly, I have a thousand apologies to make—And yet I am sure you will excuse the subject of my visit, when you consider——

Man. Your ladyship will please to sit down.

(He draws chairs, and they sit.)

L. Car. You cannot be ignorant, Mr Manly—you must know the terms of acquaintance on which Sir George Splendorville and I have been, for some time past? you were his father's agent; his chief solicitor; and although you are not employed by Sir George, yet the state of his affairs cannot be concealed from you. Has he, or has he not, any inheritance yet to come?

Man. Pardon me, madam—though not entrusted by Sir George, I will, nevertheless, keep his secrets.

L. Car. That is plainly telling me he is worth nothing.

Man. By no means—Sir George, in spite of his profusion, must still be rich. He has preserved his large estate in Wales; and as to money, I do not doubt but he has a considerable sum.

L. Car. Not a guinea. I won it all from him last night.

Man. You? You, who are to become his wife?

L. Car. I might, had I not been thus fortunate,

But why should I marry him, when his riches are mine, without that ceremony.

Man. Inconsiderate man! what will be the end of his imprudence! Yet, Heaven be praised! he has still that fine estate, I just now mentioned.

L. Car. Indeed he has not—that has belonged to me these three months.

Man. To you!

L. Car. Yes—Bought for me under another name by agents; and for half its value.

Man. Madman!—Yet your ladyship must excuse me. I know your income stinted, and till the death of the Earl, your father, where could you raise sufficient to make even half the purchase?

L. Car. From Splendorville's own prodigality—from lavish presents made to me by him.

Enter SERVANT.

Ser. Sir George Splendorville, sir, desires to speak with you; he is at the door with Mr Blackman.

L. Car. Oh Heavens! do not let him see me here.

(*She is hastening to the room where* WILLFORD *and his* DAUGHTER *are.*)

Man. I have company there—walk in here, if you please. (*Shews her another door, and she enters.*)

Man. (*to the servant.*) Desire Sir George to walk in.

Enter Sir GEORGE *and* BLACKMAN.

Man. Sir George, do me the favour to sit down.

(*He looks coolly on* BLACKMAN, *and pointing to a chair, says, " Good morning.' They sit.*)

Sir Geo. Mr Manly, my attorney, will let you know the business on which I am come.

Black. Why, yes, Mr Manly, it is extremely hard that Sir George has for so long a time been kept out of a very large part of his fortune; particularly, as he has had occasion for it.

Sir Geo. I have had occasion for it, I assure you, Mr Manly; and I have occasion for it at this very time.

Man. But so may the person, sir, from whom you would take it. In a word, Sir George, neither your lawyer nor you, shall prevail on me to give up the trust reposed in me by your father, without certain evidence, that your sister will never come to make her claim.

Black. You are not afraid of ghosts, are you?

Man. No, nor of robbers either:——you cannot frighten me, Mr Blackman.

Black. Then, depend upon it, the sister of Sir George can never appear in any other manner than as a spirit. For, here, sir, (*taking from his pocket a parcel of papers*) here are authentic letters to prove her death.   (Sir George *looks confused.*)

Man. Her death!

Black. Yes, her death. Here is a certificate from the curate of the parish in which she was buried.

Man. Buried too!

Black. Yes, sir, buried. Here is also an affidavit from the sexton of the said village, signed by the overseer and churchwardens, testifying the same.—— You see, (*shewing him the paper, and reading at the same time,*) " Died Anno Domini, one thousand seven hundred and eighty nine, the seventeenth of June.——(Mr Manly *takes the paper, and while he is reading,* Sir George *says apart*—)

Sir Geo. How near to the brink of infamy has my imprudence led me! And s'death, my confusion takes from me the power to explain, and expose the scoundrel.

Mr Manly, I will leave you for the present; but you shall hear from me shortly, when this matter shall be accounted for clearly, perfectly to your satisfaction, you may depend upon it. (*Going.*

Man. Stay, Sir George, and——

Black. Aye, Sir George, stay and see Mr Manly's objections wholly removed. He seems to doubt the evidence of paper; I must, therefore, beg leave to produce a living witness—the gentleman whom I appointed to meet me here.

Man. And who is he?

Black. The apothecary, who attended Sir George's sister in her dying illness. (SIR GEORGE *starts.*

Man. Desire him to walk in by all means. What is the matter, Sir George, you look discomposed?

Black. Sir George is something nervous, Mr Manly; and you know the very name of a medical gentleman will affect the nerves of some people.

(BLACKMAN *goes to the door, and leads on* BLUNTLY *dressed in mourning.*)

Sir Geo. (*aside*) Bluntly!—But I will see the end of this.

Man. (*Bowing to him.*) You are an apothecary, I think, sir? (BLUNTLY *looks at* BLACKMAN.)

Black. Yes, sir.

Blun. (*After seeming inclined to say,* No.) Yes, sir.

Man. Pray, sir, what disorder took the young lady, on whose account you have been brought hither, out of the world? (BLUNTLY *looks at* BLACKMAN.)

Black. Oh! the old disorder, I suppose.

Blun. The old disorder.

Man. And pray what may that be, sir? (*Blackman offers to reply.*) Mr Blackman, please to let this gentleman speak for himself. What is it you mean, pray sir, by the old disorder?

Blun. I—I—mean—Love, sir.

L 2

Man. You will not pretend to say, that love was the cause of her death?

Blun. (*Confused and hesitating.*) That—and a few fits of the gout.

Man. I fear, sir, you are not in perfect health yourself—you tremble and look very pale.

Black. That is because the subject affects him.

Man. Do you then never mention the young lady without being affected?

Blun. Never, sir—for had you seen her as I did— um—Had you seen her. She was in very great danger from the first; but after I attended her, she was in greater danger still.—I advised a physician to be called in; on which she grew worse. We had next a consultation of physicians; and then it was all over with her.

Sir Geo. (*Rising from his chair.*) Blackman, this is too much; all my calamities are inferior to this— Desist, therefore, or——

Black. (*To Bluntly.*) Desist—He cannot bear to hear the pathetic description. Consider the lady was his sister; and though he had not the pleasure of knowing her; yet, poor thing—(*Affecting to weep,*)— poor young woman! he cannot help lamenting her loss.

Blun. No more can I—for though she was not my relation—yet she was my patient. (*Pretending to weep also.*)

Sir Geo. I can bear no more. Mr Manly, you are imposed upon. But think not, however appear- ances may be against me, that I came here as the tool of so infamous a deceit. Thoughtlessness, Mr Manly, has embarrassed my circumstances; and thoughtlessness alone, has made me employ a villain to retrieve them.

Black. Mighty fine!

Sir Geo. I have no anthority, sir, to affirm that my sister is not alive ; and I am confident the account you have just now heard, of her death, is but an artifice. My indiscretions have reduced me nearly to beggary ; but I will perish in confinement—cheerfully perish—rather than owe my affluence to one dishonourable action.

Black. Grief has turned his brain.

Man. Sir George, I honour your feelings ; and as for the feelings of these gentlemen, I am extremely happy, that it is in my power to dry up their tears, and calm all their sorrows.

Sir Geo. Sir !

Black. How ?   In what way ?

Man. (*Going to the door where* WILLFORD *and his Niece are*) Come forth, young ones, to the arms of a brother, and relieve the anguish of these mourners, who are lamenting your decease. (ELEANOR *and* WILLFORD *enter.*)—Yes, Sir George, here is that sister, whom those gentlemen assure us, is dead ; and this is the brother of your father.   These are proofs, as convincing, I hope, as any Mr Blackman can produce.

Sir Geo. She, my sister !   Her pretended father my uncle too ! (*Aside.*) Blackman, you would have plunged me into an anguish I never knew before ; you would have plunged me into shame.

Blun. And so you *have* me.

Black. Pshaw.—Mr Manly, notwithstanding you are these people's voucher, this appears but a scheme. These persons are but adventurers, and may possibly have about them forgeries, such as an honest man, like myself, would shudder at.

Man. (*Going to the door.*) Who's there ? (*Enter Servant.*) Shew that—that Mr Blackman, out of my house instantly ; and take care you never admit him again.

Black. Sir George, will you suffer this?

Sir Geo. Aye, and a great deal more.

Blun. Look'ee, Blackman—If you don't fall down upon your knees, and beg my pardon at the street door, for the trick you have put upon me, in assuring me my master's sister was really dead, and that I could do her no injury, by doing him a service—if you don't beg my pardon for this, I'll give you such an assault and battery as you never had to do with in your life.

Black. Beat me—do, beat me—I'll thank you for beating me—I'd be beat every hour of the day, to recover damages. [*Exit with* BLUNTLY.

Sir Geo. My sister—with the sincerest joy I call you by that name; and while I thus embrace you, offer you a heart, that beats with all the pure and tender affection, which our kindred to each other claims. In you (*embracing his uncle,*) I behold my father; and experience an awful fear, mingled with my regard.

Wil. Continue still that regard, and even that fear —these filial sentiments may prove important; and they shall ever be repaid with my paternal watchings, friendship, and love.

Elea. My brother——

Sir Geo. I have been unworthy of you—I will be so no more, but imitate your excellence. Yet, when I reflect——

LADY CAROLINE *comes softly from the inner apartment, and attends to the discourse.*

Elea. My brother, do not imagine——

Sir Geo. Leave me, leave me to all the agonies of my misconduct. Where is my fortune? Now *all* irrecoverably gone—My last, my only resource is now to be paid to another—I have lost every thing.

L. Car. (*Coming forward.*) No, Sir George, *no-thing*—since I possess all that was yours.

Sir Geo. How ?

L. Car. Behold a friend in your necessities—a mistress whom your misfortunes cannot drive away—but who, experiencing much of your unkindness, still loves you ; and knowing your every folly, will still submit to honour, and obey you.

I received your lavish presents, but to hoard them for you—made myself mistress of your fortune, but to return it to you—and with it all my own.

Sir Geo. Can this be real ? Can I be raised in one moment, from the depths of misery to unbounded happiness ?

Enter SERVANT.

Ser. A young man, who says he is Mr Willford's son, is called to enquire for him.

Man. Shew him in.

SIR GEORGE *and* LADY CAROLINE *retire to the back part of the stage.*

Enter HENRY.

Wil. Come, Henry, and take leave of your sister for ever.

Hen. How so, sir ? What do you mean ? To be parted from her, would be the utmost rigour of fortune.

Man. The affection with which you speak, young gentleman, seems to convey something beyond mere brotherly love.

Wil. I some years since revealed to him she was *not* his sister.

Elea. And he, some years since, implied it to me. Yet, in such doubtful terms, I knew not which of us had the sorrow not to be your child. I now find it is myself; and I aver it to be a sorrow, for which, all the fortune I am going to possess will not repay me.

Sir Geo. Then, my dearest sister, indulge the hope you may yet be his daughter. This young man's merit deserves a reward, and in *time* he may learn to love you by a still nearer tie than that you have so long known to exist between you ; nay, even by a nearer tie than that of brother.

Hen. I am in doubt of what I hear—Eleanor, since our short separation, there cannot surely have been any important discovery—

Man. Be not surprised—great discoveries, which we labour in vain for years to make, are frequently brought about in one lucky moment, without any labour at all.

Sir Geo. True—for till this day arose, I had passed every hour since my birth without making one discovery to my advantage—while this short but propitious morning, has discovered to me all my former folly—and discovered to me how to be in future happy.

THE

WISE MAN OF THE EAST.

A

COMEDY,

IN FIVE ACTS.

AS PERFORMED AT THE

THEATRE-ROYAL, COVENT GARDEN.

FROM

THE GERMAN OF KOTZEBUE.

BY

Mrs. INCHBALD.

DRAMATIS PERSONÆ.

SIR RICHARD CHANCES,	*Mr Clermont.*
AVA THOANOA,	*Mr Munden.*
CLARANSFORTH,	*Mr Lewis.*
MR METLAND,	*Mr Murray.*
ENSIGN METLAND,	*Mr H. Johnston.*
TIMOTHY STARCH,	*Mr Knight.*
LAWLEY,	*Mr Waddy.*
BANKWELL,	*Mr Davenport.*
WAITBY,	*Mr Klanert.*
QUAKER SERVANT,	*Mr Simmons.*
SERVANT TO AVA,	*Mr Abbot.*
SERVANT TO LADY MARY,	*Mr Curtis.*
LADY MARY DIAMOND,	*Mrs Davenport.*
MRS METLAND,	*Mrs Johnson.*
ELLEN METLAND,	*Miss Murray.*
RACHEL STARCH,	*Mrs Mattocks.*
RUTH STARCH,	*Mrs H. Johnston.*

Servants, &c.

SCENE.—*London.*

WISE MAN OF THE EAST.

ACT THE FIRST.

SCENE I.

An apartment at CLARANSPORTH'S.

Enter SIR RICHARD CHANCES, *followed by* WAITBY.

Wai. I should be very glad to announce you, sir;
but when Mr Bankwell went into the next chamber,
he said he was going to transact business, and desired
my master and he might not be interrupted.

Sir Ri. And do you obey your master's clerk?

Wai. He is, I assure you, sir, a man of importance in this house. All the money to supply our
wants comes through his hands; and he is for ever
warning my master against extravagance, and most
partic larly against gaming.

Sir Ri. Then, perhaps, he will not come to our party to-night : but be sure to tell him he is expected at Lady Mary's in the evening, and that Sir Richard Chances himself left this card.

Wai. I will, sir. (*Laying it on the table and listening.*) I hear them very loud—my master flies from one room to another to get rid of Bankwell,—but the old man will pursue him.   Come into this room, sir.   [*Exeunt* SIR RICHARD *and* WAITBY.

Enter CLARANSFORTH, *followed by* BANKWELL.

Cla. I think, sir, I am too old to be lectur'd for my indiscretions.

Ba. Too old, perhaps, to profit by admonition ; and certainly too old for youthful excesses.

Cla. Sir, I was robbed of my early pleasures. The time of youthful happiness and folly was seiz'd from my eager grasp by the severity of a rigid father :— Why not let me have my follies at a proper age ? But it was your wise master's management to invert nature ; to force me to be a man while I was a child ;—consequently, I'm a child now I'm a man.

Ba. A counting-house was surely a proper academy for the son and heir of a merchant.

Cla. But, why so strict, that I was not permitted to live in my native country ;—but shipp'd to a gloomy town across the Atlantic, where there was no such thing as folly or misdemeanor in the whole place.—Was it not beyond all doubt, that when I returned to London, the charming novelty of doing wrong wou'd overbalance all the force of habit ?

Ba. It was your early propensity to pleasure which induc'd your father——

Cla. To forbid my tasting it.

Ba. His first wish was for your happiness.

Cla. And don't I make myself happy ?

Ba. Through improper means.   Let me intreat

you to forsake your present companions, and seek out some pretty girl——

Cla. My dear friend, with all my heart. This is a piece of advice I highly approve. Hah! I perceive your notions and mine don't differ so very widely.

Ba. Psha! Psha! I mean, seek out some sober, modest young woman, and marry.

Cla. (*Walks about*) Marry! marry!—You distress me. It's singular, Bankwell; but so it is, that of all the women I have seen, since the few months I have been in England, the woman I should prefer as a wife, I *cannot* marry.

Ba. Because she is married already, I suppose.

Cla. No; but she is not worth a guinea.

Ba. So much the better, since you are worth a million. '

Cla. Would you have me marry a servant-maid?

Ba. Sooner than I'd have you betray a servant-maid.

Cla. Betray!—What you call *betraying,* is only saying a few things, to a woman, that are not to be relied upon as truth, any more than when your servant tells an impertinent visitor you are gone out, while you are at home.

Ba. I can talk no more, and keep my temper; yet there are other subjects on which I trust we may agree. Your heart was formerly open to compassion.

Cla. Formerly, Bankwell!   (*With reproach.*)

Ba. When a school-boy.

Cla. Suppose me, in the instance of compassion, a school-boy still; and you shall be my tutor.

Ba. I have been informed that old Mr Metland is in great distress.

Cla. How can I relieve him?

Ba. Poor man! You recollect him?

Cla. I recollect he was my father's intimate friend.

Ba. You recollect also in what manner this unfortunate man lost his all?

Cla. I have heard you say, in our house.

Ba. The sudden death of your father has thrown a veil over the event, which heaven alone can see through; but for my part I am convinced myself of Mr Metland's deposition. He never told a lie.

Cla. What can I do for him?

Ba. I think it an act of duty that you support him: in what manner, I leave to your own discretion.

Cla. I will remember your advice, and determine what to do in a few days,—but at present I have such a number of petitioners, and applications of every kind.

Ba. There is another subject on which I have to speak to you. Your father passed his youth in India, and had many friends there. One of them, a native of a remote country, beyond our settlements, has been in London these four months; and at various places where he and I have met, he has given me testimony of the warm affection which, in their youth, subsisted between him and your father: he even says, he came over for the purpose of paying him a visit, when he found him in his grave. He has requested the favour of being introduced to you. He came with me now to your house, and is waiting in hopes of an interview.

Cla. Let him instantly be admitted; a friend of my father's must always be welcome.

Ba. He speaks English very well; but he is dressed in his country's fashion, and assumes the rough manners of a philosopher.   *[Exit.*

Cla. (*taking a card from the table.*) " Pharo this evening at Lady Mary Diamond's."—A more than usual solicitation to be present—Superfluous invitation! Where my Ellen resides, I could, with equal warmth, sue for admission.

Re-enter BANKWELL, *introducing an elderly gentleman, who has a dark Indian complexion, a long beard, and is dressed after the Eastern manner.*

Ba. Ava Thoanoa, a native of Cambodia, beyond the Ganges.

Cla. Sir, you do me honour ; and I only lament that your reception here is by a representative wholly unworthy of your deceased friend, my honoured father.

Av. If you speak as you think, why not make yourself worthy of him?

Ba. Ava Thoanoa uses no ceremony; he soon becomes acquainted ; and, by your permission, sir, I will leave him with you, while I step to the counting-house.   I will return immediately.   [*Exit.*

CLARANSFORTH *draws chairs, and* AVA *and he sit.*

Av. But, perhaps, sir, it is to the little resemblance you have to your father, except, indeed, in person, that you owe what you are pleased to call the honour of this visit ; for I am an unsociable man, and seldom go into company, but for some particular purpose.

Cla. Your visit to me, I understand, was merely in compliment to my father's memory.

Av. In duty to his memory.   But this is not the first time you and I have met.

Cla. I beg your pardon :—I never remember having seen you before.

Av. Because I have generally met you where there were pretty women, and they took up all your attention.

Cla. But, then, I should conceive you took up all theirs—and consequently I should attend to what they did.   M 2

Av. I engag'd their attention while I had money left. When I came first from India, I was rich, and welcome every where—but now that I am poor———

Cla. My father's friend—and reduced to poverty in a strange country! What can I do to oblige you?

Av. Reform!

Cla. How do you know that I want reformation?

Av. Because I know more than you are aware of —more than I wish to know—(*passionately.*) I have follow'd you from the pharo-table to the tavern: (*mildly,*) and sometimes from the mansions of the rich, to the huts of the poor.

Cla. Has that offended you?

Av. No; alternately I approve and condemn you. (*Passionately.*) You game, you lose large sums of money: but, when I look into your heart, I find it free from avarice.

Cla. Are you a mortal, and pretend to see my heart?

Av. You drink hard—you are frequently intoxicated: but you do this to oblige your companions.

Cla. That's true again.

Av. You gallant and toy with young women: but 'tis frequently to indulge their depravity more than your own.

Cla. Extraordinary, by heaven!

Av. You profess to love a young maiden, whom you hope to rob of her virtue.

(CLARANSFORTH *starts.*)

Av. And yet, no longer ago than yesterday, you saved an unfortunate tradesman from destruction by the gift of an hundred guineas.

Cla. I did it in secret.

Av. I was near you.

Cla. The man himself did not know me.

Av. I knew you.

Cla. Astonishing! My clerk said you were a philosopher. I pronounce you a magician. The art of magic, in the country where you were born, I know, is termed a science. I have heard my father speak of wonders he has known produced there by a certain cast of Indians. My father was rather superstitious—

Av. And his son is rather self-sufficient.

Cla. Nay, I mean to say, my father was a very good, and, in most respects, a very wise man. But he had more singularities than any Englishman I ever knew. I absolutely think he believed in ghosts.

Av. He had then cause, no doubt.

Cla. " Cause,"—Ha! ha! ha! my dear sir, I see the close acquaintance that subsisted between him and you at once; and, probably, it was to your early friendship he was indebted for some of his opinions on this subject—ha! ha! ha!

Av. No irreverent jests, sir, on my dead friend's opinions.—Your's, if they should improve, will be such as his were.

Cla. Yes—if I could see a ghost.

Av. Wou'd you believe it was one, if you did?

Cla. No!

Av. Yet you will own, wiser people than you have believed in the return of departed spirits.

Cla. I own it.

Av. And on the word of one, whom you may believe has no wish to deceive you, I once saw the spirit, the appearance of a man, whose death his friends had long lamented.

Cla. Deception! Be assur'd, deception. We are more wary in this country; and, my good friend, depend upon it, you would never think you saw such a thing in England.

Av. It was in England that I saw the apparition.

M 3

Cla. Oh! ho! In what part of England?

Av. London.—It was in my own lodgings, here in London, that the spirit came while I was merely reciting a few words, to see if I remembered the charm my Indian friends reveal'd to me: and I had proofs that I did remember it, with all the ceremony belonging to the spell, by the form that appeared.

Cla. A jocose bottle-companion, I hope.

Av. Throw off this levity. The figure which appeared to me—on the word of an old man, and a man of honour, I speak—was that of my late friend, your father.

Cla. (*Starts, then resumes his carelessness.*) And pray, when he came, what did he say to you?

Av. Very little.

Cla. Did he ask for *me*?

Av. He mentioned you.

Cla. And can you remember what he said?

Av. Perfectly.

Cla. A secret, perhaps?

Av. He did not forbid me to tell it.

Cla. Then, prythee, tell it me.

(*With some degree of anxiety.*)

Av. He said, that in the last hours of your mother's sickness, on her dying bed, she conjured him never to abandon you for any vice that your youthful frailty might commit.

Cla. Indian, you amaze me; for certainly my mother did leave this injunction, and my father revealed it to me as a secret, he would tell to no one else, lest it might give the world reason to suppose that my mother feared I *deserved* to be disinherited.

Av. You now then believe all I have uttered?

Cla. (*Hesitating.*) No—no—still, I can't—I won't believe it. Would you make a child of me? No!—no—you have only dreamt a dream, that has by chance revealed—though faith 'tis singular. But be that as it will, I don't believe a word of the ghost—not a word—no—no—not a word.

Av. To prove my veracity, *(warmly,)* will you behold the spectre which I saw ? Say but, yes, and name the hour, I'll raise it to your view.

Cla. Living, though my father stript me of my wealth, and sent me back to plod on a wretched spot, where all society is banished, still I should rejoice to see him. But dead—I wou'd not that my folly should disturb, or my curiosity even treat with irreverence, his honoured dust.

Av. You speak with propriety.

Cla. (After a pause.) But do you pretend that he said any thing further ?

Ava. He was beginning another subject, when he was interrupted—as we are now.

Enter BANKWELL.

Ba. I beg pardon, if I have left you too long, Ava Thoanoa. I have some business which takes me away instantly—shall I attend you ?

Av. (Bows gravely to CLARANSFORTH.*)* Good day, sir.

Cla. (With reserve and coolness.) Good day, sir.   [*Exeunt* BANKWELL *and* AVA.

Now, is he a wise man, or a mad man—a knave, or a fool.   [*Exit.*

SCENE II.

A room in Mr Metland's *house*—Mrs Metland
*alone knitting—A book open on the table before
her, in which, at the same time, she is reading.*

Mrs Me. When I was young, poets wrote their
sonnets of love under a thatched roof, and were contented with bread and milk. Twenty years later
this sweet contentment is turned into ridicule: but
with me it remains, and I revere it.

Enter Ensign Metland, *with a pocket-book in his
hand.*

En. Good morning, dear mother.
Mrs Me. Welcome, dear Charles! What do you
bring me?
En. My whole heart, and the half of my pay.
(Giving her a bank-note.)
Mrs Me. Dear boy, how can you content your-
self with the other half?
En. Were not you contented, mother, when, with
your small income, my father purchased my com-
mission?
Mrs Mc. We can live sparingly; but you must
do honour to your rank as an officer.
En. And if ever my general shou'd ask me, why
my regimentals look rusty, my answer will not, I
think, disgrace the service.
Mrs Me. You are young, and should enjoy life.

En. I do : By puting these little monthly savings into your hands, I am thus furnished each time with four weeks' enjoyment of life.

Mrs Me. (*Clasps him in her arms.*)   Dear Charles !

Enter ELLEN.

Ellen here also ! (*Embracing her.*)   My dear Ellen, 'tis so long since I have seen you ! Children, you give me a cheerful morning.

El. Dear brother, we have not seen each other this great while !

En. Is that my fault? Why do you forbid my coming to see you ?

El. I only wish to keep my mean situation a secret, to prevent you from being sneered at in the honourable one you hold. " Ensign Metland is " brave," I often hear your old colonel say, when he visits my lady. My eyes immediately become moist with tears, and the work I am about trembles under my hand—I am reproved for my negligence ; but that I do not mind, while I listen to my brother's praise.

En. But Lady Mary Diamond already knows—

El. Her ladyship has too many concerns of her own, and too much pride, to trouble herself about my family. She knows I have a father and mother, and where they live—and that is all: therefore I shall pursue my usual course ; and in the house of Lady Mary Diamond I shall always drop a curtsy to Ensign Metland ; while, in this house, he will ever be my dear brother Charles. And now, my dear mother, here is a small portion (*whispers*) of my savings. (*Puts into her hand two pieces of gold.*)

Mrs Me. This is too soon again, my child—I fear you deprive yourself.

El. No, indeed, dear mother.

Mrs Me. But I entreat you both not to make known to your father the assistance you give us. His mistaken pride wou'd rather let him perish than live on your bounty. Hush! I hear him coming. (*Conceals the money she had received.*)

Enter MR METLAND, *with a bundle of papers under his arm. When he comes in at the door, he starts.*

Me. Hey-day! I have just left a fine furnished house; but my own hut is more finely ornamented. (*His son and daughter meet, and* ELLEN *kisses him.*) Welcome! children, welcome! How do you do?

El. Very well, dear father.

Me. And you?

En. Tolerable.

Me. Why, but tolerable?

En. You know, Sir, that I want—

Me. A good and courageous heart is all that a soldier wants; and that I am sure you possess.

En. It is my paternal inheritance.

Me. If that is true, you are a rich heir, although my purse is empty, and these walls almost bare.

En. But—inconveniences at your time of life.

Me. What do you call inconveniences? Those who can supply their wants are well supported.

En. Can you do that?

Me. Oh yes, for I am content. Do you think your mother and I go fasting to bed? No—no— What my industry daily produces, her dear hands daily prepares; and our homely fare is made delicious by her constant cheerfulness and serenity. If ever you perceive tears in her eyes, the smoke of the kitchen fire is the cause of them.

Mrs Me. Yes, my dear husband, I should be contented; quite satisfied, if only—

Me. No one lives whose contentment is not, at times, crossed by an " if only." Let us hear the tendency of your " if only."

Mrs Me. If only—Ellen were not obliged to be a servant.

Me. And what is her servitude? Your daughter is a waiting-maid, and obliged to humour the whims and caprices of another woman, which prevents her having leisure to indulge her own.

Mrs Me. It grieves me to think she is as a stranger in our house.

Me. (*Pressing Ellen's hands.*) She will never be a stranger in our hearts. No! never, never!

Mrs Me. You have again brought home a large heap of papers, Mr Metland.

Me. Yes; heaven be thanked! there is work for a whole month; and, " if only"—There, now, I have caught myself at an " if only."

Mrs Me. Explain it—intrust its meaning to your family.

Me. I was going to say, " if only" my debts were paid—then anxiety would not alone be cast from my heart, but, what would please me much more, from the hearts of my creditors. (*Sighing.*)

En. How was it possible, my father, that, with your industry and temperance, you should have creditors?

El. How can you ask, brother? Consider the expense of our education.

Me. The expense of your education, children, has been defrayed from a capital which is inexhaustible—Parental care accomplished it. No, my dear, a misfortune that befel me a year ago, has impoverished us so much, that, at my advanced life, it will be impossible for my labour to retrieve me.

Mrs Me. We were both poor when we married; but we had, through care, saved up a handsome fortune.

Me. Twelve thousand pounds.

Mrs Me. Which your father took to the rich merchant Claransforth.

El. Claransforth !   (*In confusion.*)

Mrs. Me. The present young merchant's father.

Me. He was my friend.

En. And wronged you ?

Me. That would have hurt me much more than the loss of my money. No ; he meant me well, and was to have given me a share in his flourishing business. But it happened, that, on the very evening when I took to him my long-collected store, he was overwhelmed with letters and papers by the sudden arrival of a foreign mail, and could not at that moment give me a receipt for what I placed in his hands.

Mrs Me. That very night part of Claransforth's house was burnt to the ground, and Claransforth himself perished.

Me. I lost a proved friend.

Mrs Me. And the indefatigable earnings of twenty years.

El. (*In agitation.*) And could his son be so base as to deny the debt ?

Me. His son was abroad at the time, and a total stranger to me. On his arrival, he proves to be a man of pleasure—a fine gentleman, who neglects all kind of business. The executors judged of my case, and did their duty. I had no vouchers.

En. But Claransforth's books—your word—your oath ?

Me. None of his books were lost by the fire, and the sum was not entered in any of them. Bankwell, his trusty clerk, was questioned on the subject : he spoke to the fairness of my character ; but could say no more. Every place was searched. I described the notes, the cords they were tied with. All was in vain—nothing could be found, and I was ruined.

Mrs. Me. Enough, and already too much, of a luckless hour. I count my good fortune by years.

El. Dear father and mother, I fear I must be gone. My lady expects company to breakfast, about three this afternoon ; and ordered me to return in time to dress her.

Me. I don't like such irregular hours for meals. I hope there is nothing else irregular in your lady's family. You blush. At what hour do you go to bed ?

El. Immediately after her ladyship.

Me. There's an equivocation in that reply. I asked you the time ye went to bed—the exact time.

El. Do you mean the rest of the servants, or only me ?

Me. Again equivocation ?

Mrs Me. Dear husband ! she comes scarcely more than once a month to see us ; and, then, do not be too hard upon her—She has no meaning in her answers.

Me. So it seems.

Mrs Me. I would say, no design to deceive you : she is a good girl.   (*Shaking her hand kindly.*)

Me. I take her to be such, or she would have no business here, though she is my daughter.

En. No tears, Ellen—you will anger my father still more.

Me. What ! does she weep ? Ellen, I love you dearly ; and your person, as a female, and my child, I am bound to protect. But your *mind* you must guard yourself. Over that I have no controul, but such as you are pleased to bestow by your confidence ; and when you so trust and empower me, I'll be its guardian, or depute my son with my authority. These affectionate terms I offer, supposing you all that's amiable and good.

Mrs Me. She is ; I am sure she is.

Me. Who suspects she is not ? I am only advert-
ing to what it is possible she may hereafter be. And,
then, neither to her mind or person am I a protector,
or is this house her home.

Mrs Me. (*Supporting Ellen, who flies to her in
terror.*) You are a harsh man ; a very good, honest
man ; but too austere with those of less fortitude
than yourself.   [*Exit with* ELLEN.

Me. Charles, I have spoken something warmer to
your sister than I intended. I did not mean to
make her weep, especially as she comes so seldom
to see us. Follow her, Charles, and your mother,
and say I was a little hasty. Go—it does not become me to own myself to blame. But invite Ellen
to stay, and take some dinner with us, and I'll come
in by the time you are all sat down. You know,
Charles, I am often harsh with you ; and yet I love
you. You know I am sometimes even severe with
your mother ; yet, heaven is my witness ! this world
would be nothing to me without her mild society.
You know my temper, Charles—you know, too, that
irritable temper has met with some sharp trials.

                              [*Exeunt.*

ACT THE SECOND.

SCENE I.

A room in the house of TIMOTHY STARCH.

Enter RACHEL STARCH *and* TIMOTHY STARCH, *followed by* RUTH STARCH.

Ra. Timothy, Timothy, I say unto thee, that Claransforth, the merchant, is the man whom I have chosen, from amongst all other of her suitors, to be the spouse of thy daughter Ruth.

Tim. What will our elders say to such a marriage? For neighbour Claransforth is not one of the faithful.

Ra. But he is one of the rich.

Tim. It is asked by pious speakers, " Of what " value are riches ?"

Ra. And it is answered by other pious speakers, " Of a great deal." How can a man give to the poor, while he is poor himself?

Tim. Thou art right. What can a man give who possesseth nothing ? What produceth alms but mo-

N 2

ney? Verily, what doth money not produce? And, that my daughter shall be wedded to a rich husband, maketh me content.

Ra. It maketh me glad; and it should cause thee, maiden, to rejoice with exceeding great joy.

Ru. Verily, verily, thou has often instructed me, not to rejoice with over much gladness for that which passeth away.

Tim. And it is a precept thou art bound to follow, in imitation of thy father, who has never, since he came to man's estate, suffered himself to feel either joy or sadness, grief or merriment; but has passed his life in an uniform dullness, and insensibility to all around. And I am thankful that it is so; for, though I never felt love, I have likewise never known hate. Though I am steeled to pity, I am also proof against anger: and I never in my life did any harm, though I never did any good.

Ra. Ruth Starch, when wilt thou boast thus? And I say unto thee, Ruth, when the merchant, Claransforth, shall offer to take thee in marriage, wilt thou reject or accept him?

Ru. Peradventure he may never offer.

Tim. Then, why cometh he here to smile and to simper; to gaze and to sigh; to bow to thy mother, and shake hands with me?

Ru. Doth it follow, that a young man must marry in every house where he gazeth and shaketh hands?

Ra. Ruth, Ruth, thou art not inclined to wed Claransforth; neither any of the friends that frequent our meeting-house. To what am I to ascribe this coldness?

Ru. Verily, to the cold of which my father is composed; for I liken him unto a *snow-ball,* and myself unto a *snow-drop.*

Ra. But it is ordained that thou should'st marry.

Ru. It is also ordained that I first be wooed.

Ra. And canst thou say that Claransforth has not wooed thee ?

Ru. I can affirm that he hath never asked me to become his wife.

Ra. He will ask thee.

Ru. Then I will answer.

Ra. How—in what manner ?

Ru. As the spirit moveth.

Enter a QUAKER SERVANT.

Ser. A man bedecked in scarlet, he whom thou hast long ago desired me to watch, slily put this letter into my hand, and required of me to give it as slily to Ruth, whom he called my young mistress.

Tim. Give the letter to me. (*Servant gives him the letter.*)

Ra. (*To the servant.*) And go thou back to the man in scarlet, and say unto him, Follow me to Ruth, who wisheth to commune with thee.

[*Exit* SERVANT.

Ru. I want not to commune with any man.

Ra. But I and thy father do.

Tim. (*After reading the letter.*) Yea ; it behoveth us to rebuke this man, who is, I perceive, by his subscription, he whom we suspected—the son of the ruined Metland ; and when he cannot behold Ruth by besetting the house, writes unto her foolish epistles, called love-letters.

Enter SERVANT, *showing in* ENSIGN METLAND, *who starts.*

Thou art surprised to be brought before the parents, when thou didst only expect to see the maiden, whom thou affrontest by thy wanton love.

En. I am, I own, amazed at the deceit by which I was allured hither ; but I deny the epithet which

N 3

you have given to my passion; for it is sincere, it is pure, it is honourable.

Tim. And, in answer to all thy pretensions—I say unto thee, young man, thou wearest a red coat.

En. I scorn illiberal reproaches, or else I would say in return—

Tim. What! what would'st thou say?

En. That you—wear a brown one.

Tim. Is there any reproach in that?

En. Surely not. Who but reverences the modes of your sect, the sober decency of your habit and manners; the steady sobriety of your men, the modest demeanour of your women; that timid retiring disposition, that simple clothing, tending to form the humble handmaid, the obedient wife, the meritorious mother.

Tim. What importeth thy elocution? It is not only I, and my spouse, who dislike thee; but that damsel hath natural fear and terror of a soldier. Hast thou not, Ruth?

Ru. Yea, verily, I have fear and terror of an army of soldiers; but of one, all alone by himself, I am not much afraid.

Ra. Thou speakest unwarily: one soldier alone, in a young maiden's apartment, is more dangerous than ten thousand in the field.

Ru. Thou fillest me with astonishment! To be in the midst of a swarm of bees is perilous; but if one bee hums and buzzes about me, I think, with a little watching, I could suffer it to sip honey even from the nosegay in my bosom.

Tim. Daughter, do not compare a soldier to a harmless bee; he is a lion.

Ru. The terror of the lion is in his fangs and his paws; that of a soldier in his firelock and bayonet, but when he lays aside his arms, peradventure, he is as gentle as any other of his fellow creatures.

Tim. Ruth! Ruth! thy sayings are unwise.

Ra. And I command thee to depart from among us.

Ru. I will show obedience to my mother,—even such obedience as I would show to the husband of my choice. [*Exit.*

Tim. Come, Rachel, we will also retire. And now, friend, being left alone, I trust thou wilt likewise depart. [*Exeunt severally.*

SCENE II.

A room at LADY MARY DIAMOND'S.

Enter CLARANSFORTH, *met by a* SERVANT.

Ser. Lady Mary will wait on you immediately.
[*Exit.*

Cla. I leave this house of a night, vowing never to return to it again; and, in the morning, the first visit I pay is here. It is in vain to resist—I cannot keep away; but, not like other gamesters, I come. The cards and dice, which I seem to love, and are placed in my reach, are my abhorrence while the woman, whom I must not seem to love and is out of my reach—

Enter ELLEN.

El. Her ladyship is busy at present, sir, and desired me to say—

Cla. How fortunate! One would suppose she knew the blessing she bestowed on me, in deputing you, instead of coming herself.

El. She desired me to say, sir, that if you cannot now wait till she comes, she begs you will not disappoint her of your company in the evening.

Cla. In the evening I shall not perhaps see you ; but I owe her my company *then* for the pleasure she has given me *now*. Therefore, assure her I will be here. (*Ellen is going.*) Stay, stay, a moment! or, by heaven! I'll not come. Do you not know that you are my sole attraction to this house ; that, but for you, I should never enter it?

El. Then you have me to blame for all your ill luck at cards.

Cla. And for all my good fortune in society ; for it is the impression on my mind, of your sweetness, which makes other things pleasing to me ; of your worth, that makes other things worthy. You smile with incredulity ; but, remember, I am a merchant, and value truth and fair dealing beyond my life.

El. You mean to say, your conscience is your book-keeper.

Cla. I mean, that my heart I consider as the most valuable among all my goods.

El. Would you make merchandise of your heart ?

Cla. No ; but I would give it away.

El. Men and children give things away ; but soon take them back again.

Cla. Put me to the trial.

El. Sir, your conversation degrades you. You forget what I am.

Cla. You are not what you ought to be.

El. Do not persuade me to think so. I would fit my sentiments to my situation.

Cla. Rather alter that which fate has thrown you in. You serve, and might command.

El. I am content, while I enjoy command over myself.

Cla. Why not be the mistress of me, and of all that is mine? Why not confer happiness, while you would secure your own? Why these doubts and suspicions of a man who loves you?

El. Why this ridicule of one who has never offended you?

Cla. Ridicule! If you could see my heart, Ellen, you have too much justice to insult my passion. —Indeed, I love you! I adore you!

El. Oh, Mr Claransforth! (*in great agitation.*)

Cla. For heaven's sake! you alarm me. What's the matter?

El. I am not eighteen, you are almost twice my age, and nature has given you an understanding which education and intercourse with the world has rendered far superior to mine. Can it be wondered that your attentions have flattered my vanity; that your professions captivate my heart? Your addresses have the same weight with me that similar addresses have with similar young women; and I tremble lest the event should be the same. If I fly from you, you will pursue me; if I vow never to submit, you will determine to conquer: but here, without another struggle for victory, I claim your protection. Weapons of resistance I have none; yet do not take advantage of my weakness. Yielding, I beg for mercy, let me live with honour. (*Kneeling.*)

Cla. (*Aside.*) She has fixed on the only method; she agitates me beyond bearing. (*To her.*) You know not how you distress me. I cannot in this house explain all I wish, to prove my love to be real, my friendship lasting: leave this place, throw yourself solely on my protection. The name of wife is but a vain appendage to the union of hearts; and, under my roof—

El. You make me shudder—Can such an offer be the result of my candid declaration ? But, I thank you, sir. You have no mercy, no pity for me, and you change my love to hate.   [*Exit.*

Cla. Would mine could be so changed ! But that I fear, is fixed. Hark ! she is returning. Provoking ! her lady is with her. Now, there I could hate most cordially, without one effort.

[*Exit on the opposite side.*

Re-enter ELLEN, *followed by* LADY MARY DIAMOND.

L. Ma. Do you suppose I took you into my house for the employment I pretended ? to take care of my dresses, and fix them becomingly about my person ? Do you imagine, that with these soft engaging manners, formed to seduce the other sex, I would have had near me a rival such as you, but for some more important use ?

El. Dreadful ! (*aside.*)   What use ?

L. Ma. That which you have already been to me. Why do you think I suffered you to ride by my side through London streets, but that you might be followed by unthinking fools, who enrich our pharobank ?   You are the allurement of half those madmen who lose to me their fortune ; but of all those Claransforth is by far the richest and the least suspicious of our aim :—him, then, you must manage artfully ; and beware how you quarrel with him.

El. But, if he quarrels with me——?

L. Ma. Then make it up, kiss, and friends. Why do you start ? Tears !—then I suspect—Idiot! Fool ! Now, you have no further power, and we have lost him as a visitor. Is this your prudery ? I thought, notwithstanding your poverty, you were of a virtuous, honourable family.

El. And so I am.

L. Ma. I thought that you, yourself, were nicely delicate.

El. And so I am.

L. Ma. O! I give you joy; for then your power may not be over; but if so, of what have you to complain?

El. That his behaviour first gained my affection, and now excites my hatred.

L. Ma. Are you sure you hate him?

El. His very name gives me torture.

L. Ma. I understand, he planned your ruin. In return, I will instruct you how to accomplish his.

El. (*starts*) Not for the world!

L. Ma. You love him, it seems, then, still. So much the better. I'll point out the way you shall become his wife. Our party entertain the hope that, in an honourable way at the game of pharo, we may, perhaps, soon make him poor as you are. On this very evening's play some considerable bets are laid, that he'll not be a rich man to-morrow morning. A select company sup here this evening. You must be present; and take care that Claransforth be of the party. In the mean time, guard safely these instruments of wealth and articles of transfer between us gaming jobbers. (*Gives dice and a paper to Ellen.*) Only, my dear Ellen, draw Claransforth here to-night; and by to-morrow, reduced to poverty, he will offer you his hand in marriage.

El. That would be triumph indeed!

L. Ma. I knew you would think it so. And there will be yet, perhaps, some wreck of his fortune left, that may allow you both a comfortable support. And you, I know, with a hundred a year, and half a dozen children, will be completely happy

El. I could be happy on a less income.

L. Ma. But you must write to Claransforth immediately ; and, seeming to make all up with him,
persuade him to keep his appointment, else he'll not
be here.   Come, be cheerful, he shall be your husband still ; and, with him and virtue, you'll be as
rich as an empress.   Go, write to him.

El. No, madam ; as I have preserved myself from
his designs, I have no malice towards him, and will
not be an accomplice in his ruin.

L. Ma. I thought you wished him very ill.

El. I thought so too.

L. Ma. Ay, you relent.   But have a care ; do as
I have ordered you; and see he comes to meet the
company that expects him ; or, when all hopes of his
joining us are over, I will send you home to your parents, as unworthy of staying a moment longer
in my family, as one devoted to Claransforth ; and
the very degradation which you dread shall be the
stigma with which I will return you to your parents.
                                                    [*Exit.*

El. (Alone.) I do not think of myself.   Ruin !
beggary ! poverty ! perhaps distraction !   To see Claransforth reduced to all these.—The very apprehension has awakened all the tenderness I thought for
ever gone.   No ! it would be my duty to save any
of my fellow creatures from such calamity :—and to
save him, I find, will be my delight.   But how ? He
would not believe, were I merely to send him a letter on the subject, stating my suspicions.   He would
consider it as some new artifice, my love had contrived, to draw him back to me.   Unprincipled as
he is himself, he is wholly unsuspecting of the wicked gamesters who visit this house.   How, then, can
I convince him without proof ?   And proof is, perhaps here—(*examines what Lady Mary has put into
her hand*).   Dice ! loaded, false dice, perhaps, and
a paper signed by Sir Richard Chances, Lady Mary,

and others. A wicked plot for Claransforth's destruction. I will take all these—Yes, I will take
them all ; and with my own hands safely place them
in his—then, bid him farewell for ever.   [*Exit.*

ACT THE THIRD.

SCENE I.

Berkeley Square.

Enter CLARANSFORTH, *reading a letter.*

Cla. It is her hand, or else I could not have believed she would have acted so inconsistently. Ah !
Woman ! Woman !—Not three hours ago, she drove
me from her sight for ever, and now appoints a meeting in this square, almost at twilight. If I should
have miss'd her :—for whether she meant to be on

this, or that side, she was in too much haste to tell me.

Enter AVA, *who passeth* CLARANSFORTH.

Cla. (*turns and calls after him.*)   Ah! my Indian friend! How do you do? I am glad to meet you once again. You didn't see a young woman pass any-where here lately, did you?

Av. A young woman!

Cla. Ay, a young woman.

Av. What sort of a woman?

Cla. Why, zounds, if you must know, a pretty girl.

Av. I take no notice of pretty girls; especially in the streets of London.

Cla. No, you would prefer them at your lodgings; and 'tis better, more prudent for a man of your age.

Av. No, sir, I don't mean——

Cla. Don't be in a passion. I shall take mine to lodgings, as soon as I can find her. But you must get out of the way when she comes, for she is so timid, so bashful, and so innocent!

Av. Innocent! Then do not *you* be guilty.

Cla. Psha! an appointment like this. But tell me, my honest friend; you, who can penetrate her thoughts, my thoughts, and every body's thoughts! who can converse with spirits, and learn all their secrets! tell me, when my mistress arrives, will she be kind, or cruel?

Av. Both!

Cla. Equivocation! But oracles never speak in direct terms. However, my dear friend, as you once made the offer to show me my dead father, I'll change the mode of the obligation, and, instead of him, bring me, immediately, the girl I am waiting for.

Enter ELLEN. AVA *bows, as if he had done what he was desired, and immediately walks away.*

Cla. (*calling after him.*) Lucky rascal! Thank you a thousand times. My dear Ellen! I have been so anxious——

El. And so have I—and so frightened! I have been prevented coming till now, and now 'tis almost dark, and I tremble so!

Cla. My dearest Ellen! my charming love!

El. No flattery; but hold your hand; and let me be sure you have them safe.

Cla. What?

El. Oh! I fear'd to trust any other person; lest by some accident you shou'dn't receive them; or not attend to the warning given by other means than my word.

Cla. Dice! (*looking at what she gave him.*)

El. False dice made for your ruin, which was to be accomplish'd this very evening. Read this paper. —Instructions to the party, sign'd by Sir Richard. —You'll find I have no malice to you, Mr Claransforth; although I have formed my resolution, that we now, on this spot, end our acquaintance for ever.

Cla. (*reading the paper.*) " Credulous dupe, C'a-
" ransforth. When I throw sixes, be sure to bet—
" Our different shares not less than fifteen thousand
" pounds, besides Lady Mary's demand.

                    " Richard Chances.'

Cla. Sir Richard too! my pretended friend! And would nothing but my whole fortune content them? My escape is miraculous—Dear lovely being—My guardian angel!

El. But my lady threaten'd, should I not be accessary to this combination against you, she would send me home to my father's in disgrace.

Cla. Contemn her threats. This paper, these in-

struments of fraud, and my word, shall vindicate
your fame. But you faint, suffer me to convey you—

El. (*in a tremulous voice.*) To my father's instantly ; and let my lady's bad word follow me, if it must
be so. I will plead my own cause to my dear
parents, tell them I have only done my duty to you ;
then promise them faithfully never to see you more.

Cla. Never see me more ! Oh, Ellen ! impossible—You do not mean it. Where is your father's
house ? I'll take you to him myself, and tell him all
your wond'rous worth.

El. Oh ! not for the world. I would not, for the
world, you should accompany me. My father is a
most severe man, nicely suspicious. Only put me
in a coach, and direct me home.

Cla. Suffer me, at least, to go with you part of the
way. Where do your parents live ? Now, I hope,
you will no longer refuse to let me know your father's
name ?

El. My reasons for concealment are at this time
more strong than ever. I cannot, will not disclose
my name. Only desire the coachman to drive towards the City-Road.

Cla. Her father a severe man, nicely suspicious !
If I resign her now, she is lost to me for ever. I
cannot—'tis impossible (*aside.*) I see a coach—It's
coming this way—I'll secure it, and be with you
instantly.   [*Exit.*

El. Oh ! grant my mother may be at home, and
not my father, when I first go in. To her I can
better account, than to him, for my unexpected return, the necessity of quitting my service, and all I
have done.

CLARANSFORTH *returns with a* HACKNEY-COACH
MAN.

Cla. (*Aside to the Coachman.*) I shall tell you
" the City-Road ;" but drive to the corner house—
(*Whispers and gives him money.*) [*Exit* COACHMAN,

Fl. (*Going to* CLARANSFORTH.) You are very good.
I thank you for your trouble Oh! that my parents
may receive me kindly.

Cla. Lean on me—don't tremble so ——. (*Aside,
as he leads her off.*)   Oh, passion! passion! what a
fiend art thou!   While I practice cruelty, my heart
is torn with pity.   [*Exeunt.*

SCENE II,

A room in MR METLAND'S *house.*

Enter METLAND, *and sits.   A knocking at the doo*

Me. Come in.

Enter a LAWYER'S CLERK.

Cl. A letter, sir.
Me. From Mr Lawley, the attorney?
Cl. Yes, sir.   [*Exit*
Me. Why this dread of breaking the seal? I am
prepared for the worst. (*Opens the letter.*) " I am
" sorry to inform you, that all your intreaties have
" proved fruitless. This moment I have received
" orders from your creditors to seize your goods :
" I hasten to give you notice, that you may not feel
" the blow wholly unprepared, and that you may
" take advantage of the night to let your furniture
" be removed, in order to avoid all impertinent ob-
" servations in the neighbourhood." I thank you,

friend. " In half an hour's time I shall be with
" you." (*After a pause.*) Well, then, come and
take all! My wife, my children, and my heart, you
cannot take from me! (*Throws himself into an
arm-chair, and covers his face with his hands.*)

Enter MRS METLAND.

Mrs Me. What is the matter, dear husband?
(*Metland turns himself towards her, and holds out
his hand.*) Good heaven! what thus affects you?

Me. I was considering what you would do, should
I fall sick.

Mrs Me. How came this into your mind? I
hope you are not ill?

Me. No; but I am growing old; and that thought
makes me melancholy. How would you be able
to maintain an infirm man? What would you do?

Mrs Me. I would sell all, except your bed, and
one chair—on which I would sit by your bed-side.

Me. And sleep yourself on straw?

Mrs Me. Why not? It is a bed on which
thousands repose.

Me. And were I to get well again?

Mrs Me. We would resume our usual work: and,
when we had earned sufficient to buy the first pillow
—oh! how softly should we rest!

Me. My faithful, my good wife! we have now, at
this moment, nothing left. This very night we
sleep on straw. In a few minutes these few goods
will be seized by my creditors.

Mrs Me. (*Alarmed.*) This evening!

Me. I expect their attorney every moment. The
evening is an advantage that his humanity grants to
the delicacy of our situation.

Mrs Me. (*In great agitation, but recovers herself
by force.*) Well, well; I now thank you for the sad
introduction to this disclosure. (*Drys her tears.*)

It would have been much worse, had I been obliged to sell all, to nurse a dearly beloved husband.

Me. Thus I expected to find you ;—and thus I do find you. Yes, Eleanor, we are the persons best able to bear misfortunes; for we have done what we could to avert them. We have been diligent and frugal, and we now dare fold our hands, and pray with confidence, that heaven will assist us.

Mrs Me. Suppose you go to your son Charles for a few months, and I to my dear Ellen.

Me. Would you part from me? rob me of my only comfort? When Providence cast poverty into one scale of my life, she threw into the other the bliss of matrimony, and the last scale sunk.—We, therefore, will live together " till death do us part."

(*Embracing her.*)

Enter LAWLEY.

La. (*Speaking to some one without.*) Wait in the outer-room till I call you. (*Goes to Mr and Mrs Metland.*) Believe me, dear Mr Metland, that, during the thirteen years I have been in my profession, I never practised it so unwillingly as to-day.

Me. To shew compassion is a benefaction. Do your duty—We are prepared.

La. I am glad to find you so. I admire your fortitude ; and could almost call you happier than the rigorous men in whose names I now appear.

Mrs Me. Here are the keys to all which our house contains.

La. (*To Mrs Metland.*) You will have the goodness to point out to me what is *your* particular property.

Mrs Me. Nothing, sir.

La. In presents—plate, linen, and so forth.

Mrs Me. I was but a poor girl when my husband married me, and brought him nothing except my heart.

La. Consider, you are both now verging into years; and if deprived of every convenience—

Me. Under what pretence should we keep any thing back as presents from men who have already lost too much by us; or as gain, from a known fraud?

La. (*moved.*) I perceive that you are richer than the world supposes. Well, then, let us make a beginning.—Is this writing-desk open? (*Metland opens it.*) Won't you take out your papers?

Me. (*While he takes out the papers.*) You must know, that, of all I possess, the loss of this writing-desk grieves me most.

La. One gets accustomed to a favourite piece of furniture.

Me. It is not that. This writing-desk once belonged to my old friend, the late Claransforth. He sat before it when I saw him for the last time. After his death, I wish'd to keep something for his sake; and this desk was given to me by his executors, at the request of his old clerk, Bankwell.

La. It was but little to give, considering the great loss which, as it is said, you had just sustained.

Me. It is now empty—Here is the key.

La. Have you taken out every thing?

Me. Yes, every thing.

La. Why, here is a spring and a secret drawer.

Me. Not that I know of.

La. (*Touching a spring, which throws forth a drawer.*) A drawer, and full of papers.

Me. (*surprised.*) They don't belong to me.

La. A whole parcel of bank-notes.

Me. (*Looks at them.*) Gracious Power! that is my money.

La. Is it possible?

Me. Those are my twelve thousand pounds, tied just as I left them.

Mrs Me. God! thou art near us in the hour of trial.

Me. Mr Lawley, (*examining the notes,*) this is the same money which I carried to old Claransforth the evening before he died.

La. I understand. Now all is cleared up: the old man put by his friend's money safe enough.

Mrs Me. He was just then busily employed, and, certainly, put it hastily out of his hand into this drawer.

La. It is clear, it is clear! And I am fortunate that heaven has chosen me for the instrument of this recovery. Mr Metland, I wish you joy, with all my heart, *shakes him by the hand.*) and return home a far happier man than I came. (*Going.*)

Me. Stop, Mr Lawley. Dare I make use of this money?

La. Why not? It is your own. Is it not found, exact, as you have always described it?

Me. But have I not just said, that the papers which this writing-desk now contains, do not belong to me?

La. They do belong to you.

Me. When the executors of my old friend made me this present, did they know of its contents? And dare I call that my own, which, by chance, remained in the desk of a deceased person, whose inheritor I am not? Dare I keep silent on this occurrence? May not some other thing be in the drawer, besides these bank-notes?

La. (*Casts a look.*) Very true. And there lays a letter sure enough, which, on our first joy, escaped our notice.

Me. A letter!—To whom?

La. (*reads the direction.*) " To my son, Edward " Claransforth. Not to be opened till after my " death."

Me. Now—what now!—Must I embezzle that letter too?

La. What has this letter to do with your money?

Me. I shall carry both to young Claransforth.

La. Take my advice—Young Claransforth is unthinking and dissipated. Who knows but that he is capable of accepting the money, and, in a very easy manner, returning you thanks?

Me. In fulfilling the duty of an honest man, I do not therefore renounce my right. Yet, to invest myself with this property, without an explanation, I will not.

La. I see you are determined, and I shall say no more—Do as you please: and, if Claransforth is not dishonest, you may now pay all your debts, and live in comfort the rest of your life.—So I shall tell those who sent me, and my business here will be over; for which I shall be heartily glad. With a heavy heart I came into this house; with a light one I leave it.

[*Exit.*

Me. You do not say a single word to all this.

Mrs Me. I will not deny, that to me your virtue appears rather too strict. Is the money not unquestionably yours?

Me. This is enough for my conscience, but not for example sake.—In a word, my dear Eleanor, I feel that I could not enjoy it without the full consent of young Claransforth. Early to-morrow morning I will hasten to him, and put an end to our suspense and argument at once. (*A loud rap at the door.*)—A loud rap at this house! Can it be my son?

Mrs Me. No; for he took leave of me, going out of town on duty till to-morrow noon.

L. Ma. (*without.*) If Mr and Mrs Metland live here, I must see them immediately. (*Enter* LADY MARY.) My dear, good, worthy people, how do you both do? I beg pardon for disturbing you at this late hour; but I could not go to rest without seeing, and speaking to your daughter Ellen.

Mrs Me. Is she not at your ladyship's?

Me. She is not at home, madam.

L. Ma. (affecting surprise.) Not at home !—Are
you sure of it ?   Both sure of it ?

Me. Yes ; both.

L. Ma. Why, then, I have only to say, Heaven
bless you, good people !—and good night.

Mrs Me. Dear madam, stay and relieve my mind.

Me. (going up to her.) Tell me the worst.

L. Ma. The task is too difficult.   Excuse me—
No, I cannot.

Me. Look at my poor wife.   Kill her at once, or
relieve her.

L. Ma. Why, then, your daughter not being at
home, where I did hope, (though I must own I feared I should not find her,) confirms me that she is—

Mrs Me. Not dead ?

Me. Not worse than dead ?

L. Ma. Why, that is as you may consider it.—
Life to most people is precious—And yet, life, with
loss of honour—(*They start.*)—But don't suppose I
come to acquaint you with any thing of this kind
for *certain.*   All I know is, that your daughter, in
tears, confessed to me, this morning, her love for
a gentleman who occasionally visits at my house ; and
who had plainly declared to her, as she informed
me, that his intentions towards her were not such as
her friends would approve.—Yet, knowing this—and
after all the good advice I gave her—she was seen
this very evening, since dark, with that self-same man,
in a hackney coach ; and not returning to me by the
hour my doors are always locked, I thought it my
duty to come and state all this to you, her parents,
that no reproach may rest on my character.

Me. Tell me the villain's name with whom she is fled !

L. Ma. There I must beg to be excused.   He is a
gay man : but all men are gay now-a-days.—And
your daughter is a young woman : but all women
are young now-a-days.

Me. But, madam—the name of the libertine ?

L. Ma. I trust, Mr Metland, as a man of honour, you will not compel me to divulge that part of my story. Consider, you have a son in the army ; and were I so indiscreet as to reveal names, a duel might ensue, and you, by to-morrow, be childless.

Mrs Me. I thank you for your foresight.

Me. And I submit.—She is not worth the hazard of a brother's life. Even I would not expose myself for her, such as she *is !*—though, to have preserved her what she *was,* I would have died with joy !

L. Ma. I am sincerely glad to find you both so rational ; and, as it is very late, and a very dreadful night, and I have great compassion for my horses— (one should be kind to dumb creatures,) I'll take my leave.—Adieu ! I hope you think I have done my duty. Good night !   [*Exit.*

Me. " Good night !"—Can we have a good night ?

Mrs Me. No! The repose we promised to ourselves, from the contents of that desk, is gone for ever.

Me. (*Laying hold of her hand.*) Our daugher is gone for ever—and all the gold and gems contained in the whole world, would not repay us for her loss.

[*Exeunt*

ACT THE FOURTH.

SCENE I.

The lodgings of AVA THOANOA.

Enter AVA, *followed by a* SERVANT.

Av. Who do you say has called, since I have been out?

Ser. Only this gentleman.   (*Gives a card.*)

Av. Claransforth!—What could bring him here?

Ser. The gentleman seemed very sorry you were not at home; and said he would call again.—Here he is, sir.   [*Exit.*

Enter CLARANSFORTH.

Av. Good morning, Mr Claransforth!

Cla. Good morning, Ava!—I hope you are very well? (*Throws himself in a chair.*)

Av. You do not seem as if *you* were.

Cla. Why, yes, pretty well—I can't say I am very well.

Av. The honour of a visit from you is totally unexpected. How came you to know where I live? I don't remember your having asked me for my address.

Cla. Bankwell, my clerk; he who introduced you—I asked him for it. (*Sighs heavily.*)

Av. But, from the company I left you in last night, I could scarcely have expected to see you abroad thus early.

Cla. Ha! What you mean the pretty girl. True: after you were gone, we went to a house together.

Av. I know you did.

Cla. And to a house of ill fame.

Av. I know it.

Cla. Ay, to be sure, you know every thing!—And 'tis this very knowledge which you boast of that has brought me to you this morning, to ask your assistance.

Av. I will serve you in any thing that is honourable.

Cla. 'Sdeath, sir! do you think I would require of you any thing else?

Av. You are out of humour—displeased, uneasy.—What's the matter?

Cla. Why do you ask? Don't you know without my telling you?

Av. Perhaps I do.——But there are some things I must be told, before I hazard giving an affront by mentioning them.

Cla. Why, this is, to be sure, an affair of some delicacy; and pardon me, if in what I am going to say, I am guilty of a breach of delicacy towards you.——I suspect you are mending a broken fortune, by being the spy of some great man, or some foreign power: but, be this as it will, you certainly do possess yourself of most excellent intelligence concerning others,——as I am a proof. Now, whether this knowledge comes by natural or supernatural means, that I will not dispute with you,——it shall be as you choose: only have the friendship to take some little trouble, either through your human or your infernal agents, to find for me something I have lost.

Av. And what is the thing which you are so earnest to recover?

Cla. It is a person.

Av. A person!——And who is he?

Cla. It is not *he*; it is *she*.

Av. And who is she? (*Roughly.*)

Cla. Whenever an old man talks of *she*, how cross he speaks! In short, it is the girl you saw with me last night.

Av. (*With contempt.*) And would you employ my art to recover her?

Cla. Sooner than any thing in the world.

Av. A pretty girl is easy to be found, without the art of conjuration.

Cla. But what is another man's taste may not be mine; and her you saw with me last night I would give twenty thousand pounds you could see with me again to night.

Av. Without applying to me, a slender part of

that sum, I should conceive, would fulfil your wishes.

Cla. No!—she is virtuous, and not to be purchased.

Av. And do you pretend that the girl who accompanied you to such a house as you have mentioned——

Cla. In that she was deceived. She thought I was going to take her to her parent's house. And, oh! what aggravates my grief, my remorse, her father was *my* father's friend—a man of the strictest honour, who lost his fortune in our house—His name is Metland.—This I only learnt an hour ago from the servants of Lady Mary Diamond. The daughter, from motives of prudence, had concealed from me the name of her family.

Av. And instead of taking her to this honoured parent's house, you took her to one devoted to purposes vile as your own.

Cla. From whence, insulted by my passion, she found means to escape, while I left her for a few moments to the care of one of the family.

Av. And do you wish to pursue her to her present asylum?

Cla. What asylum?—I have sent spies to her father's, and have been myself at the lady's with whom she lived. She has returned to neither place—and where, in the midst of a cold stormy night, she could shelter——

Av. No matter where, since she was sheltered from you.

Cla. The moment I found she had escaped me, I put pistols in my pocket, and, like a madman, ran half the town over, resolute to regain her. My emissaries have been through the other half.—In vain all our efforts to find her. And now, despairing, I am come to you—You, who can search the

grave, and bring forth the dead, cannot you discover
the abode of the living ?

Av. No ! for my art is harmless.—The dead are
beyond your power to injure ;—the living you would
destroy.

Cla. I waste my time in talking to you.

Av. Still 'tis but wasted.—Your time would, probably, be worse spent in occupation.

Cla. Ava Thoanoa, in what have I offended you,
that you persist in your malignity towards me ?—As
my father's friend, I received you kindly, bore all
your reproaches with patience, and from my heart
forgave you ;—nay, for that venerable face and solemn accent, I half believed the falsities you uttered.

Av. Falsities !

Cla. Submit to 'the reproach, or raise me spec-
tres. This is the very time.—My feelings are so
painful, I want them expelled by others still more
acute. And if you have any arts to play, any
tricks to show, begin instantly. I'm in a humour to
fear nothing.

Av. This is not a humour for me to act upon.
You must be prepared, properly prepared by calmness
and reflection, before your sensual eyes can behold
an airy form—a departed spirit.

Cla. Why, then, I have an appointment within
an hour that will better than any thing else prepare
me ; for it is at one of the most retired and pious
houses in town, where nothing is seen but the purest
manners.

Av. And what could induce you to visit at such a
house ?

Cla. A pretty girl.

Av. Another pretty girl?

Cla. Oh yes—I have a thousand—but they are
none of them to compare with her I have lost ;—and
yet they must be my relief from the poignant sense
of my misfortune. And so, when I have been at

the Quaker's, and composed myself, I'll come back to you—And you engage to show me what you have promised?

Av. I do.

Cla. I thank you. Any amusement, my dear Ava, to keep me from reflection.   [*Exit.*

Aa. No! rather will I bring you to reflection.
                    [*Exit, on the opposite side.*

SCENE II.

The House of TIMOTHY STARCH.

Enter RUTH and ENSIGN METLAND.

En. At length I have watched your father and mother from the house. And now, Ruth, answer me—Is the report true of their intention to marry you to Mr Claransforth?

Ru. It is their intention, but not my will.

En. Can you then contemn all the riches of Claransforth, and prepare to take a long journey, one that will last for life, in company with a poor man? Will you not be peevish, and lament, when the roads are bad, and the ups and downs of marriage cares jolt and jostle you?

Ru. Not if they cast me against the man I love; for I would cleave unto him for support; yea, verily, I would—and think hills and dales more pleasant with him, than a smooth beaten way with any other.

En. Hark! I hear some one coming.—Perhaps your father! Let me retire into this room.   [*Exit.*

Enter CLARANSFORTH on the opposite side.

Cla. Beloved Ruth! I am not in spirits; but your charms will revive me.

Ru. Neighbour Claransforth, I am in spirits; but your presence will depress them.

Cla. My dear, enchanting, prim Ruth, where is your mother? where is your father? I hope they are well! Where are they? (*Presses her hand.*)

Ru. I wish they were here, that they might reprove thee for thy impertinence.

Cla. Impertinence! Why, that's my love, my adoration of you.

Ru. Why dost thou come to me, neighbour, to make professions of thy affection? For thou dost not love me, I can perceive by thy vacant eye, thy absent thought, and careless manners. Verily, these are no arguments of the lover.

Cla. " Verily," what maketh thee such a connoisseur in judging of love.

Ru. That which maketh a connoisseur in all the arts,—practice.

Cla. Indeed!

Ru. Yea, friend. Verily, from the first dawn of my understanding, I have had an ear for music, an eye for painting, a taste for poetry, and a heart for love.

Cla. I rejoice to hear it.

Ru. But not to love thee, friend.

Cla. Whether me or not, the picture of yourself, which you have drawn, is so enchanting, it animates me to vow upon your lips—

(*As he is going to salute her—*)

Enter RACHEL STARCH.

Ra. Neighbour Claransforth, neighbour Claransforth, is this neighbourly, thus to assail my daughter?

Cla. Friend Starch, friend Starch, is this friendly, thus to come unwarily upon me?

Ra. Dost thou mean to make my daughter thy spouse? Say, instantly, yea or nay.

Cla. Nay.

Ra. And dost thou mean, after thus dallying, to forsake her?

Cla. Yea.

Ra. Surely thou can'st not leave a maiden, whose grief at thy perfidy will continue all the days of her life. She loves thee, Edward Claransforth, and has sacrificed to thee her hopes of marriage with a man of fortune. Who is now to become her support? For her parents are poor, and can give her no portion.

Cla. 'Sdeath! (*Aside, and moved.*)

Ra. Would'st thou destroy all the prospects of an innocent woman?

Cla. No, faith, I would not! I might, perhaps, love to do a little mischief; but not a great deal, upon my honour, without thirsting to make atonement. I have plunged in misery one young woman—a repetition of the crime would be execrable. (*Aside.*) Neighbour Starch, if I have, by any incoherent expressions, misled your daughter into an error, which has lost her the prospect of marrying a wealthy man, I will make all the atonement in my power, by giving her a fortune with any other whom she may choose. And I here pledge my word, that when you call upon me——

Enter ENSIGN METLAND.

En. Hold, sir! make no rash promises. That young woman has suffered no disappointment on your account; but she is constrained to silence. Nor had she ever a man of fortune for her suitor. I am her only lover; and I am not worth a guinea. Ruth! do you love this gentleman?

Ru. (*Warmly.*) No.

En. Whom do you love?

Ru. Thee.

Cla. Sir, you ennoble poverty. I am most extremely obliged to you for the information you have given me ; and I entreat you will favour me with your address.

En. Pardon me—I wish the present meeting and conversation to be, from this day, forgotten ; particularly the part I have taken in it. This prejudiced woman will, I hope, soon perceive her mistake ; and that young woman will, I hope, soon be happily married.   [*Exit.*

Cla. But, sir—(*calls after the Ensign—then turns to Rachel*)—Grant me the only favour I shall ever ask of you—Tell me the name of that gentleman.

Ra. He hath offended me, and I will not. Follow me, Ruth Starch.

                    [*Exit* RACHEL—RUTH *following.*

Cla. He mentioned his poverty : and if it were in my power to supply his wants——

Enter TIMOTHY STARCH.

Tim. I met the military man now coming forth from this house? What means he by still visiting—

Cla. I forget that young officer's name—Pray, can you tell it me?

Tim. Dost thou mean the Ensign Metland, whom I now passed at my door?

Cla. (*Starting.*) Metland! Metland!

Tim. Yea ; son to old Metland, who lately failed in trade, and now lives in a cottage in the City-Road.

Cla. Is he his son? (*Aside.*) Oh! Oh! I had rather any one than him. (*To Timothy.*) Are you sure, certain, he is a son of Metland's?

Tim. Certain! Metland has but one son, and one daughter.

Cla. (*Anxiously.*) And where is she?

Tim. That is not at the present time known. The damsel hath fled from one Mary Diamond, with whom she lived, and has gone away with some vile man, who frequented that great and wicked house.

Cla. Heavens! (*Aside.*) And, pray, when did you hear this strange account?

Tim. But now—at my own door.

Cla. The brother did not seem acquainted with the news.

Tim. He knew it not till this instant—when his weeping mother met him, and, in my hearing, requested him to go in search of his sister, and bring her home to her bosom, whether sullied by the embraces of a seducer, or folded in the arms of death.

Cla. Oh, dreadful! And the mother lamenting in the streets!

Tim. Yea; it would have made thee weep to have listened to her lamentation. For my part, I seldom cry—and as seldom laugh. I keep my passions cool and steady, as I keep my countenance.— What is the matter with thine?

Cla. Quaker, I am a murderer. If the daughter of Metland be dead, as her mother apprehends, it is I who have caused her dissolution. It is I who seduced her from her home, and have been her murderer. Where shall I hide myself from the load that oppresses me?

Tim. Neighbour, thou must not hide thyself in my house. Why tarriest thou? Depart!

Cla. (*Inattentive to Timothy.*) Yes; I'll add suicide to murder, and end my remorse at once.

Tim. (*Going calmly up to him.*) And where would'st thou be buried, friend? Before thou committest the rash act, to whom dost thou bequeath the vast sums of which thou art possessed? Whom dost thou appoint thy pall-bearers? and what kind

of tomb-stone would'st thou have erected to thy
memory?

Cla. Your iron heart brings me to myself. While
there is a hope my Ellen lives, I will live for her.
Quaker, farewell! and, notwithstanding all the agony
I at this moment endure, I would not exchange my
sensibility for your indifference.   [*Exit.*

Tim. Verily, he speaketh foolishness.   [*Exit.*

SCENE III.

An apartment at LADY MARY'S.

Enter LADY MARY, *followed by* ELLEN.

El. If I have ever been a trusty servant—if, during the whole time I have lived in your house, this
is my first offence—if I have always paid attention
to your orders, and shown tenderness when sickness
took from you the power of command—if, till a fatal
passion seized my heart, my duty to you was as
strictly fulfilled as that to my parents—if, repentance for my past fault, and promise of amendment,
can make any atonement—oh! receive me again,
and hide my failings from my father's knowledge!

L. Ma. Failings indeed! A pretty soft term for
robbing your mistress, and passing the night with a
professed libertine.

El. I did not. I passed it under a shed, in sight of my father's door, where I dared not rap. See— my clothes have been drenched with rain, and my hair is still damp.

L. Ma. And so your lover turned you out?

El. No; he did not turn me out; he meant to keep me secure—but I escaped.

L. Ma. Then return to him again; for, be assured, no one else will receive you.

El. No; there is my last night's habitation still left, and I will return there. (*Loitering.*) Yet, madam, though you refuse to trust me again yourself, you may not wholly despair that, in another service, I may give proof of contrition, and retrieve my character. You will, then, perhaps, be so compassionate as not to reveal my indiscretions; particularly not to complain of them to my family; but suffer me, as I am now weak with fatigue and sorrow, to go home, as discharged by you this morning on account of sickness.

L. Ma. A mighty pretty plan, and a very proper contriver you are, for the embellishment of a falsehood! Would you have me impose you on your father and mother as innocent? No! So far am I from such imposition, that, at midnight, when I found you did not come home, I went to them, to let them know you were gone off with a gentleman.

El. Oh!

L. Ma. You may well sigh and mourn!—If you had seen your poor mother—and if you had heard your father—he vowed never to pardon you—and said, " Were you ever to come into his presence—"

El. I never dare.

L. Ma. And your poor mother!—She——

El. Oh! tell me what my father said! I can bear his anger, his threats; I can bear that they be put in execution—I can bear all—all things, but my mother's tears.

L. Ma. And you will not have them to bear long, if I may judge by her present grief.

El. Madam, I take my leave—gladly go—for the piercing winds, storms of hail and thunder, or the hooting of the rabble to a discarded wanderer, would not be half so wounding to my ears as your piercing words! (*Exit Lady Mary.*) Shall I follow, and kneel to her? No! her heart is hard—every heart is hardened to me—and I, who never in my life did wrong to another, am myself loaded with injuries—that will drive me to distraction!   [*Exit.*

ACT THE FIFTH.

SCENE I.

An apartment at CLARANSFORTH'S.

CLARANSFORTH *discovered, leaning disconsolately on a sopha.*

Enter BANKWELL, *and goes slowly to him.*

Ba. I am sorry to see you so out of spirits. Surely something very particular!

Cla. Yes, it is.

Ba. Lost a great sum, perhaps?

Cla. I wish I had.

Ba. I am glad you have not.

Cla. Sir, you know nothing of my concerns beyond the counting-house; nor will I suffer you to be a spy.

Ba. I beg your pardon. I did not come as a spy upon your sorrows. I come merely to deliver a message. A person, who is waiting below, requests a few minute's conversation with you.

Cla. Not now. I can see no one at present.

Ba. I was afraid so—And I would not have asked at this time for any one, except the person in question. But I was sorry to give the old man the trouble of coming again.

Cla. Oh, if it's the old Indian, you may admit him.

Ba. No, sir—it is old Mr Metland.

Cla. (*Starts.*) He! Old Metland. (*Fearfully.*) What does he want?

Ba. That he wishes to tell *you.*

Cla. No, I can't see him. I won't see him. I am ashamed to see him. (*Aside.*) Ashamed to see a man! Then am I degraded beneath one. I will have courage, and endure his reproaches.

Ba. Did you give me an answer, sir?

Cla. (*Affecting indifference.*) Yes—desire Mr Metland to walk in. Show him in.

While BANKWELL *goes out,* CLARANSFORTH *shows marks of extreme embarrassment and confusion.*

BANKWELL *re-enters, with* METLAND, *and retires immediately.*

METLAND *bows humbly to* CLARANSFORTH. CLARANSFORTH'S *confusion increases.*

Cla. Mr Metland; you do me much——Will you please to sit?

Me. No, I thank you, sir. The business on which I come will soon be over. I do not mean to detain you, sir, more than a few minutes; therefore I will proceed without ceremony. (*Takes from his pocket the notes, just as they were found in the private drawer, and lays them on the table which is standing before them.*) This money is yours.

Cla. Mine! (*Surprised.*) You to me,—money!

Me. You may, perhaps, have heard, that, on the day your father died, I brought him a sum of money which could not be found.

Cla. I heard so, with concern.

Me. After the fatal accident, which, at that time, we had to lament, I received, as a keep-sake, in memory of my friend, your father's writing-desk.— Your clerk, Bankwell, remembers the circumstance.

Cla. Probably.

Me. In this writing-desk, a secret drawer was, yesterday, by mere chance, discovered. It contained twelve thousand pounds, which, conformable to my conscience, I deliver up to you.

Cla. To me! Mr Metland! to me! Why to me?

Me. Because the writing-desk belonged to you; and because your trustees and executors, when they gave it me, were unacquainted with the treasure it contained.

Cla. Twelve thousand pounds. Is not that the amount of the sum which you entrusted to my father?

Me. Exactly.

Cla. It must then, of course, be your own money.

Me. Mr Claransforth, I know it to be my own;— and yet the manner in which I recovered it imposed a restraint upon my duty, not to consider it such, till you had acknowledged it mine.

Cla. (*aside.*) Good heaven! what a family have I wronged. Dear sir, hesitate not a moment to take it back! (*returning the money.*)

Me. You are then convinced, upon the word of an honest man, that this is my property.

Cla. I am convinced, I could not think otherwise.

Me. (*putting the notes up.*)   I thank you!

Cla. And be assured, Mr Metland, that I rejoice, and am more happy at this event than if I had saved my most valuable ships from wreck.

Me. I see my old friend is still alive. Once more I sincerely thank you, dear sir, for your generosity, although I am not, from some family afflictions, exactly in the state to enjoy it.

Cla. (*trembling.*) What afflictions! may I venture to ask?

Me. Ah! you are a young man, and an unmarried man!—You have never yet experienced either the joys or sorrows of a husband and father.

(*Struggling to conceal his tears.*)

Cla. But I can sympathise.

Me. No doubt you can. But sympathy to one, like me, cast down—wounded in the tenderest part. But I beg your pardon, I have no right to trouble you with my griefs. Yet they will, at times burst forth, in defiance of resistance, in defiance of good manners.—And now they have almost made me forget part of my errand.—Here is a letter, sir, I found in the secret drawer of which I have been speaking. It is your father's hand-writing, and addressed to you. (*Gives it, and is going.*)

Cla. A letter in my father's own hand! It may relate to the money you have brought. Stay, and hear me read it.

Me. If it's your pleasure.

Cla. With reverence I break the honoured seal, and will faithfully perform whatever he has commanded. (*Reads.*) " My dearest son, this letter " you will not receive till you have lost your father, " and I write to point out to you where to choose

Q 2

" another. Metland the elder has been my friend
" for many years. I wish him to be yours by the tie
" of relationship:—His daughter, in every endow-
" ment, resembles your deceased mother. I was
" happy in the marriage state—That you may be so,
" I recommend to you Ellen Metland for a wife. (*He*
" *shows great emotion.*) Accept of this my last ad-
" vice, as you wish me peace in my grave. With
" the hope that you will, I give my blessing to you
" both.

" Edward Claransforth."

(After reading the letter, METLAND *and* CLARANS-
FORTH *stand for some time fixed and silent.)*

Me. (*after an effort.*) Mr Claransforth, you see
before you a poor old father, sunk to the earth with
shame, disappointment, and sorrow. When your be-
neficent parent wrote that letter, I had a daughter—
now I have none. (*Bursting into a fit of tears.*)
For she has abandoned me and her mother, abandoned herself! Oh! good young man! (*taking him
by the hand.*) she is unworthy of *you.* A villain has
seduced her, has destroyed that virtuous being who
was the pride of her parents, and might have been
the happiness of a husband.

Cla. He! that villain! falls on his knees before
you, and entreats for mercy.——Metland, I saw
your daughter, and, not knowing her to be yours,
by my arts seduced her from her friends; but in
vain all my attempts to allure her from virtue.——
Wherever she is, she is pure as her guardian angel.
She fled my caresses—And, on the oath of a repent-
ant libertine, she is virtuous.

Me. Audacious profligate! But tell me where she
is, that I may fly.—Where is my child?

Enter AVA THOANOA.

Av. Thy child lies on a sick bed, attended by physicians, who despair of restoring her to health, so powerfully has affliction visited both mind and body.

Me. And yet I trust she will not die! Heaven is all merciful, and will preserve mine and my poor wife's senses! What friend to me has opened his door to a hapless wanderer.

Av. I, in my pursuit of the afflicted, I met her in a state of sorrow, bordering on distraction, and had her instantly conveyed to my apartments.—This is the address where you will find her. (*Gives a card.*) Keep it private, except to your own family.

Me. Bless you, kind sir, the way is short, and yet it will seem tedious. (*Going.*)

Cla. (*who had thrown himself distractedly on a sofa during the last speech.*) Metland! do not leave me without your forgiveness!

Me. Villain! dread an injured father's wrath!

[*Exit.*

Cla. (*to Av.*) Read that letter—You know the hand. In aggravation of my guilt, it is my wife, the wife to whom my father secretly betrothed me, that I have thrown an outcast on the world. Indian, I believe you—I now firmly believe all you have told me! My father's spirit cannot rest while his last will is directly violated, and I have the curses of those pious parents whom he hoped would bless me. I am this instant at the crisis of my fate; and, if thou hast spoken truth, precipitate me at once to better or worse, by showing me my father.

Av. (*after a pause.*) You are unworthy of the promise I made you; but my word has more weight with me than your offences. Follow me to my lodgings.   [*Exeunt.*

SCENE II.

The lodgings of AVA THOANOA.

(*Enter two* SERVANTS, *meeting.   One with lights,
which he puts down.*)

1*st Ser.* Is my master returned?

2*d Ser.* No; but I expect him every moment, and
I hope he will come soon, for we have had such
a number of cards and visitors.   (*Putting cards on
the table.   A rap at the door.*)

Enter AVA *and* CLARANSFORTH.

Av. Who have called since I have been abroad?
        (*Servants whisper him, and exeunt.*)
Your masculine vice is joined to feminine weakness:
You have prated of the art which I communicated to
you, as a secret, and every gossip and adventurer in
town apply to me, as a conjurer, to resolve their
questions.

Cla. I own I mentioned your pretended art at
Lady Mary Diamond's, and, I believe, at the house
of one Starch, a Quaker.   But I would have been
secret, had you enjoined secrecy.

Av. Truth requires none.   But here's Lady Mary
Diamond, and two or three more, my servants in-

form me, shut up in separate rooms, till I have done
with you : they do not seek truth, but falsehood.

Cla. But come, before you undeceive them, satisfy my curiosity.

Av. Are you prepared ! (*solemnly.*) Do you
think your courage will not fail you at the sight
of your father ?

Cla. I should sink to the earth were I to behold
him : But confident that I shall not, I defy both him
and you.

Av. Then to the trial. Stand firmly, and keep
your eye fixed on that entrance—that door.

Cla. Very well, I do.

Av. Would you see him alone, or shall I stay with
you ?

Cla. Alone !

Av. I'll send him to you, then, immediately.

Cla. No, hold ! you shall stay by me. I'll have
no imposition. You shall not go, and move a pup-
pet from behind a curtain. Stay by me, and call him
to come forth.

Av. I must repeat the words of the charm in private : then I'll return, and he shall follow me.

[*Exit.*

Cla. How powerful is the effect of imagination !—
The harassed state of my mind—my remorse—might
—and, above all, the venerable aspect of this man, and
the solemn language of his fictions, put me in a tremor.

*Enter a person, who, in appearance, exactly repre-
sents* AVA THOANOA.

Cla. Well !

The supposed AVA *holds up his hand to enjoin silence :
then turns towards the door, on which he and* CLA-
RANSFORTH *fix their eyes, with an anxious watchfulness, when* CLARANSFORTH (*the father*) *enters*

slow and stately. The younger CLARANSFORTH *appears amazed and shocked. The elder* CLARANSFORTH *stands fixed.*

Cla. the Younger. (*after a pause.*) It is the exact figure of my father—Exact—and almost makes me tremble. Admirable deception!—surprising ingenuity!—wonderful art!—Detain him—don't let him disappear—let me survey him nearer first. (*Claransforth the elder walks forward.*) Excellent piece of mechanism! I could even talk or kneel to that form!— 'Tis most surprising! and childish prejudices will cling about me. Yet, that you are not a ghost, I am certain.—But what, in the name of wonder, are you?——

Cla. the Elder. I am he whom you mistook for Ava, the Indian.

Cla. the Younger. Ah! my good friend Ava, himself, in the shape of my father. Then, what is this figure? He must be a ghost for certain?—(*Goes up to the person who represents* AVA. *This person takes off his beard, &c. and discovers himself to be* BANKWELL.) Bankwell engaged in a trick upon me! Then I see, I understand it all. That is not the Indian in my father's form. It was my father who put on the Indian's; my living father, who but feigned to die, that he might have the means to search into all the frailties of his son.

Cla. the Elder. Your conjecture is right, and he will punish those frailties. For, do not think, because I have descended to practise an idle deception on you, that I mean to fool on. This trifling was but to fulfil the promise I was provoked to make by your sceptic discourse. (*Cla. the Younger falls on his knees.*) No, sir, no pardon from me—

(*Enter* METLAND *and* ENSIGN METLAND.) till you have received it here.

Me. I am in astonishment.—Is it possible? Do I behold Claransforth, my former friend?

Cla. the Elder. Say your *present* friend—more firmly yours than ever.

Me. Amazement!

Cla. the Elder. My friend, I have watched you and your family, through all your sorrows, all your meritorious conduct, beneath the wrong I did you, and which it shall be now my happiness to repair. I have watched all those, too, whom I equally loved; and I have found the far greater number, such as make this world more dear, than when, in the midst of my house, in flames, my danger brought to my recollection a secret passage by which I preserved my life, yet preserved it with such hazard, that you all thought me dead. This gave, to my curious and suspicious nature, an opportunity which I could not resist. Bankwell alone has been my confidant; by his means, I have been enabled to prove all your hearts; and, I rejoice to say that, except in one instance, I have been delighted by the experiment.

Cla. the Younger. I am the exception.

Cla. the Elder. You are.

Cla. the Younger. And, yet, how I have sinned against my duty to my father is, to myself, unknown; for the inmost recesses of my heart cannot reproach me with the want of filial love.

Cla. the Elder. You have sinned against heaven and your neighbour. I take those injuries on myself.

Cla. the Younger. But heaven is merciful. So sometimes is man. (*Enter* ELLEN, *leaning on her* MOTHER.) Ellen, would'st thou forgive me?

Cla. the Elder. Dar'st thou ask it?

Cla. the Younger. Is there any other way to obtain forgiveness? If you will instruct me in any other, whatever is the penalty, I will submit to it.

Cla. the Elder. Metland ! my friend—can you ever look on this man as your son ?

Me. I can look on him as *yours,* and, as such, forgive him.

Cla. the Elder. But the rest of your family.

Mrs. Me. I love, by my husband's example.

En. And I will regard him by my sister's.

Cla. the Elder. Young woman, whom I have retrieved from desperation, and whom, from your childhood, I have loved as my own, do not deceive me. Can you forgive this man ? Can you be thoroughly reconciled to him ? Could you take him for a husband ?

CLARANSFORTH *the younger goes to her, and kneels.*

El. While heaven remits its punishment on my offence, can I be rigorous to others?

Cla. the Younger. I will deserve the confidence you place in me. I will deserve to be related to this family, whose virtues I have proved.

Cla. the Elder. And now take my hand. For while you retain all your virtuous dispositions, and will banish all your vicious ones——

Enter RUTH STARCH.

Ru. Doth one Ava Thoanoa abide in this house ?

En. Ruth ! What can bring you here ?

Ru. I came to ask the fortune-teller, if I should ever be thy wife?

Enter RACHEL *and* TIMOTHY STARCH.

Ra. Timothy ! It is as I have said unto thee ; here is the soldier and thy daughter in close communication.

Ru. Mother, I came not here to see the soldier, but to hear tidings of him from the sorcerer, who keepeth the house.

Ra. A sorcerer! Woe be unto him! Which is he?

Cla. the Elder. If I may assume the mystery of fortune-telling, this young man and woman (*pointing to the* ENSIGN *and* RUTH,) would be happy in marriage, if they could gain their friends' consent.

Me. Whatever will render my son happy, I shall not oppose.

Cla. the Elder. My neighbour Starch, what say you?

Tim. Neighbour Claransforth, they told me thou wert dead! but thou art not, I find.

Cla. the Elder. I am permitted to revisit this world, to dispose of my riches worthily; and I mean to give this young Ensign a fortune, in addition to that which his father will give him.

Tim. But, Ruth, what say'st thou to this man?

Ru. Verily, I should like to become unto this man such as my mother became unto thee.

Tim. Then, take her, young man. But I say unto thee, love her only with that discreet love with which I have loved her mother, and which made me content to marry her, and would have made me equally content if I had not.

Ra. And, verily, this is the sort of prudent love which I bear unto thee.

Cla. the Elder. What various manners and passions have I witnessed since my disguise gave me the power of judgment on the failings of my neighbours! I now, in my turn, am to be judged; and, in order to support the title of a Wise Man, I most humbly submit my character to the approbation or censure, of—Wiser Heads than my own.

PERCY,

A

TRAGEDY,

IN FIVE ACTS.

AS PERFORMED AT THE

THEATRE ROYAL, COVENT-GARDEN.

BY

HANNAH MORE.

DRAMATIS PERSONÆ.

PERCY, *Earl of Northumberland,* *Mr Lewis.*
EARL DOUGLAS,   *Mr Wroughton.*
EARL RABY, *Elwina's Father,* *Mr Aickin.*
EDRIC, *Friend to Douglas,*   *Mr Whitefield.*
HARCOURT, *Friend to Percy,* *Mr Robson.*
SIR HUBERT, *a Knight,*   *Mr Hull.*

ELWINA,   *Mrs Barry.*
BIRTHA,   *Mrs Jackson.*

Knights, Guards, Attendants, &c.

SCENE,—*Raby Castle, in Durham.*

PERCY.

ACT THE FIRST.

SCENE I.

A Gothic Hall.

Enter EDRIC *and* BIRTHA.

Bir. What may this mean ? Earl Douglas has in-
    join'd thee
To meet him here in private ?
    Ed. Yes, my sister,
And this injunction I have oft received ;
But when he comes, big with some painful secret,
He starts, looks wild, then drops ambiguous hints,
Frowns, hesitates, turns pale, and says 'twas nothing ;
Then feigns to smile, and by his anxious care

To prove himself at ease, betrays his pain.

   Bir. Since my short sojourn here, I've mark'd
       this earl,
And though the ties of blood unite us closely,
I shudder at his haughtiness of temper,
Which not his gentle wife, the bright Elwina,
Can charm to rest. Ill are their spirits pair'd;
His is the seat of frenzy, her's of softness,
His love is transport, her's is trembling duty,
Rage in his soul is as the whirlwind fierce,
While her's ne'er felt the power of that rude passion.

   Ed. Perhaps the mighty soul of Douglas mourns,
Because inglorious love detains him here,
While our bold knights, beneath the Christian stand-
      ard,
Press to the bulwarks of Jerusalem.

   Bir. Though every various charm adorns Elwina,
And though the noble Douglas dotes to madness,
Yet some dark mystery involves their fate:
The canker grief devours Elwina's bloom,
And on her brow meek resignation sits,
Hopeless, yet uncomplaining.

   Ed. 'Tis most strange.

   Bir. Once, not long since, she thought herself
      alone;
'Twas then the pent-up anguish burst its bounds;
With broken voice, clasp'd hands, and streaming
      eyes,
She call'd upon her father, call'd him cruel,
And said her duty claim'd far other recompence.

   Ed Perhaps the absence of the good Lord Raby,
Who, at her nuptials, quitted this fair castle,
Resigning it to her, may thus afflict her.
Hast thou e'er question'd her, good Birtha?

   Bir. Often,
But hitherto in vain; and yet she shews me
The endearing kindness of a sister's love;
But if I speak of Douglas——

Ed. See! he comes.
It wou'd offend him shou'd he find you here.

Enter DOUGLAS.

Dou. How! Edric and his sister in close confer-
ence?
Do they not seem alarm'd at my approach?
And see, how suddenly they part! Now Edric,
                    [*Exit* BIRTHA.
Was this well done? or was it like a friend,
When I desired to meet thee here alone,
With all the warmth of trusting confidence,
To lay my bosom naked to thy view,
And shew thee all its weakness, was it well
To call thy sister here, to let her witness
Thy friend's infirmity?—perhaps to tell her—
    Ed. My lord, I nothing know; I came to learn.
    Dou. Nay then thou dost suspect there's some-
thing wrong?
    Ed. If we were bred from infancy together,
If I partook in all thy youthful griefs,
And every joy thou knew'st was doubly mine,
Then tell me all the secret of thy soul:
Or have these few short months of separation,
The only absence we have ever known,
Have these so rent the bands of love asunder,
That Douglas should distrust his Edric's truth?
    Dou. My friend, I know thee faithful as thou'rt
brave,
And I will trust thee—but not now, good Edric,
'Tis past, 'tis gone, it is not worth the telling,
'Twas wrong to cherish what disturb'd my peace;
I'll think of it no more.
    Ed. Transporting news!
I fear'd some hidden trouble vex'd your quiet.
In secret I have watch'd——
    Dou. Ha! watch'd in secret?
A spy, employ'd, perhaps, to note my actions.

What have I said? Forgive me, thou art noble:
Yet do not press me to disclose my grief,
For when thou know'st it, I perhaps shall hate thee
As much, my Edric, as I hate myself
For my suspicions—I am ill at ease.
 Ed. How will the fair Elwina grieve to hear it!
 Dou. Hold, Edric, hold—thou hast touch'd the
   fatal string
That wakes me into madness. Hear me then,
But let the deadly secret be secured
With bars of adamant in thy close breast.
Think on the curse which waits on broken oaths;
A knight is bound by more than vulgar ties,
And perjury in thee were doubly damn'd.
Well then, the king of England—
 Ed. Is expected
From distant Palestine.
 Dou. Forbid it, Heaven!
For with him comes—
 Ed. Ah! who?
 Dou. Peace, peace,
For see Elwina's here. Retire, my Edric;
When next we meet thou shalt know all. Farewell.
         [*Exit* EDRIC.
Now to conceal with care my bosom's anguish,
And let her beauty chase away my sorrows!
Yes, I wou'd meet her with a face of smiles—
But 'twill not be.

     Enter ELWINA.

 El. Alas, 'tis ever thus!
Thus ever clouded is his angry brow. [*Aside.*
 Dou. I were too blest, Elwina, cou'd I hope
You met me here by choice, or that your bosom
Shared the warm transports mine must ever feel
At your approach.
 El. My lord, if I intrude,

The cause which brings me claims at least forgive-
          ness :
I fear you are not well, and come, unbidden,
Except by faithful duty, to inquire,
If haply in my power, my little power,
I have the means to minister relief
To your affliction ?

    Dou. What unwonted goodness !
O I were blest above the lot of man,
If tenderness, not duty, brought Elwina ;
Cold, ceremonious, and unfeeling duty,
That wretched substitute for love : but know,
The heart demands a heart ; nor will be paid
With less than what it gives. E'en now, Elwina,
The glistening tear stands trembling in your eyes,
Which cast their mournful sweetness on the ground,
As if they fear'd to raise their beams to mine,
And read the language of reproachful love.

    El. My lord, I hoped the thousand daily proofs
Of my obedience——

    Dou. Death to all my hopes !
Heart-rending word ! obedience ? what's obedience ?
'Tis fear, 'tis hate, 'tis terror, 'tis aversion,
'Tis the cold debt of ostentatious duty,
Paid with insulting caution, to remind me
How much you tremble to offend a tyrant
So terrible as Douglas.—O, Elwina——
While duty measures the regard it owes
With scrupulous precision and nice justice,
Love never reasons, but profusely gives,
Gives, like a thoughtless prodigal, its all,
And trembles then, lest it has done too little.

    El. Indeed I'm most unhappy that my cares,
And my solicitude to please, offend.

    Dou. True tenderness is less solicitous,
Less prudent and more fond ; the enamour'd heart,
Conscious it loves, and blest in being loved,
Reposes on the object it adores,

And trusts the passion it inspires and feels.——
Thou hast not learnt how terrible it is
To feed a hopeless flame.—But hear, Elwina,
Thou most obdurate, hear me.——

   El. Say, my lord,
For your own lips shall vindicate my fame,
Since at the altar I became your wife,
Can malice charge me with an act, a word,
I ought to blush at ?   Have I not still lived
As open to the eye of observation,
As fearless innocence should ever live ?
I call attesting angels to be witness,
If in my open deed, or secret thought,
My conduct, or my heart, they've aught discern'd
Which did not emulate their purity.

   Dou. This vindication ere you were accused,
This warm defence, repelling all attacks
Ere they are made, and construing casual words
To formal accusations, trust me, madam,
Shews rather an alarm'd and vigilant spirit,
For ever on the watch to guard its secret,
Than the sweet calm of fearless innocence.
Who talk'd of guilt ? Who testified suspicion ?

   El. Learn, sir, that virtue, while 'tis free from
        blame,
Is modest, lowly, meek, and unassuming;
Not apt, like fearful vice, to shield its weakness
Beneath the studied pomp of boastful phrase,
Which swells to hide the poverty it shelters;
But when this virtue feels itself suspected,
Insulted, set at nought, its whiteness stain'd,
It then grows proud, forgets its humble worth,
And rates itself above its real value.

   Dou. I did not mean to chide ! but think, O think,
What pangs must rend this fearful doting heart,
To see you sink impatient of the grave,
To feel, distracting thought ! to feel you hate me !

El. What if the slender thread by which I hold
This poor precarious being soon must break,
Is it Elwina's crime, or heaven's decree?
Yet I shall meet, I trust, the king of terrors,
Submissive and resign'd, without one pang,
One fond regret, at leaving this gay world.

Dou. Yes, madam, there is one, one man adored,
For whom your sighs will heave, your tears will flow,
For whom this hated world will still be dear,
For whom you still wou'd live——

El. Hold, hold, my lord,
What may this mean?

Dou. Ah! I have gone too far.
What have I said?—Your father, sure, your father,
The good Lord Raby, may at least expect
One tender sigh.

El. Alas, my lord! I thought
The precious incense of a daughter's sighs
Might rise to heaven, and not offend its ruler.

Dou. 'Tis true; yet Raby is no more beloved
Since he bestow'd his daughter's hand on Douglas:
That was a crime the dutiful Elwina
Can never pardon; and believe me, madam,
My love's so nice, so delicate my honour,
I am ashamed to owe my happiness
To ties which make you wretched. (*Exit* DOUGLAS.

El. Ah! how's this?
Though I have ever found him fierce and rash,
Full of obscure surmises and dark hints,
Till now he never ventured to accuse me.
Yet there is one, one man beloved, adored,
For whom your tears will flow—these were his
　　　words—
And then the wretched subterfuge of Raby—
How poor th' evasion!—But my Birtha comes.

Enter BIRTHA.

Bir. Crossing the portico I met Lord Douglas,

Disorder'd were his looks, his eyes shot fire ;
He called upon your name with such distraction,
I fear'd some sudden evil had befallen you.
  El. Not sudden ; no ; long has the storm been ga-
            thering,
Which threatens speedily to burst in ruin
On this devoted head.
  Bir. I ne'er beheld
Your gentle soul so ruffled, yet I've mark'd you,
While others thought you happiest of the happy,
Blest with whate'er the world calls great, or good,
With all that nature, all that fortune gives,
I've mark'd you bending with a weight of sorrow.
  El. O I will tell thee all ! thou cou'dst not find
An hour, a moment in Elwina's life,
When her full heart so long'd to ease its burthen,
And pour its sorrows in thy friendly bosom :
Hear then, with pity hear my tale of woe,
And, O forgive, kind nature, filial piety,
If my presumptuous lips arraign a father !
Yes, Birtha, that beloved, that cruel father,
Has doom'd me to a life of hopeless anguish,
To die of grief ere half my days are number'd,
Doom'd me to give my trembling hand to Douglas
'Twas all I had to give—my heart was—Percy's.
  Bir. What do I hear ?
  El. My misery, not my crime.
Long since the battle 'twixt the rival houses
Of Douglas and of Percy, for whose hate
This mighty globe's too small a theatre,
One summer's morn my father chased the deer
On Cheviot Hills, Northumbria's fair domain.
  Bir. On that famed spot where first the feuds com-
            menced
Between the earls ?
  El. The same. During the chace,
Some of my father's knights received an insult
From the Lord Percy's herdsmen, churlish foresters,

Unworthy of the gentle blood they served.
My father, proud and jealous of his honour,
(Thou know'st the fiery temper of our barons,)
Swore that Northumberland had been concern'd
In this rude outrage, nor wou'd hear of peace,
Or reconcilement, which the Percy offer'd ;
But bade me hate, renounce, and banish him.
O ! 'twas a task too hard for all my duty,
I strove, and wept, I strove—but still I loved.
    Bir. Indeed 'twas most unjust ; but say what fol-
        low'd ?
    El. Why shou'd I dwell on the disastrous tale ?
Forbid to see me, Percy soon embark'd
With our great king against the Saracen.
Soon as the jarring kingdoms were at peace,
Earl Douglas, whom till then I ne'er had seen,
Came to this castle ; 'twas my hapless fate
To please him.—Birtha ! thou can'st tell what fol-
        low'd :
But who shall tell the agonies I felt ?
My barbarous father forced me to dissolve
The tender vows himself had bid me form——
He dragged mo trembling, dying, to the altar,
I sigh'd, I struggled, fainted, and complied.
    Bir. Did Douglas know a marriage had been once
Proposed 'twixt you and Percy ?
    El. If he did,
He thought, like you, it was a match of policy,
Nor knew our love surpass'd our fathers' prudence.
    Bir. Should he now find he was the instrument
Of the Lord Raby's vengeance ?
    El. 'Twere most dreadful !
My father lock'd this motive in his breast,
And feign'd to have forgot the chace of Cheviot.
Some moons have now completed their slow course
Since my sad marriage.—Percy still is absent.
    Bir. Nor will return before his sov'reign comes.

El. Talk not of his return! this coward heart
Can know no thought of peace but in his absence.
How, Douglas here again? some fresh alarm!

Enter DOUGLAS, *agitated, with letters in his hand.*

Dou. Madam, your pardon—
El. What disturbs my lord?
Dou. Nothing.—Disturb! I ne'er was more at
  ease.
These letters from your father give us notice
He will be here to-night:—He further adds,
The king's each hour expected.
El. How? the king?
Said you the king?
Dou. And 'tis Lord Raby's pleasure
That you among the foremost bid him welcome.
You must attend the court.
El. Must I, my lord?
Dou. Now to observe how she receives the news!
            [*Aside.*
El. I must not,—cannot.—By the tender love
You have so oft profess'd for poor Elwina,
Indulge this one request—O let me stay!
Dou. Enchanting sounds! she does not wish to
  go—   (*Aside.*
El. The bustling world, the pomp which waits on
  greatness,
Ill suits my humble, unambitious soul ;—
Then leave me here, to tread the safer path
Of private life, here where my peaceful course
Shall be as silent as the shades around me ;
Nor shall one vagrant wish be e'er allow'd
To stray beyond the bounds of Raby Castle.
Dou. O music to my ears! [*Aside.*]—Can you
  resolve
To hide those wond'rous beauties in the shade,
Which rival kings wou'd cheaply buy with empire?
Can you renounce the pleasures of a court,

Whose roofs resound with minstrelsy and mirth ?

El. My lord, retirement is a wife's best duty,
And virtue's safest station is retreat.

Dou. My soul's in transports ! (*Aside.*)—But can
      you forego
What wins the soul of woman——admiration ?
A world, where charms inferior far to yours
Only presume to shine when you are absent ?
Will you not long to meet the public gaze ?
Long to eclipse the fair, and charm the brave ?

El. These are delights in which the mind partakes
      not.

Dou. I'll try her farther.   (*Aside.*)
      (*Takes her hand, and looks stedfastly at her as
      he speaks.*)
But reflect once more :
When you shall hear that England's gallant peers,
Fresh from the fields of war, and gay with glory,
All vain with conquest, and elate with fame,
When you shall hear these princely youths contend,
In many a tournament for beauty's prize ;
When you shall hear of revelry and masking,
Of mimic combats and of festive halls,
Of lances shiver'd in the cause of love,
Will you not then repent, then wish your fate,
Your happier fate, had till that hour reserved you
For some plumed conqueror ?

El. My fate, my lord,
Is now bound up with yours.

Dou. Here let me kneel——
Yes, I will kneel, and gaze, and weep, and wonder ;
Thou paragon of goodness !—pardon, pardon,
                (*Kisses her hand.*
I am convinced—I can no longer doubt,
Nor talk, nor hear, nor reason, nor reflect.
—I must retire, and give a loose to joy.
              (*Exit* DOUGLAS:

Bir. The king returns.

El. And with him Percy comes!
Bir. You needs must go.
El. Shall I solicit ruin,
And pull destruction on me ere its time?
I, who have held it criminal to name him?
I will not go——I disobey thee, Douglas,
But disobey thee to preserve thy honour. (*Exeunt.*

ACT THE SECOND.

SCENE I.

The Hall.

Douglas, *speaking as he enters.*

See that the traitor instantly be seized,
And strictly watch'd: let none have access to him.——
O jealousy, thou aggregate of woes!
Were there no hell thy torments wou'd create one.
But yet she may be guiltless—may? she must.
How beautiful she look'd! pernicious beauty!
Yet innocent as bright seem'd the sweet blush
That mantled on her cheek. But not for me,
But not for me those breathing roses blow!

And then she wept—What! can I bear her tears?
Well—let her weep—her tears are for another;
O did they fall for me, to dry their streams
I'd drain the choicest blood that feeds this heart,
Nor think the drops I shed were half so precious.
                    (*He stands in a musing posture.*

Enter LORD RABY.

Ra. Sure I mistake—am I in Raby Castle?
Impossible! that was the seat of smiles;
And Cheerfulness and Joy were household gods.
I used to scatter pleasures when I came,
And every servant shared his lord's delight;
But now Suspicion and Distrust dwell here,
And Discontent maintains a sullen sway.
Where is the smile unfeign'd, the jovial welcome,
Which cheer'd the sad, beguiled the pilgrim's pain,
And made Dependency forget its bonds?
Where is the ancient, hospitable hall,
Whose vaulted roof once rung with harmless mirth,
Where every passing stranger was a guest,
And every guest a friend? I fear me much,
If once our nobles scorn their rural seats,
Their rural greatness, and their vassals' love,
Freedom and English grandeur are no more.
    Dou. (*Advancing.*) My lord, you are welcome.
    Ra. Sir, I trust I am;
But yet methinks I shall not feel I'm welcome
Till my Elwina bless me with her smiles:
She was not wont with ling'ring step to meet me,
Or greet my coming with a cold embrace;
Now, I extend my longing arms in vain;
My child, my darling, does not come to fill them.
O they were happy days when she wou'd fly
To meet me from the camp, or from the chace,
And with her fondness overpay my toils!
How eager wou'd her tender hands unbrace
The ponderous armour from my war-worn limbs.

And pluck the helmet which opposed her kiss!

Dou. O sweet delights, that never must be mine!

Ra. What do I hear?

Dou. Nothing: inquire no farther.

Ra. My lord, if you respect an old man's peace,
If e'er you doted on my much-loved child,
As 'tis most sure you made me think you did,
Then, by the pangs which you may one day feel,
When you, like me, shall be a fond, fond father,
And tremble for the treasure of your age,
Tell me what this alarming silence means?
You sigh, you do not speak, nay more, you hear not;
Your lab'ring soul turns inward on itself,
As there were nothing but your own sad thoughts
Deserved regard.   Does my child live?

Dou. She does.

Ra. To bless her father!

Dou. And to curse her husband!

Ra. Ah! have a care, my lord, I'm not so old—

Dou. Nor I so base, that I should tamely bear it;
Nor am I so inured to infamy,
That I can say, without a burning blush,
She lives to be my curse!

Ra. How's this?

Dou. I thought
The lily opening to the heaven's soft dews,
Was not so fragrant, and was not so chaste.

Ra. Has she proved otherwise? I'll not believe it.
Who has traduced my sweet, my innocent child?
Yet she's too good to 'scape calumnious tongues.
I know that Slander loves a lofty mark:
It saw her soar a flight above her fellows,
And hurl'd its arrow to her glorious height,
To reach her heart, and bring her to the ground.

Dou. Had the rash tongue of Slander so presumed,
My vengeance had not been of that slow sort
To need a prompter; nor should any arm,
No, not a father's, dare dispute with mine,

The privilege to die in her defence.
None dares accuse Elwina, but—
　　Ra. But who?
　　Dou. But Douglas.
　　Ra. (*Puts his hand to his sword.*) You?—O spare
　　　　my age's weakness!
You do not know what 'tis to be a father,
You do not know, or you would pity me;
The thousand tender throbs, the nameless feelings,
The dread to ask, and yet the wish to know,
When we adore and fear; but wherefore fear?
Does not the blood of Raby fill her veins?
　　Dou. Percy;—know'st thou that name?
　　Ra. How? what of Percy?
　　Dou. He loves Elwina, and, my curses on him!
He is beloved again.
　　Ra. I'm on the rack!
　　Dou. Not the two Theban brothers bore each other
Such deep, such deadly hate as I and Percy.
　　Ra. But tell me of my child.
　　Dou. (*Not minding him.*) As I and Percy!
When at the marriage rites, O rites accursed!
I seized her trembling hand, she started back,
Cold horror thrill'd her veins, her tears flow'd fast.
Fool that I was, I thought 'twas maiden fear;
Dull, doting ignorance! beneath those terrors
Hatred for me and love for Percy lurk'd.
　　Ra. What proof of guilt is this?
　　Dou. E'er since our marriage
Our days have still been cold and joyless all;
Painful restraint, and hatred ill disguised,
Her sole return for all my waste of fondness.
This very morn I told her 'twas your will
She should repair to court; with all those graces,
Which first subdued my soul, and still enslave it,
She begg'd to stay behind in Raby Castle,
For courts and cities had no charms for her.
Curse my blind love! I was again ensnared,
And doted on the sweetness which deceived me.

Just at the hour she thought I shou'd be absent,
(For chance cou'd ne'er have timed their guilt so well,)
Arrived young Harcourt, one of Percy's knights,
Strictly enjoin'd to speak to none but her ;
I seized the miscreant ; hitherto he's silent,
But tortures soon shall force him to confess!

Ra. Percy is absent—They have never met.

Dou. At what a feeble hold you grasp for succour !
Will it content me that her person's pure ?
No, if her alien heart dotes on another,
She is unchaste, were not that other Percy.
Let vulgar spirits basely wait for proof,
She loves another—'tis enough for Douglas.

Ra. Be patient.

Dou. Be a tame convenient husband,
And meanly wait for circumstantial guilt ?
No—I am nice as the first Cæsar was,
And start at bare suspicion.   (*Going.*

Ra. (*Holding him.*) Douglas, hear me ;
Thou hast named a Roman husband ; if she's false,
I mean to prove myself a Roman father.

            (*Exit* DOUGLAS.

This marriage was my work, and thus I'm punish'd!

Enter ELWINA.

El. Where is my father ? let me fly to meet him,
O let me clasp his venerable knees,
And die of joy in his beloved embrace !

Ra. (*Avoiding her embrace.*) Elwina!

El. And is that all ? so cold ?

Ra. [*Sternly.*] Elwina !

El. Then I'm undone indeed ! How stern his looks !
I will not be repulsed, I am your child,
The child of that dear mother you adored ;
You shall not throw me off, I will grow here,
And, like the patriarch, wrestle for a blessing.

Ra. [*Holding her from him.*] Before I take thee
            in these aged arms,
Press thee with transport to this beating heart,

And give a loose to all a parent's fondnes
Answer, and see thou answer me as truly
As if the dread inquiry came from Heaven,—
Does no interior sense of guilt confound thee ?
Canst thou lay all thy naked soul before me ?
Can thy unconscious eye encounter mine ?
Canst thou endure the probe, and never shrink ?
Can thy firm hand meet mine and never tremble ?
Art thou prepared to meet the rigid Judge ?
Or to embrace the fond, the melting father ?

 El. Mysterious Heaven ! to what am I reserved !
 Ra. Shou'd some rash man, regardless of thy fame,
And in defiance of thy marriage vows,
Presume to plead a guilty passion for thee,
What wou'd'st thou do ?

 El. What honour bids me do.
 Ra. Come to my arms!   [*They embrace.*
 El. My father !
 Ra. Yes, Elwina,
Thou art my child—thy mother's perfect image.

 El. Forgive these tears of mingled joy and doubt ;
For why that question ? who should seek to please
The desolate Elwina ?

 Ra. But if any
Should so presume, canst thou resolve to hate him,
Whate'er his name, whate'er his pride of blood,
Whate'er his former arrogant pretensions ?

 El. Ha !
 Ra. Dost thou falter ? Have a care, Elwina.
 El. Sir, do not fear me ; am I not your daughter ?
 Ra. Thou hast a higher claim upon thy honour ;
Thou art Earl Douglas' wife.

 El. [*Weeps.*] I am indeed !
 Ra. Unhappy Douglas !
 El. Has he then complain'd ?
Has he presumed to sully my white fame ?

 Ra. He knows that Percy——
 El. Was my destined husband ;

By your own promise, by a father's promise,
And by a tie more strong, more sacred still,
Mine, by the fast firm bond of mutual love.

Ra. Now, by my fears, thy husband told me truth.

El. If he has told thee that thy only child
Was forced a helpless victim to the altar,
Torn from his arms who had her virgin heart,
And forced to make false vows to one she hated,
Then I confess that he has told thee truth.

Ra. Her words are barbed arrows in my heart.
But 'tis too late. (*Aside.*) Thou hast appointed Har-
    court
To see thee here by stealth in Douglas' absence?

El. No, by my life, nor knew I till this moment
That Harcourt was return'd.   Was it for this
I taught my heart to struggle with its feelings?
Was it for this I bore my wrongs in silence?
When the fond ties of early love were broken,
Did my weak soul break out in fond complaints?
Did I reproach thee? Did I call thee cruel?
No—I endured it all; and wearied Heaven
To bless the father who destroyed my peace.

Enter Messenger.

Mes. My lord, a knight, Sir Hubert as I think,
But newly landed from the holy wars,
Entreats admittance.

Ra. Let the warrior enter.   (*Exit Messenger.*
All private interests sink at his approach;
All selfish cares be for a moment banish'd!
I've now no child, no kindred but my country.

El. Weak heart, be still, for what hast thou to
    fear?

Enter Sir Hubert.

Ra. Welcome, thou gallant knight! Sir Hubert,
    welcome!

Welcome to Raby Castle!—In one word,
Is the king safe? Is Palestine subdued?

   Sir Hu. The king is safe, and Palestine subdued.

   Ra. Blest be the God of armies! Now, Sir Hubert,
By all the saints thou'rt a right noble knight!
O why was I too old for this crusade!
I think it wou'd have made me young again,
Cou'd I, like thee, have seen the hated crescent
Yield to the Christian cross.—How now, Elwina!
What! cold at news which might awake the dead!
If there's a drop in thy degenerate veins
That glows not now, thou art not Raby's daughter.
It is religion's cause, the cause of Heaven!

   El. When policy assumes religion's name,
And wears the sanctimonious garb of faith
Only to colour fraud, and license murder,
War then is tenfold guilt.

   Ra. Blaspheming girl!

   El. 'Tis not the crosier, nor the pontiff's robe,
The saintly look, nor elevated eye,
Nor Palestine destroy'd, nor Jordan's banks
Deluged with blood of slaughter'd infidels ;
No, nor the extinction of the eastern world,
Nor all the mad, pernicious, bigot rage
Of your crusades, can bribe that Power who sees
The motive with the act.   O blind to think
That cruel war can please the Prince of Peace !
He who erects his altar in the heart,
Abhors the sacrifice of human blood,
And all the false devotion of that zeal,
Which massacres the world he died to save.

   Ra. O impious rage! If thou woud'st shun my
      curse,
No more, I charge thee.—Tell me, good Sir Hubert,
Say, have our arms atchieved this glorious deed,
(I fear to ask) without much Christian bloodshed?

   El. Now   Heaven support me !   [*Aside.*

   Sir Hu. My good lord of Raby,

Imperfect is the sum of human glory!
Wou'd I could tell thee that the field was won,
Without the death of such illustrious knights
As make the high-flush'd cheek of Victory pale.
 El. Why should I tremble thus?   [*Aside.*
 Ra. Who have we lost?
 Sir Hu. The noble Clifford, Walsingham, and Grey,
Sir Harry Hastings, and the valiant Pembroke,
All men of choicest note.
 Ra. O that my name
Had been enroll'd in such a list of heroes!
If I was too infirm to serve my country,
I might have proved my love by dying for her.
 El. Were there no more?
 Sir Hu. But few of noble blood.
But the brave youth who gain'd the palm of glory,
The flower of knighthood, and the plume of war,
Who bore his banner foremost in the field,
Yet conquer'd more by mercy than the sword,
Was Percy.
 El. Then he lives!   [*Aside.*
 Ra. Did he? Did Percy?
O gallant boy, then I'm thy foe no more;
Who conquers for my country is my friend!
His fame shall add new glories to a house,
Where never maid was false, nor knight disloyal.
 Sir Hu. You do embalm him, lady, with your tears:
They grace the grave of glory where he lies—
He died the death of honour.
 El. Said'st thou—died?
 Sir Hu. Beneath the towers of Solyma he fell.
 El. Oh!
 Sir Hu. Look to the lady.
     [ELWINA *faints in her father's arms.*
 Ra. Gentle knight, retire——
'Tis an infirmity of nature in her,
She ever mourns at any tale of blood;
She will be well anon—mean time, Sir Hubert,
You'll grace our castle with your friendly sojourn.

Sir Hu. I must return with speed—health to the
    lady.   [*Exit* HUBERT.
Ra. Look up, Elwina. Shou'd her husband come!
Yet she revives not.

             Enter DOUGLAS.

  Dou. Ha——Elwina fainting!
My lord, I fear you have too harshly chid her.
Her gentle nature could not brook your sternness.
She wakes, she stirs, she feels returning life.
My love!   [*He takes her hand.*
  El. O Percy!
  Dou. [*Starts.*] Do my senses fail me?
  El. My Percy, 'tis Elwina calls.
  Dou. Hell, hell!
  Ra. Retire a while, my daughter.
  El. Douglas here,
My father and my husband?—O for pity—
  [*Exit* ELWINA, *casting a look of anguish on both.*)
  Dou. Now, now confess she well deserves my ven-
    geance!
Before my face to call upon my foe!
  Ra. Upon a foe who has no power to hurt thee—
Earl Percy's slain.
  Dou. I live again.—But hold—
Did she not weep? she did, and wept for Percy.
If she laments him, he's my rival still,
And not the grave can bury my resentment.
  Ra. The truly brave are still the truly gen'rous;
Now, Douglas, is the time to prove thee both.
If it be true that she did once love Percy,
Thou hast no more to fear, since he is dead.
Release young Harcourt, let him see Elwina,
'Twill serve a double purpose, 'twill at once
Prove Percy's death, and thy unchanged affection.
Be gentle to my child, and win her heart
By confidence and unreproaching love.
  Dou. By Heaven thou counsel'st well! it shall be
    done.

Go get him free, and let him have admittance
To my Elwina's presence.
   Ra. Farewell, Douglas.
Shew thou believest her faithful, and she'll prove so.
                          [*Exit* RABY.
   Dou. Northumberland is dead—that thought is
        peace!
Her heart may yet be mine, transporting hope!
Percy was gentle, even a foe avows it,
And I'll be milder than a summer's breeze.
Yes, thou most lovely, most adored of women,
I'll copy every virtue, every grace,
Of my bless'd rival, happier even in death
To be thus loved, than living to be scorn'd.   [*Exit.*

ACT THE THIRD.

SCENE I.

A Garden at Raby Castle, with a Bower.

Enter PERCY *and* SIR HUBERT.

   Sir Hu. That Percy lives, and is return'd in safety,
More joys my soul than all the mighty conquests
That sun beheld, which rose on Syria's ruin.
   Per. I've told thee, good Sir Hubert, by what
        wonder
I was preserved, though number'd with the slain.
   Sir Hu. 'Twas strange indeed!
   Per. 'Twas Heaven's immediate work!
But let me now indulge a dearer joy,

Talk of a richer gift of Mercy's hand;
A gift so precious to my doting heart,
That life preserved is but a second blessing.
O Hubert, let my soul indulge its softness!
The hour, the spot, is sacred to Elwina.
This was her fav'rite walk; I well remember,
(For who forgets that loves as I have loved?)
'Twas in that very bower she gave this scarf,
Wrought by the hand of love; she bound it on,
And, smiling, cried, Whate'er befal us, Percy,
Be this the sacred pledge of faith between us.
I knelt, and swore, call'd every power to witness,
No time, nor circumstance, shou'd force it from me,
But I wou'd lose my life and that together—
Here I repeat my vow.
    Sir Hu. Is this the man
Beneath whose single arm an host was crush'd?
He, at whose name the Saracen turn'd pale?
And when he fell, victorious armies wept,
And mourn'd a conquest they had bought so dear?
How has he changed the trumpet's martial note,
And all the stirring clangour of the war,
For the soft melting of the lover's lute!
Why are thine eyes still bent upon the bower?
    Per. O Hubert, Hubert, to a soul enamour'd,
There is a sort of local sympathy,
Which, when we view the scenes of early passion,
Paints the bright image of the object loved
In stronger colours than remoter scenes
Cou'd ever paint it; realizes shade,
Dresses it up in all the charms it wore,
Talks to it nearer, frames its answers kinder,
Gives form to fancy, and embodies thought.
    Sir Hu. I should not be believed in Percy's camp,
If I shou'd tell them that their gallant leader,
The thunder of the war, the bold Northumberland,
Renouncing Mars, dissolved in amorous wishes,

Loiter'd in shades, and pined in rosy bowers,
To catch a transient glance of two bright eyes.

Per. Enough of conquest, and enough of war!
Ambition's cloy'd—the heart resumes its rights.
When England's king, and England's good required,
This arm not idly the keen falchion brandish'd :
Enough—for vaunting misbecomes a soldier.
I live, I am return'd—am near Elwina!
Seest thou those turrets? Yes, that castle holds her ;
But wherefore tell thee this? for thou hast seen her.
How look'd, what said she? Did she hear the tale
Of my imagined death without emotion?

Sir Hu. Percy, thou hast seen the musk rose new-
                ly blown,
Disclose its bashful beauties to the sun,
Till an unfriendly, chilling storm descended,
Crush'd all its blushing glories in their prime,
Bow'd its fair head, and blasted all its sweetness ;
So droop'd the maid beneath the cruel weight
Of my sad tale.

Per. So tender and so true!

Sir Hu. I left her fainting in her father's arms,
The dying flower yet hanging on the tree.
Even Raby melted at the news I brought,
And envy'd thee thy glory.

Per. Then I am blest!
His hate subdued, I've nothing more to fear.

Sir Hu. My embassy dispatch'd, I left the castle,
Nor spoke to any of Lord Raby's household,
For fear the king should chide the tardiness
Of my return. My joy to find you living
You have already heard.

Per. But where is Harcourt?
Ere this he shou'd have seen her, told her all,
How I survived, return'd——and how I love!
I tremble at the near approach of bliss,
And scarcely can sustain the joy which waits me.

Sir Hu. Grant, Heaven, the fair one prove but half
   so true!
Per. O she is truth itself!
Sir Hu. She may be changed,
Spite of her tears, her fainting, and alarms.
I know the sex, know them as nature made 'em,
Not such as lovers wish and poets feign.
 Per. To doubt her virtue were suspecting Heaven,
'Twere little less than infidelity!
And yet I tremble. Why does terror shake
These firm-strung nerves? But 'twill be ever thus,
When fate prepares us more than mortal bliss,
And gives us only human strength to bear it.
 Sir Hu. What beam of brightness breaks through
   yonder gloom?
 Per. Hubert—she comes! by all my hopes she
   comes!
'Tis she—the blissful vision is Elwina!
But ah! what mean those tears?—She weeps for me!
O transport!—go.—I'll listen unobserved,
And for a moment taste the precious joy,
The banquet of a tear which falls for love.
  [*Exit* Sir Hubert. Percy *goes into the Bower.*

    Enter Elwina.

Shall I not weep? and have I then no cause?
If I could break the eternal bands of death,
And wrench the sceptre from his iron grasp;
If I could bid the yawning sepulchre
Restore to life its long-committed dust;
If I could teach the slaughtering hand of war
To give me back my dear, my murder'd Percy,
Then I indeed might once more cease to weep.
     [Percy *comes out of the Bower.*
 Per. Then cease, for Percy lives.
 El. Protect me, Heaven!
 Per. O joy unspeakable! My life, my love!
End of my toils, and crown of all my cares!

Kind as consenting peace, as conquest bright,
Dearer than arms, and lovelier than renown !

 El. It is his voice—it is, it is my Percy !
And dost thou live ?

  Per. I never lived till now.

  El. And did my sighs, and did my sorrows reach
    thee ?
And art thou come at last to dry my tears ?
How did'st thou 'scape the fury of the foe ?

  Per. Thy guardian genius hover'd o'er the field,
And turn'd the hostile spear from Percy's breast,
Lest thy fair image should be wounded there.
But Harcourt should have told thee all my fate,
How I survived——

  El. Alas ! I have not seen him.
Oh ! I have suffer'd much.

  Per. Of that no more ;
For every minute of our future lives
Shall be so bless'd, that we will learn to wonder
How we cou'd ever think we were unhappy.

  El. Percy—I cannot speak.

  Per. Those tears how eloquent !
I would not change this motionless, mute joy
For the sweet strains of angels: I look down '
With pity on the rest of human kind,
However great may be their fame of happiness,
And think their niggard fate has given them nothing,
Not giving thee ; or granting some small blessing,
Denies them my capacity to feel it.

  El. Alas ! what mean you ?

  Per. Can I speak my meaning ?
'Tis of such magnitude that words would wrong it ;
But surely my Elwina's faithful bosom
Shou'd beat in kind responses of delight,
And feel, but never question, what I mean.

  El. Hold, hold, my heart, thou hast much more to
    suffer !

  Per. Let the slow form, and tedious ceremony

Wait on the splendid victims of ambition.
Love stays for none of these.   Thy father's soften'd,
He will forget the fatal Cheviot chace;
Raby is brave, and I have served my country;
I wou'd not boast, it was for thee I conquer'd;
Then come, my love.
 El. O never, never, never!
 Per. Am I awake? Is that Elwina's voice?
 El. Percy, thou most adored, and most deceived!
If ever fortitude sustain'd thy soul,
When vulgar minds have sunk beneath the stroke,
Let thy imperial spirit now support thee.—
If thou can'st be so wond'rous merciful,
Do not, O do not curse me!—but thou wilt,
Thou must—for I have done a fearful deed,
A deed of wild despair, a deed of horror.
I am, I am—
 Per. Speak, say, what art thou?
 El. Married!
 Per. Oh!
 El. Percy, I think I begg'd thee not to curse me;
But now I do revoke the fond petition.
Speak! ease thy bursting soul; reproach, upbraid,
O'erwhelm me with thy wrongs——I'll bear it all.
 Per. Open, thou earth, and hide me from her
   sight!
Did'st thou not bid me curse thee?
 El. Mercy! mercy!
 Per. And have I 'scaped the Saracen's fell swo'd
Only to perish by Elwina's guilt?
I wou'd have bared my bosom to the foe,
I wou'd have died, had I but known you wish'd it.
 El. Percy, I loved thee most when most I wrong'd
   thee;
Yes, by these tears I did.
 Per. Married! just Heaven!
Married! to whom? Yet wherefore should I know?

It cannot add fresh horrors to thy crime,
Or my destruction.
    El. Oh! 'twill add to both.
How shall I tell? Prepare for something dreadful.
Hast thou not heard of—Douglas?
    Per. Why 'tis well!
Thou awful Power, why waste thy wrath on me?
Why arm omnipotence to crush a worm?
I cou'd have fallen without this waste of ruin.
Married to Douglas! By my wrongs I like it;
'Tis perfidy complete, 'tis finish'd falsehood,
'Tis adding fresh perdition to the sin,
And filling up the measure of offence!
    El. Oh! 'twas my father's deed! he made his child
An instrument of vengeance on thy head.
He wept and threaten'd, soothed me, and command-
        ed.
    Per. And you complied, most duteously complied!
    El. I cou'd withstand his fury; but his tears,
Ah, they undid me! Percy, dost thou know
The cruel tyranny of tenderness?
Hast thou e'er felt a father's warm embrace?
Hast thou e'er seen a father's flowing tears,
And known that thou cou'd'st wipe those tears away?
If thou hast felt, and hast resisted these,
Then thou may'st curse my weakness; but if not,
Thou canst not pity, for thou canst not judge.
    Per. Let me not hear the music of thy voice,
Or I shall love thee still; I shall forget
Thy fatal marriage and my savage wrongs.
    El. Dost thou not hate me, Percy?
    Per. Hate thee? Yes,
As dying martyrs hate the righteous cause
Of that bless'd power for whom they bleed—I hate
        thee.
       (*They look at each other in silent agony.*

Enter HARCOURT.

Har. Forgive, my lord, your faithful knight——

Per. Come, Harcourt,
Come, and behold the wretch who once was Percy.'

Har. With grief I've learn'd the whole unhappy
    tale.
Earl Douglas, whose suspicion never sleeps—

Per. What, is the tyrant jealous?

El. Hear him, Percy.

Per. I will command my rage—Go on.

Har. Earl Douglas
Knew by my arms, and my accoutrements,
That I belong'd to you; he question'd much,
And much he menaced me, but both alike
In vain, he then arrested and confined me.

Per. Arrest my knight! The Scot shall answer it.

El. How came you now released?

Har. Your noble father
Obtain'd my freedom, having learn'd from Hubert
The news of Percy's death.   The good old lord,
Hearing the king's return, has left the castle
To do him homage.
(*To* PERCY.) Sir, you had best retire;
Your safety is endanger'd by your stay.
I fear, shou'd Douglas know——

Per. Shou'd Douglas know!
Why what new magic's in the name of Douglas,
That it shou'd strike Northumberland with fear?
Go, seek the haughty Scot, and tell him—no—
Conduct me to his presence.

El. Percy, hold;
Think not 'tis Douglas—'tis—

Per. I know it well——
Thou mean'st to tell me 'tis Elwina's husband;
But that inflames me to superior madness.
This happy husband, this triumphant Douglas,

Shall not insult my misery with his bliss.
I'll blast the golden promise of his joys.
Conduct me to him—nay, 1 will have way——
Come let us seek this husband.

    El. Percy, hear me.
When 1 was robb'd of all my peace of mind,
My cruel fortune left me still one blessing,
One solitary blessing, to console me :
It was my fame.—'Tis a rich jewel, Percy,
And i must keep it spotless, and unsoil'd :
But thou wou'dst plunder what e'en Douglas spared,
And rob this single gem of all its brightness.

    Per. Go—thou wast born to rule the fate of Percy.
Thou art my conqueror still.

    El. What noise is that?

           (HARCOURT *goes to the side of the Stage.*
    Per. Why art thou thus alarm'd ?

    El. Alas ! I feel
The cowardice and terrors of the wicked,
Without their sense of guilt.

    Har. My lord, 'tis Douglas.

    El. Fly, Percy, and for ever !

    Per. Fly from Douglas ?

    El. Then stay, barbarian, and at once destroy
My life and fame.

    Per. That thought is death.   I go.
My honour to thy dearer honour yields.

    El. Yet, yet thou art not gone !

    Per. Farewell, farewell !   (*Exit* PERCY.

    El. I dare not meet the searching eye of Douglas.
I must conceal my terrors.

DOUGLAS *at the Side with his sword drawn*, EDRIC
holds him.

    Dou. Give me way.

    Ed. Thou shalt not enter.

    Dou. (*Struggling with* EDRIC.) If there were no
      hell,

It would defraud my vengeance of its edge,
And he should live.

                    (*Breaks from* EDRIC, *and comes forward.*
Cursed chance! he is not here.

El. (*Going.*) I dare not meet his fury.

Dou. See she flies
With every mark of guilt.—Go, search the bower,

                    [*Aside to* EDRIC.
He shall not thus escape. Madam, return. (*Aloud.*
Now, honest Douglas, learn of her to feign. (*Aside.*
Alone, Elwina? who just parted hence?

                    (*With affected composure.*
  El. My lord, 'twas Harcourt; sure you must have
      met him.

  Dou. O exquisite dissembler! (*Aside.*) No one else?

  El. My lord!

  Dou. How I enjoy her criminal confusion! (*Aside.*
You tremble, madam.

  El. Wherefore shou'd I tremble?
By your permission Harcourt was admitted;
'Twas no mysterious, secret introduction.

  Dou. And yet you seem alarm'd.—If Harcourt's
      presence
Thus agitates each nerve, makes every pulse
Thus wildly throb, and the warm tides of blood
Mount in quick rushing tumults to your cheek;
If friendship can excite such strong emotions,
What tremours had a lover's presence caused?

  El. Ungenerous man!

  Dou. I feast upon her terrors.   (*Aside.*
The story of his death was well contrived; (*To her.*
But it affects not me; I have a wife,
Compared with whom cold Dian was unchaste.

                    (*Takes her hand.*
But mark me well—though it concerns not you—
If there's a sin more deeply black than others,
Distinguish'd from the list of common crimes,

A legion in itself, and doubly dear
To the dark prince of hell, it is—hypocrisy.
        (*Throws her from him and exit.*
    El. Yes, I wil' bear his fearful indignation !
Thou melting heart be firm as adamant ;
Ye shatter'd nerves be strung with manly force,
That I may conquer all my sex's weakness,
Nor let this bleeding bosom lodge one thought,
Cherish one wish, or harbour one desire,
That angels may not hear and Douglas know. (*Exit.*

ACT THE FOURTH.

SCENE I.

The Hall.

Enter DOUGLAS, *his sword drawn and bloody in one
hand, in the other a letter.* HARCOURT *wounded.*

    Dou. Traitor, no more ! This letter shews thy
            office.
Twice hast thou robb'd me of my dear revenge.
I took thee for thy leader.— Thy base blood
Wou'd stain the noble temper of my sword,

But as the pander to thy master's lust,
Thou justly fall'st by a wrong'd husband's hand.
   Har. Thy wife is innocent.
   Dou. Take him away.
   Har. Percy, revenge my fall !
               (*Guards bear* HARCOURT *in.*
   Dou. Now for the letter !
He begs once more to see her.—So 'tis plain
They have already met !—but to the rest——
(*Reads.*) " In vain you wish me to restore the scarf;
Dear pledge of love, while I have life I'll wear it,
'Tis next my heart ; no power shall force it thence ;
Whene'er you see it in another's hand
Conclude me dead."—My curses on them both !
How tamely I peruse my shame ! But thus,
Thus let me tear the guilty characters
Which register my infamy ; and thus,
Thus wou'd I scatter to the winds of heaven
The vile complotters of my foul dishonour.
       (*Tears the letter in the utmost agitation.*

Enter EDRIC.

   Ed. My lord——
   Dou. (*In the utmost fury, not seeing* EDRIC.) The
      scarf !
   Ed. Lord Douglas.
   Dou. (*Still not hearing him.*) Yes, the scarf !
Percy, I thank thee for the glorious thought !
I'll cherish it ; 'twill sweeten all my pangs,
And add a higher relish to revenge !
   Ed. My lord !
   Dou. How ! Edric here ?
   Ed. What new distress ?
   Dou. Dost thou expect I shou'd recount my shame,
Dwell on each circumstance of my disgrace,
And swell my infamy into a tale ?
Rage will not let me—But—my wife is false.
   Ed. Art thou convinced ?

Dou. The chronicles of hell
Cannot produce a falser.—But what news
Of her cursed paramour?

Ed. He has escaped.

Dou. Hast thou examined every avenue?
Each spot? the grove? the bower, her favourite haunt?

Ed. I've search'd them all.

Dou. He shall be yet pursued.
Set guards at every gate.—Let none depart,
Or gain admittance here, without my knowledge.

Ed. What can their purpose be?

Dou. Is it not clear?
Harcourt has raised his arm against my life;
He fail'd; the blow is now reserved for Percy;
Then with his sword fresh reeking from my heart,
He'll revel with that wanton o'er my tomb;
Nor will he bring her aught she'll hold so dear,
As the cursed hand with which he slew her husband.
But he shall die! I'll drown my rage in blood,
Which I will offer as a rich libation
On thy infernal altar, black revenge! (*Exeunt.*

SCENE II.

The Garden.

Enter ELWINA.

El. Each avenue is so beset with guards,
And lynx-eyed Jealousy so broad awake,
He cannot pass unseen. Protect him, heaven!

Enter BIRTHA.

My Birtha, is he safe? Has he escaped?

Bir. I know not.   I dispatch'd young Harcourt to
          him,
To bid him quit the castle, as you order'd,
Restore the scarf, and never see you more.
But how the hard injunction was received,
Or what has happen'd since, I'm yet to learn.

El. O when shall I be eased of all my cares,
And in the quiet bosom of the grave
Lay down this weary head !—I'm sick at heart !
Shou'd Douglas intercept his flight !

Bir. Be calm ;
Douglas this very moment left the castle,
With seeming peace.

El. Ah, then, indeed there's danger !
Birtha, whene'er Suspicion feigns to sleep,
'Tis but to make its careless prey secure.

Bir. Shou'd Percy once again entreat to see thee,
'Twere best admit him ; from thy lips alone
He will submit to hear his final doom
Of everlasting exile.

El. Birtha, no :
If honour wou'd allow the wife of Douglas
To meet his rival, yet I durst not do it.
Percy ! too much this rebel heart is thine :
Too deeply should I feel each pang I gave ;
I cannot hate—but I will banish thee.
Inexorable duty, O forgive,
If I can do no more !

Bir. If he remains,
As I suspect, within the castle walls,
'Twere best I sought him out.

El. Then tell him, Birtha,
But, Oh ! with gentleness, with mercy tell him,
That we must never, never meet again.
The purport of my tale must be severe,
But let thy tenderness embalm the wound
My virtue gives.   O soften his despair ;
But say—we meet no more.

Enter PERCY.

Rash man, he's here !

(*She attempts to go, he seizes her hand.*

Per. I will be heard ; nay, fly not ; I will speak ;
Lost as I am, I will not be denied
The mournful consolation to complain.

El. Percy. I charge thee, leave me.

Per. Tyrant, no:
I blush at my obedience, blush to think
I left thee here alone, to brave the danger
I now return to share.

El. That danger's past :
Douglas was soon appeased ; he nothing knows.
Then leave me, I conjure thee, nor again
Endanger my repose.   Yet, ere thou goest,
Restore the scarf.

Per. Unkind Elwina, never !
'Tis all that's left me of my buried joys,
All which reminds me that I once was happy.
My letter told thee I wou'd ne'er restore it.

El. Letter ! what letter ?

Per. That I sent by Harcourt.

El. Which I have ne'er received.   Douglas per-
        haps—
Who knows ?

Bir. Harcourt, t' elude his watchfulness,
Might prudently retire.

El. Grant Heaven it prove so !

(ELWINA *going,* PERCY *holds her.*

Per. Hear me, Elwina ; the most savage honour
Forbids not that poor grace.

El. It bids me fly thee.

Per. Then ere thou goest, if we indeed must part,
To sooth the horrors of eternal exile,
Say but—thou pity'st me !

El. (*Weeps.*) O Percy—pity thee !
Imperious honour ;—surely I may pity him.

5

Yet, wherefore pity? no, I envy thee:
For thou hast still the liberty to weep,
In thee 'twill be no crime; thy tears are guiltless,
For they infringe no duty, stain no honour,
And blot no vow; but mine are criminal,
Are drops of shame which wash the cheek of guilt,
And every tear I shed dishonours Douglas.

   Per. I swear my jealous love e'en grudges thee
Thy sad pre-eminence in wretchedness.

   El. Rouse, rouse, my slumb'ring virtue! Percy,
      hear me.
Heaven, when it gives such high-wrought souls as
      thine,
Still gives as great occasions to exert them.
If thou wast form'd so noble, great, and gen'rous,
'Twas to surmount the passions which enslave
The gross of humankind.—Then think, O think,
She whom thou once didst love is now another's.

   Per. Go on—and tell me that that other's Douglas.

   El. Whate'er his name, he claims respect from me:
His honour's in my keeping, and I hold
The trust so pure, its sanctity is hurt
Ev'n by thy presence.

   Per. Thou again hast conquer'd.
Celestial virtue, like the angel spirit,
Whose flaming sword defended Paradise,
Stands guard on every charm.—Elwina, yes,
To triumph over Douglas, we'll be virtuous.

   El. 'Tis not enough to be,—we must appear so:
Great souls disdain the shadow of offence,
Nor must their whiteness wear the stain of guilt.

   Per. I shall retract—I dare not gaze upon thee;
My feeble virtue staggers, and again
The fiends of jealousy torment and haunt me.
They tear my heart-strings.——Oh!

   El. No more;
But spare my injured honour the affront
To vindicate itself.

Per. But love!

El. But glory!

Per. Enough! a ray of thy sublimer spirit
Has warm'd my dying honour to a flame!
One effort and 'tis done.   The world shall say,
When they shall speak of my disastrous love,
Percy deserved Elwina though he lost her.
Fond tears, blind me not yet! a little longer,
Let my sad eyes a little longer gaze,
And leave their last beams here.

   El. (*Turns from him.*) I do not weep.

   Per. Not weep? Then why those eyes avoiding
      mine?
And why that broken voice? those trembling accents?
That sigh which rends my soul?

   El. No more, no more.

   Per. That pang decides it.   Come—I'll die at once;
Thou Power supreme! take all the length of days,
And all the blessings kept in store for me,
And add to her account.—Yet turn once more,
One little look, one last, short glimpse of day,
And then a long dark night.—Hold, hold, my heart,
O break not yet, while I behold her sweetness;
For after this dear, mournful, tender moment,
I shall have nothing more to do with life.

   El. I do conjure thee go.

   Per. 'Tis terrible to nature!
With pangs like these the soul and body part!
And thus, but oh, with far less agony,
The poor departing wretch still grasps at being,
Thus clings to life, thus dreads the dark unknown,
Thus struggles to the last to keep his hold;
And when the dire convulsive groan of death
Dislodges the sad spirit—thus it stays,
And fondly hovers o'er the form it loved.
Once and no more—farewell, farewell!

   El. For ever!

(They look at each other for some time, then exit
PERCY. *After a pause,*
'Tis past—the conflict's past! retire, my Birtha,
I wou'd address me to the throne of grace.

 Bir. May Heaven restore that peace thy bosom
    wants!   (*Exit* BIRTHA.

 El. (*Kneels.*) Look down, thou awful, heart-in-
    specting Judge,
Look down with mercy on thy erring creature,
And teach my soul the lowliness it needs!
And if some sad remains of human weakness
Shou'd sometimes mingle with my best resolves,
O breathe thy spirit on this wayward heart,
And teach me to repent th' intruding sin
In it's first birth of thought!
(*Noise without.*) What noise is that?
The clash of swords! Shou'd Douglas be return'd!

   Enter DOUGLAS *and* PERCY *fighting.*

 Dou. Yield, villain, yield!
 Per. Not till this good right arm
Shall fail its master.
 Dou. This to thy heart then.
 Per. Defend thy own.
    (*They fight.* PERCY *disarms* DOUGLAS.
 Dou. Confusion, death, and hell!
 Ed. (*Without.*) This way I heard the noise.

 Enter EDRIC, *and many Knights and Guards from*
    every part of the Stage.

 Per. Cursed treachery!
But dearly will I sell my life.
 Dou. Seize on him.
 Per. I'm taken in the toils.
   (PERCY *is surrounded by Guards, who take his*
   sword.
 Dou. In the cursed snare
Thou laid'st for me, traitor, thyself art caught.

El. He never sought thy life.

Dou. Adulteress, peace !

The villain Harcourt too—but he's at rest.

   Per. Douglas, I'm in thy power; but do not tri-
     umph,

Percy's betray'd, not conquer'd. Come, dispatch me.

   El. (*To* Doug.) O do not, do not kill him!

   Per. Madam, forbear ;

For by the glorious shades of my great fathers,

Their godlike spirit is not so extinct,

That I should owe my life to that vile Scot.

Though dangers close me round on every side,

And death besets me, I am Percy still.

   Dou. Sorceress, I'll disappoint thee—he shall die,

Thy minion shall expire before thy face,

That I may feast my hatred with your pangs,

And make his dying groans, and thy fond tears,

A banquet for my vengeance.

   El. Savage tyrant !

I would have fallen a silent sacrifice,

So thou had'st spared my fame.—I never wrong'd
     thee.

   Per. She knew not of my coming ;—I alone

Have been to blame—Spite of her interdiction,

I hither came.   She's pure as spotless saints.

   El. I will not be excused by Percy's crime ;

So white my innocence it does not ask

The shade of others' faults to set it off;

Nor shall he need to sully his fair fame

To throw a brighter lustre round my virtue.

   Dou. Yet he can only die—but death for honour !

Ye powers of hell, who take malignant joy

In human bloodshed, give me some dire means,

Wild as my hate, and desperate as my wrongs !

   Per. Enough of words. Thou know'st I hate thee,
     Douglas ;

'Tis stedfast, fix'd, hereditary hate,

As thine for me ; our fathers did bequeath it
As part of our unalienable birthright,
Which nought but death can end.—Come, end it
     here.

    El. (*Kneels.*) Hold, Douglas, hold !—not for my-
     self I kneel,
I do not plead for Percy, but for thee :
Arm not thy hand against thy future peace,
Spare thy brave breast the tortures of remorse,—
Stain not a life of unpolluted honour,
For, oh ! as surely as thou strik'st at Percy,
Thou wilt for ever stab the fame of Douglas.

    Per. Finish the bloody work.

    Dou. Then take thy wish.

    Per. Why dost thou start ?

      (PERCY *bares his bosom.* DOUGLAS *advances to*
       stab him, and discovers the scarf.

    Dou. Her scarf upon his breast !
The blasting sight converts me into stone ;
Withers my powers like cowardice or age,
Curdles the blood within my shiv'ring veins,
And palsies my bold arm.

    Per. (*Ironically to the Knights.*) Hear you, his
     friends !
Bear witness to the glorious, great exploit,
Record it in the annals of his race,
That Douglas the renown'd—the valiant Douglas,
Fenced round with guards, and safe in his own cas-
    tle,
Surprised a knight unarm'd, and bravely slew him.

    Dou. (*Throwing away his dagger.*) 'Tis true—I
     am the very stain of knighthood.
How is my glory dimm'd !

    El. It blazes brighter !
Douglas was only brave—he now is generous !

    Per. This action has restored thee to thy rank,
And makes thee worthy to contend with Percy.

Dou. Thy joy will be as short as 'tis insulting.
                                        (*To* ELWINA.
And thou, imperious boy, restrain thy boasting.
Thou hast saved my honour, not removed my hate,
For my soul loaths thee for the obligation.
Give him his sword.

    Per. Now thou'rt a noble foe,
And in the field of honour I will meet thee,
As knight encount'ring knight.

    El. Stay, Percy, stay,
Strike at the wretched cause of all, strike here,
Here sheathe thy thirsty sword, but spare my hus-
      band.

    Dou. Turn, madam, and address those vows to me,
To spare the precious life of him you love.
Even now you triumph in the death of Douglas,
Now your loose fancy kindles at the thought,
And wildly rioting in lawless hope,
Indulges the adultery of the mind.
But I'll defeat that wish.—Guards, bear her in.
Nay, do not struggle.   (*She is borne in.*

    Per. Let our deaths suffice,
And reverence virtue in that form inshrined.

    Dou. Provoke my rage no farther.—I have kind-
      led
The burning torch of never-dying vengeance
At love's expiring lamp.—But mark me, friends,
If Percy's happier genius should prevail,
And I should fall, give him safe conduct hence,
Be all observance paid him.—Go, I follow thee.
                                        (*Aside to* EDRIC.
Within I've something for thy private ear.

    Per. Now shall this mutual fury be appeased!
These eager hands shall soon be drench'd in slaughter!
Yes—like two famish'd vultures snuffing blood,
And panting to destroy, we'll rush to combat ;
Yet I've the deepest, deadliest cause of hate,
I am but Percy, thou'rt—Elwina's husband.
                                        [*Exeunt*

ACT THE FIFTH.

SCENE I.

ELWINA'S *Apartment.*

El. Thou who in judgement still remember'st
　　　mercy,
Look down upon my woes, preserve my husband!
Preserve my husband! Ah, I dare not ask it;
My very prayers may pull down ruin on me!
If Douglas should survive, what then becomes
Of—him—I dare not name? And if he conquers,
I've slain my husband. Agonizing state!
When I can neither hope, nor think, nor pray,
But guilt involves me. Sure to know the worst
Cannot exceed the torture of suspense,
When each event is big with equal horror.
　　　　　　　　　　　　(*Looks out.*
What, no one yet? This solitude is dreadful!
My horrors multiply!

Enter BIRTHA.

Thou messenger of woe!
　Bir. Of woe indeed!
　El. How, is my husband dead?
Oh, speak!
　Bir. Your husband lives.
　El. Then farewell Percy!

He was the tenderest, truest!—Bless him, Heaven,
With crowns of glory and immortal joys!

Bir. Still are you wrong; the combat is not over.
Stay, flowing tears, and give me leave to speak.

El. Thou sayest that Percy and my husband live;
Then why this sorrow?

Bir. What a task is mine!

El. Thou talk'st as if I were a child in grief,
And scarce acquainted with calamity.
Speak out, unfold thy tale whate'er it be,
For I am so familiar with affliction,
It cannot come in any shape will shock me.

Bir. How shall I speak? Thy husband——

El. What of Douglas?

Bir. When all was ready for the fatal combat,
He call'd his chosen knights, then drew his sword,
And on it made them swear a solemn oath,
Confirm'd by every rite religion bids,
That they would see perform'd his last request,
Be it whate'er it would. Alas! they swore.

El. What did the dreadful preparation mean?

Bir. Then to their hands he gave a poison'd cup,
Compounded of the deadliest herbs and drugs;
Take this, said he, it is a husband's legacy;
Percy may conquer—and—I have a wife!
If Douglas falls, Elwina must not live.

El. Spirit of Herod! Why, 'twas greatly thought!
'Twas worthy of the bosom which conceived it!
Yet 'twas too merciful to be his own.
Yes, Douglas, yes, my husband, I'll obey thee,
And bless thy genius which has found the means
To reconcile thy vengeance with my peace,
The deadly means to make obedience pleasant.

Bir. O spare, for pity spare my bleeding heart:
Inhuman to the last! Unnatural poison!

El. My gentle friend, what is there in a name?
The means are little where the end is kind.
If it disturb thee do not call it poison;

Call it the sweet oblivion of my cares,
My balm of woe, my cordial of affliction,
The drop of mercy to my fainting soul,
My kind dismission from a world of sorrow,
My cup of bliss, my passport to the skies.
    Bir. Hark! what alarm is that?
    El. The combat's over!   (BIRTHA *goes out.*
(ELWINA *stands in a fix'd attitude, her hands clasp'd.*
Now, gracious Heaven, sustain me in the trial,
And bow my spirit to thy great decrees!

Re-enter BIRTHA.

    (ELWINA *looks stedfastly at her without speaking.*
    Bir. Douglas is fallen.
    El. Bring me the poison.
    Bir. Never.
    El. Where are the knights? I summon you—ap-
        proach!
Draw near, ye awful ministers of fate,
Dire instruments of posthumous revenge!
Come—I am ready; but your tardy justice
Defrauds the injured dead.—Go, haste, my friend,
See that the castle be securely guarded,
Let every gate be barr'd—prevent his entrance.
    Bir. Whose entrance?
    El. His—the murderer of my husband.
    Bir. He's single, we have hosts of friends.
    El. No matter;
Who knows what love and madness may attempt?
But here I swear by all that binds the good,
Never to see him more.—Unhappy Douglas!
O if thy troubled spirit still is conscious
Of our past woes, look down, and hear me swear,
That when the legacy thy rage bequeath'd me
Works at my heart, and conquers struggling nature,
Ev'n in that agony I'll still be faithful.
She who could never love, shall yet obey thee,
Weep thy hard fate, and die to prove her truth.

Bir. O unexampled virtue !   (*A noise without.*
El. Heard you nothing ?
By all my fears the insulting conqueror comes.
O save me, shield me !

Enter DOUGLAS.

Heaven and earth, my husband !
    Dou. Yes——
To blast thee with the sight of him thou hat'st,
Of him thou hast wrong'd, adulteress, 'tis thy hus-
        band.
    El. (*Kneels.*) Blest be the fountain of eternal
        mercy,
This load of guilt is spared me ! Douglas lives !
Perhaps both live ! (*To* BIRTHA.) Could I be sure
        of that,
The poison were superfluous, joy would kill me.
    Dou. Be honest now, for once, and curse thy stars;
Curse thy detested fate which brings thee back
A hated husband, when thy guilty soul
Revell'd in fond, imaginary joys
With my too happy rival; when thou flew'st,
To gratify impatient, boundless passion,
And join adulterous lust to bloody murder ;
Then to reverse the scene ! polluted woman !
Mine is the transport now, and thine the pang.
    El. Whence sprung the false report that thou had'st
        fallen ?
    Dou. To give thy guilty breast a deeper wound,
To add a deadlier sting to disappointment,
I raised it—I contrived—I sent it thee.
    El. Thou seest me bold, but bold in conscious vir-
        tue.
—That my sad soul may not be stain'd with blood,
That I may spend my few short hours in peace,
And die in holy hope of Heaven's forgiveness,
Relieve the terrors of my lab'ring breast,
Say I am clear of murder—say he lives,

Say but that little word, that Percy lives,
And Alps and oceans shall divide us ever,
As far as universal space can part us.

Dou. Canst thou renounce him?

El. Tell me that he lives,
And thou shalt be the ruler of my fate,
For ever hide me in a convent's gloom,
From cheerful day-light, and the haunts of men,
Where sad austerity and ceaseless prayer
Shall share my uncomplaining day between them.

Dou. O, hypocrite! now, Vengeance, to thy office.
I had forgot—Percy commends him to thee,
And by my hand——

El. How—by thy hand?

Dou. Has sent thee
This precious pledge of love.

> (*He gives her* PERCY's *scarf.*

El. Then Percy's dead!

Dou. He is.—O great revenge, thou now art
mine!
See how convulsive sorrow rends her frame!
This, this is transport!—injured honour now
Receives its vast, its ample retribution.
She sheds no tears, her grief's too highly wrought;
'Tis speechless agony.—She must not faint—
She shall not 'scape her portion of the pain.
No! she shall feel the fulness of distress,
And wake to keen perception of her loss.

Bir. Monster! Barbarian! leave her to her sorrows.

El. (*In a low broken voice.*) Douglas—think not
I faint, because thou see'st
The pale and bloodless cheek of wan despair.
Fail me not yet, my spirits; thou cold heart,
Cherish thy freezing current one short moment,
And bear thy mighty load a little longer.

Dou. Percy, I must avow it, bravely fought,—
Died as a hero shou'd;—but, as he fell,

(Hear it, fond wanton !) call'd upon thy name,
And his last guilty breath sigh'd out—Elwina !
Come—give a loose to rage, and feed my soul
With wild complaints, and womanish upbraidings.

 El. (*In a low solemn voice.*) No .
The sorrow's weak that wastes itself in words,
Mine is substantial anguish—deep, not loud;
I do not rave.——Resentment's the return
Of common souls for common injuries.
Light grief is proud of state, and courts compassion ;
But there's a dignity in cureless sorrow,
A sullen grandeur which disdains complaint ;
Rage is for little wrongs—Despair is dumb.

    (*Exeunt* ELWINA *and* BIRTHA.
 Dou. Why this is well !—her sense of woe is strong!
The sharp, keen tooth of gnawing grief devours her,
Feeds on her heart, and pays me back my pangs.
Since I must perish, 'twill be glorious ruin :
I fall not singly, but, like some proud tower,
I'll crush surrounding objects in the wreck,
And make the devastation wide and dreadful.

Enter RABY.

 Ra. O whither shall a wretched father turn ?
Where fly for comfort ? Douglas, art thou here ?
I do not ask for comfort at thy hands.
I'd but one little casket, where I lodged
My precious hoard of wealth, and, like an idiot,
I gave my treasure to another's keeping,
Who threw away the gem, nor knew its value,
But left the plunder'd owner quite a beggar.

 Dou. What ! art thou come to see thy race disho-
   nour'd ?
And thy bright sun of glory set in blood ?
I would have spared thy virtues, and thy age,
The knowledge of her infamy.

 Ra. 'Tis false.
Had she been base, this sword had drank her blood.

 Dou. Ha ! dost thou vindicate the wanton ?

Ra. Wanton?
Thou hast defamed a noble lady's honour—
My spotless child—in me behold her champion :
The strength of Hercules will nerve this arm,
When lifted in defence of innocence.
The daughter's virtue for the father's shield,
Will make old Raby still invincible. (*Offers to draw.*

Dou. Forbear.

Ra. Thou dost disdain my feeble arm,
And scorn my age.

Dou. There will be blood enough ;
Nor need thy wither'd veins, old lord, be drain'd,
To swell the copious stream.

Ra. Thou wilt not kill her ?

Dou. Oh, 'tis a day of horror !

Enter EDRIC *and* BIRTHA.

Ed. Where is Douglas ?
I come to save him from the deadliest crime
Revenge did ever meditate.

Dou. What meanest thou ?

Ed. This instant fly, and save thy guiltless wife.

Dou. Save that perfidious——

Ed. That much-injured woman.

Bir. Unfortunate indeed, but O most innocent !

Ed. In the last solemn article of death,
That truth-compelling state, when even bad men
Fear to speak falsely, Percy clear'd her fame.

Dou. I heard him—'Twas the guilty fraud of love.
The scarf, the scarf ! that proof of mutual passion,
Given but this day to ratify their crimes !

Bir. What means my lord ? This day ? that fatal
          scarf
Was given long since, a toy of childish friendship ;
Long ere your marriage, ere you knew Elwina.

Ra. 'Tis I am guilty

Dou. Ha !

Ra. I,—I alone.
Confusion, honour, pride, parental fondness,

Distract my soul,—Percy was not to blame,
He was—the destined husband of Elwina!
He loved her—was beloved,—and I approved.
The tale is long.—I changed my purpose since,
Forbad their marriage—

Dou. And confirm'd my mis'ry!
Twice did they meet to-day—my wife and Percy.

Ra. I know it.

Dou. Ha! thou knew'st of my dishonour?
Thou wast a witness, an approving witness,
At least a tame one!

Ra. Percy came, 'tis true,
A constant, tender, but a guiltless lover!

Dou. I shall grow mad indeed! a guiltless lover!
Percy, the guiltless lover of my wife!

Ra. He knew not she was married.

Dou. How? is't possible?

Ra. Douglas, 'tis true; both, both were innocent:
He of her marriage, she of his return.

Bir. But now, when we believed thee dead, she
vow'd
Never to see thy rival. Instantly,
Not in a start of momentary passion,
But with a martyr's dignity and calmness,
She bade me bring the poison.

Dou. Had'st thou done it,
Despair had been my portion! Fly, good Birtha,
Find out the suffering saint—describe my penitence,
And paint my vast extravagance of fondness,
Tell her I love as never mortal loved—
Tell her I know her virtues, and adore them—
Tell her I come, but dare not seek her presence,
Till she pronounce my pardon.

Bir. I obey. (*Exit* BIRTHA.

Ra. My child is innocent! ye choirs of saints,
Catch the blest sounds—my child is innocent!

Dou. O I will kneel, and sue for her forgiveness,
And thou shalt help me plead the cause of love,
And thou shalt weep—she cannot sure refuse

A kneeling husband and a weeping father.
Thy venerable cheek is wet already.
  Ra. Douglas! it is the dew of grateful joy!
My child is innocent! I now wou'd die,
Lest fortune shou'd grow weary of her kindness,
And grudge me this short transport.
  Dou. Where, where is she?
My fond impatience brooks not her delay;
Quick, let me find her, hush her anxious soul,
And sooth her troubled spirit into peace.

Enter BIRTHA.

  Bir. O horror, horror, horror!
  Dou. Ah! what mean'st thou?
  Bir. Elwina—
  Dou. Speak—
  Bir. Her grief wrought up to frenzy,
She has, in her delirium, swallow'd poison.
  Ra. Frenzy and poison!
  Dou. Both a husband's gift;
But thus I do her justice.

As DOUGLAS *goes to stab himself, enter* ELWINA *distracted, her hair dishevelled,* PERCY'S *scarf in her hand.*

  El. (*Goes up to* DOUGLAS.) What, blood again?
      We cannot kill him twice!
Soft, soft—no violence—he's dead already;—
I did it—Yes—I drown'd him with my tears;
But hide the cruel deed! I'll scratch him out
A shallow grave, and lay the green sod on it;
Ay—and I'll bind the wild briar o'er the turf,
And plant a willow there, a weeping willow—
          (*She sits on the ground.*
But look you tell not Douglas, he'll disturb him;
He'll pluck the willow up—and plant a thorn.
He will not let me sit upon his grave,
And sing all day, and weep and pray all night.
  Ra. Dost thou not know me?

El. Yes—I do remember
You had a harmless lamb.

    Ra. I had indeed!

    El. From all the flock you chose her out a mate,
In sooth a fair one—you did bid her love it—
But while the shepherd slept the wolf devour'd it.

    Ra. My heart will break. This is too much, too
        much!

    El. (*Smiling.*) O 'twas a cordial draught—I drank
        it all.

    Ra. What means my child?

    Dou. The poison! Oh the poison!
Thou dear wrong'd innocence—

    El. Off—murderer, off!
Do not defile me with those crimson hands.

                    [*Shews the scarf.*
This is his winding sheet—I'll wrap him in it—
I wrought it for my love—there—now I've drest him.
How brave he looks! my father will forgive him,
He dearly loved him once—but that is over.
See where he comes—beware, my gallant Percy,
Ah! come not here, this is the cave of death,
And there's the dark, dark palace of Revenge!
See, the pale king sits on his blood-stain'd throne!
He points to me—I come, I come, I come.

    [*She faints, they run to her,* DOUGLAS *takes up his
       sword and stabs himself.*

    Dou. Thus, thus I follow thee.

    Ed. Hold thy rash hand!

    Dou. It is too late.   No remedy but this
Cou'd medicine a disease so desperate.

    Ra. Ah she revives!

    Dou. [*Raising himself.*] She lives! bear, bear
      me to her!
We shall be happy yet.

           [*He struggles to get to her, but sinks down.*
It will not be—
O for a last embrace—Alas I faint—
She lives—Now death is terrible indeed—

Fair spirit, I loved thee—O—Elwina!   [*Dies*

   El. Where have I been? The damps of death are
      on me.

   Ra. Look up, my child! O do not leave me thus!
Pity the anguish of thy aged father.
Hast thou forgot me?

   El. No—you are my father;
O you are kindly come to close my eyes,
And take the kiss of death from my cold lips!

   Ra. Do we meet thus?

   El. We soon shall meet in peace.
I've but a faint remembrance of the past—
But something tells me—O those painful struggles!
Raise me a little—there—
          [*She sees the body of* DOUGLAS.
What sight is that?
A sword, and bloody? Ah! and Douglas murder'd!

   Ed. Convinced too late of your unequall'd virtues,
And wrung with deep compunction for your wrongs,
By his own hand the wretched Douglas fell.

   El. This adds another, sharper pang to death.
O thou Eternal! take him to thy mercy,
Nor let this sin be on his head, or mine!

   Ra. I have undone you all—the crime is mine!
O thou poor injured saint, forgive thy father,
He kneels to his wrong'd child.

   El. Now you are cruel.
Come near, my father, nearer—I wou'd see you,
But mists and darkness cloud my failing sight.
O Death! suspend thy rights for one short moment,
Till I have ta'en a father's last embrace—
A father's blessing.—Once—and now 'tis over.
Receive me to thy mercy, gracious Heaven!
          [*She dies.*

   Ra. She's gone! for ever gone! cold, dead and
      cold.
Am I a father? Fathers love their children——
I murder mine! With impious pride I snatch'd

The bolt of vengeance from the hand of Heaven.
My punishment is great—but oh! 'tis just.
My soul submissive bows.   A righteous God
Has made my crime become my chastisement.

                              [*Exeunt omnes.*

A

TRIP TO SCARBOROUGH,

A

COMEDY.

AS PERFORMED AT THE

THEATRE-ROYAL, DRURY LANE.

ALTERED FROM

VANBURGH'S RELAPSE, OR VIRTUE IN DANGER.

BY

RICHARD BRINSLEY SHERIDAN, Esq.

DRAMATIS PERSONÆ.

LORD FOPPINGTON,	*Mr Dodd.*
YOUNG FASHION,	*Mr Palmer.*
LOVELESS,	*Mr Smith.*
COLONEL TOWNLY,	*Mr Brereton.*
SIR TUNBELLY CLUMSY,	*Mr Moody.*
PROBE,	*Mr Parsons.*
LORY,	*Mr Baddely.*
LA VAROLE,	*Mr Burton.*
Shoemaker,	*Mr Carpenter.*
Tailor,	*Mr Baker.*
Hosier,	*Mr Norris.*
Jeweller,	*Mr La Mash.*

Servants, &c.

BERINTHIA,	*Miss Farren.*
AMANDA,	*Mrs Robinson.*
MRS COUPLER,	*Mrs Booth.*
Nurse,	*Mrs Bradshaw.*
MISS HOYDEN,	*Mrs Abington.*

TRIP TO SCARBOROUGH.

ACT THE FIRST.

SCENE I.

The Hall of an Inn.

Enter YOUNG FASHION *and* LORY—*Postillion following with a portmanteau.*

Y. Fash. Lory, pay the post-boy, and take the portmanteau.

Lory. Faith, sir, we had better let the post-boy take the portmanteau and pay himself.

Y. Fash. Why sure there's something left in it?

Lory. Not a rag, upon my honour, sir—we eat the last of your wardrobe at Newmalton; and if we had had twenty miles farther to go, our next meal must have been off the cloak-bag.

Y. Fash. Why, 'sdeath! it appears full.

Lory. Yes, sir—I made bold to stuff it with hay, to save appearances, and look like baggage.

Y. Fash. What the devil shall I do!——Hark'e, boy, what's the chaise?

Boy. Thirteen shillings, please your honour.

Y. Fash. Can you give me change for a guinea?

Boy. O yes, sir.

Lory. Soh, what will he do now?—Lord, sir, you had better let the boy be paid below.

Y. Fash. Why, as you say, Lory, I believe it will be as well.

Lory. Yes, yes; tell them to discharge you below, honest friend.

Boy. Please your honour, there are the turnpikes too.

Y. Fash. Ay, ay, the turnpikes by all means.

Boy. And I hope your honour will order me something for myself.

Y. Fash To be sure, bid them give you a crown.

Lory. Yes, yes—my master doesn't care what you charge them—so get along, you—

Boy. Your honour promised to send the hostler——

Lory. Pshaw! damn the hostler—would you impose upon the gentleman's generosity?—[*Pushes him out.*]—A rascal, to be so curst ready with his change!

Y. Fash. Why faith, Lory, he had near posed me.

Lory. Well, sir, we are arrived at Scarborough, not worth a guinea!—I hope you'll own yourself a happy man—You have outlived all your cares.

Y. Fash. How so, sir?

Lory. Why you have nothing left to take care of.

Y. Fash. Yes, sirrah, I have myself and you to take care of still.

Lory. Sir, if you could prevail with somebody else to do that for you, I fancy we might both fare the better for't—But now, sir, for my Lord Foppington, your elder brother.

Y. Fash. Damn my elder brother !

Lory. With all my heart ; but get him to redeem your annuity, however.—Look you, sir, you must wheedle him, or you must starve.

Y. Fash. Look you, sir, I will neither weedle him nor starve.

Lory. Why, what will you do then ?

Y. Fash. Cut his throat, or get some one to do it for me.

Lory. Gad-so, sir, I'm glad to find I was not so well acquainted with the strength of your conscience as with the weakness of your purse.

Y. Fash. Why, art thou so impenetrable a block-head as to believe he'll help me with a farthing ?

Lory. Not if you treat him *de haut en bas*, as you used to do.

Y. Fash. Why, how would'st have me treat him ?

Lory. Like a trout—tickle him.

Y. Fash. I can't flatter.

Lory. Can you starve ?

Y Fash. Yes.

Lory. I can't—Good-bye t'ye, sir.

Y. Fash. Stay—thou'lt distract me.—But who comes here—my old friend, Colonel Townly,

Enter COLONEL TOWNLY.

Y. Fash. My dear colonel, I am rejoiced to meet you here.

Town. Dear Tom, this is an unexpected pleasure —What, are you come to Scarbro' to be present at your brother's wedding ?

Lory. Ah, sir, if it had been his funeral, we should have come with pleasure.

Town. What, honest Lory, are you with your master still ?

Lory. Yes, sir, I have been starving with him ever since I saw your honour last.

Y. Fash. Why, Lory is an attach'd rogue; there's
no getting rid of him.

Lory. True, sir, as my master says, there's no se-
ducing me from his service,—till he's able to pay
me my wages. 　　　　　　　　　　　　*[Aside.*

Y. Fash. Go, go, sir—and take care of the baggage.

Lory. Yes, sir—the baggage!—O Lord!—I suppose, sir, I must charge the landlord to be very particular where he stows this.

Y. Fash. Get along, you rascal.
　　　　　　　[Exit LORY, *with the portmanteau.*
But, colonel, are you acquainted with my proposed
sister-in-law?

Town. Only by character—her father, Sir Tunbelly Clumsy, lives within a quarter of a mile of this
place, in a lonely old house, which nobody comes
near. She never goes abroad, nor sees company at
home; to prevent all misfortunes, she has her breeding within doors; the parson of the parish teaches
her to play upon the dulcimer, the clerk to sing, her
nurse to dress, and her father to dance:—in short,
nobody has free admission there but our old acquaintance, Mother Coupler, who has procured
your brother this match, and is, I believe, a distant
relation of Sir Tunbelly's.

Y. Fash. But is her fortune so considerable?

Town. Three thousand a year, and a good sum
of money independent of her father beside.

Y. Fash. 'Sdeath! that my old acquaintance
dame Coupler could not have thought of me as well
as my brother for such a prize!

Town. Egad, I wouldn't swear that you are too
late: his lordship, I know, hasn't yet seen the lady,
and, I believe, has quarrelled with his patroness.

Y. Fash. My dear colonel, what an idea have
you started!

Town. Pursue it if you can, and I promise you you shall have my assistance; for, besides my natural contempt for his lordship, I have at present the enmity of a rival towards him.

Y. Fash. What, has he been addressing your old flame, the sprightly widow Berinthia?

Town. Faith, Tom, I am at present most whimsically circumstanced—I came here near a month ago to meet the lady you mention; but she failing in her promise, I, partly from pique, and partly from idleness, have been diverting my chagrin by offering up chaste incense to the beauties of Amanda, our friend Loveless's wife.

Y. Fash. I have never seen her, but have heard her spoken of as a youthful wonder of beauty and prudence.

Town. She is so indeed; and Loveless being too careless and insensible of the treasure he possesses, my lodging in the same house has given me a thousand opportunities of making my assiduities acceptable; so that, in less than a fortnight, I began to bear my disappointment from the widow with the most Christian resignation.

Y. Fash. And Berinthia has never appeared?

Town. O there's the perplexity; for, just as I began not to care whether I ever saw her again or not, last night she arrived.

Y. Fash. And instantly reassumed her empire?

Town. No faith—we met—but the lady not condescending to give me any serious reasons for having fool'd me for a month, I left her in a huff.

Y. Fash. Well, well, I'll answer for't she'll soon resume her power, especially as friendship will prevent your pursuing the other too far—But my coxcomb of a brother is an admirer of Amanda's too, is he?

Town. Yes; and I believe is most heartily despised by her—but come with me, and you shall see her and your old friend Loveless.

Y. Fash. I must pay my respects to his lordship—
perhaps you can direct me to his lodgings?

Town. Come with me, I shall pass by it.

Y. Fash I wish you could pay the visit for me;
or could tell me what I should say to him.

Town. Say nothing to him—apply yourself to his
bag, his sword, his feather, his snuff-box; and, when
you are well with them, desire him to lend you a
thousand pounds, and I'll engage you prosper.

Y. Fash. 'Sdeath and furies! why was that coxcomb thrust into the world before me? O Fortune!
Fortune! thou art a jilt, by gad.   [*Exit*.

SCENE II

A Dressing Room.

LORD FOPPINGTON, *in his Night Gown, and* LA
VAROLE.

Ld Fop. Well, 'tis an unspeakable pleasure to be
a man of quality—strike me dumb!—even the boors
of this northern spa have learn'd the respect due to
a title—La Varole!

La Var. Mi lor—

Ld Fop. You ha'n't yet been at Muddy-moat-hall
to announce my arrival, have you?

La Var. Not yet, mi lor.

Ld Fop. Then you need not go till Saturday.—
                    [*Exit* LA VAR.

As I am in no particular haste to view my intended
sposa, I shall sacrifice a day or two more to the
pursuit of my friend Loveless's wife—Amanda is a
charming creature—strike me ugly; and if I have

any discernment in the world, she thinks no less of my Lord Foppington.

Enter LA VAROLE.

La Var. Mi lor, de shoemaker, de tailor, de hosier, de semptress, de peru, be all ready, if your lordship please to dress.

Ld Fop. 'Tis well, admit them.

La Var. Hey, messieurs, entrez!

Enter Tailor, &c. &c.

Ld Fop. So, gentlemen, I hope you have all taken pains to shew yourselves masters in your professions?

Tai. I think I may presume to say, sir—

La Var. My lor, you clown you!

Tai. My lord, I ask your lordship's pardon, my lord. I hope, my lord, your lordship will please to own I have brought your lordship as accomplished a suit of clothes as ever peer of England wore, my lord——will your lordship please to try 'em now?

Ld Fop. Ay; but let my people dispose the glasses so that I may see myself before and behind; for I love to see myself all round.

Whilst he puts on his clothes, enter YOUNG FASHION *and* LORY.

Y. Fash. Hey-day! What the devil have we here? Sure my gentleman's grown a favourite at court, he has got so many people at his levee.

Lory. Sir, these people come in order to make him a favourite at court—they are to establish him with the ladies.

Y. Fash. Good Heaven! to what an ebb of taste are women fallen, that it should be in the power of a laced coat to recommend a gallant to them!

Lory. Sir, tailors and hair-dressers are now become

the bawds of the nation—'tis they that debauch all the women.

Y. Fash. Thou say'st true; for there's that fop, now, has not, by nature, wherewithal to move a cook maid; and by the time these fellows have done with him, egad he shall melt down a countess—But now for my reception.

Ld Fop. Death and eternal tortures! Sir—I say the coat is too wide here by a foot.

Tai. My lord, if it had been tighter, 'twould neither have hook'd nor button'd.

Ld Fop. Rat the hooks and buttons, sir! can any thing be worse than this?—As gad shall judge me, it hangs on my shoulders like a chairman's surtout.

Tai. 'Tis not for me to dispute your lordship's fancy.

Lory. There, sir, observe what respect does.

Y. Fash. Respect!—D—mn him for a coxcomb!—but let's accost him.—Brother, I'm your humble servant.

Ld Fop. O lard, Tam, I did not expect you in England—Brother, I'm glad to see you—but what has brought you to Scarbro', Tam?—Look you, sir, (*To the Tailor.*) I shall never be reconciled to this nauseous wrapping gown; therefore, pray get me another suit with all possible expedition; for this is my eternal aversion.—Well, but Tam, you don't tell me what has driven you to Scarbro'?—Mrs Calico, are not you of my mind?

Semp. Directly, my lord.—I hope your lordship is pleased with your ruffles?

Ld Fop. In love with them, stap my vitals!—Bring my bill, you shall be paid to-morrow.

Semp. I humbly thank your lordship.

[*Exit* SEMP.

Ld Fop. Hark thee, shoemaker, these shoes an't ugly, but they don't fit me.

Shoe. My lord, I think they fit you very well.

Ld Fop. They hurt me just below the instep.

Shoe. (*Feeling his foot.*) No, my lord, they don't hurt you there.

Ld Fop. I tell thee they pinch me execrably.

Shoe. Why then, my lord, if those shoes pinch you I'll be d——'d !

Ld Fop. Why, wilt thou undertake to persuade me I cannot feel ?

Shoe. Your lordship may please to feel what you think fit, but that shoe does not hurt you.   I think I understand my trade.

Ld Fop. Now, by all that's good and powerful, thou art an incomprehensible coxcomb——but thou makest good shoes, and so I'll bear with thee.

Shoe. My lord, I have worked for half the people of quality in this town these twenty years, and 'tis very hard I shou'dn't know when a shoe hurts, and when it don't.

Ld Fop. Well, pr'ythee be gone about thy business.
                                                    (*Exit Shoe.*

Mr Mendlegs, a word with you.   The calves of these stockings are thickened a little too much; they make my legs look like a porter's.

Mend. My lord, methinks they look mighty well.

Ld Fop. Ay, but you are not so good a judge of those things as I am.   I have studied them all my life; therefore, pray let the next be the thickness of a crown piece less.

Mend. Indeed, my lord, they are the same kind I had the honour to furnish your lordship with in town.

Ld Fop. Very possible, Mr Mendlegs; but that was in the beginning of the winter; and you should always remember, Mr Hosier, that if you make a nobleman's spring legs as robust as his autumnal calves, you commit a monstrous impropriety, and make no allowance for the fatigues of the winter.

Jew. I hope, my lord, these buckles have had the

unspeakable satisfaction of being honoured with your lordship's approbation ?

Ld Fop. Why, they are of a pretty fancy ; but don't you think them rather of the smallest ?

Jew. My lord, they could not well be larger to keep on your lordship's shoe.

Ld Fop. My good sir, you forget that these matters are not as they used to be formerly ; indeed, the buckle was a sort of machine intended to keep on the shoe ; but the case is now quite reversed, and the shoe is of no earthly use but to keep on the buckle. Now give me my watches, and the business of the morning will be pretty well over.

Y. Fash. Well, Lory, what dost think on't ?——a very friendly reception from a brother, after three years absence !

Lory. Why, sir, 'tis your own fault—here you have stood ever since you came in, and have not commended any one thing that belongs to him.

Y. Fash. Nor ever shall while they belong to a coxcomb.—Now your people of business are gone, brother, I hope I may obtain a quarter of an hour's audience of you ?

Ld Fop. Faith, Tam, I must beg you'll excuse me at this time, for I have an engagement which I would not break for the salvation of mankind.   Hey there ! —is my carriage at the door ? You'll excuse me, brother.   (*Going.*

Y. Fash. Shall you be back to dinner ?

Ld Fop. As gad shall jedge me, I can't tell, for it is passible I may dine with some friends at Donner's.

Y. Fash. Shall I meet you there ? for I must needs talk with you.

Ld Fop. That, I'm afraid, mayn't be quite so praper ; for those I commonly eat with are a people of nice conversation ; and you know, Tam, your education has been a little at large—but there are other ordinaries in town—very good beef ordinaries.   I suppose, Tam, you can eat beef?—However, dear Tam, I'm glad to see thee in England, stap my vitals!   [*Exit.*

Y. Fash. Hell and furies! Is this to be borne?

Lory. Faith, sir, I could almost have given him a knock o' the pate myself.

Y. Fash. 'Tis enough; I will now shew you the excess of my passion by being very calm.   Come, Lory, lay your loggerhead to mine, and, in cold blood, let us contrive his destruction.

Lory. Here comes a head, sir, would contrive it better than us both, if she would but join in the confederacy.

Y. Fash. By this light, Madam Coupler! she seems dissatisfied at something: let us observe her.

Enter COUPLER.

Coup. Soh! I am likely to be well rewarded for my services, truly; my suspicions, I find, were but too just—What! refuse to advance me a paltry sum, when I am upon the point of making him master of a galloon! But let him look to the consequences, an ungrateful, narrow-minded coxcomb!

Y. Fash. So he is, upon my soul, old lady: it must be my brother you speak of?

Coup. Hah!—stripling, how came you here? What, hast spent all, hey? and art thou come to dun his lordship for assistance?

Y. Fash. No:—I want somebody's assistance to cut his lordship's throat, without the risque of being hang'd for him.

Coup. Egad, sirrah, I could help thee to do him almost as good a turn, without the danger of being burnt in the hand for't.

Y. Fash. How—how, old Mischief?

Coup. Why you must know I have done you the kindness to make up a match for your brother.

Y. Fash. I'm very much beholden to you, truly.

Coup. You may before the wedding-day yet: the

lady is a great heiress, the match is concluded, the
writings are drawn, and his lordship is come hither to
put the finishing hand to the business.

Y. Fash. I understand as much.

Coup. Now you must know, stripling, your brother's a knave.

Y. Fash. Good.

Coup. He has given me a bond of a thousand
pounds for helping him to this fortune, and has promised me as much more in ready money upon the
day of the marriage : which, I understand by a
friend, he never designs to pay me ; and his just
now refusing to pay me a part is a proof of it : If,
therefore, you will be a generous young rogue, and
secure me five thousand pounds, I'll help you to the
lady.

Y. Fash. And how the devil wilt thou do that?

Coup. Without the devil's aid, I warrant thee.
Thy brother's face not one of the family ever saw ;
the whole business has been managed by me, and
all the letters go through my hands. Sir Tunbelly
Clumsy, my relation, (for that's the old gentleman's
name) is apprised of his lordship being down here,
and expects him to-morrow to receive his daughter's
hand; but the peer, I find, means to bait here a few
days longer, to recover the fatigue of his journey, I
suppose. Now you shall go to Muddy-moat-hall in
his place. I'll give you a letter of introduction; and
i you don't marry the girl before sun-set, you deserve to be hang'd before morning.

Y. Fash. Agreed, agreed : and for thy reward—

Coup. Well, well ; though I warrant thou hast not
a farthing of money in thy pocket now—no—one
may see it in thy face.

Y. Fash. Not a sous, by Jupiter.

Coup. Must I advance then ?—well, be at my lodging next door this evening, and I'll see what may be
done—We'll sign and seal, and when I have given

thee some farther instructions, thou shalt hoist sail
and be gone.   (*Exit* COUP.

Y. Fash. So, Lory; Providence, thou seest, at last
takes care of merit : we are in a fair way to be
great people.

Lory. Ay, sir, if the devil don't step between the
cup and the lip, as he uses to do.

Y. Fash. Why, faith, he has played me many a
damned trick to spoil my fortune ; and, egad, i'm
almost afraid he's at work about it again now ; but
if I should tell thee how, thou'dst wonder at me.

Lory. Indeed, sir, I should not.

Y. Fash. How dost know ?

Lory. Because, sir, I have wondered at you so often, I can wonder at you no more.

Y. Fash. No ! what would'st thou say if a qualm
of conscience should spoil my design ?

Lory. I would eat my words, and wonder more
than ever !

Y. Fash. Why faith, Lory, though I am a young
rakehell, and have played many a roguish trick, this
is so full-grown a cheat, I find I must take pains to
come up to't——I have scruples.

Lory. They are strong symptoms of death. If you
find they increase, sir, pray make your will.

Y. Fash. No, my conscience sha'n't starve me
neither : but thus far I'll listen to it.   Before I execute this project, I'll try my brother to the bottom.
If he has yet so much humanity about him to assist
me (though with a moderate aid) I'll drop my project
at his feet, and shew him how I can do for him much
more than what I'd ask he'd do for me.   This one
conclusive trial of him I resolve to make————

  Succeed or fail, still victory's my lot;
  If I subdue his heart, 'tis well—if not,
  I will subdue my conscience to my plot.   [*Exeunt.*

ACT THE SECOND.

SCENE I.

Enter LOVELESS *and* AMANDA.

Love. How do you like these lodgings, my dear? For my part, I am so well pleased with them, I shall hardly remove whilst we stay here, if you are satisfied.

Aman. I am satisfied with every thing that pleases you, else I had not come to Scarbro' at all.

Love. O! a little of the noise and folly of this place will sweeten the pleasures of our retreat; we shall find the charms of our retirement doubled when we return to it.

Aman. That pleasing prospect will be my chiefest entertainment, whilst, much against my will, I engage in those empty pleasures which 'tis so much the fashion to be fond of.

Love. I own most of them are indeed but empty; yet there are delights, of which a private life is destitute, which may divert an honest man, and be a harmless entertainment to a virtuous woman: good music is one; and truly, (with some small allowance) the plays, I think, may be esteemed another.

Aman. Plays, I must confess, have some small

charms, and would have more, would they restrain that loose encouragement to vice, which shocks, if not the virtue of some women, at least the modesty of all.

Love. But, till that reformation can be wholly made, 'twould surely be a pity to exclude the productions of some of our best writers, for want of a little wholesome pruning ; which might be effected by any one who possessed modesty enough to believe that we should preserve all we can of our deceased authors, at least till they are outdone by the living ones.

Aman. What do you think of that you saw last night ?

Love. To say truth, I did not mind it much ; my attention was for some time taken off to admire the workmanship of Nature, in the face of a young lady who sat some distance from me, she was so exquisitely handsome.

Aman. So exquisitely handsome !

Love. Why do you repeat my words, my dear ?

Aman. Because you seemed to speak them with such pleasure, I thought I might oblige you with their echo.

Love. Then you are alarmed, Amanda ?

Aman. It is my duty to be so, when you are in danger.

Love. You are too quick in apprehending for me. I viewed her with a world of admiration, but not one glance of love.

Aman. Take heed of trusting to such nice distinctions.   But were your eyes the only things that were inquisitive ? Had I been in your place, my tongue, I fancy, had been curious too.   I should have asked her where she lived, yet still without design—Who was she, pray ?

Love. Indeed I cannot tell.

Aman. You will not tell.

Love. By all that's sacred then, I did not ask.

Aman. Nor do you know what company was with her?

Love. I do not; but why are you so earnest?

Aman. I thought I had cause.

Love. But you thought wrong, Amanda; for turn the case, and let it be your story; should you come home and tell me you had seen a handsome man, should I grow jealous because you had eyes?

Aman. But should I tell you he was *exquisitely* so, and that I had gazed on him with admiration, should you not think 'twere possible I might go one step further, and inquire his name?

Love. (*Aside.*) She has reason on her side, I have talked too much; but I must turn off another way. (*To her.*) Will you then make no difference, Amanda, between the language of our sex and yours? There is a modesty restrains your tongues, which makes you speak by halves when you commend, but roving flattery gives a loose to ours, which makes us still speak double what we think. You should not, therefore, in so strict a sense, take what I said to her advantage.

Aman. Those flights of flattery, sir, are to our faces only; when women are once out of hearing, you are as modest in your commendations as we are; but I sha'n't put you to the trouble of farther excuses; —if you please, this business shall rest here, only give me leave to wish, both for your peace and mine, that you may never meet this miracle of beauty more.

Love. I am content.

Enter Servant.

Serv. Madam, there is a lady at the door in a chair, desires to know whether your ladyship sees company? her name is Berinthia.

Aman. O dear!—'tis a relation I have not seen these five years; pray her to walk in. (*Exit Serv.*

Here's another beauty for you ; she was, when I saw her last, reckoned extremely handsome.

Love. Don't be jealous now, for I shall gaze upon her too.

Enter BERINTHIA.

Love. (*Aside.*) Ha! by heavens the very woman!

Berin. (*Saluting* AMANDA.) Dear Amanda, I did not expect to meet with you in Scarbro'.

Aman. Sweet cousin, I'm overjoyed to see you. (*To* LOVE.) Mr Loveless, here's a relation and a friend of mine I desire you'll be better acquainted with.

Love. (*Saluting* BERINTHIA.) If my wife never desires a harder thing, madam, her requests will be easily granted.

Enter Servant.

Serv. Sir, my Lord Foppington presents his humble service to you, and desires to know how you do. He's at the next door, and if it be not inconvenient to you, he'll come and wait upon you.

Love. Give my compliments to his lordship, and I shall be glad to see him. (*Exit Serv.*) If you are not acquainted with his lordship, madam, you will be entertained with his character.

Aman. Now it moves my pity more than my mirth, to see a man whom nature has made no fool be so very industrious to pass for an ass.

Love. No, there you are wrong, Amanda ; you should never bestow your pity upon those who take pains for your contempt ; pity those whom nature abuses, never those who abuse nature.

Enter LORD FOPPINGTON.

Ld Fop. Dear Loveless, I am your most humble servant.

Love. My lord, I'm yours.

Ld Fop. Madam, your ladyship's very humble slave.

Love. My lord, this lady is a relation of my wife's.

Ld Fop. (*Saluting her.*) The beautifullest race of people upon earth, rat me! Dear Loveless, I am overjoyed that you think of continuing here. I am, slap my vitals. (*To* AMANDA.) For Gad's sake, madam, how has your ladyship been able to subsist thus long under the fatigue of a country life?

Aman. My life has been very far from that, my lord, it has been a very quiet one.

Ld Fop. Why that's the fatigue I speak of, madam; for 'tis impossible to be quiet without thinking; now thinking is to me the greatest fatigue in the world.

Aman. Does not your lordship love reading then?

Ld Fop. Oh, passionately, madam, but I never think of what I read.

Berin. Why, can your lordship read without thinking?

Ld Fop. O Lard, can your ladyship pray without devotion, madam?

Aman. Well, I must own, I think books the best entertainment in the world.

Ld Fop. I am so much of your ladyship's mind, madam, that I have a private gallery in town, where I walk sometimes, which is furnished with nothing but books and looking-glasses. Madam, I have gilded them, and ranged them so prettily, before Gad, it is the most entertaining thing in the world to walk and look at them.

Aman. Nay, I love a neat library too, but 'tis, I think, the inside of a book should recommend it most to us.

Ld Fop. That, I must confess, I am not altogether so fond of, far to my mind the inside of a book is to entertain one's self with the forced product of another man's brain. Now, I think a man of quality and breeding may be much more diverted with the natu-

ral sprauts of his own ; but, to say the truth, madam,
let a man love reading never so well, when once he
comes to know the tawn, he finds so many better ways
of passing away the four-and-twenty hours, that it
were ten thousand pities he should consume his time
in that.   Far example, madam ; now my life, my life,
madam, is a perpetual stream of pleasure, that glides
through with such a variety of ertertainments, I believe the wisest of our ancestors never had the least
conception of any of 'em.   I rise, madam, when in
town, about twelve o'clock.   I don't rise sooner, because it is the worst thing in the world for the complexion ; nat that I pretend to be a beau, but a man
must endeavour to look decent, lest he makes so odious a figure in the side-bax, the ladies should be compelled to turn their eyes upon the play ; so, at twelve
o'clock, I say, I rise.   Naw, if I find it a good day, I
resalve to take the exercise of riding, so drink my
chocolate, and draw on my boots by two.   On my
return, I dress ; and after dinner, lounge perhaps to
the Opera.

Berin. Your lordship, I suppose, is fond of music ?

Ld Fop. O, passionately, on Tuesdays and Satur-
days, provided there is good company, and one is
not expected to undergo the fatigue of listening.

Aman. Does your lordship think that the case at
the Opera ?

Ld Fop. Most certainly, madam : there is my
Lady Tattle, my Lady Prate, my Lady Titter, my
Lady Sneer, my Lady Giggle, and my Lady Grin,
—these have boxes in the front, and while any favourite air is singing, are the prettiest company in
the waurld, stap my vitals ! Mayn't we hope for the
honour to see you added to our society, madam ?

Aman. Alas, my lord, I am the worst company in
the world at a concert, I'm so apt to attend to the
music.

Ld Fop. Why, madam, that is very pardonable in

the country, or at church ; but a monstrous inattention in a polite assembly.   But I am afraid I tire the
company?

Love. Not at all ; pray go on.

Ld Fop. Why then, ladies, there only remains to
add, that I generally conclude the evening at one
or other of the clubs, nat that I ever play deep ; indeed I have been for some time tied up from losing
above five thousand paunds at a sitting.

Love. But isn't your lordship sometimes obliged
to attend the weighty affairs of the nation ?

Ld Fop. Sir, as to weighty affairs, I leave them to
weighty heads; I never intend mine shall be a burthen
to my body.

Berin. Nay, my lord, but you are a pillar of the
state.

Ld Fop. An ornamental pillar, madam ; for, sooner than undergo any part of the burthen, rat me, but
the whole building should fall to the ground.

Aman. But, my lord, a fine gentleman spends a
great deal of his time in his intrigues ; you have given
us no account of them yet.

Ld Fop. (*Aside.*) Soh! She would inquire into
my amours, that's jealousy ; poor soul! I see she's
in love with me. (*To her.*) Why, madam, I should
have mentioned my intrigues, but I am really afraid
I begin to be troublesome with the length of my
visit.

Aman. Your lordship is too entertaining to grow
troublesome any where.

Ld Fop. (*Aside.*) That now was as much as if she
had said, pray make love to me. I'll let her see I'm
quick of apprehension. (*To her.*) O Lard, madam, I
had like to have forgot a secret I must needs tell
your ladyship. (*To Lov.*) Ned, you must not be so
jealous now as to listen.

Love. Not I, my lord, I am too fashionable a husband to pry into the secrets of my wife.

Ld Fop. (*To* AMAN, *squeezing her hand.*) I am in love with you to desperation, strike me speechless!

Aman. (*Giving him a box o' the ear.*) Then thus I return your passion,—an impudent fool!

Ld Fop. Gad's curse, madam, I'm a peer of the realm.

Love. Hey, what the devil, do you affront my wife, sir? Nay, then——   (*Draws and fight.*

Aman. Ah! What has my folly done?—Help! murder! help! Part them, for Heaven's sake!

Ld Fop. (*Falling back, and leaning on his sword.*) Ah! quite through the body, stap my vitals!

Enter Servants.

Love. (*Running to him.*) I hope I ha'n't killed the fool, however—bear him up—where's your wound?

Ld Fop. Just through the guts.

Love. Call a surgeon, there——unbutton him quickly.

Ld Fop. Ay, pray make haste.

Love. This mischief you may thank yourself for.

Ld Fop. I may so: love's the devil, indeed, Ned.

Enter PROBE and Servant.

Serv. Here's Mr Probe, sir, was just going by the door.

Ld Fop. He's the welcomest man alive.

Probe. Stand by, stand by, stand by: pray, gentlemen, stand by; Lord have mercy upon us! did you never see a man run through the body before? Pray, stand by.

Ld Fop. Ah! Mr Probe, I'm a dead man.

Probe. A dead man, and I by! I should laugh to see that, egad.

Love. Pr'ythee, don't stand prating, but look upon his wound.

Probe. Why, what if I won't look upon his wound this hour, sir?

Love. Why then he'll bleed to death, sir.

Probe. Why then I'll fetch him to life again, sir.

Love. 'Slife! he's run through the guts, I tell thee.

Probe. I wish he was run through the heart, and I should get the more credit by his cure.—Now I hope you are satisfied?—Come, now let me come at him —now let me come at him—(*Viewing his wound.*) Oons! what a gash is here!—Why, sir, a man may drive a coach and six horses into your body!

Ld Fop. Oh!

Probe. Why, what the devil, have you run the gentleman through with a scythe?—(*Aside.*) A little scratch between the skin and the ribs, that's all.

Love. Let me see his wound.

Probe. Then you shall dress it, sir—for if any body looks upon it, I won't.

Love. Why thou art the veriest coxcomb I ever saw.

Probe. Sir, I am not master of my trade for nothing.

Ld Fop. Surgeon!

Probe. Sir!

Ld Fop. Are there any hopes?

Probe. Hopes! I can't tell—What are you willing to give for a cure?

Ld Fop. Five hundred paunds with pleasure.

Probe. Why then perhaps there may be hopes; but we must avoid a further delay—here—help the gentleman into a chair, and carry him to my house presently—that's the properest place (*Aside.*) to bubble him out of his money.——Come, a chair—a chair quickly—there, in with him—(*They put him into a chair.*)

Ld Fop. Dear Loveless, adieu: if I die, I forgive thee; and if I live, I hope thou wilt do as much by me. I am sorry you and I should quarrel, but I hope there's an end on't; for, if you are satisfied, I am.

Love. I shall hardly think it worth my prosecuting any farther, so you may be at rest, sir.

Ld Fop. Thou art a generous fellow, strike me dumb!—(*Aside.*) but thou hast an impertinent wife, stap my vitals!

Probe. So—carry him off—carry him off——we shall have him prate himself into a fever by and by—carry him off.

(*Exeunt* LORD FOPPINGTON *and* PROBE.

Aman. Now on my knees, my dear, let me ask your pardon for my indiscretion—my own I never shall obtain.

Love. Oh, there's no harm done—you served him well.

Aman. He did indeed deserve it; but I tremble to think how dear my indiscreet resentment might have cost you.

Love. O, no matter—never trouble yourself about that.

Enter COLONEL TOWNLY.

Town. So, so, I am glad to find you all alive—I met a wounded peer carrying off—for Heaven's sake what was the matter?

Love. O, a trifle—he would have made love to my wife before my face, so she obliged him with a box o' the ear, and I run him through the body, that was all.

Town. Bagatelle on all sides!—But pray, madam, how long has this noble lord been an humble servant of yours?

Aman. This is the first I ever heard on't—so I suppose 'tis his quality more than his love has brought him into this adventure.   He thinks his title an authentic passport to every woman's heart below the degree of a peeress.

Town. He's coxcomb enough to think any thing,

but I would not have you brought into trouble for him.—I hope there's no danger of his life?

Love. None at all—he's fallen into the hands of a roguish surgeon, who, I perceive, designs to frighten a little money out of him—but I saw his wound—'tis nothing—he may go to the ball to-night if he pleases.

Town. I am glad you have corrected him without farther mischief, or you might have deprived me of the pleasure of executing a plot against his lordship, which I have been contriving with an old acquaintance of yours.

Love. Explain——

Town. His brother, Tom Fashion, is come down here, and we have it in contemplation to save him the trouble of his intended wedding; but we want your assistance. Tom would have called, but he is preparing for his enterprize, so I promised to bring you to him—so, sir, if these ladies can spare you—

Love. I'll go with you with all my heart—(*Aside.*) though I could wish, methinks, to stay and gaze a little longer on that creature—Good gods! how engaging she is—but what have I to do with beauty? I have already had my portion, and must not covet more—(*To* TOWNLY.) Come, sir, when you please.

Town. Ladies, your servant.

Aman. Mr Loveless, pray one word with you before you go.

Love. (*To* TOWNLY.) I'll overtake you, colonel. (*Exit* TOWNLY.) What would my dear?

Aman. Only a woman's foolish question;—how do you like my cousin, here?

Love. Jealous already, Amanda?

Aman. Not at all—I ask you for another reason.

Love. (*Aside.*) Whate'er her reason be, I must not tell her true. (*To her.*) Why, I confess she's handsome—but you must not think I slight your kinswoman, if I own to you, of all the women who may claim that character, she is the last would triumph in my heart.

Aman. I am satisfied.

Love. Now tell me why you ask'd?

Aman. At night I will—Adieu.

Love. (*Kissing her.*) I'm yours.—   [*Exit.*

Aman. (*Aside.*) I'm glad to find he does not like her, for I have a great mind to persuade her to come and live with me.

Berin. (*Aside.*) Soh! I find my colonel continues in his airs; there must be something more at the bottom of this than the provocation he pretends from me.

Aman. For Heaven's sake, Berinthia, tell me what way I shall take to persuade you to come and live with me?

Berin. Why one way in the world there is—and but one.

Aman. And pray what is that?

Berin. It is to assure me—I shall be very welcome.

Aman. If that be all, you shall e'en sleep here tonight.

Berin. To-night!

Aman. Yes, to-night.

Berin. Why the people where I lodge will think me mad.

Aman. Let 'em think what they please.

Berin. Say you so, Amanda?—Why then they shall think what they please—for I'm a young widow, and I care not what any body thinks.—Ah, Amanda, it's a delicious thing to be a young widow.

Aman. You'll hardly make me think so.

Berin. Puh! because you are in love with your husband—but that is not every woman's case.

Aman. I hope 'twas your's at least.

Berin. Mine, say you?—Now I have a great

mind to tell you a lie, but I shall do it so awkwardly, you'd find me out.

Aman. Then e'en speak the truth.

Berin. Shall I?—then, after all, I did love him, Amanda, as a nun does penance.

Aman. How did you live together?

Berin. Like man and wife—asunder—he loved the country—I the town.—He hawks and hounds—I coaches and equipage.—He eating and drinking—I carding and playing.—He the sound of a horn—I the squeek of a fiddle—We were dull company at table—worse a-bed: whenever we met we gave one another the spleen, and never agreed but once, which was about lying alone.

Aman. But, tell me one thing truly and sincerely —notwithstanding all these jars, did not his death at last extremely trouble you?

Berin. O yes.—I was forced to wear an odious widow's band a twelve-month for't.

Aman. Women, I find, have different inclinations: —prythee, Berinthia, instruct me a little farther—for I'm so great a novice, I'm almost ashamed on't.— Not, Heaven knows, that what you call intrigues have any charms for me—the practical part of all unlawful love is—

Berin. O 'tis abominable—but for the speculative, that we must all confess is entertaining enough.

Aman. Pray, be so just then to me, to believe, 'tis with a world of innocence I would inquire, whether you think those we call women of reputation do really escape all other men, as they do those shadows of beaus?

Berin. O no, Amanda—there are a sort of men make dreadful work amongst 'em—men that may be called the beaus' antipathy—for they agree in nothing but walking upon two legs. These have brains—the beau has none.—These are in love with their mistress— the beau with himself.—They take care of their re-

5

putation—he's industrious to destroy it.—They are decent—he's a fop.—They are men—he's an ass.

Aman. If this be their character, I fancy we had here e'en now a pattern of 'em both.

Berin. His lordship and Colonel Townly?

Aman. The same.

Berin. As for the lord, he's eminently so ; and for the other, I can assure you there's not a man in town who has a better interest with the women, that are worth having an interest with.

Aman. He answers then the opinion I ever had of him—Heavens! what a difference there is between a man like him, and that vain nauseous fop, Lord Foppington!—(*Taking her hand.*) I must acquaint you with the secret, cousin—'tis not that fool alone has talked to me of love—Townly has been tampering too.

Berin. (*Aside.*) So, so—here the mystery comes out!—Colonel Townly!—impossible, my dear!

Aman. 'Tis true, indeed!—though he has done it in vain; nor do I think that all the merit of mankind combined could shake the tender love I bear my husband; yet I will own to you, Berinthia, I did not start at his addresses, as when they came from one whom I contemned.

Berin. (*Aside*) O this is better and better—well said, innocence!—and you really think, my dear, that nothing could abate your constancy and attachment to your husband?

Aman. Nothing, I am convinced.

Berin. What if you found he loved another woman better?

Aman. Well!

Berin. Well!—why, were I that thing they call a slighted wife, somebody should run the risk of being that thing they call—a husband.

Aman. O fie, Berinthia! no revenge should ever

be taken against a husband—but to wrong his bed is a vengeance which of all vengeance—

Berin. Is the sweetest! ha, ha, ha!—don't I talk madly?

Aman. Madly indeed!

Berin. Yet I'm very innocent.

Aman. That I dare swear you are. I know how to make allowances for your humour; but you resolve then never to marry again?

Berin. O no! I resolve I will.

Aman. How so?

Berin. That I never may.

Aman. You banter me.

Berin. Indeed I don't, but I consider I'm a woman, and form my resolutions accordingly.

Aman. Well, my opinion is, form what resolution you will, matrimony will be the end on't.

Berin. I doubt it—but ah, Heavens!—I have business at home, and am half an hour too late.

Aman. As you are to return with me, I'll just give some orders, and walk with you.

Berin. Well, make haste, and we'll finish this subject as we go. [*Exit* AMANDA.] Ah! poor Amanda, you have led a country life! Well, this discovery is lucky! Base Townly! at once false to me, and treacherous to his friend! and my innocent demure cousin too! I have it in my power to be revenged on her, however. Her husband, if I have any skill in countenance, would be as happy in my smiles as Townly can hope to be in her's. I'll make the experiment, come what will on't. The woman who can forgive the being robb'd of a favour'd lover must be either an idiot or a wanton.

[*Exeunt.*

ACT THE THIRD.

SCENE I.

Enter LORD FOPPINGTON *and* LA VAROLE.

Ld Fop. Hey, fellow, let my vis-a-vis come to the door.

La Var. Will your lordship venture so soon to expose yourself to the weather?

Ld Fop. Sir, I will venture as soon as I can to expose myself to the ladies.

La Var. I wish your lordship would please to keep house a little longer; I'm afraid your honour does not well consider your wound.

Ld Fop. My wound! I would not be in eclipse another day, though I had as many wounds in my body as I have had in my heart. So mind, Varole, let these cards be left as directed. For this evening I shall wait on my father-in-law, Sir Tunbelly, and I mean to commence my devoirs to the lady, by giving an entertainment at her father's expence; and, hark thee, tell Mr Loveless I request he and his company will honour me with their presence, or I shall think we are not friends.

La Var. I will be sure.   [*Exit.*

Enter YOUNG FASHION.

Y. Fash. Brother, your servant, how do you find yourself to-day ?

Ld Fop. So well, that I have ordered my coach to the door ; so there's no danger of death this baut, Tam.

Y. Fash. I'm very glad of it.

Ld Fop. (*Aside.*) That I believe's a lie.—Pr'ythee, Tam, tell me one thing, did your heart cut a caper up to your mauth, when you heard I was ran through the bady ?

Y. Fash. Why do you think it should ?

Ld Fop. Because I remember mine did so when I heard my uncle was shot through the head.

Y. Fash. It then did very ill.

Ld Fop. Pr'ythee, why so ?

Y. Fash. Because he used you very well.

Ld Fop. Well !—Naw, strike me dumb, he starved me—he has let me want a thausand women for want of a thausand paund.

Y. Fash. Then he hindered you from making a great many ill bargains ; for I think no woman worth money that will take money.

Ld Fop. If I was a younger brother, I should think so too.

Y. Fash. Then you are seldom much in love ?

Ld Fop. Never, stap my vitals.

Y. Fash. Why then did you make all this bustle about Amanda ?

Ld Fop. Because she was a woman of an insolent virtue, and I thought myself piqued in honour to debauch her.

Y. Fash. (*Aside.*) Very well. Here's a rare fellow for you to have the spending of five thousand pounds a year ! But now for my business with him. —Brother, though I know to talk of business (especially of money) is a theme not quite so entertain-

ing to you as that of the ladies, my necessities are
such, I hope you'll have patience to hear me.

Ld Fop. The greatness of your necessities, Tam,
is the worst argument in the warld for your being
patiently heard.   I do believe you are going to make
a very good speech, but, strike me dumb, it has the
worst beginning of any speech I have heard this
twelvemonth.

Y. Fash. I'm sorry you think so.

Ld Fop. I do believe thou art—but come, let's
know the affair quickly.

Y. Fash. Why then, my case in a word is this—
The necessary expences of my travels have so much
exceeded the wretched income of my annuity, that I
have been forced to mortgage it for five hundred
pounds, which is spent; so, unless you are so kind
as to assist me in redeeming it, I know no remedy
but to take a purse.

Ld Fop. Why, faith, Tam, to give you my sense
of the thing, I do think taking a purse the best remedy in the warld; for if you succeed you are relieved that way, if you are taken—you are relieved
t' other.

Y. Fash. I'm glad to see you are in so pleasant a
humour; I hope I shall find the effects on't.

Ld Fop. Why, do you really then think it a reasonable thing that I should give you five hundred
paunds?

Y. Fash. I do not ask it as a due, brother, I am
willing to receive it as a favour.

Ld Fop. Then thou art willing to receive it any
how, strike me speechless.—But these are d—ned
times to give money in; taxes are so great, repairs
so exorbitant, tenants such rogues, and bouquets so
dear, that, the devil take me, I am reduced to that
extremity in my cash, I have been forced to retrench
in that one article of sweet pawder, till I have brought

it dawn to five guineas a maunth—now judge, Tam, whether I can spare you five hundred paunds?

Y. Fash. If you can't I must starve, that's all. (*Aside.*) Damn him!

Ld Fop. All I can say is, you should have been a better husband.

Y. Fash. Ouns!—If you can't live upon ten thousand a year, how do you think I could do't upon two hundred?

Ld Fop. Don't be in a passion, Tam, for passion is the most unbecoming thing in the warld—to the face—Look you, I don't love to say any thing to you to make you melancholy, but upon this occasion I must take leave to put you in mind, that a running horse does require more attendance than a coach horse.—Nature has made some difference 'twixt you and me.

Y. Fash. She has made you older. (*Aside.*) Plague take her!

Ld Fop. That is not all, Tam.

Y. Fash. Why, what is there else?

Ld Fop. (*Looking first upon himself and then upon his brother.*) Ask the ladies.

Y. Fash. Why, thou essence-bottle, thou musk-cat,—dost thou then think thou hast any advantage over me but what fortune has given thee?

Ld Fop. I do, stap my vitals!

Y. Fash. Now, by all that's great and powerful, thou art the prince of coxcombs.

Ld Fop. Sir, I am proud at being at the head of so prevailing a party.

Y. Fash. Will nothing then provoke thee?—Draw, coward!

Ld Fop. Look you, Tam, you know I have always taken you for a mighty dull fellow; and here is one of the foolishest plats broke out that I have seen a lang time. Your poverty makes life so burthensome to you, you would provoke me to a quarrel, in hopes

either to slip through my lungs into my estate, or to
get yourself run through the guts, to put an end to
your pain; but I will disappoint you in both your designs; far, with the temper of a philasapher, and the
discretion of a statesman—I shall leave the room with
my sword in the scabbard.   (*Exit.*

Y. Fash. So!-farewell, brother; and now, Conscience, I defy thee.——Lory!

Enter LORY.

Lory. Sir?

Y. Fash. Here's rare news, Lory; his lordship has
given me a pill has purged off all my scruples.

Lory. Then my heart's at ease again; for I have
been in a lamentable fright, sir, ever since your conscience had the impudence to intrude into your company.

Y. Fash. Be at peace; it will come there no
more; my brother has given it a wring by the nose,
and I have kicked it down stairs. So run away to
the inn, get the chaise ready quickly, and bring it to
Dame Coupler's without a moment's delay.

Lory. Then, sir, you are going straight about the
fortune?

Y. Fash. I am.—Away—fly, Lory.

Lory. The happiest day I ever saw. I'm upon the
wing already.   (*Exeunt severally.*

SCENE II.

A Garden.

Enter LOVELESS *and Servant.*

Love. Is my wife within ?

Serv. No, sir, she has been gone out this half hour.

Love. Well, leave me. [*Exit Servant.*] How strangely does my mind run on this widow—never was my heart so suddenly seized on before—that my wife should pick out her, of all woman-kind, to be her play-fellow !—But what fate does let fate answer for—I sought it not—soh!—by heavens! here she comes.

Enter BERINTHIA.

Berin. What makes you look so thoughtful, sir ? I hope you are not ill ?

Love. I was debating, madam, whether I was so or not; and that was it which made me look so thoughtful.

Berin. Is it then so hard a matter to decide? I thought all people were acquainted with their own bodies, though few people know their own minds.

Love. What if the distemper I suspect be in the mind ?

Berin. Why then I'll undertake to prescribe you a cure.

Love. Alas ! you undertake you know not what.

Berin. So far at least then you allow me to be a physician ?

Love. Nay, I'll allow you to be so yet farther; for I have reason to believe, should I put myself into your hands, you would increase my distemper.

Berin. How?

Love. Oh, you might betray my complaints to my wife.

Berin. And so lose all my practice.

Love. Will you then keep my secret?

Berin. I will.

Love. I'm satisfied. Now hear my symptoms, and give me your advice. The first were these; when I saw you at the play, a random glance you threw at first alarmed me. I could not turn my eyes from whence the danger came—I gazed upon you till my heart began to pant——nay, even now, on your approaching me, my illness is so increased, that if you do not help me, I shall, whilst you look on, consume to ashes.   (*Taking her hand.*

Berin. (*Breaking from him.*) O Lord, let me go, 'tis the plague, and we shall be infected!

Love. Then we'll die together, my charming angel.

Berin. O Gad! the devil's in you! Lord, let me go—here's somebody coming!

Enter Servant.

Serv. Sir, my lady's come home, and desires to speak with you.

Love. Tell her I'm coming.   (*Exit Servant.*

(*To* BERINTHIA.) But before I go, one glass of nectar to drink her health.

Berin. Stand off, or I shall hate you, by heavens!

Love. (*Kissing her.*) In matters of love, a woman's oath is no more to be minded than a man's.

                                   (*Exit* LOVE.

Berin. Um!

Enter TOWNLY.

Town. Soh! what's here?—Berinthia and Loveless,

—and in close conversation!—I cannot now wonder at her indifference in excusing herself to me!—O, rare woman!—Well then, let Loveless look to his wife, 'twill be but the retort courteous on both sides. (*To* BERINTHIA.) Your servant, madam, I need not ask you how you do, you have got so good a colour.

Berin. No better than I used to have, I suppose.

Town. A little more blood in your cheeks.

Berin. I have been walking.

Town. Is that all? Pray was it Mr Loveless went from here just now?

Berin. O yes; he has been walking with me.

Town. He has!

Berin. Upon my word, I think he is a very agreeable man; and there is certainly something particularly insinuating in his address!

Town. So, so! she hasn't even the modesty to dissemble! Pray, madam, may I, without impertinence, trouble you with a few serious questions?

Berin. As many as you please; but pray let them be as little serious as possible.

Town. Is it not near two years since I presumed to address you?

Berin. I don't know exactly; but it has been a tedious long time.

Town. Have I not, during that period, had every reason to believe that my assiduities were far from being unacceptable?

Berin. Why, to do you justice, you have been extremely troublesome; and I confess I have been more civil to you than you deserved.

Town. Did I not come to this place at your express desire? and for no purpose but the honour of meeting you? and, after wasting a month in disappointment, have you condescended to explain, or in the slightest way apologize for your conduct?

Berin. O heavens! apologize for my conduct!—apologize to you!—O, you barbarian!—But, pray now, my good serious colonel, have you any thing more to add?

Town. Nothing, madam. but that, after such behaviour, I am less surprised at what I saw just now; it is not very wonderful that the woman who can trifle with the delicate addresses of an honourable lover, should be found coquetting with the husband of her friend.

Berin. Very true—no more wonderful than it was for this *honourable* lover to divert himself, in the absence of this coquet, with endeavouring to seduce his friend's wife! O colonel, colonel, don't talk of honour or your friend, for heaven's sake!

Town. 'Sdeath! how came she to suspect this?—Really, madam, I don't understand you.

Berin. Nay—nay—you saw I did not pretend to misunderstand you.—But here comes the lady—perhaps you would be glad to be left with her for an explanation.

Town. O, madam, this recrimination is a poor resource; and, to convince you how much you are mistaken, I beg leave to decline the happiness you propose me.—Madam, your servant.

Enter AMANDA. (TOWNLY *whispers* AMANDA, *and exit.*)

Berin. He carries it off well, however—upon my word—very well!—how tenderly they part!—So, cousin,—I hope you have not been chiding your admirer for being with me. I assure you we have been talking of you.

Aman. Fie, Berinthia!—my admirer!—will you never learn to talk in earnest of any thing?

Berin. Why, this shall be in earnest, if you please; for my part I only tell you matter of fact.

Aman. I'm sure there's so much jest and earnest in what you say to me on this subject, I scarcely know how to take it. I have just parted with Mr Loveless

Perhaps it is my fancy; but I think there is an alteration in his manner, which alarms me.

Berin. And so you are jealous? is that all?

Aman. That all!—is jealousy then nothing?

Berin. It should be nothing, if I were in your case.

Aman. Why what would you do?

Berin. I'd cure myself.

Aman. How?

Berin. Care as little for my husband as he did for me. Look you, Amanda, you may build castles in the air, and fume and fret, and grow thin and lean, and pale, and ugly, if you please; but I tell you, no man worth having is true to his wife, or ever was, or ever will be so.

Aman. Do you then really think he's false to me? for I did not suspect him.

Berin. Think so!—I am sure of it.

Aman. You are sure on't?

Berin. Positively—he fell in love at the play.

Aman. Right—the very same—but who could have told you this?

Berin. Um—O—Townly!—I suppose your husband has made him his confidant.

Aman. O base Loveless!—and what did Townly say on't?

Berin. So, so—why should she ask that?—(*Aside*)—Say!—why, he abused Loveless extremely, and said all the tender things of you in the world.

Aman. Did he?—Oh! my heart—I'm very ill.—I must go to my chamber—dear Berinthia, don't leave me a moment. [*Exit.*

Berin. No;—don't fear.—So!—there is certainly some affection on her side, at least, towards Townly. If it prove so, and her agreeable husband perseveres—Heaven send me resolution!—Well—how this business will end I know not; but I seem to be in as fair a way to lose my gallant colonel, as a boy is to be a rogue when he's put clerk to an attorney. [*Exit.*

SCENE III.

A Country House.

Enter YOUNG FASHION *and* LORY.

Y. Fash. So—here's our inheritance, Lory, if we can but get into possession—but methinks the seat of our family looks like Noah's ark, as if the chief part on't were designed for the fowls of the air and the beasts of the field.

Lory. Pray, sir, don't let your head run upon the orders of building here—get but the heiress, let the devil take the house.

Y. Fash. Get but the house! let the devil take the heiress, I say—but come, we have no time to squander, knock at the door—

[LORY *knocks two or three times.*
What the devil, have they got no ears in this house? —knock harder.

Lory. Egad, sir, this will prove some enchanted castle—we shall have the giant come out by and by with his club, and beat our brains out. (*Knocks again.*

Y. Fash. Hush—they come—(*From within.*) Who is there?

Lory. Open the door and see—is that your country breeding?

Serv. (*Within.*) Ay, but two words to that bargain —Tummas, is the blunderbuss primed?

Y. Fash. Ouns! give 'em good words, Lory, or we shall be shot here a fortune-catching!

Lory. Egad, sir, I think you're in the right on't— ho!—Mr What-d'ye-callum—will you please to let us

in ? or are we to be left here to grow like willows by
your moat side ?

(*Servant appears at the window with a blunderbuss.*)

Serv. Weel naw, what's ya're business ?

Y. Fash. Nothing, sir, but to wait upon Sir Tunbelly, with your leave.

Serv. To weat upon Sir Tunbelly !—why you'll
find that's just as Sir Tunbelly pleases.

Y. Fash. But will you do me the favour, sir, to
know whether Sir Tunbelly pleases or not ?

Serv. Why look you, d'ye see, with good words
much may be done.—Ralph, go thy waes, and ask
Sir Tunbelly if he pleases to be waited upon—and,
dost hear ? call to nurse that she may lock up Miss
Hoyden before the geat's open.

Y. Fash. D'ye hear that, Lory ?

Enter SIR TUNBELLY, *with Servants, armed with guns,
clubs, pitchforks, &c.*

Lory (*Running behind his master.*) O Lord, O, O
Lord, Lord, we are both dead men !

Y. Fash. Take heed, fool,—thy fear will ruin us.

Lory. My fear, sir ! 'sdeath, sir ! I fear nothing !—
(*Aside*) Would I were well up to the chin in a horse-
pond !

Sir Tun. Who is it here has any business with me ?

Y. Fash. Sir, 'tis I, if your name be Sir Tunbelly
Clumsy ?

Sir Tun. Sir, my name is Sir Tunbelly Clumsy,
whether you have any business with me or not—
so you see I am not ashamed of my name, nor my face
either.

Y. Fash. Sir, you have no cause that I know of.

Sir Tun. Sir, if you have no cause either, I desire
to know who you are ; for 'till I know your name, I
sha'n't ask you to come into my house : and when I
do know your name, 'tis six to four I don't ask you
then.

Y. Fash. (*Giving him a letter.*) Sir, I hope you'll find this letter an authentic passport.

Sir Tun. God's my life, from Mrs Coupler!—I ask your lordship's pardon ten thousand times—(*To his Servant*)—Here, run in a doors quickly ; get a Scotch coal fire in the great parlour—set all the Turkey-work chairs in their places ; get the brass candlesticks out, and be sure stick the socket full of laurel, run—(*Turning to* YOUNG FASHION.) My lord, I ask your lordship's pardon—(*To Servant.*) and, do you hear ? run away to nurse, bid her let Miss Hoyden loose again.   [*Exit Servant.*
(*To* YOUNG FASHION.) I hope your honour will excuse the disorder of my family—we are not used to receive men of your lordship's great quality every day—Pray where are your coaches and servants, my lord ?

Y. Fash. Sir, that I might give you and your daughter a proof how impatient I am to be nearer akin to you, I left my equipage to follow me, and came away post with only one servant.

Sir Tun. Your lordship does me too much honour——It was exposing your person to too much fatigue and danger, I protest it was——but my daughter shall endeavour to make you what amends she can—and, though I say it that should not say it, Hoyden has charms.

Y. Fash Sir, I am not a stranger to them, though I am to her : common fame has done her justice.

Sir Tun. My lord, I am common fame's very grateful humble servant.—My lord, my girl's young—Hoyden is young, my lord ; but this I must say for her, what she wants in art she has by nature,—what she wants in experience she has in breeding—and what's wanting in her age is made good in her constitution—so pray, my lord, walk in, pray, my lord, walk in.

Y. Fash. Sir, I wait upon you.
                                    [*Exeunt through the gate.*

Miss Hoyden *sola.*

Miss Hoy. Sure, nobody was ever used as I am. I know well enough what other girls do, for all they think to make a fool of me. It's well I have a husband a coming, or I'cod I'd marry the baker, I would so.—Nobody can knock at the gate, but presently I must be lock'd up—and here's the young greyhound can run loose about the house all the day long, so she can.— Tis very well— (*Nurse without opening the door.*)

Nurse. Miss Hoyden, Miss, Miss, Miss, Miss Hoyden !

Enter Nurse.

Miss Hoy. Well, what do you make such a noise for, ha ?—what do you din a body's ears for ?—can't one be at quiet for you ?

Nurse. What do I din your ears for !—here's one come will din your ears for you.

Miss Hoy. What care I who's come ?—I care not a fig who comes, nor who goes, as long as I must be lock'd up like the ale-cellar.

Nurse. That, Miss, is for fear you should be drank before you are ripe.

Miss Hoy. O don't you trouble your head about that, I'm as ripe as you, though not so mellow.

Nurse Very well—now I have a good mind to lock you up again, and not let you see my lord to-night.

Miss Hoy. My lord ! why is my husband come ?

Nurse. Yes, marry is he, and a goodly person too.

Miss Hoy. (*Hugging Nurse.*) O, my dear nurse, forgive me this once, and I'll never misuse you again ; no, if I do, you shall give me three thumps on the back and a great pinch by the cheek.

Nurse. Ah ! the poor thing, see how it melts ! it's as full of good-nature as an egg's full of meat.

Miss Hoy. But, my dear nurse, don't lie now ; is he come by your troth ?

Nurse. Yes, by my truly is he.

Miss Hoy. O Lord! I'll go and put on my laced tucker, though I'm lock'd up a month for't.

[*Exit running.*

ACT THE FOURTH.

SCENE I.

Enter MISS HOYDEN *and Nurse.*

Nurse. Well, Miss, how do you like your husband that is to be?

Miss Hoy. O Lord, nurse, I'm so overjoy'd, I can scarce contain myself.

Nurse. O but you must have a care of being too fond, for men now-a-days hate a woman that loves 'em.

Miss Hoy. Love him! why do you think I love him, nurse? I'cod, I would not care he was hang'd, so I were but once married to him.—No, that which pleases me, is to think what work I'll make when I get to London; for when I am a wife and a lady both, I'cod I'll flaunt it with the best of 'em. Ay, and I shall have money enough to do so too, nurse.

Nurse. Ah! there's no knowing that, Miss; for, though these lords have a power of wealth indeed, yet, as I have heard say, they give it all to their sluts and their trulls, who joggle it about in their coaches, with a murrain to 'em, whilst poor madam sits sighing and wishing, and has not a spare half-crown to buy her a Practice of Piety.

Miss Hoy. O, but for that, don't deceive yourself, nurse, for this I must say of my lord, he's as free as an open house at Christmas. For this very morning he told me I should have six hundred a year to buy pins. Now, nurse, if he gives me six hundred a year to buy pins, what do you think he'll give me to buy fine petticoats?

Nurse. Ah, my dearest, he deceives thee foully, and he's no better than a rogue for his pains. These Londoners have got a gibberage with 'em would confound a gipsey. That which they call pin-money is to buy their wives every thing in the versal world, down to their very shoe-knots—Nay, I have heard folks say, that some ladies, if they will have gallants, as they call 'em, are forced to find them out of their pin-money too. But, look, look, if his honour be not coming to you.—Now, if I were sure you would behave yourself handsomely, and not disgrace me that have brought you up, I'd leave you alone together.

Miss Hoy. That's my best nurse, do as you'd be done by—trust us together this once, and if I don't shew my breeding, may I never be married, but die an old maid.

Nurse. Well, this once I'll venture you.—But if you disparage me—

Miss Hoy. Never fear.   [*Exit Nurse.*

Enter YOUNG FASHION.

Y. Fash. Your servant, madam; I'm glad to find you alone, for I have something of importance to speak to you about.

Miss Hoy. Sir, (my lord I meant) you may speak to me about what you please, I shall give you a civil answer.

Y. Fash. You give me so obliging a one, it encourages me to tell you in a few words what I think both for your interest and mine.   Your father, I suppose you know, has resolved to make me happy in being your husband, and I hope I may depend on your consent to perform what he desires.

Miss Hoy. Sir, I never disobey my father in any thing but eating green gooseberries.

Y. Fash. So good a daughter must needs be an admirable wife—I am therefore impatient till you are mine, and hope you will so far consider the violence of my love, that you won't have the cruelty to defer my happiness so long as your father designs it.

Miss Hoy. Pray, my lord, how long is that?

Y. Fash. Madam—a thousand years—a whole week.

Miss Hoy. A week!—Why I shall be an old woman by that time.

Y. Fash. And I an old man.

Miss Hoy. Why I thought it was to be to-morrow morning, as soon as I was up. I'm sure nurse told me so.

Y. Fash. And it shall be to-morrow morning, if you'll consent.

Miss Hoy. If I'll consent! Why I thought I was to obey you as my husband?

Y. Fash. That's when we are married; till then I'm to obey you.

Miss Hoy. Why then if we are to take it by turns, it's the same thing—I'll obey you now, and when we are married you shall obey me.

Y. Fash. With all my heart. But I doubt we must get nurse on our side, or we shall hardly prevail with the chaplain.

Miss Hoy. No more we sha'n't indeed, for he loves her better than he loves his pulpit, and would always be a preaching to her by his good-will.

Y. Fash. Why then, my dear, if you'll call her hither, we'll try to persuade her presently.

Miss Hoy. O Lord, I can tell you a way how to persuade her to any thing.

Y. Fash. How's that?

Miss Hoy. Why tell her she's a handsome, comely woman, and give her half-a-crown.

Y. Fash. Nay, if that will do, she shall have half a score of them.

Miss Hoy. O Gemini, for half that she'd marry you herself.—I'll run and call her.   [*Exit.*

Y. Fash. So, matters go swimmingly. This is a rare girl, i'faith. I shall have a fine time on't with her at London. But no matter—she brings me an estate will afford me a separate maintenance.

Enter LORY.

Y. Fash. So, Lory, what's the matter?

Lory. Here. sir; an intercepted packet from the enemy—your brother's postillion brought it—I knew the livery, pretended to be a servant of Sir Tunbelly's, and so got possession of the letter.

Y. Fash. (*Looking at it.*) Ouns!—He tells Sir Tunbelly here that he will be with him this evening, with a large party to supper—'Egad ! I must marry the girl directly.

Lory. O zounds, sir, directly to be sure ! Here she comes.   [*Exit* LORY.

Y. Fash. And the old Jezabel with her. She has a thorough procuring countenance however.

Enter MISS HOYDEN *and Nurse.*

Y. Fash. How do you do, Mrs Nurse ?—I desired your young lady would give me leave to see you, that I might thank you for your extraordinary care and conduct in her education; pray accept of this small acknowledgement for it at present, and depend upon my farther kindness when I shall be that happy thing her husband.

Nurse. (*Aside.*) Gold, by Maakins!—Your honour's goodness is too great.   Alas! all I can boast of is, I gave her pure milk, and so your honour would have said, an you had seen how the poor thing thrived—and how it would look up in my face—and crow and laugh it would.

Miss Hoy. (*To Nurse, taking her angrily aside.*) Pray one word with you. Pr'ythee, nurse, don't stand ripping up old stories, to make one ashamed before one's love; do you think such a fine proper gentleman as he is cares for a fiddle-come tale of a child? If you have a mind to make him have a good opinion of a woman, don't tell him what one did then, tell him what one can do now. (*To him.*) I hope your honour will excuse my mis-manners to whisper before you, it was only to give some orders about the family.

Y. Fash. O every thing, madam, is to give way to business; besides, good housewifery is a very commendable quality in a young lady.

Miss Hoy. Pray, sir, are young ladies good housewives at London town? Do they darn their own linen?

Y. Fash. O no;—they study how to spend money, not to save.

Miss Hoy. I'cod, I don't know but that may be better sport, ha, nurse?

Y. Fash. Well, you shall have your choice when you come there.

Miss Hoy. Shall I?—then by my troth I'll get there as fast as I can. (*To Nurse.*) His honour desires you'll be so kind as to let us be married to-morrow.

Nurse. To-morrow, my dear madam!

Y. Fash. Ay faith, nurse, you may well be surprised at Miss's wanting to put it off so long—to-mor-

row ! no, no,—'tis now, this very hour, I would have
the ceremony perform'd.

Miss Hoy. I'cod with all my heart.

Nurse. O mercy ! worse and worse.

Y. Fash. Yes, sweet nurse, now, and privately.
For all things being signed and sealed, why should
Sir Tunbelly make us stay a week for a wedding
dinner ?

Nurse. But if you should be married now, what
will you do when Sir Tunbelly calls for you to be
wedded ?

Miss Hoy. Why then we will be married again.

Nurse. What ! twice, my child ?

Miss Hoy. I'cod, I don't care how often I'm married, not I.

Nurse. Well—I'm such a tender-hearted fool, I find
I can refuse you nothing ; so you shall e'en follow
your own inventions.

Miss Hoy. Shall I ?—(*Aside.*) O Lord, I could leap
over the moon !

Y. Fash. Dear nurse, this goodness of your's sha'n't
go unrewarded. But now you must employ your
power with the chaplain, that he may do his friendly
office too, and then we shall be all happy. Do you
think you can prevail with him ?

Nurse. Prevail with him !—or he shall never prevail with me, I can tell him that.

Y. Fash. I'm glad to hear it : however, to strength-
en your interest with him, you may let him know I
have several fat livings in my gift, and that the first
that falls shall be in your disposal.

Nurse. Nay then, I'll make him marry more folks
than one, I'll promise him.

Miss Hoy. Faith do, nurse, make him marry you
too, I'm sure he'll do't for a fat living.

Y. Fash. Well, nurse, while you go and settle matters with him, your lady and I will go and take a
walk in the garden.   [*Exit Nurse.*

Y. Fash. (*Giving her his hand.*) Come, madam, dare you venture yourself alone with me?

Miss. O dear, yes, sir, I don't think you'll do any thing to me I need be afraid on.   [*Exeunt.*

SCENE II.

Enter AMANDA, *her Woman following.*

Maid. If you please, madam, only to say whether you'll have me buy them or not?

Aman. Yes—no—go—teazer! I care not what you do—pr'ythee leave me.   (*Exit Maid.*

Enter BERINTHIA.

Berin. What in the name of Jove's the matter with you?

Aman. The matter, Berinthia? I'm almost mad; I'm plagued to death.

Berin. Who is it that plagues you?

Aman. Who do you think should plague a wife but her husband?

Berin. O ho! is it come to that?—we shall have you wish yourself a widow by and bye.

Aman. Would I were any thing but what I am!— a base ungrateful man, to use me thus!

Berin. What, has he given you fresh reasons to suspect his wandering?

Aman. Every hour gives me reason.

Berin. And yet, Amanda, you perhaps at this moment cause in another's breast the same tormenting doubts and jealousies which you feel so sensibly yourself.

Aman. Heaven knows I would not!

Berin. Why, you can't tell but there may be some

2

one as tenderly attached to Townly, whom you boast
of as your conquest, as you can be to your husband.

Aman. I'm sure I never encouraged his pretensions.

Berin. Pshaw ! pshaw !—no sensible man ever
perseveres to love without encouragement. Why
have you not treated him as you have Lord Foppington ?

Aman. Because he has not presumed so far. But
let us drop the subject. Men, not women, are rid-
dles. Mr Loveless now follows some flirt for variety,
whom I'm sure he does not like so well as he does
me.

Berin. That's more than you know, madam.

Aman. Why, do you know the ugly thing?

Berin. I think I can guess at the person—but she's
no such ugly thing neither.

Aman. Is she very handsome ?

Berin. Truly I think so.

Aman. Whate'er she be, I'm sure he does not like
her well enough to bestow any thing more than a
little outward gallantry upon her.

Berin. (*Aside.*) Outward gallantry !—I can't bear
this—Come, come, don't you be too secure, Amanda; while you suffer Townly to imagine that you do
not detest him for his designs on you, you have no
right to complain that your husband is engaged elsewhere. But here comes the person we were speaking of.

Enter TOWNLY.

Town. Ladies, as I come uninvited, I beg, if I intrude, you will use the same freedom in turning me
out again.

Aman. I believe, sir, it is near the time Mr Loveless said he would be at home. He talked of accepting of Lord Foppington's invitation to sup at Sir
Tunbelly Clumsy's.

Town. His lordship has done me the honour to invite me also. If you'll let me escort you, I'll let you into a mystery as we go, in which you must play a part when we arrive.

Aman. But we have two hours yet to spare—the carriages are not ordered till eight, and it is not a five minutes drive. So, cousin, let us keep the colonel to play piquet with us, till Mr Loveless comes home.

Berin. As you please, madam, but you know I have a letter to write.

Town. Madam, you know you may command me, though I'm a very wretched gamester.

Aman. O, you play well enough to lose your money, and that's all the ladies require—and so, without any more ceremony, let us go into the next room, and call for cards and candles.   (*Exeunt.*

SCENE III.

BERINTHIA's *Dressing-Room.*

Enter LOVELESS.

Love. So—thus far all's well—I have got into her dressing-room, and it being dusk, I think nobody has perceived me steal into the house. I heard Berinthia tell my wife she had some particular letters to write this evening, before we went to Sir Tunbelly's, and here are the implements for correspondence—How shall I muster up assurance to shew myself when she comes?—I think she has given me encouragement—and, to do my impudence justice, I have made the most of it.—I hear a door open, and some one com-

ing; if it should be my wife, what the devil should I
say?—I believe she mistrusts me, and, by my life, I
don't deserve her tenderness; however, I am determined to reform, though not yet.   Hah!—Berinthia
—so I'll step in here till I see what sort of humour
she is in.   (*Goes into the closet*.

Enter BERINTHIA.

Berin. Was ever so provoking a situation!—To
think I should sit and hear him compliment Amanda
to my face!—I have lost all patience with them both.
I would not for something have Loveless know what
temper of mind they have piqued me into, yet I can't
bear to leave them together.   No—I'll put my papers
away, and return to disappoint them.   (*Goes to the
closet.*) O Lord! a ghost! a ghost! a ghost!

Enter LOVELESS.

Love. Peace, my angel!—'tis no ghost—but one
worth a hundred spirits.
Berin. How, sir, have you had the insolence to
presume to—run in again, here's somebody coming.

Enter Maid.

Maid. O Lord, ma'am, what's the matter?
Berin. O, Heavens, I'm almost frightened out of
my wits!—I thought verily I had seen a ghost, and
'twas nothing but a black hood pinned against the wall.
—You may go again, I am the fearfullest fool!
                                       (*Exit Maid.*

Re-enter LOVELESS.

Love. Is the coast clear?
Berin. The coast clear!—Upon my word I wonder
at your assurance.
Love. Why then you wonder before I have given
you a proof of it.   But where's my wife?
Berin. At cards.

Love. With whom ?

Berin. With Townly.

Love. Then we are safe enough.

Berin. You are so !—Some husbands would be of another mind were he at cards with their wives.

Love. And they'd be in the right on't too—but I dare trust mine.

Berin. Indeed!—And she, I doubt not, has the same confidence in you. Yet do you think she'd be content to come and find you here ?

Love. 'Egad, as you say, that's true—then, for fear she should come, hadn't we better go into the next room out of her way ?

Berin. What—in the dark ?

Love. Ay—or with a light, which you please.

Berin. You are certainly very impudent.

Love. Nay then—let me conduct you, my angel.

Berin. Hold, hold, you are mistaken in your angel, I assure you.

Love. I hope not, for by this hand I swear—

Berin. Come, come, let go my hand or I shall hate you; I'll cry out as I live.

Love. Impossible !—you cannot be so cruel.

Berin. Ha !—here's some one coming—be gone instantly.

Love. Will you promise to return if I remain here ?

Berin. Never trust myself in a room with you again while I live.

Love. But I have something particular to communicate to you.

Berin. Well, well, before we go to Sir Tunbelly's I'll walk upon the lawn. If you are fond of a moonlight evening, you will find me there.

Love. I'faith, they're coming here now.—I take you at your word. (*Exit* LOVELESS *into the closet.*

Berin. 'Tis Amanda, as I live—I hope she has not heard his voice. Though I mean she should have her share of jealousy in turn.

Enter AMANDA.

Aman. Berinthia, why did you leave me?

Berin. I thought I only spoiled your party.

Aman. Since you have been gone, Townly has at‑tempted to renew his importunities——I must break with him—for I cannot venture to acquaint Mr Love‑less with his conduct.

Berin. O no—Mr Loveless mustn't know of it by any means.

Aman. O not for the world—I wish, Berinthia, you would undertake to speak to Townly on the sub‑ject.

Berin. Upon my word it would be a very pleasant subject for me to talk to him on—But come—let us go back, and you may depend on't I'll not leave you together again if I can help it.   (*Exeunt.*

Enter LOVELESS.

Love. So—so!—a pretty piece of business I have overheard—Townly makes love to my wife—and I'm not to know it for the world—I must inquire into this—and, by Heaven, if I find that Amanda has in the smallest degree——Yet what have I been at here?—O, 'sdeath! that's no rule.

> That wife alone unsullied credit wins,
> Whose virtues can atone her husband's sins;
> Thus while the man has other nymphs in view,
> It suits the woman to be doubly true.   [*Exit.*

ACT THE FIFTH.

SCENE I.

A Garden—Moon-light.

Enter LOVELESS.

Love. Now, does she mean to make a fool of me or not ?—I sha'n't wait much longer, for my wife will soon be inquiring for me to set out on our supping party—Suspence is at all times the devil—but of all modes of suspence, the watching for a loitering mistress is the worst—but let me accuse her no longer— she approaches with one smile to overpay the anxiety of a year.

Enter BERINTHIA.

O, Berinthia, what a world of kindness are you in my debt !—had you stayed five minutes longer——

Berin. You would have been gone, I suppose.

Love. (*Aside.*) Egad she's right enough.

Berin And I assure you 'twas ten to one that I came at all. In short, I begin to think you are too dangerous a being to trifle with; and, as I shall probably only make a fool of you at last, I believe we had better let matters rest as they are.

Love. You cannot mean it, sure ?

Berin. No !—why, do you think you are really so irresistible, and master of so much address, as to deprive a woman of her senses in a few days acquaintance ?

Love. O, no, madam ; 'tis only by your preserving your senses that I can hope to be admitted into your favour—your taste, judgment, and discernment, are what I build my hopes on.

Berin. Very modest upon my word !—and it certainly follows, that the greatest proof I can give of my possessing those qualities would be my admiring Mr Loveless !

Love. O that were so cold a proof——

Berin. What shall I do more ?—Esteem you ?

Love. O, no—worse and worse.—Can you behold a man, whose every faculty your attractions have engrossed—whose whole soul, as by enchantment, you have seized on—can you see him tremble at your feet, and talk of so poor a return as your esteem ?

Berin. What more would you have me give to a married man ?

Love. How doubly cruel to remind me of a misfortune !

Berin. A misfortune to be married to so charming a woman as Amanda !

Love. I grant all her merit, but—'sdeath ! now see what you have done by talking of her—she's here, by all that's unlucky !

Berin. O Ged, we had both better get out of the way, for I should feel as awkward to meet her as you.

Love. Ay—but, if I mistake not, I see Townly coming this way also—I must see a little into this matter.   (*Steps aside.*

Berin. O, if that's your intention—I am no woman if I suffer myself to be outdone in curiosity.

                                    (*Goes on the other side.*

Enter AMANDA.

Aman. Mr Loveless come home and walking on the lawn!—I will not suffer him to walk so late, though perhaps it is to shew his neglect of me.—Mr Loveless —ha!—Townly again!—how I am persecuted!

Enter TOWNLY.

Town. Madam, you seem disturbed!

Aman. Sir, I have reason.

Town. Whatever be the cause, I would to Heaven it were in my power to bear the pain, or to remove the malady.

Aman. Your interference can only add to my distress.

Town. Ah, madam, if it be the sting of unrequited love you suffer from, seek for your remedy in revenge ; weigh well the strength and beauty of your charms, and rouse up that spirit a woman ought to bear—disdain the false embraces of a husband—see at your feet a real lover—his zeal may give him title to your pity, although his merit cannot claim your love!

Lov. (*Aside.*) So, so, very fine, i'faith !

Aman. Why do you presume to talk to me thus? —is this your friendship to Mr Loveless ? I perceive you will compel me at last to acquaint him with your treachery.

Town. He could not upbraid me if you were; he deserves it from me, for he has not been more false to you than faithless to me.

Aman. To you!

Town. Yes, madam ; the lady for whom he now deserts those charms which he was never worthy of, was mine by right · and I imagined, too, by inclination. Yes, madam, Berinthia, who now—

Aman. Berinthia!—impossible !

Town. 'Tis true, or may I never merit your attention. She is the deceitful sorceress who now holds your husband's heart in bondage.

Aman. I will not believe it.

Town. By the faith of a true lover, I speak from conviction. This very day I saw them together, and overheard—

Aman. Peace, sir! I will not even listen to such slander; this is a poor device to work on my resentment, to listen to your insidious addresses. No, sir; though Mr Loveless may be capable of error, I am convinced I cannot be deceived so grossly in him, as to believe what you now report; and for Berinthia, you should have fixed on some more probable person for my rival than she who is my relation and my friend: for, while I am myself free from guilt, I will never believe that love can beget injury, or confidence create ingratitude.

Town. If I do not prove this to you—

Aman. You never shall have an opportunity— From the artful manner in which you first shew'd yourself to me, I might have been led, as far as virtue permitted, to have thought you less criminal than unhappy; but this last unmanly artifice merits at once my resentment and contempt.   [*Exit.*

Town. Sure there's divinity about her; and she has dispensed some portion of honour's light to me: yet can I bear to lose Berinthia without revenge or compensation?—Perhaps she is not so culpable as I thought her. I was mistaken when I began to think lightly of Amanda's virtue, and may be in my censure of my Berinthia—Surely I love her still; for I feel I should be happy to find myself in the wrong.
          [*Exit.*

Enter LOVELESS *and* BERINTHIA.

Berin. Your servant, Mr Loveless.

Love. Your servant, madam.

Berin. Pray, what do you think of this ?

Love. Truly, I don't know what to say.

Berin. Don't you think we steal forth two contemptible creatures ?

Love. Why, tolerably so, I must confess.

Berin. And do you conceive it possible for you ever to give Amanda the least uneasiness again ?

Love. No, I think we never should, indeed.

Berin. We !—why, monster, you don't pretend that I ever entertain'd a thought—

Love. Why then, sincerely and honestly, Berinthia, there is something in my wife's conduct which strikes me so forcibly, that if it were not for shame, and the fear of hurting you in her opinion, I swear I would follow her, confess my error, and trust to her generosity for forgiveness.

Berin. Nay, pr'ythee don't let your respect for me prevent you; for as my object in trifling with you was nothing more than to pique Townly, and as I perceive he has been actuated by a similar motive, you may depend on't I shall make no mystery of the matter to him.

Love. By no means inform him ; for though I may chuse to pass by his conduct without resentment, how will he presume to look me in the face again ?

Berin. How will you presume to look him in the face again ?

Love. He—who has dared to attempt the honour of my wife !

Berin. You—who have dared to attempt the honour of his mistress !—Come, come, be ruled by me who affect more levity than I have, and don't think of anger in this cause. A readiness to resent injuries is a virtue only in those who are slow to injure.

Love. Then will I be ruled by you, and when you shall think proper to undeceive Townly, may

your good qualities make as sincere a convert of
him as Amanda's have of me.   When truth's extended from us, then we own the robe of virtue is a
sacred habit.

> Could women but our secret counsels scan—
> Could they but reach the deep reserve of man—
> To keep our love, they'd rate our virtue high—
> They live together, and together die !   [*Exeunt.*

SCENE II.

SIR TUNBELLY's *House.*

Enter MISS HOYDEN, *Nurse, and* YOUNG FASHION.

Y. Fash. This quick dispatch of the chaplain's I
take so kindly, it shall give him claim to my favour
as long as I live, I assure you.

Miss Hoy. And to mine too, I promise you.

Nurse. I most humbly thank your honours ; and
may your children swarm about you like bees about
a honey-comb.

Miss Hoy. I'cod with all my heart—the more
the merrier, I say, ha, nurse ?

Enter LORY, *taking* YOUNG FASHION *hastily aside.*

Lory. One word with you, for Heaven's sake.

Y. Fash. What the devil's the matter ?

Lory. Sir, your fortune's ruin'd, if you are not
married—yonder's your brother, arrived with two
coaches and six horses, twenty footmen, and a coat
worth fourscore pounds, so judge what will become
of your lady's heart.

Y. Fash. Is he in the house yet?

Lory. No, they are capitulating with him at the

gate. Sir Tunbelly luckily takes him for an impostor, and I have told him that we had heard of this plot before.

Y. Fash. That's right. (*To Miss.*) My dear, here's a troublesome business my man tells me of, but don't be frighten'd, we shall be too hard for the rogue. Here's an impudent fellow at the gate (not knowing I was come hither incognito) has taken my name upon him, in hopes to run away with you.

Miss Hoy. O the brazen-faced varlet! it's well we are married, or may be we might never have been so.

Y. Fash. (*Aside.*) Egad like enough —Pr'ythee, nurse, run to Sir Tunbelly, and stop him from going to the gate before I speak with him.

Nurse. An't please your honour, my lady and I had best lock ourselves up till the danger be over.

Y. Fash. Do so, if you please.

Miss Hoy. Not so fast—I won't be lock'd up any more now I'm married.

Y. Fash. Yes, pray, my dear, do, till we have seiz'd this rascal.

Miss Hoy. Nay, if you'll pray me, I'll do any thing.
(*Exeunt Miss and Nurse.*

Y. Fash. (*To* Lory.) Hark you, sirrah, things are better than you imagine—the wedding's over.

Lory. The devil it is, sir!

Y. Fash. Not a word—all's safe—but Sir Tunbelly don't know it, nor must not yet ; so I am resolved to brazen the business out, and have the pleasure of turning the imposture upon his lordship, which I believe may easily be done.

Enter Sir Tunbelly *and Servants, armed with clubs, pitchforks, &c.*

Y. Fash. Did you ever hear, sir, of so impudent an undertaking?

Sir Tun. Never, by the mass—but we'll tickle him, I'll warrant you.

Y. Fash. They tell me, sir, he has a great many people with him, disguised like servants.

Sir Tun. Ay, ay, rogues enow—but we have mastered them.—We only fired a few shot over their heads, and the regiment scowered in an instant.—— Here, Thomas, bring in your prisoner.

Y. Fash. If you please, Sir Tunbelly, it will be best for me not to confront the fellow yet, till you have heard how far his impudence will carry him.

Sir Tun. Egad, your lordship is an ingenious person. Your lordship then will please to step aside.

Lory. (*Aside.*) 'Fore Heaven, I applaud my master's modesty!   (*Exeunt* YOUNG FASHION *and* LORY.

Enter Servants, with LORD FOPPINGTON, *disarmed.*

Sir Tun. Come—bring him along, bring him along.

Ld Fop. What the pax do you mean, gentlemen? is it fair time, that you are all drunk before supper?

Sir Tun. Drunk, sirrah!—here's an impudent rogue for you! Drunk or sober, bully, I'm a justice of the peace, and know how to deal with strollers.

Ld Fop Strollers!

Sir Tun. Ay, strollers.—Come, give an account of yourself—What's your name? Where do you live? Do you pay scot and lot? Come, are you a freeholder or a copyholder?

Ld Fop. And why dost thou ask me so many impertinent questions?

Sir Tun. Because I'll make you answer 'em before I have done with you, you rascal you.

Ld Fop. Before Gad, all the answers I can make to 'em is, that you are a very extraordinary old fellow, stap my vitals!

Sir Tun Nay, if thou art for joking with deputy lieutenants, we know how to deal with you—Here, draw a warrant for him immediately.

Ld Fop. A warrant!—What the devil is't thou wou'd'st be at, old gentleman?

Sir Tun. I would be at you, sirrah, (if my hands were not tied as a magistrate,) and with these two double fists beat your teeth down your throat, you dog you.

Ld Fop. And why would'st thou spoil my face at that rate?

Sir Tun. For your design to rob me of my daughter, villain.

Ld Fop. Rob thee of thy daughter! Now do I begin to believe I am in bed and asleep, and that all this is but a dream. Pr'ythee, old father, wilt thou give me leave to ask thee one question?

Sir Tun. I can't tell whether I will or not, till I know what it is.

Ld Fop. Why then it is, whether thou did'st not write to my Lord Foppington to come down and marry thy daughter?

Sir Tun. Yes, marry did I, and my Lord Foppington is come down, and shall marry my daughter before she's a day older.

Ld Fop. Now give me thy hand, old dad—I thought we should understand one another at last.

Sir Tun. This fellow's mad—here, bind him hand and foot.   (*They bind him.*

Ld Fop. Nay, pr'ythee, knight, leave fooling—thy jest begins to grow dull.

Sir Tun. Bind him, I say—he's mad—bread and water, a dark room, and a whip, may bring him to his senses again.

Ld Fop. Pr'ythee, Sir Tunbelly, why should you take such an aversion to the freedom of my address, as to suffer the rascals thus to skewer down my arms like a rabbit? 'Egad, if I don't waken quickly, by all that I can see, this is like to prove one of the most impertinent dreams that ever I dreamt in my life.

(*Aside.*

Enter Miss Hoyden *and Nurse.*

Miss Hoy. (*Going up to him.*) Is this he that would
have run away with me? Fough! how he stinks of
sweets!—Pray, father, let him be dragged through
the horse-pond.

Ld Fop. (*Aside.*) This must be my wife, by her
natural inclination to her husband.

Miss Hoy. Pray, father, what do you intend to do
with him—hang him?

Sir Tun. That at least, child.

Nurse. Ay, and it's e'en too good for him too.

Ld Fop. (*Aside.*) Madame la Governante, I presume; hitherto this appears to me to be one of the
most extraordinary families that ever man of quality matched into.

Sir Tun. What's become of my lord, daughter?

Miss Hoy. He's just coming, sir.

Ld Fop. (*Aside.*) My lord!—What does he mean
by that now?

Enter Young Fashion *and* Lory.

Ld Fop. Stap my vitals, Tam! now the dream's out.

Y Fash. Is this the fellow, sir, that designed to
trick me of your daughter?

Sir Tun. This is he, my lord; how do you like
him? is not he a pretty fellow to get a fortune?

Y. Fash. I find by his dress he thought your
daughter might be taken with a beau.

Miss Hoy. O gemini! Is this a beau? Let me see
him again.   Ha! I find a beau is no such ugly thing
neither.

Y. Fash. 'Egad, she'll be in love with him presently—I'll e'en have him sent away to gaol. (*To* Lord
Fop.) Sir, though your undertaking shews you a person of no extraordinary modesty, I suppose you ha'n't
confidence enough to expect much favour from me?

Ld Fop. Strike me dumb, Tam, thou art a very impudent fellow!

Nurse. Look if the varlot has not the frontery to call his lordship plain Thomas !

Sir Tun. Come, is the warrant writ ?

Chap. Yes, sir.

Ld Fop. Hold, one moment, pray, gentlemen— My Lord Foppington, shall I beg one word with your lordship ?

Nurse. O, ho, it's my lord with him now ; see how afflictions will humble folks !

Miss Hoy. Pray, my lord, don't let him whisper too close, lest he bite your ear off.

Ld Fop. I am not altogether so hungry as your ladyship is pleased to imagine. (*To* Y. FASHION.) Look you, Tam, I am sensible I have not been so kind to you as I ought, but I hope you'll forgive what's past, and accept of the five thousand pounds I offer. Thou may'st live in extreme splendour with it, stap my vitals !

Y. Fash. It's a much easier matter to prevent a disease than to cure it. A quarter of that sum would have secured your mistress, twice as much won't redeem her.   (*Leaving him.*

Sir Tun. Well, what says he ?

Y. Fash. Only the rascal offered me a bribe to let him go.

Sir Tun. Ay, he shall go, with a halter to him— Lead on, constable.

Enter Servant.

Serv. Sir, here is Muster Loveless, and Muster Colonel Townly, and some ladies, to wait on you.

Lory. (*Aside.*) So, sir, what will you do now ?

Y. Fash. Be quiet—they are in the plot. (*To* SIR TUNBELLY.) Only a few friends, Sir Tunbelly, whom I wish to introduce to you.

Ld Fop. Thou art the most impudent fellow, Tam, that ever nature yet brought into the world. Sir Tunbelly, strike me speechless, but these are my friends and my guests, and they will soon inform thee, whether I am the true Lord Foppington or not.

Enter LOVELESS, TOWNLY, AMANDA, *and* BERINTHIA.

Y. Fash. So, gentlemen, this is friendly; I rejoice to see you.

Town. My lord, we are fortunate to be the witnesses of your lordship's happiness.

Love. But your lordship will do us the honour to introduce us to Sir Tunbelly Clumsy?

Aman. And us to your lady?

Ld Fop. Ged take me, but they are all in a story!

Sir Tun. Gentlemen, you do me great honour; my Lord Foppington's friends will ever be welcome to me and mine.

Y. Fash. My love, let me introduce you to these ladies.

Miss Hoy. By goles, they look so fine and so stiff, I am almost ashamed to come nigh 'em.

Aman. A most engaging lady indeed!

Miss Hoy. Thank ye, ma'am!

Berin. And I doubt not will soon distinguish herself in the beau monde.

Miss Hoy. Where is that?

Y. Fash. You'll soon learn, my dear.

Love. But, Lord Foppington—

Ld Fop. Sir!

Love. Sir! I was not addressing myself to you, sir; pray who is this gentleman? he seems rather in a singular predicament.

Sir Tun. Ha, ha, ha!—So these are your friends and your guests, ha, my adventurer?

Ld Fop. I am struck dumb with their impudence, and cannot positively say whether I shall ever speak again or not.

Sir Tun. Why, sir, the modest gentleman wanted to pass himself upon me for Lord Foppington, and carry off my daughter.

Love. A likely plot to succeed, truly, ha, ha!

Ld Fop. As Gad shall judge me, Loveless, I did not expect this from thee: Come, pr'ythee confess the joke; tell Sir Tunbelly that I am the real Lord Foppington, who yesterday made love to thy wife; was honoured by her with a slap on the face, and afterwards pink'd through the bady by thee.

Sir Tun. A likely story, truly, that a peer wou'd behave thus!

Love. A curious fellow indeed! that wou'd scandalize the character he wants to assume; but what will you do with him, Sir Tunbelly?

Sir Tun. Commit him certainly, unless the bride and bridegroom chuse to pardon him.

Ld Fop. Bride and bridegroom! for Gad's sake, Sir Tunbelly, 'tis tarture to me to hear you call 'em so!

Miss Hoy. Why, you ugly thing, what would you have him call us? dog and cat?

Ld Fop. By no means, Miss: for that sounds ten times more like man and wife than t'other.

Sir Tun. A precious rogue this, to come a wooing!

Enter Servant.

Serv. There are some more gentle folks below, to wait upon Lord Foppington.

Town. 'Sdeath, Tom! what will you do now?

Ld Fop. Now, Sir Tunbelly, here are witnesses, who, I believe, are not corrupted.

Sir Tun. Peace, fellow!—Wou'd your lordship chuse to have your guests shewn here, or shall they wait till we come to 'em?

Y. Fash. I believe, Sir Tunbelly, we had better not have these visitors here yet—'Egad, all must out!
(*Aside.*

Love. Confess, confess, we'll stand by you.

Ld Fop. Nay, Sir Tunbelly, I insist on your calling evidence on both sides, and if I do not prove that fellow an impostor——

Y. Fash. Brother, I will save you the trouble, by now confessing that I am not what I have passed myself for:—Sir Tunbelly, I am a gentleman, and I flatter myself a man of character ; but 'tis with great pride I assure you I am not Lord Foppington.

Sir Tun. Ouns !—what's this ?—an impostor !—a cheat !—fire and faggots, sir !—if you are not Lord Foppington, who the devil are you ?

Y. Fash. Sir, the best of my condition is, I am your son-in-law, and the worst of it is, I am brother to that noble peer.

Ld Fop. Impudent to the last !

Sir Tun. My son-in-law ! Not yet I hope ?'

Y. Fash. Pardon me, sir, thanks to the goodness of your chaplain, and the kind offices of this old gentlewoman.

Lory. 'Tis true, indeed, sir ; I gave your daughter away, and Mrs Nurse here was clerk.

Sir Tun. Knock that rascal down !—But speak, Jezebel, how's this ?

Nurse. Alas, your honour, forgive me !—I have been overreached in this business as well as you ; your worship knows, if the wedding dinner had been ready, you would have given her away with your own hands.

Sir Tun. But how durst you do this without acquainting me ?

Nurse. Alas, if your worship had seen how the poor thing begged and prayed, and clung and twined about me like ivy round an old wall, you wou'd say I, who had nursed it and reared it, must have had a heart of stone to refuse it.

Sir Tun. Ouns ! I shall go mad ! Unloose my lord there, you scoundrels !

Ld Fop. Why, when these gentlemen are at leisure, I should be glad to congratulate you on your son-in-law with a little more freedom of address.

Miss Hoy. 'Egad though—I don't see which is to be my husband, after all.

Love. Come, come, Sir Tunbelly, a man of your understanding must perceive, that an affair of this kind is not to be mended by anger and reproaches.

Town. Take my word for it, Sir Tunbelly, you are only tricked into a son-in-law you may be proud of: my friend, Tom Fashion, is as honest a fellow as ever breathed.

Love. That he is, depend on't, and will hunt or drink with you most affectionately; be generous, old boy, and forgive them.

Sir Tun. Never—the hussy!—when I had set my heart on getting her a title!

Ld Fop. Now, Sir Tunbelly, that I am untrussed, give me leave to thank thee for the very extraordinary reception I have met with in thy damned, execrable mansion, and at the same time to assure you, that of all the bumpkins and blockheads I have had the misfortune to meet with, thou art the most obstinate and egregious, strike me ugly!

Sir Tun. What's this!—Ouns! I believe you are both rogues alike!

Ld Fop. No, Sir Tunbelly, thou wilt find to thy unspeakable mortification, that I am the real Lord Foppington, who was to have disgraced myself by an alliance with a clod; and that thou hast matched thy girl to a beggarly younger brother of mine, whose title deeds might be contained in thy tobacco-box.

Sir Tun. Puppy, puppy!—I might prevent their being beggars if I chose it; for I could give 'em as good a rent-roll as your lordship.

Town. Well said, Sir Tunbelly.

Ld Fop. Ay, old fellow, but you will not do it:

for that would be acting like a Christian, and thou
art a thorough barbarian, stap my vitals!

Sir Tun. Udzookers! now six such words more,
and I'll forgive them directly.

Love. 'Slife, Sir Tunbelly! you should do it, and
bless yourself; ladies, what say you?

Aman. Good Sir Tunbelly, you must consent.

Berin. Come, you have been young yourself, Sir
Tunbelly.

Sir Tun. Well, then, if I must, I must; but turn
that sneering lord out, however; and let me be revenged on somebody; but first, look whether I am
a barbarian, or not; there, children, I join your hands,
and when I'm in a better humour, I'll give you my
blessing,

Love. Nobly done, Sir Tunbelly; and we shall
see you dance at a grandson's wedding yet.

Miss Hoy. By goles though, I don't understand
this; what, an't I to be a lady after all? only plain
Mrs—what's my husband's name, nurse?

Nurse. 'Squire Fashion.

Miss Hoy. 'Squire, is he?—Well, that's better than
nothing.

Ld Fop. Now will I put on a philosophic air, and
shew these people that it is not possible to put a
man of my quality out of countenance. Dear Tam,
since things are thus fallen out, pr'ythee give me
leave to wish thee joy; I do it *de bon coeur,* strike
me dumb! You have married into a family of great
politeness and uncommon elegance of manners; and
your bride appears to be a lady beautiful in person,
modest in her deportment, refined in her sentiments,
and of nice morality, split my windpipe!

Miss Hoy. By goles, husband, break his bones, if
he calls me names.

Y. Fash. Your lordship may keep up your spirits
with your grimace, if you please; I shall support
mine by Sir Tunbelly's favour, with this lady, and
three thousand pounds a year.

Ld Fop. Well, adieu, Tam; ladies, I kiss your hands; Sir Tunbelly, I shall now quit thy den; but, while I retain my arms, I shall remember thou art a savage, stap my vitals!   (*Exit.*

Sir Tun. By the mass, 'tis well he's gone, for I shou'd ha' been provoked by and by to ha' dun'un a mischief.—Well, if this is a lord, I think Hoyden has luck o' her side in troth.

Town. She has indeed, Sir Tunbelly,—but I hear the fiddles; his lordship, I know, had provided 'em.

Love. O, a dance, and a bottle, Sir Tunbelly, by all means.

Sir Tun. I had forgot the company below—Well, what—we must be merry then, ha?—and dance and drink, ha?—Well, 'fore George, you sha'n't say I do things by halves; son-in-law there looks like a hearty rogue, so we'll have a night of it; and which of these gay ladies will be the old man's partner, ha?—Ecod, I don't know how I came to be in so good a humour.

Berin. Well, Sir Tunbelly, my friend and I both will endeavour to keep you so; you have done a generous action, and are entitled to our attention; and if you shou'd be at a loss to divert your new guests, we will assist you to relate to them the plot of your daughter's marriage, and his lordship's deserved mortification, a subject which, perhaps, may afford no bad evening's entertainment.

Sir Tun. 'Ecod, with all my heart; though I am a main bungler at a long story.

Berin. Never fear, we will assist you, if the tale is judged worth being repeated; but of this you may be assured, that while the intention is evidently to please, British auditors will ever be indulgent to the errors of the performance.   [*Exeunt.*

END OF VOLUME SEVENTH.

THE MODERN THEATRE

THE

MODERN THEATRE;

THE MODERN THEATRE

A collection of plays

selected by

MRS. ELIZABETH INCHBALD

First published London, 1811

in ten volumes

Reissued in 1968
in five volumes
by Benjamin Blom, Inc.

Benjamin Blom, Inc.

New York

THE

MODERN THEATRE;

A COLLECTION OF

SUCCESSFUL MODERN PLAYS,

AS ACTED AT

THE THEATRES ROYAL, LONDON.

PRINTED FROM THE PROMPT BOOKS UNDER THE AU-
THORITY OF THE MANAGERS.

SELECTED BY

MRS INCHBALD.

———

IN TEN VOLUMES.

VOL. VIII.

MATILDA.   FUGITIVE.
MARY, QUEEN OF SCOTS.   HE WOU'D BE A SOLDIER.
ENGLAND PRESERVED.

LONDON:

PRINTED FOR LONGMAN, HURST, REES, ORME, AND RBOWN,
PATERNOSTER-ROW.

1811.

First published London, 1811
Reissued 1968,
by Benjamin Blom, Inc. Bx 10452

Library of Congress Catalog Card No. 67-13004

MATILDA;

A

TRAGEDY,

IN FIVE ACTS.

AS PERFORMED AT THE

THEATRE-ROYAL, DRURY-LANE.

BY THE

AUTHOR OF THE EARL OF WARWICK.

VOL. VIII.   A

DRAMATIS PERSONÆ.

MORCAR,	*Mr Reddish.*
EDWIN,	*Mr Smith.*
SIWARD,	*Mr Palmer.*
OFFICERS, *&c.*	
MATILDA,	*Miss Younge.*
BERTHA,	*Miss Platt.*

SCENE,—*Morcar's Camp, and the Environs near Nottinghám.*

MATILDA.

ACT THE FIRST.

SCENE I.

MATILDA's *Tent, with a view of the distant country.*

Enter MATILDA *and* BERTHA.

Mat. I thank thee, gentle Bertha, for thy good-
   ness ;
If aught could sooth the anguish of my soul,
Or raise it from the horrors of despair
To hope and joy, 'twould be thy gen'rous friend-
   ship :
But I am sunk so deep in misery,
That comfort cannot reach me.
 Ber. Talk not thus,
My sweet Matilda ; innocence, like thine,
Must be the care of all-directing heav'n.
Already hath the interposing hand

Of providence redeem'd thee from the rage
Of savage war, and shelter'd thee within
This calm asylum. Mercia's potent Earl,
The noble Morcar, will protect thy virtues;
And, if I err not, wishes but to share
His conquests with thee.

 Mat. O my friend, ofttimes
The flow'ry path that tempts our wand'ring steps
But leads to misery; what thou fondly deem'st
My soul's best comfort, is its bitterest woe.
Earl Morcar loves me. To the generous mind
The heaviest debt is that of gratitude,
When 'tis not in our power to repay it.

 Ber. Oft have I heard thee say, to him thou ow'st
Thy honour and thy life.

 Mat. I told thee truth.
Beneath my father's hospitable roof,
I spent my earlier, happier days, in peace
And safety: when the Norman conq'ror came,
Discord, thou know'st, soon lit her fatal torch,
And spread destruction o'er this wretched land.
The loyal Ranulph flew to William's aid,
And left me to a faithful peasant's care,
Who liv'd, sequester'd, in the fertile plains
Of rich Northumbria: There awhile I dwelt
In sweet retirement, when the savage Malcolm
Rush'd on our borders.

 Ber. I remember well
The melancholy hour. Confusion rag'd
On ev'ry side, and desolation spread
Its terrors round us. How didst thou escape?

 Mat. A crew of desperate ruffians seiz'd upon me,
A helpless prey: For, O! he was not there,
Who best could have defended his Matilda.
Then had I fall'n a wretched sacrifice
To brutal rage, and lawless violence,
Had not the generous Morcar interposed

To save me: Though he joined the guilty cause
Of foul rebellion, yet his soul abhorr'd
Such violation.   At his awful voice
The surly ruffians left me, and retired.
He bore me, half expiring, in his arms,
Back to his tent; with ev'ry kind attention
There strove to sooth my griefs, and promis'd, soon
As fit occasion offer'd, to restore me
To my afflicted father.
    Ber. Something sure
Was due to generous Morcar for his aid,
So timely given.
    Mat. No doubt: But mark what follow'd.
In my deliverer too soon I found
An ardent lover sighing at my feet.
    Ber. And what is there the proudest of our sex
Could wish for more? To be the envied bride
Of noble Morcar, first of England's peers
In fame and fortune.
    Mat. Never trust, my Bertha,
To outward show.   'Tis not the smiles of fortune,
The pomp of wealth, or splendour of a court,
Can make us happy.   In the mind alone,
Rests solid joy, and true felicity,
Which I can never taste: For, O my friend!
A secret sorrow weighs upon my heart.
    Ber. Then pour it in the bosom of thy friend:
Let me partake it with thee.
    Mat. Generous maid!
Know then, for nought will I conceal from thee,
I honour Mercia's Earl, revere his virtues,
And wish I could repay him with myself;
But, blushing, I acknowledge it, the heart
His vows solicit, is not mine to give.
    Ber. Has then some happier youth——
    Mat. Another time
I'll tell thee all the story of our loves.

But, O my Bertha! didst thou know to whom
My virgin faith is plighted, thou wouldst say,
I am indeed unhappy.

   Ber. Could Matilda
Bestow the treasure of her heart on one
Unworthy of her choice ?

   Mat. Unworthy! No.
I glory in my passion for the best,
The loveliest of his sex.   O ! he was all
That bounteous nature, prodigal of charms,
Did on her choicest fav'rite e'er bestow.
His graceful form and sweet deportment spoke
The fairer beauties of his kindred soul,
Where ev'ry grace and ev'ry virtue shone.
But thou wilt tremble, Bertha, when I tell thee,
He is Earl Morcar's —— brother.

   Ber. Ha ! his brother !
The noble Edwin ! Often have I heard
My father——

   Mat. Did Lord Edrick know him then ?

   Ber. He knew his virtues, and his fame in arms,
And often would lament the dire effects
Of civil discord, that could thus dissolve
The ties of nature, and of brethren make
The bitt'rest foes.   If right I learn, Lord Edwin
Is William's firmest friend, and still supports
His royal master.

   Mat. Yes, my Bertha, there
I still find comfort : Edwin ne'er was stain'd,
As Morcar is, with foul disloyalty,
But stands betwixt his sov'reign and the rage
Of rebel multitudes, to guard his throne.
If nobly fighting in his country's cause,
My hero falls, I shall not weep alone ;
The king he lov'd and honour'd will lament him,
And grateful England mix her tears with mine.

   Ber. And doth Earl Morcar know of Edwin's love?

Mat. O, no! I would not for a thousand worlds
He should suspect it, lest his fiery soul
Should catch th' alarm, and kindle to a flame
That might destroy us all.

    Ber. I know his warmth
And vehemence of temper, unrestrain'd
By laws, and spurning at the royal pow'r
Which he contemns, he rules despotic here.

    Mat. Alas! how man from man, and brother oft
From brother differs! Edwin's tender passion
Is soft and gentle as the balmy breath
Of vernal zephyrs; whilst the savage north,
That curls the angry ocean into storms,
Is a faint image of Earl Morcar's love:
'Tis rage, 'tis fury all.   When last we met,
He knit his angry brow, and frown'd severe
Upon me; then, with wild distracted look,
Bade me beware of trifling with his passion,
He would not brook it—trembling I retir'd,
And bath'd my couch in tears.

    Ber. Unhappy maid!
But time, that softens ev'ry human woe,
Will bring some blest event, and lighten thine.

    Mat. Alas! thou know'st not what it is to love.
Haply thy tender heart hath never felt
The tortures of that soul-bewitching passion.
Its joys are sweet and poignant, but its pangs
Are exquisite, as I have known too well:
For, O! my Bertha, since the fatal hour
When Edwin left me, never hath sweet peace,
That us'd to dwell with all its comforts here,
E'er deign'd to visit this afflicted breast.

    Ber. Too plain, alas! I read thy sorrows; grief
Sits in sad triumph on thy faded cheek,
And half obscures the lustre of thy beauties.

    Mat. Talk not of beauty, 'tis our sex's bane,
And leads but to destruction.   I abhor

The fatal gift.   O ! would it had pleas'd heav'n
To brand my homely features with the mark
Of foul deformity, or let me pass
Unknown, and undistinguish'd from the herd
Of vulgar forms, save by the partial eye
Of my lov'd Edwin ; then had I been blest
With charms unenvied, and a guiltless love.

   Ber. Where is thy Edwin now ?
   Mat. Alas ! I know not.
'Tis now three years since last these eyes beheld
Their dearest object.   In that humble vale,
Whence, as I told thee, Malcolm's fury drove me,
There first we met.   O ! how I cherish still
The fond remembrance ! There we first exchanged
Our mutual vows, the day of happiness
Was fixt ; it came, and in a few short hours
He had been made indissolubly mine,
When fortune, envious of our happiness,
And William's danger, call'd him to the field.

   Ber. And since that parting have ye never met ?
   Mat. O never, Bertha, never but in thought.
Imagination, kind anticipator
Of love's pleasures, brings us oft together.
Oft, as I sit within my lonely tent,
And cast my wishful eyes o'er yonder plain,
In ev'ry passing traveller I strive
To trace his image, hear his lovely voice
In ev'ry sound, and fain would flatter me
Edwin still lives, still loves his lost Matilda !

   Ber. Who knows but fate, propitious to thy love,
May guide him hither ?
   Mat. Gracious heav'n forbid !
Consider, Bertha, if the chance of war
Should this way lead him, he must come in arms
Against his brother : Oh ! 'tis horrible
To think on.   Should they meet, and Edwin fall,
What shall support me ? And if vict'ry smiles

Upon my love, how dear will be the purchase
By Morcar's blood ! Then must I lose my friend,
My guardian, my protector—ev'ry way
Matilda must be wretched.
 Ber. Is there ought
In Bertha's power ?
 Mat. Wilt thou dispatch, my friend,
Some trusty messenger with these ?—Away.
        (Gives her letters.
I'll meet thee in my tent—farewel. [*Exit* BER.
 Mean time
One hope remains, the gen'rous Siward—he
Might save me still. His sympathetic heart
Can feel for the afflicted.— have heard,
(Such is the magic pow'r of sacred friendship)
When the impetuous Morcar scatters fear
And terror round him, he, and he alone,
Can stem the rapid torrent of his passion,
And bend him, though reluctant, to his will ;
And see, in happy hour, he comes this way.
Now, Fortune, be propitious ! if there be,
As I have heard, an eloquence in grief,
And those can most persuade, who are most wretch-
   ed,
I shall not pass unpitied.

    Enter SIWARD.

 Siw. Ha ! in tears,
Matilda ! What new grief, what cruel foe
To innocence and beauty, thus could vex
Thy gentle spirit ?
 Mat. Canst thou ask the cause,
When thou beholdst me still in shameful bonds,
A wretched captive, friendless and forlorn,
Without one ray of hope to sooth my sorrows.
 Siw. Can she, whose beauteous form, and fair
   demeanour,

Charm ev'ry eye, and conquer ev'ry heart,
Can she be wretched? can she want a friend,
Whom Siward honours, and whom Morcar loves?
O! if thou knew'st with what unceasing ardour,
What unexampled tenderness and truth,
He doats upon thee, sure thou might'st be wrought
At least to pity.

   Mat. Urge no more, my lord,
Th' ungrateful subject; but too well I know
How much thy friend deserves, how much, alas!
I owe him!—If it be Earl Morcar's wish
To make me happy, why am I detain'd
A pris'ner here, spite of his solemn promise
He would restore me to my royal master,
Or send me back to the desiring arms
Of the afflicted Ranulph, who, in tears
Of bitt'rest anguish, mourns his long-lost daughter?
Surely, my lord, it ill becomes a soldier
To forfeit thus his honour and his word.

   Siw. I own it; yet the cause pleads strongly for
       him.
If, by thy own too pow'rful charms misled,
He deviates from the paths of rigid honour,
Matilda might forgive. Thou know'st he lives
But in thy smiles; his love-enchanted soul
Hangs on those beauties he would wish to keep
For ever in his sight.

   Mat. Indulgent heav'n
Keep me for ever from it! O, my lord,
If e'er thy heart with gen'rous pity glow'd
For the distress'd; if e'er thy honest zeal
Could boast an influence o'er the man you love;
O! now exert thy pow'r, assist, direct,
And save thy friend from ruin and Matilda.
There are, my lord, who most offend, where most
They wish to please. Such often is the fate
Of thy unhappy friend, when he pours forth

His ardent soul in vows of tend'rest passion ;
'Tis with such rude and boist'rous violence
As suits but ill the hero or the lover.

   Siw. I know his weakness, know his follies all,
And feel 'em but too well : He loves with trans-
        port,
And hates with fury. Warm'd with fierce desire,
Or strong resentment, his impetuous soul
Is hurried on, till reason quits her seat,
And passion takes the loosely-flowing rein ;
Then all is rage, confusion, and despair.
And yet, when cool reflection hath remov'd
The veil of error, he will weep his faults
With such a sweet contrition, as would melt
The hardest heart to pity and forgiveness.
O ! he has virtues that may well atone
For all his venial rashness,—that deserve
A sov'reign's love, and claim a nation's praise ;
Virtues that merit happiness and thee.
Why wilt thou thus despise my noble friend ?
His birth and fortune, with the rank he bears
Amongst the first of England's peers, will raise thee
As far above thy sex, in wealth and pow'r,
As now thou art in beauty.

   Mat. O, my lord !
'Tis not the pride, the luxury of life,
The splendid robe and glitt'ring gem, that knits
The lasting bonds of mutual happiness :
Where manners differ, where affections jar,
And will not kindly mix together, where
The sweet harmonious concord of the mind
Is wanting, all is misery and woe.

   Siw. By heav'n, thou pleadst thy own and vir-
        tue's cause,
With such bewitching eloquence, the more
Thy heart, alarm'd by diffidence, still urges

Against this union with my friend, the more
I wish to see him blest with worth like thine.

Mat. My lord, it must not be : for grant him all
The fair perfections you already see,
And I could wish to find, there is a bar
That must for ever disunite us—Born
Of Norman race, and from my earliest years
Attach'd to William's cause, I love my king,
And wish my country's peace : That king, my lord,
Whom Morcar wishes to dethrone ; that peace
Which he destroys : Had he an angel's form,
With all the virtues that adorn his sex,
With all the riches fortune can bestow,
I would not wed a traitor.

Siw. Call not his errors by so harsh a name ;
He has been deeply wrong'd, and souls like his
Must feel the wounds of honour, and resent them.
Alas ! with thee I weep my country's fate,
Nay wish, perhaps, as well to William's cause,
And England's peace, as can the loyal daughter
Of gallant Ranulph, and would, therefore, joy
To see Matilda lend a gracious ear
To Morcar's suit. Thy reconciling charms
Might sooth his troubled soul, might heal the wounds
Of bleeding England, and unite us all
In one bright chain of harmony and love.
The gallant Edwin too—

Mat. Ha ! what of him ?
Know'st thou that noble youth ?

Siw. So many years
Have past since last we met, by diff'rent views,
And our unhappy feuds, so long divided,
I should not recollect him ; but report
Speaks loudly of his virtues. He, no doubt,
If yet he lives——

Mat. Yet lives ?—Why, what, my lord ?
Siw. You seem much mov'd.

Mat. Forgive me; but whene'er
This sad idea rises to my mind,
Of brother against brother arm'd, my soul
Recoils with horror.

Siw. 'Tis a dreadful thought:
Would I could heal that cruel breach! but then
Thou might'st do much, the task is left for thee.

Mat. For me? Alas! it is not in my power.

Siw. In thine, and thine alone. O think, Matilda!
How great thy glory, and how great thy praise,
To be the blessed instrument of peace,
The band of union 'twixt contending brothers!
Thou see'st them now like two descending floods,
Whose rapid torrents meeting, half o'erwhelm
The neighb'ring plains: Thy gentle voice might
    still
The angry waves, and bid their waters flow
In one united stream, to bless the land.

Mat. That flatt'ring thought beams comfort on
    my soul
Amidst my sorrows; bear me witness, heav'n!
Could poor Matilda be the happy means
Of reconcilement: Could these eyes behold
The noble youths embracing, and embrac'd
In the firm cords of amity and love;
O! it would make me ample recompence
For all my griefs, nor would I more complain,
But rest me in the silent grave, well pleas'd
To think, at last, I had not liv'd in vain.

Siw. Cherish that virtuous thought, illustrious
    maid,
And let me hope my friend may still be happy.

Mat. I wish it from my soul: But see, my lord,
Earl Morcar comes this way, with hasty steps,
Across the lawn. I must retire: Farewel!
You'll not forget my humble suit.

Siw. O! no,

I will do all that loveliest innocence
And worth, like thine, deserve.   Farewel: Mean
          time
Remember, Siward's ev'ry wish, the bliss
Of Morcar, Edwin's life, the public peace,
And England's welfare, all depend on thee.
                                        [*Exit* MAT.
 Siw. (*Alone.*) There's no alternative but this; my
          friend
Must quit Matilda, or desert the cause
We've rashly promis'd to support—Perhaps
The last were best—both shall be tried—he comes.

Enter MORCAR.

 Mor. O, Siward! was not that
The fair Matilda whom you parted from?
 Siw. It was.
 Mor. What says she? the dear, cruel maid!
Is she still deaf? inexorable still?
 Siw. You must not think of her.
 Mor. What say'st thou, Siward?
Not think of her!
 Siw. No.   Root her from thy heart,
And gaze no more.   I blush to see my friend
So lost to honour: Is it for a man,
On whom the fate of England may depend,
To quit the dangerous post, where duty calls,
And all the bus'ness of the war, to sigh
And whine in corners for a captive woman?
Resume the hero, Morcar, and subdue
This idle passion.
 Mor. Talk not thus of love,
The great refiner of the human heart,
The source of all that's great, of all that's good;
Of joy, of pleasure—If it be a weakness,
It is a weakness which the best have felt:
I would not wish to be a stranger to it.

Siw. Let me entreat thee, if thou valuest life,
Or fame, or honour, quit Matilda.
    Mor. Yes:
I thank you for your council.   'Tis the advice
Of cold, unfeeling wisdom, kindly meant
To make me prudent, and to leave me wretched:
But thus it is, that proud exulting health
Is ever ready to prescribe a cure
For pain and sickness which it never knew.
    Siw. There too thou err'st; for I have known its
            joys
And sorrows too.   In early life I lost
The partner of my soul.   E'er since that hour
I bade adieu to love, and taught my soul
To offer her devotions at the shrine
Of sacred friendship; there *my* vows are paid:
Morcar best knows the idol of my worship.
    Mor. I know and love thee for it: But, O! my
            friend,
I cannot force this tyrant from my breast;
E'en now I feel her here, she sits enthron'd
Within the foldings of my heart, and he
Who tears her thence must draw the life-blood from
            me.
My morning slumbers, and my midnight dreams,
Are haunted by Matilda.
    Siw. To be thus
The slave of one that scorns thee, O! 'tis base,
Mean, and unworthy of thee.
    Mor. I will bear
That scorn no longer: Thou hast rous'd me, Si-
            ward;
I will enjoy the glorious prize; she's mine,
By right of conquest mine.   I will assert
A victor's claim, and force her to be happy.
    Siw. That must not be.   It ill becomes the man
Who takes up arms against a tyrant's pow'r,

To adopt a tyrant's maxims ; force and love
Are terms that never can be reconciled.
You will not, must not do it.

Mor. Must not! who
Shall dare oppose me ?

Siw. Honour, conscience, love,
The sense of shame, your virtue, and your friend.
Whilst I have life, or pow'r, I will not see
Matilda wrong'd.

Mor. You are her champion then
It seems, her favour'd, happy friend ;—perhaps
Her fond admirer too.   I'll-fated Morcar !
I see it but too well.   I'm lost, abandon'd ;
Alike betray'd by friendship and by love.
I thank you, sir, you have perform'd your office,
And merit your reward.

Siw. Unkind reproach !
Did I for this desert my sov'reign's cause,
My peaceful home, and all its joys, to serve
Ungrateful Morcar ? Why did I rebel?
The naughty William never injur'd me.
For thee alone I fought, for thee I conquer'd ;
And, but for thee, long since I had employ'd
My gallant soldiers to a nobler purpose,
Than loit'ring thus in idle camp to hear
A love-sick tale, and sooth a mad man's phrenzy.

Mor. You could? Away, and leave me then:
                    withdraw
Your boasted aid, and bid Northumbria's sons
Bend to the tyrant's yoke, whilst I alone
Defend the cause of freedom and my conntry.
Here let us part.   Remove your loiterers,
And join the usurper.

Siw. Mark the diff'rence now
Betwixt blind passion and undaunted friendship :
You are impatient of the keen reproof,

Because you merit :—I can bear it all,
Because I've not deserv'd it.

Enter an OFFICER.

Offi. Good my lords,
Forgive this rough intrusion, but the danger,
I trust, will plead my pardon.   As I watch'd,
From yonder tow'r, a dusky cloud appear'd,
As if from distant troops advancing, soon
I saw their armour glitter in the sun ;
With rapid motion they approach'd ; each moment
We must expect them here.
   Siw. Why, let 'em come,
Already I have order'd fit disposal
Of all our little force.   Away, good Osmond,
Be silent and be ready.   [*Exit* OFFICER.
Now, my friend,
Thou art as welcome to thy Siward's breast,
As dear as ever.—When the man I love,
Walks in the paths of error, I reprove him
With honest freedom ; but when danger comes
Upon him, I forget his faults, and flee
With all a lover's ardour to his rescue ;
His sorrows and his wants alone remember'd,
And all his follies buried in oblivion.
   Mor. Thou hast disarm'd me now.   This pierces
            more
Than all the bitter poison of reproach
Which thou hast pour'd upon me.   O ! 'twas trea-
            son
Against the sacred majesty of friendship,
To doubt thy honour, or suspect thy virtue.
Thou wilt forgive : But when the wounded mind
Is torn with passion, ev'ry touch is pain ;
You should not probe so deeply.
   Siw. 'Twas my duty.
But come, no more of that.   The foe advances.

If we succeed, as my prophetic soul
Foretels we shall—I have some comfort for you—
If not, we'll borrow courage from despair,
And die like men.   Thou stand'st upon the rock
Of danger, and the yawning precipice
Opens before us ; I will snatch thee from it,
Or leap the gulph, and perish with my friend.

ACT THE SECOND.

SCENE I.

A Fortress belonging to MORCAR.

EDWIN *alone (in chains.)*

Edw. It is the will of heav'n, and must be done.
The hard-fought field is lost, and here I am
A pris'ner in my brother's camp: alas!
That fortune thus should guide me to a foe
Whom most I wish'd to shun ! We little thought
The troops, by Morcar led, had this way bent
Their ill-directed course: but providence
Hath so ordain'd, perhaps, to heal the wounds
Of civil discord. O ! unhappy Edwin,
For what art thou reserv'd ? No matter what.
Since fate depriv'd me of my dear Matilda,
Whom I for three long years have sought in vain,
Life hath been irksome to me: this, perchance,
May end it—For, who knows if nature yet
May live within the conq'ror's breast, to plead
A brother's pardon ? Yet he knows me not,
But soon he must—Ha! who comes here? Earl
   Siward !—
The second in command, to whom, o'erpower'd
By circling foes, and fainting with my wounds,

I yielded up my sword. If fame say true,
He bears a mind too great to look with scorn
On the oppress'd, or triumph o'er misfortune.

Enter SIWARD.

Siw. Stranger, whoe'er thou art, be comforted;
Thy fate hath thrown thee into noble hands,
Who know thy merit. May I ask thy name ?
Edw. I am a poor abandon'd wretch, the sport
Of Fortune; one whose least affliction is
To be a captive, and from ev'ry eye
Would wish to hide the story of my fate:
Too soon my name and sorrows will be known.
Siw. Respect is ever due to misery :
I will not urge thee further; all I hope,
That gen'rous pity could afford to sooth
Calamity like thine, by my command
Hath been extended to thee. Here awhile
You must remain a pris'ner, but e'er long
I hope to greet thee by a fairer name,
And rank thee as our friend.
Edw. Your gen'rous orders
Have been obey'd, and I acknowledge it
With grateful heart. May I not ask the fate
Of him who fought so nobly by my side,
That brave old man ?
Siw. The gallant Ranulph—
Edw. Yes;
My fellow captive.
Siw. He is safe and free.
Edw. Ha! free! Thank heav'n!
Siw. The gen'rous Morcar, urg'd
By my entreaties, pardon'd and releas'd him,
Though much our soldiers murmur'd, and demanded
His life and yours; a sacrifice, they said,
Due to the manes of their slaughter'd friends;
But mercy has prevail'd.

Edw. Whate'er becomes
Of an unhappy wanderer, like me,
For your kind treatment of the aged Ranulph,
Accept my thanks; it was a precious boon;
Morcar may find me not unworthy of it.
To-day I am his captive, but to-morrow
May see me his deliverer: for know
My royal master, the victorious William,
With eagle swiftness, soon will follow me
With twenty times your force.   As this shall prove
Or true, or false, so deal with me; remember
I warn'd you of it.

Siw. And remember thou
That I with joy receive the welcome news :
Welcome to me, for I am William's friend.

Edw. Thou canst not then be mine, or England's
          foe :
With such a heart as thine, so nobly form'd
To feel for the afflicted, satisfied,
For thou seem'st, of William's royal right,
What could engage thee in this foul revolt,
This base rebellion ?

Siw. What but the great bond
Of kindred souls, inviolable friendship !
The only solid bliss on this side heav'n,
That doubles all the joys of human life,
And, by dividing, lessens ev'ry woe.

Edw. Who knows but this day's sad event may
          prove
The happy means to heal a nation's wounds,
And sooth our jarring factions into peace ?

Siw. Had Morcar thought with me, long since
          that end
Had been obtain'd ; but Morcar is—

Edw. Inexorable.
So I have heard, and therefore little hope
To change his nature.   O ! could he be wrought

To sweet oblivion of his wrongs ; to bury
His deep resentment.   Mine should be the task,
A task, heav'n knows, I would with joy perform,
To reconcile offended majesty :
To soften all his errors, plead his pardon,
And give my sov'reign one brave soldier more.
 Siw. When next we meet I trust it shall be so :
Mean time, let me prepare him for the change ;
Retire a while—e'er long we'll send for thee,
For ev'ry moment I expect him here :
Thy freedom and thy happiness shall be
My first concern, for thou hast well deserv'd it.
  Edw. Farewel.   Be quick in your resolves ; the
    time
Requires it ; and be wise e'er 'tis too late.
           [*Exit* EDWIN.
  Siw. (*Alone.*) I hope we shall.   This well-tim'd
    victory,
If rightly us'd, may smooth our way to peace.
Now, Morcar, all thy happiness depends
Upon thyself alone.   Now, friendship, raise
Thy pow'rful voice, and force him to be happy.
He will, he must—he comes—

Enter MORCAR.

 Siw. My conq'ror, welcome !
 Mor. Thrice welcome to my arms, my noble
   Siward ;
At length we meet in joy, the day is ours ;
Thanks to thy friendly aid.
 Siw. We must not boast ;
'Twas hardly purchas'd, and has cost us dear :
You follow'd 'em too close.
 Mor. I own 'twas rash ;
My youthful ardour urg'd the keen pursuit
Too far ; and but for thee I had been lost.
In war, thy arm protects me ; and in peace,

Thy counsels guide. O! how shall I return
Thy goodness? Thou wert born to save thy friend.
   Siw. Away. I'll not be thank'd. I've done my
       duty ;
And if thou think'st thyself indebted for it,
Repay me not with flattery, but with love.
E'er since my soul, with thine congenial, met
In social bands, and mark'd thee for her own,
Thy int'rest and thy happiness have been
My first ambition ; and when thou art blest
With all thy soul can wish for, Siward then,
And then alone, will have his full reward.
   Mor. O unexampled faithfulness and truth!
But say, my Siward, is our loss so great?
   Siw. The flow'r of half our troops. But 'tis not
      now
A time to weep, for I have glorious tidings,
That much import thy happiness.
   Mor. Ha! what?
   Siw. Know that amongst our captives I have ta'en
A noble prize, will make us full amends
For ev'ry loss—the gallant Ranulph.
   Mor. Ha!
Matilda's father! then I'm satisfied.
The wily chief! by heav'n he shall repay me
For her unkindness : Give him to my rage,
To my resentment, to my injur'd love.
Where is he, Siward?
   Siw. I have set him free.
   Mor. Ha! free! Thy ill-timed mercy hath be-
      tray'd
Our cause. The tyrant would have ransom'd him
With half his kingdom.
   Siw. Still thy rapid passions
O'erpow'r thy reason. What, if it should serve
A better purpose ; smooth thy paths to bliss,
And gain Matilda for thee!

Mor. O, my friend!
My Siward, do not flatter me: By heav'n,
Her kind consent would give my ravish'd soul
More true and heart-felt happiness than could
A thousand vict'ries o'er the proud usurper.

Siw. Know then, I gave him liberty and life
On these conditions—That he should withdraw
His pow'rs from William's aid, and never more
Assist his cause; the time would come, I told him,
That he should know to whom he ow'd the boon,
And how he might repay it.

Mor. That was kind,
Indeed, my Siward, that was like a friend.
O! thou reviv'st my drooping heart; but tell me,
Did my Matilda, let me call her mine,
Did she acknowledge, did she thank thee for it?

Siw. O! I assum'd no merit but to thee,
And to thy gen'rous, unexampled love
Did I attribute all.   She sigh'd, and wept,
Pour'd forth a thousand blessings on thy head——

Mor. And dost thou think, my Siward, that one
        ray
Of hope remains?

Siw. The clouds already vanish,
The prospect brightens round thee; haste, and seize
The lucky moment.   When the gen'rous mind
Is sooth'd by obligation, soon it opens
To the mild dictates of humanity,
And softens into sympathy and love.

Mor. O, Siward! couldst thou teach me but to win
That lovely maid ——

Siw. The task is half perform'd
Already, and my friend shall soon be bless'd.
One thing, and one alone, remains to fix
Her doubtful heart, if yet a doubt remains.

Mor. O! name it, Siward; if 'tis in the pow'r
Of wealth to purchase, or of victory

In the fair field of glory to acquire,
It shall not long be wanting.
    Siw. It requires
No price, but such as Morcar well can pay;
No vict'ry, but the vict'ry o'er thyself,
And thy own passions—Give up thy resentment,
Make peace with William, and Matilda's thine.
    Mor. Matilda mine! and must I purchase her
At the dear price of honour? with the loss
Of all my soul holds dear, my country's welfare?
My word ——
    Siw. Away! whilst prudence warranted
Our honest zeal, I was the first to aid
Thy just revenge; but valour, ill-advis'd,
And ill-exerted in a hopeless cause,
Degen'rates into rashness. You mistake
The pride of honour for the pride of virtue.
    Mor. And wouldst thou have me bend beneath
        the yoke
Of ignominious slav'ry, quit the cause
Of heav'n-born freedom, and betray my friends?
    Siw. I'd have thee just and happy—We have been
Successful, let us now be generous,
Whilst we have something to bestow; nor wait
Till fickle fortune from our brows shall tear
The blasted wreath, and leave us nought to give.
Too long already have we sacrific'd,
At proud ambition's altar, to revenge;
Now let us offer at the shrine of peace,
And sacrifice ——
    Mor. To love, and to Matilda;
It shall be so—the struggle's past—away,
My Siward, haste, and tell her, I obey;
Her laws, her king, her master shall be mine;
I have no will but hers, and in her eyes
Will read my duty—Yet a moment stay.
What will my brave companions of the war,
    VOL. VIII.   C

My fellow soldiers, say? Will they approve
This unexpected change?

   Siw. I know them firm
In their obedience, and resolv'd to act
As you command—But I will see 'em strait,
And urge such pow'rful reasons as may best
Secure them to our purpose. Fare thee well.

   Mor. Siward, thy kind anticipating care
Prevents my ev'ry wish—But say, my friend,
Where is the gallant chief whom we subdu'd,
Who fought so hardly, and so nobly fell?

   Siw. In yonder tent, a wretched pris'ner still,
He counts the tedious hours; a heavy gloom
Sits on his brow, as if some deep-felt sorrow
Oppress'd his noble mind—We must release him.

   Mor. Thou know'st, my Siward, thrice we had
        o'erpow'r'd
His troops, and thrice his single valour turn'd
The fortune of the day: Since first I trod
The paths of glory, ne'er did I behold
Such deeds of valour wrought by mortal hand;
I almost envied, though I conquer'd him.
He wore his beaver up, nor could I trace
His features, but he bears a noble form;
Know'st thou his quality or name?

   Siw. Not yet;
He seems industrious to conceal them both
From ev'ry eye.

   Mor. Some deity protects him,
As its peculiar care: for, as I rais'd
My sword against him, whether the soft passion
That triumphs o'er me, had unmann'd my soul,
I know not; but, bereft of all its pow'r,
My nerveless arm dropp'd ineffectual down,
And let him 'scape me.

   Siw. 'Tis most true, I saw
And wonder'd at it. When you left the field,

With desperate rage he rush'd intrepid on,
And seem'd to court his fate, till circling foes
Compell'd him to resign, and yield his sword.
 Mor. Away. I burn with ardour to forgive,
To free, and to embrace him: fly, my Siward.
Let him approach, he could not wish to meet,
In happier hour, the master of his fate,
For now, methinks, I could be reconcil'd
To ev'ry foe. Away, my Siward, haste
And send him to me.
 Siw. Treat him like a friend,
He may be useful. Such distinguish'd merit
Must have its influence: he commands, no doubt,
The royal ear, and may procure such terms
As William may with honour yield, and we
Without a blush accept.   [*Exit* SIWARD.
 Mor. (*Alone.*) Farewel. And now
How stands the great account? Can I quit
Myself, or shall I be condemn'd before
Thy great tribunal, all-repaying justice ?
But fair Matilda wipes out ev'ry stain,
'Tis she commands me to forgive, and she
Must be obey'd; I'm not the first apostate
From honour's cause the tyrant love has made.
My friend too urg'd the change—
   [*Guards bring in* EDWIN *chained.*
He's here—Strike off
Those ignominious chains—he has deserv'd
A better fate.   [*Guards unchain him.*
Stranger, whoe'er thou art,   [*Turning to* EDWIN.
Thy gallant bearing in th' unequal conflict,
For we had twice thy numbers, hath endear'd
A soldier to a soldier. Vulgar minds
To their own party, and the narrow limits
Of partial friendship, meanly may confine
Their admiration ; but the brave will see,
And seeing, praise the virtues of a foe.

Edw. (*Aside.*)   O, powerful nature, how thou
  work'st within me!

Mor. Still silent! still conceal'd! perchance thou
  fear'st,

Knowing thy rank and name, I might recal
My promis'd pardon; but be confident,
For by that sacred honour, which I hold
Dearer than life, I promise here to free,
And to protect thee;—did'st thou hide from me
My deadliest foe; should William's self appear
Before me, he who hath so deeply wrong'd me,
So long oppos'd: Nay, should I hear the voice
Of that advent'rous, rash, misguided youth,
Whom yet I cannot hate—my cruel brother—
I could forgive him.

  Edw. (*Discovering himself.*) Then—behold him
  here.

  Mor. Edwin! Amazement! By what wond'rous
  means,

Mysterious Providence, dost thou unfold
Thy secret purposes?   I little thought,
When last we met, what heav'n-protected victim
Escap'd my sword.

  Edw. With horror I recal
The dreadful circumstance.   Throughout the battle
I knew, and carefully avoided thee.

  Mor. O, Edwin! how, on this propitious day,
Have victory, fame and friendship, fortune, love,
And nature, all conspir'd to make me blest!
We have been foes too long—Of that no more.
My Edwin, welcome!   Once more to thy arm
Receive a brother.

  Edw. Yet a moment stay:
By Nature touch'd, the same accordant string,
That vibrates on thy heart, now beats on mine;
But honour, and the duty which I owe
The best of kings, restrains the fond embrace

I wish to share, and bids me ask, if yet
In Morcar I behold my sov'reign's foe.
If it be so, take back thy proffer'd freedom,
Take back my forfeit life : I would not wish
To be indebted for it to—a traitor.

   Mor. Perhaps I may deserve a better name;
Perhaps I may be changed.

   Edw. I hope thou art ;
For this I came, for this I yielded to thee,
To tell thee William's strength is ev'ry hour
Increasing : if thou mean'st to make thy peace,
Now is the crisis—

   Mor. Edwin, stop, nor urge
Such mean unworthy motives as alone
Could thwart my purpose.   Morcar cannot fear,
But Morcar can be generous ; for know,
Before I saw thee here I had resolv'd
To sheath my sword, and be the conq'ror's friend ;
For, O ! there is a cause——

   Edw. Whate'er the cause,
Th' effect is glorious.   Now thou art again
My brother.   Here, let us once more unite
The long-dissever'd cord.   [*They embrace.*

   Mor. And never more
May blind resentment, faction, party rage,
Envy, or jealous fear, dissolve the tie !
And now, my Edwin, blushing, I confess,
Not to thy tender care for Morcar's safety,
To friendship's counsel, or to reason's voice,
Owe we this wish'd-for change.   A female hand
Directs and wills it.

   Edw. Ha ! a woman !

   Mor. Yes,
If such I ought to call that form divine,
Which triumphs here, who rules my ev'ry thought,
My ev'ry action guides.   In yonder tent
A beauteous captive dwells, who hath enslav'd

Her conq'ror : She demands the sacrifice ;
She would not give her hand to William's foe,
And therefore, only, Morcar is his friend.

 Edw. I could have wish'd that this important
   change
Were to the hero, not the lover, due.

 Mor. I am above deceit, and own my weakness ;
But thou shalt see her—Yes, my Edwin, thou
Shalt bear the welcome tidings to my love.
Thy presence will bear witness to the change ;
Thy freedom, and the joyful news thou bring'st
Of our blest union, will confirm it to her.
Wilt thou, my Edwin—

 Edw. Do not ask me what
I must refuse. I would do much to serve
A friend and brother ; but a task of joy
Ill suits a soul oppress'd with griefs like mine.
O ! I could tell thee—but 'twould be unkind,
When thou art ent'ring on the paths of bliss,
To stop thee with my melancholy tale.

 Mor. Whate'er thy griefs, I pity, and hereafter
May find the means to lessen or remove them ;
Mean time this tender office may divert
Thy sorrows ; nay, if thou deny'st me, Edwin,
I shall not think our union is sincere.

 Edw. Then be it so.

 Mor. I'll send a trusty slave
That shall conduct thee to her. Soon I mean
To follow thee—away—begone and prosper.
But, O my brother ! if thou hast a heart
That is not steel'd with stoic apathy
Against the magic of all-conq'ring love,
Beware of beauty's pow'r ; for she has charms
Would melt the frozen breast of hoary age,
Or draw the lonely hermit from his cell
To gaze upon her.

 Edw. Know, thy fears are vain ;

For long, long since, by honour's sacred ties,
United to the loveliest of her sex,
Edwin, like Morcar, is to one alone
Devoted, and my heart is fix'd as thine.
    Mor. Then I am blest.   Thy sympathetic soul,
With warmer feelings, shall express my passion,
Wak'd by the fond remembrance of thy own.

Go then, thy kind returning friendship prove,
Go, plead with all the eloquence of love ;
And as thou dost thy brother's anguish tell,
Still on thy lips may soft persuasion dwell !
Urge my fond suit with energy divine,
Nor cease till thou hast made the lovely captive
      mine.

ACT THE THIRD.

SCENE I.

MATILDA's *Tent, with a distant view of the Camp.*

MATILDA, BERTHA.

Mat. O Bertha! I have had such frightful
    dreams,
They harrow'd up my soul.
    Ber. It is the work
Of busy fancy in thy troubled mind;
Give it no heed.
    Mat. O! It was more, much more
Than fancy ever form'd; 'twas real all;
It haunts me still, and ev'ry circumstance
Is now before me; but I'll tell thee all.
Scarce had I clos'd my eyes, to seek that rest
Which long had been a stranger, when methought
Alone I wander'd through a mazy wood,
Beset with thorns and briars on ev'ry side,
The mournful image of my wretched state:
When, from a winding walk, the beauteous form
Of my lov'd Edwin seem'd to glide across,
And ran with haste to meet me: But, behold!
A tiger rush'd between, and seiz'd upon him:
I shriek'd aloud.

Ber. 'Twas terrible.

Mat. But mark
What follow'd : for a gleam of light broke in,
And sav'd me from despair : When cross the glade
A gen'rous lion, as with pity mov'd
At the unequal conflict, darted forth,
And sprung with vengeance on the spotted beast,
Who turn'd with fury on his natural foe,
And loos'd my Edwin ; he escap'd, and fled :
I wak'd in agonies.

Ber. Be comforted ;
The dream presages good : Some gen'rous friend
Shall save him from the perils of the war,
And give him to thy longing arms again.

Mat. O, never, never !

Enter an OFFICER.

Offi. Noble lady, one
From William's camp, by Morcar's orders sent,
Would crave a minute's conference, and says
He bears some news that may be welcome.

Mat. Ha !
From William's camp ! O flatt'ring hope ! who knows
But he may bring some tidings of my love !
Tidings, perhaps, I may not wish to hear.
Perhaps he comes to speak of Edwin's death ;
Or Edwin's falsehood—Be it as it may,
I cannot be more wretched than I am.
Conduct him hither.   [*Exit Officer.*
O my fluttering heart !
Look yonder ! how imagination forms
What most we wish for ; see he comes—It is,
It is my Edwin—Save me, Bertha ! O !
                    (*As he enters she faints.*

Enter EDWIN.

Edw. What do I see ? Matilda here ! she faints !

Am I deserted then ? abandon'd, lost,
Betray'd by her I love? She breathes, she lives!
But not for me—for Morcar; for my brother.
  Mat. *(To Ber.)* Where is he? O! it was delu-
      sion all;
The form deceiv'd me.   Had it been my love,
He would have flown with rapture to me—See
He stands far off, and will not look upon me.
  Edw. I dare not.
  Mat. Is it thus we meet again ?
Is this the kind, the tender, faithful Edwin?
  Edw. Art thou Matilda? Speak; for I am lost
In wild astonishment.   It cannot be.
In Morcar's camp! Is this the lovely captive
That I should meet?
  Mat. All-seeing heav'n,
Bear witness for me: If, from that sad hour
When last we parted, this devoted heart
Hath ever wander'd, ever cast one thought,
Or form'd a wish for any bliss but thee,
Despise me, Edwin; slight me, cast me off
To infamy and shame.
  Edw. I must, I must
Believe thee; Yet, 'tis strange—when thou shalt
      know
From whom I came, and what my errand here.
Thou wilt not call me cruel or unkind,
When I shall tell thee I am come to claim
Another's right,—O! heav'n, another's right
To my Matilda;—to request thy hand
For Morcar.
  Mat. For thy brother!
  Edw. Yes, ev'n now
We parted.—Here he told me I should meet
A beauteous captive; little did I think
It was Matilda, whom he long had woo'd;
Whose gen'rous heart, he hop'd, would now accept

A convert made to loyalty by love;
She only waited for that blest event,
With mutual ardour to return his passion.
Can it be thus? Alas! thy presence here
Confirms it but too well.

   Mat. Appearance oft,
By strange events, and causeless jealousy,
Confounds the guilty with the innocent.
But sure my Edwin's noble mind disdains
To cherish low suspicion; 'tis a vice
Abhorrent to thy nature, and Matilda
Will never practise it on thee.   True love
Knows not distrust, or diffidence, but rests
On its own faith secure, and hopes to meet
The truth it merits.

   Edw. Can this be the voice
Of falsehood?—Can those lips?—

   Mat. Mistaken man!
Couldst thou e'er credit the delusive tale?
Couldst thou believe I had so soon forgot
My plighted faith? But since I am suspected,
Return, and bear this answer back to Morcar.
First say, I thank him for the choice he made
Of thee to be the herald of his love:
For what is there Matilda can refuse,
That Edwin could request?

   Edw. O! that recals
A thousand tender thoughts——

   Mat. Go tell him too,
Whate'er I rashly promis'd but to gain
A few short moments, to preserve my king,
And save a father's life, I never meant
To feign a passion which I could not feel;
For I was destin'd to another's arms;
To one, who, now regardless of his vows
To poor Matilda, after three long years

Of cruel absence from her, comes at last
To doubt her honour, and suspect her love.

    Edw. O! never, never. Sooner will I doubt
The pow'rs of nature, and believe these eyes
Can misinterpret ev'ry object here,
Than think thee false. O! take me to thy arms,
And bury all my doubts.—Canst thou forgive
The jealous warmth of agonizing passion?

    Mat. I can; I must. But say, to what blest
        chance
Am I indebted for this happy moment?

    Edw. The chance of war. I am a prisoner here,
And but for thee—

    Mat When I shall tell thee all
That I have suffer'd since we parted last,
Thou wilt not blame, but pity, poor Matilda.
Meanwhile be calm; it is not now a time
For idle doubts and visionary fears,
When real dangers threat. I see already,
By thy imperfect tale, what misery
Must soon await us, when the fiery Earl
Shall know this strange event.

    Edw. And wherefore know it?
Why not conceal our passion, till some means
Of freedom offer?

    Mat. I abhor the thought.
No, Edwin, no. The crisis of our fate
Approaches. Never let us stain our loves
With crooked fraud and base dissimulation.
Hark! didst thou hear a voice in yonder grove?
Siward in conf'rence with the haughty Earl;
Behold them—see—they part—and Morcar hastes,
With quick impatient step, to know his fate.
Now summon all thy pow'rs.

    Edw. I am prepared.
He comes: a few short minutes will determine

Whether Matilda plays the hypocrite,
Or is deserving of her Edwin's love.

Enter MORCAR.

Mor. At length I hope Matilda's satisfied.
Edwin has told thee what a sacrifice
My heart hath made.   Ambition, glory, pride,
And fierce resentment, bend beneath thy power,
And yield the palm to all-subduing love.
Yes, thou hast conquered.   I am William's friend;
The struggle's past.   I have performed the task
Assigned, and come to claim my just reward.

Mat. By virtuous acts, the self-approving mind
Is amply paid, nor seeks a recompence
From ought beside.   You have redeemed your
    honour,
Turned to the paths of duty, and discharged
The debt you owe your country and your king :
England and William will be grateful for it.
What can you wish for more ?

Mor. There is a prize,
More welcome far, beyond whate'er a king
Or kingdom can bestow—thy love—

Mat. My lord !

Mor. If to have saved thee from the brutal rage
Of pitiless ruffians ; if to have renounced
A victor's claim, and be myself the slave
Of her I conquered ; if to have released
My bitterest foe, because allied to thee ;
If, after all my cruel wrongs, to accept
The proud oppressor's hand, can merit ought,
I am not quite unworthy of the boon.

Mat. The good and just, my lord, demand our
    praise,
And generous deeds will claim the tribute due,
The debt of humble gratitude ; but love,
Love, that must mark the colour of our days

For good or ill, for happiness or woe,
'Tis not the gift of fortune, or of fame,
Nor earned by merit, nor acquired by virtue.
All the rich treasures, which, or wealth, or power,
Have to bestow, can never purchase that
Which the free heart alone itself must give.

   Mor. Give it with freedom then to him who most
Hath studied to deserve—

   Mat. You talk, my lord,
As if the right of conquest could bestow
A right more precious, and a dearer claim;
But know, for now 'tis time to throw aside
The veil that long hath hid from Morcar's eyes
The secret of my soul; and say at last
I never can be thine.

   Mor. Ha! Never! O,
Recal that word!

   Mat. I must not: Edwin knows
There is a bar of adamant between,
That must for ever part us.

   Mor. Ha! for ever!
Distraction! can it be? Take heed, Matilda,
I am not to be mocked thus. O my brother!
Didst thou not hear her? But astonishment
Has closed thy lips in silence—Never mine!
And wherefore not be mine? [*Turning to* MATILDA.

   Mat. Because I am
Another's—Well I know our hapless sex,
So custom wills, and arbitrary man,
Is taught in fearful silence to conceal
The honest feelings of a tender heart:
Else, wherefore should Matilda blush to own
A virtuous passion for the best of men?

   Mor. A virtuous passion! grant me patience,
      heaven!
I am betrayed, abandoned, lost. Another's!
Some fawning slave, some Norman plunderer,

Rich with the ravished spoils of English valour,
Hath snared her easy heart, and tortured mine.
But I will drag him from his dark abode ;
Where'er he lurks, he shall not 'scape my vengeance.
Thou hear'st her, Edwin.

　　Edw. Aye : Who would not wish
To hear the voice of Nature, and of Love,
Thus nobly pleading by the lips of Truth ?

　　Mor. Amazement ! Thou art linked with the vile
　　　　slave
That hath usurped my right.　All, all conspire
To make me wretched.

　　Edw. Why should Morcar think
That lovely maid would act beneath herself,
And make so mean a choice ?　Now, on my soul,
I doubt not but the object of her love
Hath earned the glorious prize, and will be found
Deserving of it.

　　Mor. Thou know'st him then ?

　　Edw. I do ;
Know him as brave, as noble as thyself :
One who would scorn, howe'er the outward act
Might seem unworthy of him, to do ought
That should disgrace his family and name.
A man he is of yet untainted honour,
Of birth and valour equal to thy own,
Though fortune frowns upon him.

　　Mor. Now by heaven,
But that I know thy eyes were never blest
With my Matilda's charms, I should suspect
Thou hadst betrayed the sacred trust reposed
In thy false heart, by unsuspecting friendship,
And wert thyself the traitor.

　　Edw. Think so still.
Let Fancy, ever busy to torment
The jealous mind, alarm thee with the thought
Of seeing him whom thou hast thus reviled ;

Stand forth, and dare the proof; suppose him here
Before thee, ready to assert his claim,
His prior right to all the joys that love
And fair Matilda can bestow : Then look
On me, and know thy rival in—thy brother.

    Mor. Confusion! horror! misery! O heaven!
Canst thou behold such complicated guilt,
Such unexampled perfidy, and yet
Withhold thy vengeance? Let thy lightnings blast
The base betrayer! O Matilda! false,
Deceitful, cruel woman!

    Mat. 'Tis the lot
Of unprotected innocence to meet
The cruel censure, which to guilt alone
Is due. I've not deceived, I've not betrayed thee;
And wouldst thou listen to the artless tale
I could unfold—

    Mor. Away! I will not hear,
Nor see, nor think of thee. Deceitful villain!
Was this thy kind concern for Morcar's safety?
Was it for this that subtle Edwin came
A willing captive? boasted William's strength,
And lured me to a base, inglorious peace?
That, like a midnight ruffian, he might steal,
Unseen and unsuspected on my love,
And rob me of Matilda.

    Edw. I abhor
A thought so mean; the bare suspicion stains,
With such foul blot, my honour, and my name,
I will not deign to answer thee. My birth
Alone might prove, to any sense but thine,
That I disdain it : 'Tis enough to say
I am Earl Morcar's brother.

    Mor. I disclaim
All ties of nature or of friendship with thee,
And henceforth hold thee as my deadliest foe:
As such I will pursue thee, slave; for know,

Thou art my prisoner still—Who waits there ? Seize
And guard this traitor——

            [Guards enter and seize on EDWIN.

   Mat. (*Kneeling to* MORCAR.) O my Lord ! if e'er
Soft pity touched thy breast, if e'er thy heart
Felt the warm glow of sympathetic grief
For the unhappy, do not let the rage
Of thoughtless passion urge thee to a deed
Of horror, which, too late, thou wilt repent.
O ! spare a guiltless brother, spare thyself
The bitter pangs of sad remorse that soon
Shall harrow up thy soul, when radiant truth
Shall flash conviction on thee. O ! forgive
And pity.——

   Edw. Rise, Matilda : 'Tis beneath
The dignity of innocence to kneel
Before proud guilt, and supplicate a tyrant.

   Mat. (*Rising.*) I feel the just reproach—Forgive
       me, Edwin ;
Henceforth I never will disgrace thy love
By mean submission. Morcar, if thou hop'st
For future peace, or pardon, set us free.

   Mor. I'll hear no more ; convey her to her tent.

   Mat. Edwin, adieu ! If honour, virtue, truth,
And mutual love, protect the innocent,
We yet shall meet in happiness—farewel !

            [Exit MATILDA *guarded.*

   Mor. Let none have entrance there, but faithful
       Siward.
Would he were here that I might pour my sorrows
Into his friendly bosom ! O Siward !
Where art thou?—Ha, he comes !

       Enter SIWARD.

   Siw. My Lord, the troops,
Flushed with their late success, refuse all terms
Of peace with Willliam, and cry out for war
And vengeance.

Mor. They shall have it. Now, by heaven,
Thou bringest me glorious tidings—well, what more ?
    Siw. They have discovered that the noble pris'ner,
Who had surrendered, is thy brother Edwin ;
This hath alarmed them ; they suspect you both
Of vile collusion, to betray their cause,
And yield them to the tyrant. If, they say,
You mean them fair, let Edwin be confined,
And answer for the treason with his life.
    Mor. And so he shall : They could not ask a boon
Which Morcar would more readily bestow ;
Already their request is granted.—See
The traitor is secured. All-seeing heaven !
Thou see'st how justice will o'ertake the wicked !
    Siw. What can this mean ? Since last I saw my
            friend,
How the fair day, that shone so bright upon us,
Is suddenly o'ercast.
    Mor. Alas, my Siward !
When thou shalt know—but 'tis enough to say
Matilda's false, and Edwin is—a villain.
    Siw. Amazement ! can it be ?
    Mor. It is too true ;
And I am lost for ever. O Matilda !
Deceitful woman !
    Siw. 'Tis not now a time
For idle plaints : Consult your safety : Fly
This moment to the camp—your presence there,
And that alone, may quell the rising storm :
Leave Edwin to my care.
    Mor. I go, my Siward,
Safe in thy friendship ; I entrust to thee
My just revenge. Yon moss-grown tower that hangs
O'er the deep flood—'tis under thy command—
Place double guard—he must not 'scape—his fate
Shall be determined soon. Whate'er it prove,
It cannot be more wretched than my own.
                                [*Exit* MORCAR.

Edw. (*Pointing to the guards.*) Where is my
  dungeon ? My conductors here
Wait but your orders ; give 'em their commission ;
For you, it seems, sir, are to execute
The friendly office : Do it, and be happy.
 Siw. Guards, set your pris'ner free—Thou little
  know'st
Of Siward's soul, to think it joys in aught
That gives another pain. I've learnt too well,
In sad affliction's hard, but wholesome school,
The lesson of humanity.
 Edw. O generous Siward, if thou hast a heart
To feel for others miseries, pity mine,
And poor Matilda's : She has not deserved
A fate like this.
 Siw. Alas ! it rives my soul
To see the tender bonds of amity
Thus torn asunder by the very means
I fondly thought for ever would unite them ;
And the fair structure, which my hopes had raised,
Of love and friendship, in a moment shrunk
From its weak base, and buried all in ruin.
If thou canst prove thy innocence, as yet
I hope thou wilt, for in that noble mien
I read a conscious pride, that would not stoop
To ought that's base ; still may I hope to heal
These bleeding wounds, and sooth him to forgive-
  ness.
Meantime be free.   Give me thy sacred word,
The soldier's oath, thou wilt be found whene'er
I call upon thee ; and yon tent alone
Shall be thy prison ; free to range around,
Far as my guard extends.
 Edw. Accept my thanks,
The humble tribute of a grateful heart ;
'Tis all I have to give.   The time may come
When Edwin shall repay thee as he ought.

 Siw. Is there ought more, which honour, and the
   duty
I owe my friend, permits me to bestow,
That thou wouldst ask?
 Edw. O, grant me to behold
That injured maid, to take my last farewel;
Then act as fate and Morcar shall determine.
I give the pledge of safety thou requir'st,
And will be found—speak, wilt thou listen to me?
 Siw. Of that we'll talk hereafter—come—within
I'll hear thy story—Thou but know'st me yet
As Morcar's friend; hereafter thou may'st find
I am still more the friend of Truth and Virtue.

ACT THE FOURTH.

SCENE I.

An Apartment belonging to SIWARD, *opening to a
wood.*

EDWIN, MATILDA.

Edw. Thanks to the noble Siward's generous pity
For the distressed ; once more we meet, Matilda,
But only meet, alas ! to mourn our fate,
To feel each other's woes, and to be wretched.

Mat. Eternal blessings wait on him who thus
Could sweeten sorrow's bitter draught, and make
Captivity a blessing.　O my Edwin,
A few short moments spent with those we love,
Is worth an age of common life.

Edw. With thee
Indeed it is ; but we are on the verge
Of a dark precipice, and every step
Is dangerous.　If Morcar should return,
And find us here together, we are lost
For ever ; thou hast seen, and seen with horror,
The desperate rage of his tumultuous soul,
Let us avoid it, let us——

Mat. What, my love ?
Thou art my guide, protector, guardian, all

I have to boast on earth ! O ! teach me where
To find some blest asylum for my woes,
And guide my footsteps to the paths of peace.

   Edw. Let me entreat thee then——

   Mat. O, speak ! thou know'st
I have no will but thine.

   Edw. Then leave me, leave
This hated roof : I have a friend within,
Who shall conduct thee to the royal camp
In safety ; bear this signet to the king,
He will protect thee, and whatever fate
Decrees for me, Matilda may be happy.

   Mat. O ! never, never : safety dwells with thee,
And thee alone. Without my faithful Edwin,
The peopled city, and the crowded court,
Would be a desert to me. No, my love,
We will not part : The same benignant power
That led thee hither, that, beyond my hopes,
Brought my lost Edwin to these arms again,
Will still protect that virtue which it loves.

   Edw. Didst thou not tell me, that this very
      morn
Thou hadst determined, as the only means
To shun my brother's love, on sudden flight ?

   Mat. But then I should have fled in search of
      thee.

   Edw. Thou winning softness ! how shall I re-
      ward
Such unexampled tenderness and truth !

   Mat. By flying with me. Come, my love, lead
      on,
I'll follow thee to dangers and to death ;
Nor perils shall affright, nor labours tire,
When thou art with me.

   Edw. No : It must not be.

   Mat. Why ? What should keep thee here ?

   Edw. The ties of honour.

Mat. And are they stronger than the bonds of
　　love?

Edw. To Siward's kind indulgence, well thou
　　know'st,
I owe this little interval of peace,
This transient gleam of happiness with thee;
And should I break my sacred word, his life
Might answer for it; wouldst thou have me thus
Repay his kindness? No, my love: I may
Be wretched, but I cannot be ungrateful.

Mat. Must thou return then to that hateful pri-
　　son
When Morcar comes?

Edw. I must.   O! think when I
Am pent within a loathsome dungeon, who
Shall shelter then thy unprotected virtue?
No Edwin there to succour thee: Who knows
What brutal lust and power may dare to act
On a deserted, beauteous, friendless woman?
Distracting thought! A monarch's vengeance then
Would come too late; would make me poor amends
For my Matilda's violated charms.

Mat. He cannot be so mean, so base of soul;
Or if he should, I have a dagger here
To save me from dishonour.

Edw. What! by death?
Dreadful alternative! O! hazard not
Thy precious life, but seize the lucky moment
Which fortune gives us, e'er it be too late.

Mat. Urge me no more; already I have felt,
Too deeply felt, the pangs of absence from thee:
Another separation would be worse
Than death, and all its terrors.   No, my love;
We are embarked on a tumultuous sea,
And must abide the fury of the storm.
The waves of angry fortune may o'erwhelm,
But shall not part us: We will stem the torrent,

Brave the proud ocean's rage, and gain the harbour
Of peace and happiness—or sink together.

Edw. Thou hast foretold the tempest, and behold
It rushes on us.

Enter MORCAR *and* HAROLD.

Mat. Ha! Earl Morcar here!

Mor. Harold, I thank thee; thy intelligence
Was but too true.   [*Turning to* EDWIN.
Traitor! who set thee free?
They would have 'scap'd my vengeance—false Ma-
          tilda!
'Tis thus I am rewarded for my love,
My ill-timed mercy to a thankless brother.
Back to thy dungeon, slave. Guards drag him
          hence
To prison, and to death.   [*To the soldiers.*

Edw. Or death, or life,
Are equal to me, if I must be torn
From my Matilda. But, whate'er thy purpose,
Be speedy in thy vengeance, nor delay
The cruel work; for know, thy master comes,
William approaches—to revenge my cause.

Mor. But not to save thee.

Edw. Then farewel, Matilda,
Perhaps for ever—If we meet no more
Thou wilt remember—But I will not doubt
Thy honour, or thy love. I know thy truth;
Know thou wilt act as best becomes thy fate,
Whate'er it be, and worthy of thyself.

Mat. Of thee, my Edwin; rather say of thee.
Yes; I will copy well thy bright example;
I'll not disgrace thy love with woman's weakness,
But part without a tear. I will but stay
To tell thy tyrant brother how I hate,
How I despise him, and then follow thee.

Mor. I'll hear no more—begone!—away with
   him.   [*Exeunt guards with* EDWIN.
For thee, Matilda——
 Mat. What for me remains
I know too well; thy odious love, reproach
Unmerited, and threats which I despise.
Thou think'st I have deceived thee—think so still.
Enjoy thy error. Thou believ'st us guilty;
'Twill make thee happy now—Perchance to find
Us innocent, may be thy punishment hereafter.
 Mor. Aye, 'twas a proof of innocence to fly,
Thou and thy paramour together.
 Mat. No;
I scorn a thought so mean. Could I have left
My Edwin, long e'er this I might have been
Beyond the reach of tyranny; beyond
Thy hated power; and safe, beneath the wing
Of sacred majesty, in William's care.
 Mor. In William's care!
 Mat. Thy conqueror's—for know
The hero comes—to scatter blessings round him,
To heal his country's wounds, chastise rebellion,
And punish false perfidious slaves like thee.
 Mor. By heav'ns! she braves my wrath, insults
   my weakness,
And triumphs o'er her slave.
 Mat. There was a time,
When with an eye of pity I beheld
Thy hopeless love; when I concealed my passion
For the dear idol of my heart, because
I feared 'twould make thee wretched; but thy rage,
Thy cruel treatment of a guiltless brother,
Has cancelled all.
 Mor. Then, mark me: If thou hop'st
For Edwin's freedom, shake off this vile passion;
Yield thy proud heart to him who best deserves it,
And meet me at the altar—Two hours hence

I shall expect thee there—Beyond that time
He may not live to thank thee for thy bounty.

   Mat. Then let him perish—glut thy tyrant soul
With vengeance : bathe it in a brother's blood.
All ruffian, all barbarian, as thou art ;
Thou canst not murder his immortal fame :
Thou canst not rob him of Matilda's love.
But know—when he, for whom alone this pulse
Would wish to beat, this lazy blood to flow
Within my veins, when he shall be no more ;
Another life shall satiate thy revenge ;
Another victim shall attend thy triumph.

   Mor. Thou talk'st it nobly—'tis the common
       trick,
The affectation of thy sex, to boast
A fancied firmness, which ye never knew ;
But with affrighted nature thou wouldst shrink
When death approaches.

   Mat. Put me to the proof.
If thou wouldst punish Edwin, know he lives
Within this breast—strike home, and pierce him
      there.

   Mor. Imperious woman ! thou defiest my power,
And let it crush thee.   If thy country bleeds
In every vein ; if perjur'd Edwin falls,
As soon he shall, a victim to my rage,
Thou art the murd'rer ; thou the parricide ;
I stand absolved ; the guilt is all thy own.

   Mat. If it be guilt to suffer keen reproach,
Pain, persecution, terror, chains, and death,
For him I love, rather than stain my soul
With foul disloyalty, I am indeed
The guiltiest of my sex, and well deserve
The pangs I feel.

   Mor. Thou'st driven me to the pit
Of black despair, and I will drag thee down
To share the dreadful ruin thou hast made.

Mat. I know thy savage purpose; but remember,
The hour approaches when thou shalt repent
This base, unmanly triumph. William comes:
Hear that and tremble, thou unnat'ral brother;
Nor rocks, nor caves shall hide thee from his ven-
　　　geance;
Inglorious, and unpitied, shalt thou fall,
And after ages shall consign thy name
To endless scorn, and infamy immortal.
　　　　　　　　　　　[*Exit* MATILDA.

Mor. Inexorable judge! I stand condemned,
And shall await my doom; but not alone
Or unreveng'd shall Morcar fall—henceforth
I bid adieu to Love, and all his train
Of fond delusions—Vengeance! I am thine,
And thine alone: Thou daughter of despair!
Destructive goddess! come, possess my soul
With all thy terrors—Yes; it shall be so.
A few short hours are all that niggard fate
Will deign to spare me; I'll employ 'em well,
For I will crowd into the narrow circle
A little age of misery and horror.
Ha! Siward here! what brought thee hither?

Enter SIWARD.

Siw. Pity
For the distressed. I knew thou wert unhappy,
And came, where duty called, to pour the balm
Of friendship in, and heal thy wounded heart.

Mor. O, they have pierced too deep; even thou,
　　　, my friend,
Thou hast betrayed me: was it not unkind
To set my pris'ner free; to let him meet
Matilda, and conspire against my life?

Siw. Impossible! By heaven! the artful story
He told, so wrought upon my easy soul,
I thought him innocent.

Mor. Hast thou not heard——

Siw. From Harold only an imperfect tale,
So strange I could not credit it.

Mor. Alas!
'Tis all too true: I am the veriest slave,
The meanest wretch that e'er was trampled on
By an imperious woman: O my friend!
My Siward! I have nought on earth but thee:
Shouldst thou forsake me in this hour of terror!
But sure thou wilt not.

Siw. No: Whate'er the will
Of wayward Fortune may determine for us,
Behold me ready to partake thy fate.
If we must sue for peace, let Siward bear
The olive for thee: if once more we cast
The desperate die of battle, let me perish
By Morcar's side. Come, let us on together;
Shake off this load of unavailing sorrow,
And seek the field; there, if we fall, we fall
With honour: if we rise, we rise to glory.

Mor. Talk not of glory to a wretch like me,
Bereft of every hope. There was a time
When that enlivening call would have awaked
My active spirit, and this drooping heart
Bounded with joy; but my Matilda's lost:
Revenge alone——

   [*Enter a messenger to* SIWARD *with letters.*

Siw. From Walstcoff these;
'Tis well—retire.   [*Exit messenger.*
(*Reads*)——How's this? then all is lost.
He writes me here, that William's fame in arms,
Spite of his cruel and oppressive laws,
Hath raised him friends in every part: already
The northern rebels are dispersed, and thousands
Flock to the royal standard. To resist
Were madness.

Mor. And to yield were cowardice
More shameful——

    Siw. What must we resolve on?

    Mor. Death :
The wretch's only hope, the wish'd-for end
Of every care; but I would meet him clothed
In all his terrors, with his reeking spear
Dipt in the blood of an ungrateful mistress,
And a false, happy rival : Then, my Siward,
Shalt thou behold me welcome the kind stroke,
And smile in agony.

    Siw. Unhappy youth !
The storm beats hard upon thee ; but our fate
Will soon be fixt, for William comes to-morrow.

    Mor. To-morrow ! ha ! then something must be
        done,
And quickly too.   If William comes, he comes
To triumph over us: then, my Siward, who
Shall punish Edwin ? who shall wed Matilda !
I cannot bear it—If thou lov'st me, Siward,
For now I mean to try thy virtue, swear
By all the powers that wait on injured honour,
Whate'er my anxious soul requests of thee,
Thou'lt not refuse it.

    Siw. By the hallowed flame
Of sacred friendship, that within this breast,
Since the first hour I sealed thee for my own,
With unremitted ardour still hath glow'd,
I will not—Speak, my Morcar, here I swear
To aid thy purpose.

    Mor. 'Tis enough; and now
Come near and mark me: Thou command'st the
        tower
Where Edwin is confined.

    Siw. I do.

    Mor. Methinks
It were an easy task—you understand me—

Justice is slow, and—William comes to-morrow.
Thy friendly hand——

    Siw. My lord!—

    Mor. Thou tremblest—Well, another time, my
        Siward,

We'll talk on't—shall we not? Thou mean'st to do
As thou hast promised?

    Siw. Certainly.

    Mor. Then speak,

And do not trifle with me.

    Siw. Sure, my lord,

You cannot mean to—

    Mor. Is he not a villain?

    Siw. I fear he may be so.

    Mor. A hypocrite.

    Siw. He hath, perhaps, deceived you, and de-
        serves—

    Mor. To perish.

    Siw. No; to suffer, not to die;

Or, if to perish, not by Morcar's hand,
Or Siward's—O! 'tis horrible to shed
A brother's blood—

    Mor. A rival's.

    Siw. Nature—

    Mor. Love—

    Siw. Humanity—

    Mor. Matilda——

    Siw. (*Aside.*) Gracious heaven!

That passion thus should root up every sense
Of good and evil in the heart of man,
And change him to—a monster!

    Mor. Hence! away,

And leave me—From this moment I will herd
With the wild savage in yon leafless desert,
Nor trust to friendship—but another hand—

    Siw. (*Musing.*) Ha! that alarms me—then it
        must be so;

And yet how far—

Mor. You pause.

Siw. I am resolved.

Mor. On what ?

Siw. To serve, to honour, to—obey you.
Edwin shall ne'er disturb thy peace again.

Mor. O glorious instance of exalted friendship !
My other self, my best, my dear-lov'd Siward—
Conscience ! thou busy monitor, away,
And leave me—Siward, when shall it be done ?
To-night, my Siward, shall it not ?

Siw. Or never.

Mor. Let me but see the proud Matilda weep ;
Let me but hear the music of her groans,
And sate my soul with vengeance—For the rest,
'Tis equal all. But tell me, Siward, say,
How shall I know the bloody moment ? What
Shall be the welcome signal ?

Siw. When thou hear'st
The solemn curfeu sound, conclude
The business done—Farewell. When I return,
With tears of joy thou shalt my zeal commend,
And own that Siward was indeed thy friend.

ACT THE FIFTH.

SCENE I.

A Gothic Hall.

MORCAR, HAROLD.

Mor. Treason and foul rebellion in my camp !
But I was born to be for ever wretched,
The sport of Fortune.   These base mutineers——
   Har. Your presence on the battlements, my lord,
Dispersed 'em soon ; they hang their heads in silence,
And all is peace.
   Mor. (*To himself.*) It is not so within !
Would it were done, or——
   Har. What, my lord ?
   Mor. No matter.
What urged my soldiers to rebel ?
   Har. 'Tis thought
The gallant captive did by secret means
Excite them to revolt.
   Mor. It must be so.
By heaven! thou mak'st me happy with the tidings :
His head shall pay the forfeit.
   Har. Whilst he lives
We are not safe.

Mor. No more we are, good Harold;
'Tis fit he perish—is it not? What say'st thou?
　Har. Prudence demands his life to save your own.
　Mor. O! thou hast given such comfort to my
　　　　soul—
　Har. My lord—
　Mor. Be watchful: Bring me early notice
Of every motion: Go. 　　　　[*Exit* HAROLD.
Or I must fall,
Or Edwin—Hence ye visionary fears;
Ye vain chimeras, hence—It is no matter:
Conscience, I heed thee not; 'tis self-defence,
Nature's first law, and I must stand acquitted.
The prudent Siward seemed to hesitate,
As if he wished, but knew not how to shun
The office. He who could behold my tortures
With all that cold tranquillity, would ne'er
Have ventured to remove them. But I've trusted
The sword of vengeance to a safer hand.
What ho! Who waits?

　　　　　Enter an OFFICER.

That soldier whom thou saw'st
In private conference with me, is he gone
As I directed him?
　Off. My Lord, even now
I saw him hastening toward the tower.
　Mor. 'Tis well.
When he returns conduct him to me—Stay;
If Siward comes this way, I'm not at leisure:
I will not see him. *(Starts.)* Hark! didst thou not
　　　　hear
The solemn curfeu?
　Off. No, my Lord.
　Mor. Not hear it?
It shocks my soul with horror—Hark! again!

Hollow and dreadful! Sure thy faculties
Are all benumbed.

    Offi. Indeed, I heard it not.

    Mor. Away, and leave me to myself. [*Exit* OFFICER.
Methought
I heard a voice cry—stop—it is thy brother:
We loved each other well; our early years
Were spent in mutual happiness together:
Matilda was not there—I do remember,
One day, in sportive mood, I rashly plunged
Into the rapid flood, which had well nigh
O'erwhelmed me; when the brave, the gallant Ed-
       win,
Rushed in and saved me—Shall I, in return,
Destroy my kind preserver? Horrid thought!
Forbid it heaven! *(Pauses.)* I am myself again.
All powerful Nature! once more I am thine.
He shall not die—Who's there—

Enter an OFFICER.

    My Oswald! fly,
Fly to the tower this moment, haste, and save
My brother—Some base ruffian—

    Offi. If, my Lord,
You mean the noble pris'ner there, I fear
It is too late: This moment, as I passed
The citadel, I saw a mangled corpse
Drawn forth by Siward's order—

    Mor. Slave, thou liest.
Away this moment, bring me better news
On peril of thy life.   [*Exit* OFFICER.

    Who knows but heaven,
In gracious pity, still may interpose
And save me from the guilt? It is not done;
It shall not—must not be—All's quiet yet;
I have not heard the signal.   [*The bell tolls.*
Hark! he's dead:

My brother's dead—O! cover me, ye shades
Of everlasting night! Hide, if ye can,
A murtherer from himself. Ha! see, he comes:
His wounds are bleeding still; his angry eyes
Glare full upon me.   Speak—what wouldst thou
              have?
Matilda shall be thine: He smiles and leaves me—
            [*He pauses and recovers himself.*
'Twas but the error of my troubled soul,
O! guilt, guilt, guilt!   [*Throws himself down.*
Here will I lay me down,
And end my days in bitterness and anguish.

Enter SIWARD.

Who's there! ha! Siward here.   [*Rises.*
Speak, murtherer, speak,
Where is my brother? Villain, thou hast snared
My soul; my honour's stain'd, my fame destroyed,
And my sweet peace of mind is lost for ever.
     Siw. Matilda will restore it.
     Mor. Never, never,
The price of blood! No: Could Matilda bring
The vanquished world, in dowry with her charms,
I would not wed her. O! could I recal
One hasty moment, one rash, cruel act—
But 'twas thy savage hand that—
     Siw. I received
Your orders: 'twas my duty to obey them.
     Mor. Where slept thy friendship then? Thou
              know'st despair
And madness urged me to it—but for thee—
Thy callous heart had never felt the pangs,
The agonies of disappointed love;
Thou didst not know Matilda—Curs'd obedience
How often has thy insolence opposed
Thy master and thy prince? how often dared
To thwart my will, and execute thy own:

But when I bade thee do a deed of horror,
And shed a brother's blood, thou couldst obey me.
   Siw. Away! this is a trick of self-delusion,
The common cant of hypocrites, who rail
At others guilt, to mitigate their own.
I've been the mean, the servile instrument
Of thy base vengeance; but thou hadst prepared
Another, a low ruffian, to perform
The bloody office; I detest thee for it,
Despise, abhor thee.
   Mor. Thou wert once my friend.
   Siw. Henceforth I am thy foe—Thou hast de-
      stroyed
The best of brothers, and the best of men.
   Mor. Despised by Siward—then my cup of sor-
      row
Is full indeed—But this shall—
   [*Attempts to kill himself,* SIWARD *wrests the*
      sword from him.
Ha! disarm'd!
But coward guilt is weak as infancy;
It was not so before I murdered Edwin.
   Siw. The murderer's punishment should be to
      live,
And shall be thine; thou know'st not half thy guilt,
Nor half thy sorrows: I shall rend thy soul.
Prepare thee for another, deeper wound,
And know that Edwin loved thee; in his hand,
Whilst mine was lifted up for his destruction,
I found this paper; 'tis the counterpart
Of one he had dispatched to William; read it,
And tremble at thy complicated guilt.
   Mor. (*Taking the paper.*) What's here? He pleads
      my pardon with the king,
Ascribes my frantic zeal, in Edgar's cause,
To ill-advised warmth; and recommends
His—murderer to mercy: Horrid thought!

I am the vilest, most abandoned slave
That e'er disgraced humanity—O Siward!
If thou hast yet, among the dying embers
Of our long friendship, one remaining spark
Of kind compassion for the wretched Morcar,
Lend me thy aid to shake off the sad load
Of hated life, that presses sore upon me.
    Siw. Though thou'rt no longer worthy of my
        friendship,
Deaf to the cries of Nature, and the voice
Of holy Truth, that would have counselled thee
To better deeds, yet hath my foolish heart
Some pity for thee—After crimes like these,
There is but one way left—Say, wilt thou patient
        wait
Till I return?
    Mor. I will.
    Siw. Remember, Morcar,
You promised me—I have a draught within,
Of wondrous power, that in a moment lulls
The tortured soul to sweet forgetfulness
Of all its woes; I'll haste and bring it thee;
'Twill give thee rest and peace.   [*Exit* SIWARD,
    Mor. I hope for ever.
But where's the lost Matilda? who shall comfort
That dear, unhappy maid, whom I have robb'd
Of every bliss.   O save me from the sight,
Ye pitying powers!

Enter MATILDA.

She comes—distraction!
    Mat. O!
My Lord, permit—
    Mor. Away—I know thee not.
    Mat. Not know me! 'tis the poor distress'd Ma-
        tilda,
Who comes to ask forgiveness for the rage

Of frantic love ; the madness of despair,
That urged me to such wrath and bitterness
Of keen reproach ; but pardon,   [*Kneels.*
Generous Morcar,
A woman's weakness : speak, and make me blest.
Alas ! he hears me not.

 Mor. Matilda, rise ;
I pray thee leave me.   [*Weeps.*

 Mat. Gracious heaven ! he weeps ;
Propitious omen ! O my Lord ! those tears
Are the soft marks of sympathizing woe,
And seem to say, I shall not plead in vain.

 Mor. Ask what thou wilt, for know, so dear I
    hold
Matilda's happiness, that here I swear,
If all the kingdoms of the peopled earth
Were mine to give, I'd lay them at her feet ;
But much I fear they would not make her happy.

 Mat. Alas ! my Lord, Matilda's happiness
Is center'd all in one dear precious jewel ;
'Tis in thy keeping—Edwin—

 Mor. What of him ?

 Mat. Is innocent.

 Mor. I know it.

 Mat. Just and good ;
He never meant to injure thee ; indeed
He did not.

 Mor. I believe it ; for his nature
Was ever mild and gentle.

 Mat. Good my Lord,
You mock me.

 Mor. No, Matilda ; speak, go on,
And praise him : I could talk to thee for ever
Of Edwin's virtues—

 Mat. Then thou wouldst not hurt
His precious life, thou wouldst not—

 Mor. I would give
A thousand worlds to save him.

Mat. Wouldst thou? then
My prayers are heard, thou hast forgiven all,
And I am happy.   Speak, is Edwin free?
    Mor. From every care—would I were half so
        blest!
    Mat. What mean you? Ha! thy eyes are fixt
        with horror,
Thy looks are wild.   What hast thou done? O!
        speak.
    Mor. Matilda, if thou com'st for Edwin's life,
It is too late—for Edwin is no more.
    Mat. And is my Edwin slain?
    Mor. Aye: Basely murder'd.
O! 'twas the vilest, most unnat'ral deed
That ever—
    Mat. Blasted be the cruel hand
That dealt the blow! O, may his guilty heart
Ne'er taste of balmy peace, or sweet repose!
    Mor. But ever, by the vulture conscience torn,
Bleed inward, still unpitied, till he seek
For refuge in the grave.
    Mat. Nor find it there.
    Mor. 'Tis well: Thy curses are accomplished all;
I feel 'em here within—for know—'twas I.
I gave the fatal order, and my friend,
My Siward, has too faithfully performed it.
    Mat. Siward! impossible! There dwells not then,
In human breast, or truth or virtue—O!
Unnatural brother!—but I will be calm.
    Mor. Alas! thy fate is happiness to mine;
For thou art innocent.
    Mat. And soon, I hope
To be rewarded for it.   O! my Edwin,
Matilda soon shall follow thee—thou think'st
I am unarmed, deserted, doomed like thee
To hated life; but know, I have a friend,

A bosom-friend, and prompt, as thine, to enter
On any bloody service I command.

         [*Draws a dagger.*

 Mor Command it then for justice, for revenge,
Behold! my bosom rises to the blow;
Strike here, and end a wretched murderer.—

 Mat. No;
That were a mercy thou hast not deserv'd;
I shall not seek revenge in Morcar's death,
In mine thou shalt be wretched.—

  [*Attempts to stab herself;* MORCAR *lays hold of*
    the dagger.

 Mor. Stop, Matilda—
Stop thy rash hand; the weight of Edwin's blood
Sits heavy on my heart.   O! do not pierce it
With added guilt.

 Mat. No more, I must be gone
To meet my Edwin, who already chides
My lingering steps, and beckons me away.

 Mor. Yet hear me! O! if penitence and prayer,
If deep contrition, sorrow, and remorse,
Could bring him back to thy desiring eyes,
O! with what rapture would I yield him now
To thee, Matilda—bear me witness—Ha!   [*Starts.*
'Tis he—Look up, dear injured maid—he comes
To claim my promise

 Mat. It is, it is my Edwin!

  Enter SIWARD *and* EDWIN : EDWIN *runs and*
    embraces MATILDA.

 Mor. O unexpected bliss! what gracious hand—
 Siw. Behold the cordial draught I promised you!
I knew thy noble nature, when the storm
Of passion had subsided, would abhor
A deed so impious—'Tis the only time
That Siward ever did deceive his friend.
Canst thou forgive?

Mor. Forgive thee ! O thou art
My guardian angel, sent by gracious heaven
To save me from perdition.   O my brother !
I blush to stand before thee—wilt thou take
From these polluted hands one precious gift ?
'Twill make thee full amends for all thy wrongs.
Accept her, and be happy.

   [*He joins the hands of* EDWIN *and* MATILDA:
           then, turning to SIWARD.

              That vile slave
Whom I employed—

   Siw. I guessed his horrid purpose,
Watched every step, and as the villain aimed
His poniard at the guiltless Edwin's breast,
Turned sudden round, and plunged it in his own.
The bloody corse was dragged—

   Mor. I know the rest.
O Siward ! from what weight of endless woe
Hath thy blest hand preserved me !

   Edw. O my Matilda ! how shall we repay
Our noble benefactor ? Much I owe
To gallant Siward, but to Morcar more :
Thou gav'st me life, but my kind, generous brother
Enhanced the gift, and blessed me with Matilda.

   Mat. (*To* MORCAR.) Words are too poor to thank
            thee as I ought
Accept this tribute of a grateful heart,
These tears of joy; and, O! may every curse
My frantic grief for Edwin poured upon thee,
Be changed to dearest blessings on thy head !

   Mor. Alas : thy blessings cannot reach me. Guilt
May plead for pardon, but can never boast
A claim to happiness : I only ask
A late forgiveness.   If a life of sorrow,
And deep remorse, can wash my crimes away,
Let 'em be buried with me in oblivion,

And do not curse the memory of Morcar.

                   [Turning to EDWIN.

O Edwin ! say, canst thou forgive the crime
Of frantic love, of madness and despair ?

    Edw. As in my latest hour from heaven I hope
Its kind indulgence for my errors past,
Even so, my brother, from my soul I pardon
And pity thee.

    Mor. Then I shall die in peace.

    Edw. Talk not of death, my brother, thou must
         live
To see our happiness complete, to hear
My sweet Matilda pour forth all her heart
In rapturous thanks to thee, and to thy friend;
And grateful Edwin bless thee for thy bounties.

    Mor. It must not be : I know too much already
Of Morcar's weakness, and Matilda's power ;
They are not to be trusted.   No, my Edwin,
Morcar shall never interrupt thy joys.
Far from thy sight, and from the haunts of men,
In some deep distant solitude retired,
To pious sorrow will I dedicate
My short remains of wretched life, and strive
To make my peace with heaven and wronged Ma-
        tilda.

And if perchance in after times some bard,
Struck with the native horrors of my tale,
Should bid the historic muse record it—let him,
By my example, teach a future age
The dire effects of loose, unbridled rage ;
Teach thoughtless men their passions to controul,
And curb the sallies of the impetuous soul,
Lest they experience worse than Morcar's woe,
Nor find a Siward—to prevent the blow.

MARY QUEEN OF SCOTS;

A

TRAGEDY,

IN FIVE ACTS.

AS PERFORMED AT THE

THEATRE-ROYAL, DRURY-LANE.

BY THE

HON. JOHN ST JOHN.

DRAMATIS PERSONÆ.

DUKE OF NORFOLK,	*Mr Kemble.*
SIR WILLIAM CECIL,	*Mr Aikin.*
LORD HERRIES,	*Mr Barrymore.*
DAVISON,	*Mr Parker.*
EARL OF SHREWSBURY,	*Mr Benson.*
EARL OF HUNTINGDON,	*Mr Phillimore.*
SIR AMIAS PAULET,	*Mr Fawcett.*
BETON,	*Mr Williams.*
NAWE,	*Mr Alfred.*
LIEUTENANT OF THE TOWER,	*Mr Lyons.*
SHERIFF,	*Mr Chaplin.*
QUEEN MARY,	*Mrs Siddons.*
QUEEN ELIZABETH,	*Mrs Ward.*
LADY DOUGLAS,	*Mrs Farmer.*
LADY SCROPE,	*Miss Tidswell.*

MARY QUEEN OF SCOTS.

ACT THE FIRST.

SCENE I.

The Gateway of Bolton Castle.

Enter BETON, *who perceives* LORD HERRIES *arriving.*

Bet. Sure 'tis Lord Herries ! O my noble friend !
How have we daily prayed for your return !
Your royal mistress, from yon turret's height,
By hourly watch, hath strained her beauteous eyes,
Till gushing tears o'erwhelmed her sight.—But say,
What tidings bring you from the English court?
  L. Her. Beton ! if faith and zeal in a good cause
Could have secured success, it had been thine ;
Your claim of simple audience for a queen
Was founded on a royal pledge.   The ring
Which graced your embassy was sent with vows
To Mary from Elizabeth, that she would aid

Her royal sister's cause—But, O good Beton!
It needs not our experience to foresee
The gulf 'twixt vows and their accomplishment.

 Bet. But the result?

 L. Her. Evasions and chicane;
Base terms propos'd; then treacherous advice
That Mary should in policy submit
To this strange trial; heaven forbid! until
She's heard in person.

 Bet. Still deny her presence?
Still urge these poor pretences! Grant our queen
Were liable to imputations—Grant
Whate'er hate, envy list—'twill but enforce
Her claim to face the accuser.

 L. Her. I shall entreat
Permission to revoke this rash appeal.

 Bet. Would it were done! Our country is de-
   based!
While our anointed queen submits her cause
To foreign jurisdiction, and betrays
At once her own and Scotland's dignity.

 L. Her. Thus shall I urge; you know her spirit
   well;
Touch but that string, 'twill vibrate o'er her frame;
She has a soul that wakes at Honour's voice;
Alive, with eager trembling at the sound,
She flies to its embrace; let Shame approach!
Straight she recoils, and shrinks within herself;
No plant so sensitive, no shade so fleet.
May heav'n still guard her! which way is the queen?
          [*Exeunt.*

SCENE II.

The Hall in Bolton Castle.

Enter LADY SCROPE, *meeting* LADY DOUGLAS.

L. Scr. How fares my royal guest this morn,
    sweet maid?
You meet me on my accustomed daily course
To attend your queen, and wait her high com-
    mands.
    L. Doug. My gentle Lady Scrope, you are too
    kind;
Such courteous words but ill besuit the state
Of my poor fallen mistress—Rather say,
Is she secure? Who guards the castle gates?
Is every arrow-slit and loop-hole watched?
    L. Scr. Tax me not, Douglas! with severity—
    L. Doug. 'Tis but your duty, which you exer-
    cise
With tender feeling, and more true respect
Than those at first deputed to receive her
With all the forms and pomp of royal state.
For, O! what aggravating mockery!
Bows, smiles, and court-like phrases never sooth
The pangs of princes in imprisonment.
But your high mind would scorn to pay base court
By acts of rigour on the wretched.
    L. Scr. Yes!
I know too well the dues of sovereignty:
While she is with me, under the Lord Scrope's
    roof,
His wife, and Norfolk's sister, ne'er shall hear
A queen's complaints with cold indifference.

L. Doug. O, nobly spoken! worthy your great
   birth!
O ' how your sentiments and voice recal
Your brother's image! would he now were here
For my poor mistress' sake—But see she comes.

Enter MARY.

L. Scr. May health and comfort to your majesty
Return with this propitious morn!
  Q. Mary. Alas!
My noble hostess, your civility
Touches a grateful mind more pointedly—
Is more affecting—melts my spirits more
Than a less kind reception could have done.
You owe not me this visit; for I came
In strict obedience to your queen's high will,
Under a promise from her royal self
That she would meet me ere I should arrive;
But in her place, behold! she sends her guards
To do me honour—O, my faithful maid!
You've seen me travel with a prouder suit,
When all the gallant youth of France pressed on,
Led forward by the princes of Lorrain,
Striving who foremost should escort their queen
From Paris to the sea—The gorgeous train,
Sweeping along the plains of Picardy,
Like some bright comet in its pathless course,
Illumined all the country as it passed:
But what avail these thoughts? for other scenes
I must behold—Yet, truly, this fair seat
Might well befit a royal residence,
And suits my fancy—but that I perceive
Some features in it which awake my mind
To strange misgivings—Wherefore, Lady Scrope,
Do centinels surround the battlements?
  L. Scr. Madam, be not alarmed; and rest as-
   sured

All comforts, honours, free access of friends,
And every privilege that can assuage
Misfortune, shall be found within these walls.
Seek then no rescue, nor attempt a flight.

 Q. Mary. Flight! said you, lady Scrope? I must
   not fly?
Then there's no farther doubt—Ah! 'tis too plain!
I'm in confinement here! a prisoner!
O horrid word! O monstrous perfidy!
O perjured, false Elizabeth! Is this
The faith of England? these the plighted vows
Of queen to queen? the bond of sisterhood,
And sacred rights of hospitality?
If justice has not fled the earth and skies,
Requite it, heaven! O my kind keeper, now
No more my hostess; you are merciful;
Your kind indulgence mitigates my lot;
Softens and blunts the sharp edge of that hour,
The painful but short hour, that goes between
The imprisonment of princes and their end:
You did assure me I should see my friends;
Your brother Norfolk is my dearest friend.
Shall I?—

Enter HERRIES.

 L. Scr. Here's one to put me to the proof—
Heaven knows the issue! we'll retire and pray
For peace and concord, amity and love.
  [*Exeunt* LADY SCROPE *and* LADY DOUGLAS.
 Q. Mary. Herries, my friend! companion of my
   flight!
Best counsellor who bade me shun this land,
What answer have you brought from this proud
   queen?
 L. Her. This is the purport: England's queen
   declares,
That, as a friend, and not a judge, she hears

This cause.   Your restoration to achieve
If you renounce all title to her crown,
During her life and issue—give up France;
Ally yourself with her; renounce the mass.

 Q. Mary. Heavens, what a height of insolence is
   this!
I see her aim : and now, no more than this—
Will she in person hear her sister queen?

 L. Her. She still declines to see you, till you are
   cleared
Of this foul charge ; which she herself abets,
Basely suborning forgeries ; mean time,
Full of professions of sincerest love,
She waits impatient to embrace with joy
Her vindicated sister—But till then,
Most sanctimoniously abhors the sight
Of one whose honour she herself betrays
By her false calumnies.

 Q. Mary. Perfidious wretch !

 L. Her. Know you that Murray, your base bro-
   ther, dwells
At England's court, consulted, closeted ;
While you, a queen, her equal in all points,
Are in a vile durance—

 Q. Mary. Grant me patience, heaven !

 L. Her. Were he your equal, why this preference
To him who should plead guilty, not accuse ?

 Q. Mary. 'Tis all mere mockery and artifice
To cheat the world, and gain its confidence
By semblance of fair justice.

 L. Her. Rather say
Plain, undisguis'd injustice : might I speak,
Your majesty should arrogate your right,
As a supreme and independent queen.

 Q. Mary. And yet, my trusty guide, can I recede ;

Decline the inquiry; scorn the public voice;
Leave the licentious world to its own thoughts,
And my fair fame, a prey to wild conjecture?
    L. Her. The world's more just than to expect a
        queen
To plead to vassals in a foreign land;
Hold up her hand, and bend her knee to those
Whose proudest head, at sight of her approach,
Should prostrate fall, and humbly kiss the dust.
    Q. Mary. And yet what other clearance can I
        have?
Shall I sit down under this heavy load?
Shall conscious innocence reject the means
Of wiping off this stain? No! I ll resign
All, but the first of titles, a fair name.
    L. Her. 'Tis not yourself, but Scotland you be-
        tray;
Rights of a sovereign realm, transmitted through
A hundred kings; rights which yourself were borne,
And which you've sworn to uphold.
    Q. Mary. Truth will prevail;
Herries! you may return to England's queen:
Tell her I here recal my late appeal,
As all beneath my name and dignity.
Tell her I came invited to this land
By her fair words, and sought a refuge here;
That refuge is a prison—then repeat
My wish in person to submit my cause;
(Wherein I show her honour and respect
Exceeding all example). If, at last,
This woman, so forgetful of herself,
Deaf to the claims of blood and royalty,
Against a sister shall make fast the door,
Admitting her accuser: let her know,
The queen of Scotland claims her liberty;
Demands her birthright; nor will e er resign
That freedom Heaven and Nature gave to all.
If this just suit's denied, defy her then;

Challenge her worst ; dare her to keep me here ;
Bid her unhinge, and set at naught the laws
Of Nature and of Nations; let her pride
Exult in barbarous disregard of right,
And emulate the unlettered Turk and Moor,
Till in one common cause, and with one voice,
All Christendom shall rise to rescue me.

                [*Exit* HERRIES.

Enter NORFOLK.

D. Nor. Pardon this bold intrusion of your slave,
Whose steps are guided by resistless charms,
And every sentiment that purest love
Breathes in the hearts of her true votaries.

    Q. Mary. Are you then come, brave, generous
            man ! My joy,
Norfolk, at sight of thee, dispels my fears :
Yet were it known you sought my presence here—

    D. Nor. Is it then treason to approach these
            walls ?
Must I presume your guilt, who, through this veil,
See your bright innocence ?

    Q. Mary. Heaven knows 'tis such ;
But circumvented thus by perjuries,
By bold bad men, what can a woman hope,
A helpless, unbefriended exile ?

    D. Nor. O !
Canst thou pronounce those words, and look on me?

    Q. Mary. No ! thou didst guard me from the im-
            pending wrath
Of Murray, that inhuman enemy.
O ! thou hast lavished unrequited aid,
Most angel-like !—Now first I feel my loss :
The fall of power ne'er wounds the breast so deep,
As when, from hearts who swell with gratitude,
It severs all the means of recompence.

D. Nor. What do I hear? No means of recom-
       pence?
Why, what reward can heaven? a beauteous queen,
The paragon and envy of her sex,
The wonder and delight of all mankind;
Sent from the skies to dazzle all below
With rays too bright for mortal sight to bear.

Q. Mary. Terms such as these apply not to a
       wretch,
A poor, unfortunate, degraded wretch,
Doomed to captivity.

D. Nor. Captivity!
It cannot, must not, shall not be; such acts
Are not within the reach of Envy's grasp:
Cold-blooded tyrants may conceive such thoughts;
But, trust me, mankind is not yet so lost
To honour, decency, and generous love;
The manners of the age, the face of things,
Would not endure to see the pride of the age,
And all the living beauty of the world,
Led like a sacrifice to night and hell,
And buried quick—nay, in the bloom of youth;
And such a bloom as blasts the blushing rose
Of England's maids so famed—a form that mars
All other claim to grace or dignity.

Q. Mary. You mock me, sure! Alas, what
       would these flights?

D. Nor. Yourself, and this fair hand; here on
       this earth
I ask, in one rash prayer, all heaven can grant.
                         [*Kneeling.*

Q. Mary. Let not despair or confidence take
       place,
Where fickle Fortune reigns.

D. Nor. O, joyful words!
I am not to despair; hence, hence, I date
All joys of life, and flattering hopes to come;

And dedicate all honour, service, love,
Henceforth, unto the mistress of my soul.

    Q. Mary. Another mistress claims thy services,
A proud, inquisitive, revengeful queen;
One full of envy; doomed through life to feed
On gall and spleen; nor taste love's generous
       draught.
Watchful she is, and jealous in the extreme:
Beware how she's inform'd!

    D. Nor. Why should we fear?
Her ministers approve; proud Leicester's self,
Her favourite, will procure her full consent.

    Q. Mary. Great minds are unsuspicious to their
       ruin;
Trust not to Leicester's words—Nor dream that she
Will loose these chains, and fasten Hymen's bands,
For one she hates, fears, views with envious eyes.
Will she, so wise, join me to all your power?
It cannot be; prepare then for the worst;
And, if we fail, and I remain a slave,
Perhaps in faster chains, they shall but add
Fresh rivets to our love—This token keep!
                        [*Delivering a token.*
If closer walls await me, this may serve
To instruct some faithful servant of your name,
And of my wish for your access—Adieu!

    D. Nor. Farewell, thou pattern of all excellence!
                        [*Exit* NORFOLK.

    Q. Mary. (*Sola.*) Now, heavens! as you regard
       our mortal cares,
If innocence claims mercy in your sight,
Expand your guardian wings, and cover me
From this black storm! avert the dire approach
Of this too subtle serpent's crooked pace,
That glides to my destruction! How have I
Deserved her venom? Is it that I am young?
Born to one crown, and married to another?

Or that, in me, she sees with jaundiced eyes
Her lineal successor?   Aye! there's the crime
Meanness cannot forgive—Poor narrow soul!
That wanting courage to submit to fate,
Seeks, like her father, to perpetuate
A mortal throne, and reign when she's no more:
There's no distemper so incurable
As thirst of power—Here then for life I'm fixed,
Unless I work my way through walls of stone.—
Alas! these hands are weak!   But I'll find some
Shall tear up by the roots these thick-ribb'd towers;
I'll from my dungeon scream, till to my cries
All Europe echoes—Norfolk! thou shalt rouse
That insuppressive spirit of this isle,
Which hates injustice, succours innocence,
Appals the tyrant, and protects the oppressed.

ACT THE SECOND.

SCENE I.

Whitehall.

ELIZABETH *seated on her Throne, attended by her*
Court and Guards.

Enter CECIL.

Q. Eliz. Cecil, your haste tells me you bring ad-
  vice
Of the result of this day's conference
On Mary's cause.
  Sir W. Cec. My liege, the conference
By Norfolk, your own delegate, this hour
Is suddenly dissolved. The partial duke,
When Herries claimed an audience for his queen,
Dismissed the court, and justified the claim.
  Q. Eliz. Mary will never be in want of friends,
While Norfolk lives.
  Sir W. Cec. And how long that may be,
I know not ! but can never wish long life
To England's foes.—
  Q. Eliz. Of Norfolk say you that ?
  Sir W. Cec. Not as a charge direct of any crime

Within the grasp of law; but when a duke,
So highly honoured by his queen, shall plot
In state affairs—

   Q. Eliz. What mean these hints? Explain.
                   [*Descending from her Throne.*
   Sir W. Cec. The duke arrives from Bolton, the
      Lord Scrope's.
   Q. Eliz. Indeed! I own the visit was ill timed.
   Sir W. Cec. Or flowed it purely from fraternal
      love?
   Q. Eliz. Why, Cecil, you delight in dark surmise!
Norfolk's an open, undesigning man;
His friendships and dislikes are all avowed.
   Sir W. Cec. Soft clay takes deep impression—
      flexible
To any shape, is moulded easily;
And facile, honest minds, when caught by love,
Exchange their native qualities for those
Which suit their new designs—
   Q. Eliz. Speak you of love?
   Sir W. Cec. Aye, mutual, in all its forms de-
      clared;
Close correspondence.
   Q. Eliz. O, accursed news!
O, all-seducing harlot!—Wanton wretch!
Can none escape the fascinating looks
Of this attracting basilisk? must she—
Cecil! this instant issue my commands
For closer custody; seek Shrewsbury;
Tell him to take her from the Lady Scrope,
Her Norfolk's sister, and from Bolton, straight
Proceed to Tutbury's strong fortress: there
Let her be guarded safe—begone—no stop—
Cecil, be sure you do not trifle here.
I would not have your wary character
Blemished, by joining in the babbling cry

Of every politic officious knave,
Seeking reward for premature reports:—
What proof have you of this?

Sir W. Cec. Ere long complete;
Till then, my faithful word; but let not haste
Mar the discovery—Plots there are besides
Of blacker die, not flowing from the duke,
But from the restless spirit of the church,
Whose midnight conclave, brooding in the dark,
Devises stratagems and massacres
For those who break her fetters.

Q. Eliz. Now dispatch,
Use all your zeal—forget not Shrewsbury.

[*Exit* CECIL.

(*Sola.*) The events begin to multiply, which tend
All to my point—This close imprisonment
Will now be sanctified in people's eyes.
I'll spread the fame of this conspiracy;
But for the Duke's intrigue there needs no haste;
As yet 'tis in the bud, and may lie hid
Till farther light shall ripen and expand
Its native colours.—Here he comes at length.

Enter NORFOLK.

D. Nor. I fear I'm come full late; though not
            the last
In love and duty to my gracious queen.

Q. Eliz. My Lord, we know your fame for loyalty;
For honour, justice, generosity;
We think ourselves have not been wanting yet,
In owning and rewarding your deserts;
Nor can we doubt your faith and gratitude.

D. Nor. Forbid it, heaven! that there should be
            just cause!

Q. Eliz. Norfolk, you are our first commissioner.

   D. Nor. As such, I trust, I've not disgraced my
        charge,
Or England's justice.
   Q. Eliz. You are not accus'd ;
Think not we wish for blind subserviency
In the exercise of such a trust; but say
Frankly, what colour wears this wondrous cause ?
   D. Nor. On Mary's side, fair as her beauteous
        front.
   Q. Eliz. How ! to my face ?   [*Aside.*
My Lord, you never speak
But from the heart ; such frankness pleases me,
And much becomes your family and name ;
Which, in good truth, I wish were well secur'd
In the right line ; your noble wife, my Lord,
Hath lately left us to lament her loss ;
You should repair it : who would not be proud
To boast of Norfolk's heart ? Why not aspire
To ask a royal hand ?—The queen of Scots
Is not, I guess, displeasing in your sight.
   D. Nor. Aspire to gain the queen of Scots !
        shall I,
So highly countenanced by your good grace,
Court one in bondage, fallen, and accused ?
   Q. Eliz. Is, then, a diadem so small a prize ?
   D. Nor. Pardon me, madam, if I have no wish
To wed a prisoner.—Gods, when I reflect
On all the comforts I enjoy at home,
How can I wish to seek a land of strife;
And purchase, at the price of wealth and ease,
A barren sceptre and a fruitless crown ?
   Q. Eliz. Then England boasts a peer who scorns
        the match ?
   D. Nor. Such are the gifts of bounteous Provi-
        dence,
Such my condition in my native land,
That when surrounded by the numerous throng

Of my retainers, at my plenteous board,
Or in the crowded field at country sports,
I, your liege subject, sometimes rate myself
As high as many princes.—

Enter DAVISON.

    Dav. Madam, I come
From the Earl of Leicester, who, by illness seiz'd,
Despairs of life, yet frequently repeats
Your royal name, and seems as if he wished
To impart some weighty matter.—
    Q. Eliz. Say I'll come.   [*Exit* DAV.
(*Aside.*) So Leicester has some secret to divulge
Upon his death-bed, though I trust to heaven
He doth not yet upon his death-bed lie!—
(*Addressed to* NORFOLK.) And on what pillow Nor-
    folk lays his head,
Let him beware!—   [*Exit* ELIZ.
    D. Nor. (*Solus.*) What may this caution mean?
Beware what pillow! ha! why, more is meant:
I mark'd her cold, dry looks, her pregnant sneers;
All is not well—surely she has not heard—
She has, and I'm undone—all confidence,
All faith is rotten—Leicester is my friend:
But who knows what in sickness he'll confess?
Somehow I am betrayed: 'Tis Cecil sure;
The prying, penetrating Cecil, aye!
He at a glance views all this busy world,
And reads our very hearts. I'll to him straight.
              [*Exit* NORFOLK.

SCENE II.

Enter CECIL, *meeting Lord* HERRIES *in haste.*

Sir W. Cec. Whither so fast, my Lord?
L. Her. No matter, sir,
If far from regions whence all faith is flown,
All reverence to royal rights—
Sir W. Cec. How's this?
L. Her. England's no more a civiliz'd estate;
The savage Afric tyrant may expose
His subject's liberty to public sale,
Seize, bind, and sell the human race like beasts,
Mow down their heads like thistles in the path;
He is untutored; yet not more than you,
Barbarian, reckless of all faith and law.
Sir W. Cec. What breach of law? what wrong-
        ful judgment's this?
L. Her. None: for you cannot, dare not judge
        our queen.
Why is she then detained? Curse on this land
And all its savage race; your cursed shores,
Placed like a trap to intercept the course
And passage of the sea, had well nigh caught
My mistress on her way; Henceforth what sail
Will not, through rocks and sands, avoid your coast?
Soon as the mariner shall from afar
Descry your hated cliffs, though spent with toil,
Consumed with sickness, and distressed for food,
He'll turn his leaky vessel, and escape
The seat of treacherous Circe's cruel reign,

Yet, ere I go, mark this, the hour's at hand
When foreign vengeance shall dismay your isle,
Scare all its coasts, and make its centre shake
At sight of such a buoyant armament,
As never pressed the bosom of the main.
Beware!　　　　　　　　　　　　[*Exit* HERRIES.
　　Sir W. Cec. (*Solus.*) Aye; and in spite of thee,
　　　　proud Scot!
Let Scotland, France, and Spain blow up the
　　　storm,
I'll weather it, if no sinister wind,
No inland gust, o'erset me suddenly:
Mary's secure; and Norfolk's shallow brains
Are wrapt in dreams of vanity and love;
His plots I find have yet no farther scope.
　　　　　　　　　　　　　　[*Exit* CECIL.

SCENE III.

ELIZABETH *entering her chamber with the* LIEU-
TENANT *of the* Tower.

　　Q. Eliz. Lieutenant, now you've had your orders,
　　　　haste!
　　Lieut. The duke is still below—I'll guard him
　　　　well.　　　　　　　　　　[*Exit.* LIEUT.
　　Q. Eliz. (*Sola.*) So! this design is riper than I
　　　　thought:
Leicester informs me that the contract's signed.
The Tower is now the fittest residence
For this intriguing Lord, who thinks to mix
The statesman's and the lover's part unseen,

Enter CECIL, *throwing himself at* ELIZABETH's *feet.*

Sir W. Cec. Most gracious queen! thus at your
  royal feet
I crave a boon. E'en as I entered now,
The Duke was seized; O, yet suspend your wrath!
 Q. Eliz. Can Cecil plead for Norfolk? Rise! and
  say,
What means this double aspect? this quick change?
This aguish heat and cold? your steady mind,
Which used to point the safest road, now veers,
Turns, like the shifting vane, at every blast.
 Sir W. Cec. When have these eyes e'er viewed
  your enemies
But with an even, stedfast look of hate?
 Q. Eliz. Why, Cecil! are not all the Catholics
United in this cause? the ambassadors
Of France and Spain haunt me from morn to night
With their petitions for this captive queen.
 Sir W. Cec. Yet Norfolk's neither Catholic nor
  foe;
Vouchsafe to hear him!——
 Q. Eliz. Since you are so prompt
In his defence;—who waits? [*Enter Attendant.*
Call in the Duke.   [*Exit Attendant.*
 Sir W. Cec. Had he designs against your govern-
  ment
I ne'er had sued for him; but he, poor dupe!
Intent on his vain-glorious enterprise,
Aimed at no farther harm: and to be plain,
He is so popular, that 'tis not safe
To keep his person long in custody—
But here he comes.

Enter NORFOLK, *throwing himself at* ELIZABETH's
    feet.

 D. Nor. My Mistress! O my queen!

Here let me, prostrate on this ground, assert
My faith and loyalty !

   Q. Eliz. You may arise;
'Tis done already; honest Cecil proved
Your plots were not designed against ourselves.

   D. Nor. Though justice is of right, yet he who
       feels
Not thankful for't, betrays a narrow mind,
Forgets the general pravity of man,
Nor prizes virtues for their rarity.

   Q. Eliz. Norfolk, attend ! this caution now re-
       mains ;
What falls from high should deep impression make;
Beware how you take part in Mary's cause !
Remember this forgiveness, and engage,
That henceforth you'll give over these attempts.

   D. Nor. This act of justice claims my solemn
       vow.

   Q. Eliz. Cecil, attend us ——   [*Exit.* ELIZ.
   Sir W. Cec. Norfolk, this escape
Should serve to warn you from this idle chase :
Now seek some other fair—take her to wife ;
Fly not at game so high ; the falcon's safe
Who for the lesser quarry scuds the plain,
But if he's struck, towering to chase the hern,
He falls, to rise no more.   [*Exit* CECIL.

   D. Nor. (*Solus.*) So ! this wise man
Thus condescends to waste his thoughts on me !
Advice is easier given than pursued.
It is no trifling task to quit at once
All that makes life engaging, all I love !
What have I promised ? Heavens, I dread to think !
Yet it must be ! for when did Norfolk e'er
Infringe his word ? Nay, to his queen, his kind
Indulgent mistress—What ! for mercy sue,
And break the fair conditions of the grant ?

The very thought's a crime—Nature may change;
All creatures may their elements forsake;
The universe dissolve and burst its bonds;
Time may engender contrarieties,
And bring forth miracles—but none like this,
That I should break my word—I'll to my love,
Lament our fate, and take my last farewell.

ACT THE THIRD.

SCENE I.

Before Tutbury Castle.

Enter the EARL *of* SHREWSBURY *and* BETON.

Bet. I am charged with royal thanks to Shrews-
          bury
For his humanity and gentleness.
    E. Shr. Alas, good Beton ! 'tis a grievous task
Thus to confine a queen.   Humanity,
Where 'tis so due, claims less acknowledgment.
I am enjoined to keep her close, because
The neighbourhood abounds with Catholics.
I was in search of Bagot, the high sheriff,
With orders on that point.
    Bet. I learn from him
That the Earl of Huntingdon will soon arrive ;
I fear his surly, proud, imperious mind
Will bring no comfort to my mistress here.
    E. Shr. You know he claims succession to the
          crown
Before the queen of Scots : this strange conceit
May swell his native pride and violence
With envious malice ; but I'll temper it

By all the indulgences and gentle means
Our rigid orders suffer.   Now farewell.

[*Exeunt.*

SCENE II.

Tutbury Castle, MARY's *chamber*—MARY *and* LADY
DOUGLAS *discovered.*

Q. Mary. No, not another tear ! our fate's decreed ;
Our lot is cast; here in this sad abode,
E'en here, we may enjoy a dread repose—
Better by far than the tumultuous throbs
Of my poor aching heart, while yet it dreamt
Of liberty, and visionary crowns,
Whene'er I slumbered, mocked my troubled sight.
Here then, at last, in these dark, silent dens,
We shall be proof against anxiety,
And feverous Expectation's agonies.
    L. Doug. My royal mistress, still there is hope,
        though this
May seem the mansion of despair; so cold,
So comfortless, and fit for scenes of woe ;
Such deep, low, winding vaults ; such towers aloft
Impending o'er their base, like broken cliffs,
Whose shapeless, weather-beaten summits hang
In rude excrescence, threatening instant fall :
Perhaps, in each of them, some wretch, pent up,
Lives here suspended between heaven and earth.
    Q. Mary. I like these dismal cells; this awful
        gloom's
Congenial to my soul—each yawning cave
Looks like the entrance to the shades of death,
And promises oblivion of this world.
Rude as this castle is, here held his state

Old John of Gaunt; hither flocked all the pride
Of chivalry; around the lists sat all
The beauties of the court; each knight in arms,
Intent to catch a glance from some bright eye,
Exulting in her champion's victory:
Our eyes are now to other uses doomed;
To read and weep by turns—Alas, my dear!
Your pretty eyes are far too young and bright
To waste their lustre on these sights of woe.

    L. Doug. Lose not a thought on me! while I be-
        hold
My royal mistress' face, my heart's at rest:
Not all the gaieties and bravery,
Which once you say these walls were witness to,
Have charms for me; 'tis all I ask, to sit,
Long, wintry, sleepless nights, and cheer awhile
The heavy hours that hang around your head.

    Q. Mary. Heavens! how have I deserved such
        kindness? No!
This must not be; you must depart, my girl;
Fly quickly, shun this seat of wretchedness;
For else, who knows but you may be involved
In that sad fate which hourly threatens me?
O! 'tis a sorry sight to see thee sit
At meals with me, who never can insure
One morsel at our scanty board from fear
Of deadly poison: fly ere 'tis too late;
The prelude of imprisonment is short;
Soon, very soon, we must expect to hear
The assassin's wary step, fixed on his point,
Yet trembling still with horror and remorse
And faultering in the deed——Ah! who comes
    here?

        Enter SHREWSBURY.

    E. Shr. Madam! it grieves me that my presence
    here

Should give you such alarm; I hoped, that if
In any point I varied from my trust,
'Twas not in cruelty.
 Q. Mary. O, no, my Lord!
Far otherwise; 'twas somewhat else, indeed;
Perhaps an idle fear, at least while you
Continue in your charge.
 E. Shr. If I remain—
 Q. Mary. Why, there's no doubt, I hope?
 E. Shr. None: but report
Now adds the name of Huntingdon.
 Q. Mary. Alas!
Why is that monster sent? Are there no racks
Or torturing engines made to plague mankind?
No! I defy all art to find a tool
So fit for her ingenious cruelty;
The sharpest instruments which tyrants use
Can ne'er impart such pain, as the blunt edge
Of that unpolished fool's impertinence.
 E. Shr. I shall not fail to enforce all due respect.
 Q. Mary. 'Tis vain to preach civility to brutes.
These tidings quite oppress my sinking soul.
Now I've no comfort left; my Douglas! now
You and I shall no longer sit all day,
Consoling one another's miseries,
Telling old stories, to beguile the time,
Of things that passed, when I was queen, and you
The brightest jewel in my court.
 L. Doug. Indeed
We have a kind of melancholy joy
Indulging in our grief.
 E. Shr. For that, alas!
I bring fresh food.
 Q. Mary. How so?
 E. Shr. This hour I learn
A strange account of some conspiracy
Detected at Whitehall; wherein your name

Was joined with Norfolk's, who, with other Lords,
Stands now committed to the Tower.

    Q. Mary. Ha, me!
Merciful Heaven! What say'st thou, Shrewsbury?
Is Norfolk in the Tower on my account?
Recal those words! O, they shot through my brain
Like lightning! Say you do not believe them,
      man!
Speak, prythee! O, you hesitate! I'm lost!
He's gone! I see the cruel lioness
Has seized the noble hart; he bleeds beneath
Her horrid fangs.   [*Leaning on* LADY DOUGLAS.

    L. Doug. Alas! her memory fails?
Excuse this transient weakness, sir, in one
So cruelly oppressed, and made the sport
Of cross and wayward fortune.

    E. Shr. Why this haste?

Enter NAWE *hastily.*

    Nawe. This moment brings a messenger, who
      tells
That Norfolk, Pembroke, Lumley, Arundel,
Each to his several dungeon was confined
For Norfolk's treason; that, on farther proof,
The Duke was cleared; who now, restored to grace
Lives in full splendour, fame, and liberty.

    E. Shr. Look to the queen! she faints.
      [*Here* MARY, *having changed from horror to
        joy, faints, and falls into* LADY DOUGLAS'S
        arms.*

    L. Doug. Help! help!
    E. Shr. Who waits?

Enter MARY'S *attendants.*

Convey her softly: Thus, alas! she's dead.
      [*They carry her to a conch.*

L. Doug. My mistress! O my mistress! O my
  queen!
She breathes! she breathes! yet there is life, O
  heav'ns!
E. Shr. Patience awhile!
L. Doug. Be silent all, I pray!
Her troubled spirit must not be disturbed;
These shocks have stopped the current of her blood;
And nature seeks a momentary pause:
Excessive joy succeeding grief so quick
Now o'erwhelms her mind; but balmy sleep,
With tears that make the drowning tide to ebb,
Will ease the load that weighs upon her heart.
 E. Shr. Give her repose a while, and watch her
  well.
  [*Exeunt, leaving* MARY *asleep, surrounded by*
  LADY DOUGLAS *and her maids.*

SCENE III.

Before Tutbury Castle.

Enter BETON *and* NAWE.

Nawe. I trust the queen will soon regain her
  strength.
 Bet. No doubt, if this were all; but still I fear
Farther vicissitudes.   The crazy times
Are big with strange events; each teeming hour
Is fruitful of new mischief—Who goes there?

Enter NORFOLK *in disguise.*

 D. Nor. One born to freedom, and not bound to
  tell,
Whether he comes or goes.

Nawe. What would you here?

Bet. Let's take him to the governor.

D. Nor. Villains,
Stand off.

Bet. No villains serve the queen of Scots;
Learn that, base ruffian.

    [*They draw their swords, and seize* NORFOLK.

D. Nor. Hold, are you the queen's?
Serve you queen Mary? then a word with you:
Know you this signet?

Nawe. Ha! the token sure!

Bet. The very token! it is the Duke!

D. Nor. My friends!

Bet. No more; this is a dangerous place; retire
Below the drawbridge, to that sally-port,
Half choaked with ruins; there wait patiently
Till we can execute the queen's commands.

                           [*Exeunt.*

SCENE IV.

MARY *discovered on her Couch, surrounded by* LADY
DOUGLAS *and her Maids.*

Q. Mary. Am I awake? Methinks the clouds
      disperse;
A watery gleam of light breaks through the mist;
The tepid sunbeams play, and 'gin to shed
Their all-enlightning, vivifying rays,
To chear the world, and dissipate its gloom;
All nature seems restored. My gentle maids,
Have you been with me whilst I slept! No doubt;
For I have dreamed I was in heaven; and you
Were surely the fair angels that I saw
Surrounding me in bliss. Douglas! I think

The last word that I heard was liberty;
Norfolk is set at liberty?
   L. Doug. No doubt;
That was the purport of our joyful news.
   Q. Mary. Then I'm alive again, my hopes and
      all;
Once more I'll dream of comfort, and indulge
Each fond delusion ;—I shall see my love ;
He'll soon be here ;—Norfolk won't tarry long.

    SHREWSBURY *and* HUNTINGDON *entering.*

   E. Shr. Gently, my Lord ! perhaps the queen's
     at rest.
   E. Hun. We must use all dispatch.
   E. Shr. Awhile ! my Lord !—
Madam ! the Earl of Huntingdon, who is joined
In trust with me—
      [*Presenting* LORD HUNTINGDON *to the queen.*
   Q. Mary. (*Aside.*) Alas ! are these my dreams
Of joy and comfort ?   My Lords, I still rely
On your humanity and gentleness.
   E. Hun. Our first instruction is to hold her safe.
      [*Turning to* SHREWSBURY.
   E. Shr. Aye, but in that beware how we trans-
     gress
The bounds of mercy : mercy is the due
Of all who breathe on England's soil ; it grows
From the same root, and is entwined around
The sceptre of our queen ; we are to her
Subjects and servants.
   Q. Mary. I am neither, Lords !
I am, like her, a queen ; nor will consent
To take, as mercy, what I claim as right,
Justice, and liberty.
   E. Hun. This is no time
For such high strains; learn your condition here.
   Q. Mary. Is this a language suited to your birth?
    VOL. VIII.   I

    E. Hun. High birth is ne'er disgraced by truth,
        I hope;
And for my tongue, 'twere better fail in that,
Than use my hands to perpetrate such deeds
As queens have sometimes done.
    E. Shr. O! shame; such words,
If they were true—
    E. Hun. Talk not of words! I come
To execute my orders. First, 'tis said,
This castle, till of late, was used to hold
The county prisoners.
    L. Doug. How! would you place a queen—
A lady formed in Nature's fairest mould,
Reared like the tenderest plant, shaped by each
        grace,
Each exquisite last touch of polished art—
Among a tribe of felons?
    E. Shr. What! immured
With all the refuse of the human race,
The outcasts of the earth?
    E. Hun. My Lord, I know
My duty; sure you have forgot the charge.
Who are all these that make the prison show
More like a royal court?
                [*Pointing at* MARY's *Attendants.*
    Q. Mary. Mean, abject slave!
    E. Hun. I here dismiss one half of this same train:
Begone!   [*To the Attendants.*
    Q. Mary. No, stop! inhuman wretch, forbear!
On me direct your vengeance—let not these
Poor helpless maids be driven from their home,
Though 'tis a poor disconsolate abode:
For still they wait with pleasure on their queen,
Proud to participate in all her woes:
But these are sentiments thou canst not feel.
Go, ask your mistress, whether such a train
Is all too proud to attend upon the crowns

Of France and Scotland ? ask what retinue
I should have deemed becoming her estate
With me, at Paris, or at Holyrood ?

 E. Hun. Those days are past—without more idle
    words,
There's one condition, and but one, by which
You may be nobly entertained, and have
All freedom and respect—Give up your crown ;
Confirm Earl Murray regent ; and reside
In England with your son—

 Q. Mary. No more ! perform
The part that suits thee, jailor !—Thou lackest wit
To tempt me to resign my native crown ;
To sacrifice at once myself, and son ;
And make the world believe I own her charge.
No ! I prefer her dungeons—Death itself.

 E. Hun. Then be it so !   Attendants, follow me ;
Leave her to ruminate in solitude.

    [*Exeunt* SHREWSBURY *and* HUNTINGDON,
     with the attendants following reluctantly.

 Q. Mary. (*Sola.*) Give up my crown ; my son ;
    support my foe,
My mortal, base, unnatural enemy !
'Tis a plain challenge to a queen—Resign
All sense of honour, claims of birth, all thoughts
Of eminence, in early youth imbibed,
And grown habitual, to those whom chance
Has in derision decked with mortal crowns ;
Or else prepare, and summon fortitude
To brave the threats of power, the taunts, the scorn,
The worst indignities that envy breeds ;
That bitterest produce of the meanest plant
That grows in mortal breasts—Perhaps still more ;
Perhaps her iron hand may rend these limbs.
This cruel wretch, this Huntingdon, is sent
To view my torments with unaltered eyes ;
To sit, preside, direct the torturer's knife,

Glutting his greedy soul with scenes of blood,
While dying shrieks are music to his ears.
'Tis hard for female spirits to bear up,
And stand the fiery trial—Ah ! who's that ?
Spare me !

Enter Norfolk *in disguise.*

D. Nor. O, fear me not, my life ! 'tis I;
'Tis Norfolk at your feet.
     Q. Mary. O heavens ! once more
Save my poor intellects ! O Norfolk, O !
My guardian angel ! How shall I relate
All that befel me since ? Yet rather say,
How have you 'scaped the jaws of that fell tigress ?
How got you hither ?
     D. Nor. By the gift you gave ;
Your token known, they straight conducted me,
By secret ways, through these old walls, and thus
These eyes at once are dazzled with a sight
Dangerous to look on.
     Q. Mary. Danger is no more
When my brave Norfolk's come ; we'll talk of love,
Of future bliss, and paint gay scenes of joy,
Counting our happy days before their time.
     D. Nor. Alas ! that's all, I fear, we e'er can hope.
     Q. Mary. Let not your noble spirit, Norfolk, fail !
     D. Nor. Spirit will fail when reason cannot hope.
     Q. Mary. Norfolk cannot despond in Mary's cause.
     D. Nor. O, think no more of such a worthless
          wretch ;
A base, mean villain, traitor to my queen.
     Q. Mary. Is love for me such treason in her sight?
     D. Nor. My treason is not 'gainst my lawful
          queen,
But against her, to whom I'm bound by ties
Dearer than dull cold duty.
     Q. Mary. Mean you me ?

Doubtless you made confession of your love;
Was that a treason against me? 'twas great,
Worthy yourself; magnanimous to scorn
Her utmost rage, and brave her dire revenge.

    D. Nor. (*Aside.*) How shall I wound her gene-
        rous, noble heart?
Her, whose pure mind, whose unsuspicious thoughts
Dress up my sins in virtuous robes; thereby
But making them more hideous in my sight;
And me more hateful to myself.—O, fool!
That could be brought to purchase this vile life,
By quitting all that's dear to me on earth!

    Q. Mary. What do I hear? O, say not so, my
        love!
You are not capable of such a thought.

    D. Nor. Alas, I've pledged my word; I've sworn
        to it.

    Q. Mary. Extorted vows are void, mere idle
        breath.

    D. Nor. Mine have not been so hitherto—an oath,
A sacred oath—

    Q. Mary. Had I no oath from you?

    D. Nor. (*Aside.*) Ah! there's the dreadful maze,
        the double road,
Where each path leads to ruin and disgrace.

    Q. Mary. O Norfolk, do not leave me! do not
        forsake
Your poor, forlorn, and faithful prisoner;
Already lost to all the world but thee;
My only comfort, refuge, under heaven.
O, 'twould belie the tenor of your life:
What would I not for thee? Let all the kings,
The rival princes that have wooed in vain,
Here in my prison recommence their suit,
Would I not spurn them all for thee? Yet fly,
I'm lost; but you are born to better fates.

    D. Nor. (*Aside.*) Be, firm, my soul! O, torture!

Q. Mary. Cruel man !
To cast me off because I'm here confined :
What sent me hither but my love for thee ?
When last I saw you, then you were a man,
Replete with courage, gentleness, and love.
What have I done to change your nature thus ?
If I'm in fault, strike at this wretched heart ;
Let it not break !   Or leave me to my fate,
To chains and dungeons, insults and hard words ;
Let savage Huntingdon dismiss my train.

  D. Nor. The horror of my crimes comes thick
   upon me.
Could I then leave thee thus, a prey to grief,
The sport of ruffian tongues ! Why did not heaven
Blast with its lightning, and benumb these limbs,
So slow in striving to break ope the gates
Of this accursed cell ?   O foul disgrace !
Where shall I escape the pointing hand of Shame ?
Here let me sue for pardon.   All I ask,
Is to devote my life to rescue thee ;
To stem the torrent, and oppose the flood,
Defy the deluge of o'erwhelming fate,
And snatch thee from the waves of misery.

  Q. Mary. Are you then still my Norfolk ? Do I
   dream ?

  D. Nor. No, while there's life in this poor frame,
   and while——

  Q. Mary. Enough, my Norfolk, I am the debtor
   now :
Your noble resolution doth restore
The genial current of my frozen blood ;
The blood of many hundred kings doth rise
To chase despondency, and swell my soul
With thoughts of nobler deeds, and times to come.
Mary shall once more triumph in her turn.

  D. Nor. Then farewell, beautiful and injured
   saint !

Good angels hover round this dark abode,
And guard you till the cries of honour's voice
Shake these old battlements, and rend this roof;
Burst wide these bars, and once more charm the
   world
With radiant light of matchless beauty's beams.
Adieu, my love!
 Q. Mary. Remember me—Farewell!

ACT THE FOURTH.

Whitehall.

Enter ELIZABETH *and* CECIL.

Q. Eliz. Cecil! what more? the Duke, you say,
  is secur'd.
Sir W. Cec. Aye! beyond escape, my liege!—
  he's on his way;
Perhaps has reached the Tower.
 Q. Eliz. Sir, he may thank
Your intercession for that liberty
Which proved his bane.
 Sir W. Cec. Reproaches from my queen,
So just, fall like the chastisement of heaven
On those it favours.
 Q. Eliz. Heaven favours none
But those who see their errors, and repent.
 Sir W. Cec. If I repent me not the part I took,
May I be sharer in his punishment.
 Q. Eliz. We know your faith; 'twas error, we're
  convinced;
Let assiduity atone for it;
Probe this infernal plot.

Sir W. Cec. 'Tis done ! Behold
This train of correspondence, betwixt the duke,
The pope, the queen of Scots.

Q. Eliz. The treason is clear:
Cecil, my foes are numerous and strong.

Sir W. Cec. Were they in number as the sum-
mer leaves,
Their autumn doth approach ; they soon shall fall,
Blasted, and driven by the wind.

Q. Eliz. This day
One falls at least ; this faithless Lord no more
Shall dupe me with his promises ; let him
Await his doom—yet stay ! his birth and name—

Sir W. Ccc. Are but fresh motives for example
sake.

Q. Eliz. Then be it so.

Sir W. Cec. And her ambassador,
Who would have forced the Tower, and seized
yourself?

Q. Eliz. That must be nicely weighed ; for so-
vereignty,
Aye, but the shadow of it, claims regard :
'Tis not for us to extinguish hastily
That emanation from the royal light ;
Although the source from whence it springs may
seem
Somewhat obscured and clouded.

Sir W. Cec. But if threats
Produce confession, we may learn to guard
'Gainst farther harm.

Q. Eliz. Proceed.   [*Exit* CECIL.
He needs no spur ;
Nay, he anticipates my inmost thoughts.
The ambitious Duke's disposed of ; such halfpaced,
Soft, scrupulous fools, make poor conspirators.
Mary yet lives : but for the ambassadors,
I should have sent her cross the Tweed ere now,

To Murray's care : I would it had been done,
When first she threw herself into my hands ;
It seemed a consummation of success,
A period to my cares : but now this prize,
This precious prize, so unexpectedly
Entangled in my toils, proves a fierce snake
Which I can neither safely hold or loose ;
While yet I have her in my grasp, she slips,
Twining her folds around my limbs—Alas !
I live in fear of my own prisoner,
And tremble on my throne.   [*Exit* ELIZ.

SCENE II.

Enter DAVISON *to* CECIL.

Dav. The fatal order's sent ; e'en now the Duke
Prepares for death.
    Sir W. Cec. O Davison ! these times
Demand dispatch ; patience must have its bounds,
Or change its nature, and degenerate
To dangerous weakness.
    Dav. Yet the piteous fall
Of this beloved, generous Duke, will rend
The hearts of all his countrymen : the streets
Are thronged with weeping multitudes ; and groans
Betray more deep-felt sorrow than the tongue
Dares, in these days, to utter.
    Sir W. Cec. Such esteem,
And general sympathy, denote his sway
And empire o'er the affections of the land ;
And should have served to other ends than strife,
For the romantic honour and renown
Of liberating helpless, captive queens.   [*Exeunt.*

SCENE III.

The Tower.

NORFOLK *and the* LIEUTENANT *discovered.*

D. Nor. No, good lieutenant; I am at a point,
The very point and summit of my path,
Up life's steep rough ascent; and now must leap
The dreadful precipice.

Lieut. Yet, still, my Lord,
There's room for mercy; and if fame speaks true,
Good cause for it. 'Tis said your grace did save
Her majesty's own person from assault.

D. Nor. As I'm a Christian man, and doomed to
die,
'Tis true; and never have I aught devised
Against her sacred self: but 'tis in vain
To sue for mercy; nor is it my wish
To ask that mercy which I've once abus'd.
Could I but, during this sad interval,
Could I but send one——

Enter a servant, delivering a paper to the LIEUTE-
NANT.

Ha! what's that I see?

Lieut. (*Reading.*) Alas!——

D. Nor. Enough! I read it in your looks:
My hour is come——

Lieut. My Lord, the guards attend.

Enter SHERIFF *and Guards.*

D. Nor. I am content, thank heaven! to meet my
fate;

Not from indifference to life, or claim
To innocence ; far otherwise in both :
But knowing mercy's infinite extent,
I cast the world behind me—One farewell!
And then—

    Sher. My Lord, in truth, we may not wait.

    D. Nor. I go—and, good lieutenant, tell the queen,
That he who lately stood in highest rank,
(Now sunk below the meanest citizen)
Though he's pronounced a traitor by his peers,
Whom yet he blames not, still appeals to heaven
In his last moments, that there lives not one
More true to his religion, country, queen,
Than dying Thomas Howard—Then implore
Her kind compassion to my orphan babes.
Say that my dying words were, " Peace be with
    her !"
And as I am the first to fall by the axe,
So may I be the last, in her blest reign !
May she do justice, and protect the oppressed !
So may her fame reach all posterity !
And by her hand, do thou, O gracious heaven !
Build up the walls of England !

    Sher. Alas ! my Lord !
Delay is at our peril ; we beseech—

    D. Nor. A little moment! I had something yet,
But let it pass !—here ! here ! it rests; while yet
Life's current flows, while yet my nerves perform
Their functions—Mary ! I must think on thee !
Bless thee with my last breath : may heaven afford
That succour which this mortal arm in vain
Attempted ! may'st thou never feel such pangs
As he who dies for thee ! and now, e'en now,
Flies with impatience from this hell to seek
A refuge in the cold embrace of death.—
Lead on!—O, Mary ! Mary ! Mary !   [*Exeunt.*

SCENE IV.

Whitehall.

Enter ELIZABETH *and* CECIL.

Q. Eliz. Cecil! our last commands have been
    performed?
Sir W. Cec. Madam, they have.
Q. Eliz. And how behaved the Duke?
Sir W. Cec. With manly, decent constancy; and
    seemed
Most penitent in that he broke his word;
But still disclaiming fully all designs
Against your crown and person; at the last,
His parting soul seemed bent on his own fate
Less than on Mary's——
Q. Eliz. (*Aside.*) How! how's this! intent
On her at last? must her attractions reach
Even to the very brink of death? Alas!
That each progressive circumstance of woe
Tends but to prove the power of her charms.
    Sir W. Cec. Her minister, the bishop, hath
    confessed
His share of guilt, and opened all the plot
'Twixt him and Alva, Philip and the pope.
    Q. Eliz. Then bid him instantly depart my
    realm;
If he beholds to-morrow's setting sun
On English ground, his privilege is gone,
He dies a traitor's death; and from his queen,
No more ambassadors I'll entertain;
Or risk my life to grace my prisoner.
    VOL. VIII.   K

Sir W. Cec. The French king's minister, of late,
  is grown
Importunate for fresh indulgences;
That she may be allowed to take the air,
With fit attire and decent retinue :
All this is asked of grace, not as a part
Of Anjou's marriage treaty.
  Q. Eliz. If that serve
To amuse and hoodwink France, she'll think no
  more
On Mary.—Davison ! what brings thee thus ?

    Enter DAVISON.

 Dav. Dispatches from your minister in France.
 Q. Eliz. Of weighty matter ?
 Dav. Heavier far, and worse,
Than mortal ears can bear ; heaven guard us all
From such disasters as no tongue can tell !
A visitation which the world, till now,
Ne'er saw or heard of———
 Q. Eliz. Speak ! no more delay.
 Dav. Then hear the fate of all our friends in
  France,
Swept from the face of the earth, exterminate,
In one black night, at one infernal blow,
Dealt by the hand of Rome : there scarcely lives
A protestant to tell the massacre.
 Q. Eliz. and Sir W. Cec. The massacre !
 Dav. I said the word : the tale
Runs thus :—That signals from the Louvre top
Proclaimed the time of slaughter ; Paris first,
And 'tis supposed, within an hour, that all
The cities of that kingdom streamed with blood.
Nor age, nor sex, was spared ; old men, nay babes,
Fast in their helpless mother's arms, were pierced
With the same weapon ; sick men in their beds,
Brave warriors in their sleep, were butchered ; one,

One only checked their course—The first who fell,
Brave Coligni, whose very name appals
The bigot's heart—At sight of his grey locks,
So known where'er the thickest battle raged,
They stood aghast, till one more hardened wretch,
With eyes averted, stabbed him to the heart.

 Q. Eliz. O! let me shed one tear for that great
   man!

 Dav. Marshals of France, and bishops, led the
   band,
Invoking heaven, yet calling out for blood;
And, O eternal infamy! the king
Looked on, encouraged, nay imbrued his hands,
His sacred hands, in his own subjects' blood;
Pointing his carabine at those who fled
Apart, like stricken deer—while he, in sport,
At his balcony revelled, 'midst a throng
Of ladies, praising his dexterity,
Taught, like himself, by his more cruel mother,
From early youth, to jest at homicide.

 Q. Eliz. No more, the tale's too dreadful, I'll re-
   tire.
May heaven preserve my people from this curse!
War, famine, pestilence, are trifles all,
Compared to this corruption of the mind,
This degradation of humanity.
I'll to my closet; let none dare approach;
No cares of state presume to interrupt
My holy solitude.   [*Exit* ELIZABETH.

 Dav. The queen's retired
Most opportunely, for I've that to tell,
Which to no ear but thine——

 Sir W. Cec. What, Davison,
Hast thou, that can the least attention claim,
After thy dreadful tale?

 Dav. That which demands
All your dispatch, prudence, activity;

The queen's in danger, and each hour lost
Appears an age; ruffians there are——
   Sir W. Cec. How's this?
Her life in danger? say by whom? and how?
   Dav. These ruffians came from Rheims, a semi-
        nary
Intoxicated with the omnipotence
Of papal power, and Rome's accursed decrees,
Thinking, that if they perished in the attempt
They gained a glorious crown of martyrdom.
This motley crew, composed of soldiers, priests,
Of various orders, mad enthusiasts,
So confident in their iniquity,
Cast lots for weapons; then in full career
Of riot, 'midst their cups, for frolic sake,
Were painted in one portrait, each with the arms
That fell to him by lot.—These villains all
Are seized.
   Sir W. Cec. Can you no farther trace the plot?
Are you so slack a friend? Till now I thought
That if you gained the clue, your zeal would soon
Tread back the windings of the labyrinth,
And from her dark recess drag forth to light
This sorceress.
   Dav. Mistrust not yet that zeal:
Behold this fruit of it.—These lines I've gained
                [*Delivering Letters.*
From Gifford, a corrupt, abandon'd priest,
Who sold his fellow-traitors—these are said
To be the writing of Queen Mary's hand;
And whether true——
   Sir W. Cec. Enough! they strongly bear
The semblance—now 'tis done—thanks, Davison!
I'll to the queen, nor heed her prohibition.
      [CECIL *knocks at the closet-door,* ELIZABETH
        enters from thence.

Q. Eliz. Who dares with sacrilegious steps ap-
  proach,
And intervene betwixt his sovereign's prayers
And heaven's impending vengeance on our race?
 Sir W. Cec. 'Twas not without just cause—
 Q. Eliz. No cause, I trust,
Warrants plain disobedience of my word,
My strict commands, Sir ;——
 Sir W. Cec. Madam, these events
Brook no delay——
 Q. Eliz. Events! why, what events?
Canst thou add flames to Ætna's raging fire?
Imagination can no sequel find
Worthy the tale he told.
 Sir W. Cec. This hour Davison
Fears for your royal self.
 Q. Eliz. Speak, Davison!
 Dav. I trust
All will be well, for the conspirators
Are almost all secured.
 Q. Eliz. Conspirators!
 Dav. Aye, most inveterate, implacable!
Hell never sent such fiends to curse mankind,
Taught by religious zeal to emulate,
Nay to contest the prize of parricide.
 Q. Eliz. You say they are secured?
 Sir W. Cec. Know you their names?
 Dav. Their chief is Babington; a youth whose
  zeal
For Mary springs from a distemper'd brain,
Inflamed by love.—And more, 'tis fully proved
That Mary's in the league.
 Sir W. Cec. An associate
In this conspiracy.
 Q. Eliz. Remove her straight
From gentle Shrewsbury's care to Fotheringay ;

Let her no more be treated as a queen.

[*Exit* DAVISON.

Cecil, am I not just ? why, to what length
Will she abuse my patience ?

Sir W. Cec. How many crimes
Which now disgrace the annals of the world
Owe their existence to false clemency,
And weak procrastination ? She must die ;
Or you, a willing sacrifice, must yield
Your life to save her.

Q. Eliz. Mean you, that through fear,
I should assume her part, and basely turn
Assassin ?

Sir W. Cec. Heaven forbid ! are we then sunk
Below the level of the pagan world ?
For they have justice ; justice is the right
Of all beneath the sun ; and shall not you,
The source and fountain of it, be allowed
What you dispense to all ? Are royal lives
Worth less than those of subjects ? or is she,
This mighty captive, paramount to laws,
Divine and human ?

Q. Eliz. Whither tends this theme ?

Sir W. Cec. To justice ; to the fair, impartial
course
Of justice——

Q. Eliz. Cecil ! you forget yourself,
And her whom you address : is this your zeal,
Your reverence for royalty ? What law
Can render her amenable to me ?

Sir W. Cec. Nature has laws ; instinct, alike to
all,
Promulgates them.—Assassination needs
No human statutes to declare its guilt ;
They are but feeble, artificial props,
The patchwork of society, which serve

Only to swell the catalogue of crimes
By inefficient sanguinary means.
Thank heaven! no mortal is exempt from law
Who shall attempt the life of England's queen.

    Q. Eliz. Aye in this island; but the general voice
Of Europe would cry shame!—Presumptuous man!
No more—Let not your forwardness o'erstep
The bounds of our forbearance, nor abuse
Your sovereign's ear with base suggestions! cease!

Enter DAVISON.

What fresh disaster now? hate, fear, and death,
Revolt, and treason, mark thy ominous steps.

    Dav. No prince was ever more beloved and
        feared;
Your people, in one bond associated,
Join to defend your life, and with one voice
Call for immediate justice on her head,
Whose life is incompatible with yours.

    Q. Eliz. For that alternative, if that were all,
Freely I'd pardon all her injuries:
But for my people's sake, it cannot be:
Heaven has entrusted them, and their true faith,
To my defence.

    Dav. Our lives, religion, all!
Grant, O! grant justice!

    Q. Eliz. Have I not sworn to it,
When I succeeded to the imperial crown?
You have our leave, our royal warrant, Davison.
[Exit DAVISON.
(*Aside.*) Heavens, what have I pronounced! I
        dare not think!
Then I must act, and leave slow timorous thought;
This is no time for scruples and remorse.
Cecil, 'tis done! since nothing but her blood
Can satisfy your thirsty souls.

Sir W. Cec. My liege,
Your grateful people will applaud the deed ;
Bless the defender of their faith.

Q. Eliz. 'Tis false ;
The universal world will curse the deed ;
All future ages execrate the name
Of her who brought anointed royalty
To such disgrace : yet there is time—who waits ?

Enter SERVANT.

Fly quickly ; call back Davison—Alas !

[*Exit* SERVANT.

Alas, poor queen ! cruel, perfidious man !
Your baneful counsel prompted me to this.

Enter DAVISON.

O, are you come ?—Davison ! I recal
The horrid sentence.

Sir W. Cec. Such are now the thanks,
And ever were, of those who weakly strive
To save a prince determined on his fall.
Madam ! since, inattentive to my prayers,
You thus devote yourself—let me retire,
Unaccessary to your fate.

Q. Eliz. Cecil !
I must not lose your service.

Sir W. Cec. Why should I
Stay to endure that vengeance, which will fall
On all your ministers, when Mary's plots
Rob England of her queen ?

Dav. Till that's atchieved,
She'll never rest ; her object is your crown.
Has she renounced her claim ? No ; to this hour
She sometimes boasts her title to your throne,
As confidently as she used in France,
When she with her first husband's fleurs-de-lis
Quartered the arms of England.

Q. Eliz. That indeed——
That was an early pledge ; with her first milk
She drank the seeds of hate : still, as she grew,
The inveterate poison spread ; and now she pours,
Full in my bosom, all the venomous store.

Sir W. Cec. O, 'tis not mercy, it is cruelty
To spare her, when the safety of your realm
Hangs on her fate ; what, if her voice should pierce
The prison walls, and through the nation sound
A signal for a second massacre ?

Q. Eliz. Ah, there is the word ! that word recals
   my mind,
Chills all my blood, and drives its current back.
Heaven doth exact a sacrifice to those
Who fell for our true faith : 'tis heaven's decree—
It is resolved—She dies—Fly, Davison !
Outstrip the winds, and with the winged speed
Of lightning, let the thunderbolt of heaven
Strike her devoted head !—Away ! Away !
        [Exeunt.

ACT THE FIFTH.

SCENE I.

Fotheringay Castle.

Enter LADY DOUGLAS *and* BETON.

L. Doug. Beton, alas ! you prophesy too well ;
Each moment brings some melancholy proof
Of your foreboding spirit.
    Bet. Could I doubt
The consequence of such facility ?
You know how oft and earnestly I urged
The danger of submission ; but to plead,
A queen, in her own person, thus to plead !
    L. Doug. Had she not pleaded, this prejudging
            court,
As by confession, had pronounced her doom.
And yet, could she suspect that such a list
Of all the great nobility, such names,
The warriors, heroes, patriots of the land,
Could so disgracefully be led to join
In concert to her ruin ?
    Bet. O ! too oft
Servile compliances are brought about
By joining numbers and great names, where none,

No single, worthy individual
Would show his face, or lend his honest fame.
Know you what urged her to appear in court ?

   L. Doug. 'Twas to defend her honour that she
       came,
In all the majesty of innocence ;
Descending from a throne, she offered up
Her dignity, a willing sacrifice,
To her fair fame ; impelled by conscious pride,
That inward pride which purity of mind
Inspires, and prompts to dare corruption's art,
To face, upon unequal terms, the wiles
Of perjured treachery.—O ! 'twas a sight
New to the world ; so strange, that mortal eyes
Their credit lost ; none who beheld, believed :
But, Beton, such a mockery as this
Can ne'er be realized ?

   Bet. O, surely not ;
'Tis but an artifice to justify
Past cruelties ; and what I fear the most,
Perhaps still closer custody.

   L. Doug. Alas !
They dare not sure proceed to take her life ?

   Bet. O, no ! 'twould rouse all Europe ; shake all
       thrones ;
Loosen the deepest-rooted monarchies :—
They dare not think of it—you see they're gone
For farther counsel to the Star Chamber.

   L. Doug. 'Tis time to attend the queen ; heaven
      guard her still !   [*Exeunt.*

SCENE II.

MARY's *Chamber, Fotheringay Castle.*

Enter LADY DOUGLAS *to the* QUEEN.

Q. Mary. Douglas ! come hither, Douglas ! sit by
    me ;
Thou art the constant solace of my woes.
I am almost worn out with grief and care ;
And, as you sometimes hint, I plainly find
My health is much impaired—I had not strength
Or spirits to do justice to my cause
Before this court.
    L. Doug. O my royal mistress !
How could you condescend to plead to them ?
    Q. Mary. Alas ! too confident in innocence,
I undervalued human treachery ;
Suffered my ears to catch the specious sound
Of Hatton's soft persuasive eloquence ;
Who, fair and false as Belial, from his tongue
Shed manna, which beguiled my silly heart,
Brought me to compromise my dignity
By condescensions, which the petulance
Of rancorous Burleigh's bitter enmity
Had ne'er effected.—O accursed fraud !
    L. Doug. Fraud ! aye, and open force ; did they
    not seize
Your papers, burst your cabinet, and rob,
Aye, basely pilfer all your little hoard,
The remnant of your treasure, which you saved
To pay your poor domestics, and for acts
Of charity ?

Q. Mary. But that, you know, of late
Has been prohibited ; because 'twas found
One still remaining source of happiness.
    L. Doug. Infernal, unexampled infamy !
Yes, my dear mistress, 'twas a cruelty
More felt by you than by the poor themselves
Who lost your daily charity.
    Q. Mary. Douglas !
Forsaken as I am, I could not think
That my own secretary would have turned
Against his mistress ; and in that, where he,
Above all others, knew me innocent :
I never much esteemed the man ; but yet
I did not think the viper would have bit
The hand that fed it.—He first came to me
From my poor uncle, the late Cardinal.
My uncle was the prop of all my counsels;
Alas ! he's gone ; and Charles, my brother, now
No longer reigns in France—he too is lost !
His end was wretched and unnatural.
And for my son, my only child, he reigns
In Scotland, patient of a mother's wrongs ;
I am forbid to hear from him.—Alas !
Had he the heart or spirit of a man—

Enter BETON.

    Bet. Pardon the messenger of dismal news !
    L. Doug. (*Aside.*) O me, what now ?
    Bet. And, O ! prepare to hear
The heaviest tidings.
    Q. Mary. I've been long prepared.
    Bet. Your own misfortunes you have ever borne
With fortitude, but other's sufferings—
    Q. Mary. What, others ? speak ! alas ! I guess.
    Bet. Too well
I fear.
    Q. Mary. The Duke ?

Bet. His troubles are no more ;
He rests in peace, beyond the tyrant's sway,
Where mortal envy cannot reach : alas !
Poor man ! he fell a victim to his love ;
His dying breath still blessed you.
 Q. Mary. O just heavens !
Since it has pleased you thus to visit him
For my offences, let my prayers ascend
In his behalf : yet stay ; he's risen now,
Whence he looks down with pity and contempt
On worldly cares ; views with serenity
Her despicable malice. O mean wretch !
Why dared you not let fall your vengeance here ?
He dies at last in my defence ! to save
This poor forlorn existence. Fie upon't !
Why lingers yet my breath ? Out, out, for shame !
Seek the wide air, and catch my Norfolk's soul.

SCENE III.

The Hall.

Enter BETON, *meeting* SIR AMIAS PAULET.

Bet. (*Aside.*) Paulet arrived ! What is your plea-
 sure here ?
Sir A. Paul. I am about to seek your mistress,
 Sir.
Bet. The queen is ill at ease, and needs repose.
Sir A. Paul. Sir, I have business to communicate—
Bet. Concerning her ?
Sir A. Paul. Aye, very nearly too ?
Bet. From Westminster ?

Sir A. Paul. From the Star Chamber, Sir;
No less than that her secretaries both
Have now confessed the plot, and sworn to it.

Bet. O perjured, venal slaves ! They never dared
Confront her with these murderous lies—the sight
Of injured innocence had choked their speech.

Sir A. Paul. Say rather, their repentance has pro-
    duced
Full proof to justify the course of law.

Bet. Who, but a judge determined to convict,
Would credit those whose faith is forfeited
By plain, avowed desertion of their trust?
'Twere a judicial murder—the worst crime
This sinful world has known : first, as the judge
Is, for his purity and wisdom, placed
In high authority, and charged to guard
Fair innocence ; then, as the sufferer
By such injustice, feels disgrace and shame
Added to all the bitterness of death.

Sir A. Paul. Is she, who claims protection, above
    law ?

Bet. Call you imprisonment protection ? O !
Mere subterfuges, worthy of your queen :
This last exploit of bribing evidence
Was an achievement suiting her great power,
Her riches, her wise ministers—O, shame !

Sir A. Paul. Is this the language, Sir, of Mary
    Stuart,
Late queen of Scotland ? She shall answer for it :
I must proceed to her—

Bet. Mean, servile wretch !
Paulet ! if you're a man, some future day
You'll not refuse atonement for these words.

SCENE IV.

The Queen's Chamber.

QUEEN MARY, LADY DOUGLAS, *Two Maids, and*
SIR AMIAS PAULET.

Q. Mary. Are these your orders, Sir, before my
    face
To take my canopy ?
    Sir A. Paul. No doubt they are.
    Q. Mary. And you're instructed thus to insult a
    queen !
    Sir A. Paul. I am instructed to consider you
As one attempting to destroy a queen.
    Q. Mary. 'Tis false, by all that's sacred ! Heaven
    well knows
I would not touch the meanest life on earth,
Much less the queen's, for all that she enjoys,
All her great empire—No ; on my royal word.
    Sir A. Paul. Henceforth, no more let convicts
    idly dream
Of forfeit titles—Farewell, Mary Stuart !
    Q. Mary. Thinks she that such indignities de-
    grade
My native titles !   Tell her, she doth fix
Eternal shame, contempt, and ridicule,
On her own name, by these low practices ;
And say, though she may rob me of my life,
Mary will die the lawful queen of Scots.
                [*Exit* SIR A. PAULET.
    L. Doug. O my dear mistress ! heed not such
    base men,

They are beneath your care.

Q. Mary. They harass me ;
My spirits are worn out.; I'll lay me down—
                [MARY *reclines on her sopha.*
Methinks soft music would compose my nerves :
I once had music at command—But, O !
The lute's unstrung that smoothed the brow of care;
Cold is the tongue that charmed with living fire.

    L. Doug. Allow your faithful maid to try her
        voice.

      [*Here* QUEEN MARY's *Lamentations should
        be sung by* LADY DOUGLAS, *or one of the
        maids.*

    Q. Mary. These plaintive strains bring quiet to
        my mind,
Balm to my troubled soul ; they sooth my woes,
Recal old times, and tell me what I was.
Douglas ! while yet I was in infancy,
The cruel father of this cruel queen
Asked me in marriage, from my native land,
For his own son ; and failing in his suit,
Waged war with Scotland : afterwards, you know,
It was my fate to mount the throne of France,
As consort of young Francis ; on whose death,
(O, ever lamentable, fatal loss !)
I staid in France, till, by the jealousy
And cruel arts of Catherine, I was driven
To seek my own hereditary crown.—
Dost thou remember how reluctantly
I left the gay and sprightly court of France?

    L. Doug. Aye, as 'twere yesterday—I see you
        still,
Fixed like a statue at the vessel's stern,
With eyes intent upon the Gallic shore,
Watching each lessening object, till the coast,
The wide-extended coast, and distant spires
Of Calais, glittering in the evening skies,

Alone remained in view; darkness came on,
And tears incessant, till the morning calm
Gave one faint glimpse of the departing scene:
O! then you beat your breast, and waved your
    hand,
While intermingled tears and sobs half-choked
Your ill-articulated, last adieu.

    Q. Mary. O, what a change for a young queen of
    France!
From all the pleasures of that splendid court,
To the morose, sour aspect, the dull cant,
And furious zeal, of Scotland's puritans!

    L. Doug. What barbarous, fanatic insolence!

    Q. Mary. O, I was destined in my native land
To heavier ills; to Darnley's cruelty;
Murray's ambition; Morton's treachery;
My subjects' mean desertion of their queen;
Their base revolt, and baser calumnies.

    L. Doug. The time shall come, when the impar-
    tial world
Shall nobly vindicate your injured fame.

    Q. Mary. Long since, dear Douglas, I've resign-
    ed this world,
With all its vanities, and fixed my heart
On heaven alone—Ah me! who's this?—

Enter DAVISON.

    L. Doug. Who art thou?

    Dav. One whose approach forebodes a blacker
    storm
Than e'er struck terror in the human breast.

    Q. Mary. Know you this man?

    L. Doug. No; but I fear he brings
Fresh insults and new rigours.

    Q. Mary. Whence come you?

    Dav. From the queen's self; who, most reluc-
    tantly,

Nor without many bitter sighs and tears—
  L. Doug. Tears of a crocodile—
  Dav. I say, with tears
The queen dispatched me to announce the fate,
The fate contained within this warrant—
                       [*Delivering a warrant.*
  Q. Mary. Ha!   [*Reading the warrant.*

Enter BETON.—*A Drum is heard beating a slow*
March.

  Bet. O mercy, heavens! alas, my queen; I fear
Some dreadful fate; the Earls of Shrewsbury
And Huntingdon, attended by the guards,
Are at the castle gate.
  L. Doug. Ah, here they come!
The array of death! Ah! is it come to this?

Enter SHREWSBURY *and* HUNTINGDON, *with Guards,*
Executioner, &c.

  E. Shr. The painful office which I now perform—
  Q. Mary. I know your business—
  E. Shr. Ah! know you, alas!
With what dispatch we're ordered to proceed?
  L. Doug. O murder! murder! cruel murderers,
    stay!
  Q. Mary. Patience, my child! I did not think, I
    own,
My sister queen would have proceeded thus;
But if my body cannot sustain one blow,
My soul deserves not those eternal joys
In heaven my holy faith has promised me.
  E. Hun. 'Tis your accursed faith that seals your
    doom;
While you're on earth, there is no surety
For our true faith—
  Q. Mary. What do I hear? good heaven!
Say you that I'm to suffer for my faith?
O, happy and glad tidings! glorious news!

Repeat that word, thou messenger of joy !
Angels, descending from their blest abodes,
Could not have hailed me with more welcome
                sounds—
Then it hath pleased the gracious heavens at last
To hear my prayers, and recompense my woes.
Now, in one blessed moment, all my pain,
All my long sufferings are exchanged for bliss.
These ears have heard me thus proclaimed a saint ;
And Mary's, aye, poor Mary's weeping eyes
Have lived to see her crown of martyrdom.
I'll make short preparation ; and mean while,
Let all my servants be in readiness ;
And bid my confessor to follow me.

    L. Doug. We will obey—
                [*Exit Lady* DOUGLAS, *with the Maids.*
    E. Hun. This may not be allowed ;
We came not here to see our holy faith
Mocked by the tricks and superstitious forms
Of papal ceremony—Your confessor
Must not approach—

    Q. Mary. Sir, I was born to reign ;
I am your mistress's kinswoman ; like her,
Descended from King Henry—Dowager
Of France, and Scotland's lawful queen ; as such,
I pray you, treat me.

              [*Exit* MARY *to her oratory.*
    Bet. Inhuman tyranny,
That would extend its barbarous cruelties
Beyond the grave !

    E. Shr. We may not violate
Our strict commands—

    Bet. Heaven will remember them :
You are, then, ordered to refuse a queen,
In the last moments of her life, those rites,
That consolation, which is always given
To the most hardened, graceless criminals,

That e'er insulted justice, or brought shame
On human nature ?—
   E. Hun. Nay, urge not that ; for, lo !
A pious prelate now attends without
To offer his assistance—I'll propose—
      [HUNTINGDON *offers to go towards the oratory.*
   Bet. If you're not lost to all humanity,
Disturb not her last meditations thus.
               [*Stopping* HUNTINGDON.

Enter Lady DOUGLAS, *with four Maids, a Physician, and an Almoner.*—BETON *places himself with them.*

   E. Hun. Why are you all assembled here ?
   L. Doug. You see
The sad remains of her poor family.
   E. Hun. You are, at best, but useless, idle show ;
Perhaps employed for superstitious use ;
Retire !—
   L. Doug. You cannot mean to hinder us
From this last, wretched office ?—
   E. Hun. Nay, begone !
   Bet. Infernal savage !
   L. Doug. Yet have mercy, Lords !
O ! you are far more gentle, Shrewsbury !
Drive not her few, poor faithful maids from her ;
Let them receive her blessing, and behold
Their dying mistress' looks, and close her eyes.
In pity, nay in decency, comply ;
Is't fit the person of a royal queen
Should lie a mangled and unheeded corse,
Without her maids to shroud those precious limbs,
Which kneeling princesses were proud to adorn ?
   E. Shr. 'Tis not in nature to resist the claim.

Enter MARY *from her oratory, dressed gorgeously,*
with a cross and beads.

 Q. Mary. This world to me is as a thing that's
   past ;
A burden shaken off—The retrospect
Exhibits nothing but a wearisome
And tedious pilgrimage—What is to come
Opens a scene of glory to my eyes :
Therefore with joy I hasten to begin
This course of triumph——O ! my faithful friends !
Ye all—all of you, my poor followers,
Have sacrificed your days to share my woes.
Now let me ask forgiveness for the past ;
Pardon my many negligences !—
 L. Doug. O !
Thus, on our knees, we crave your blessing all.
 Q. Mary. Yes, I will bless you with my latest
   breath ;
'Tis all I have to give : except, perchance,
Some trifles, which I here bequeath among you.
        [Delivering her will.
Beton, accept this ring—take that.   And thou !
  [Giving a ring to BETON, *and her Physician,*
   and her Almoner.
These tokens may remind you of my love.
Come hither, all my maids !
      [The Maids rise and approach.
Farewel, sweet friends.
      MARY *kisses each of them.*
We soon shall meet.   Come, Douglas ! let me bind
Thine arm with this my bracelet ; that so oft
As you behold it, you may think on me.
      Clasping her in her arms.
Now let me hold thee thus—Nay, do not weep,
That I'm translated from this scene of care
To endless joy.   Once more, farewel !—lead on

[MARY *makes a sign for the procession to go on,
and is proceeding, when* MELVIN, *an old man
with grey locks, throws himself at her feet, in
tears.*

Mel. O, mercy! mercy, heaven! alas, my queen!
That I should live to such an age for this,
To see this sight, and carry back this tale!

Q. Mary. Melvin! my faithful servant, Melvin,
    here!
In my last moment—They have kept thee long
Out of thy mistress' sight—thou comest in time
For her poor blessing—Good old man, return;
Commend me to my son—tell him I've done
No prejudice to Scotland's crown—tell him
My latest words were those of Scotland's queen.

                MELVIN *tries to speak, and is unable.*
Poor soul, thy griefs have chok'd thy speech!
    Adieu!
Bear witness, all! tell it throughout the world,
But chiefly to my family in France,
That I die firmly in their holy faith!
And you, ye ministers from England's queen!
Tell her, she hath my pardon; and relate,
That, with my dying breath, I do beseech
Her kindness to my servants; and request
Safe conduct for them into France; that done,
I've nought to ask, but that my poor remains
May be bestowed in Lorrain, or in France,
Where I may hope for pious obsequies;
For here the tombs of my progenitors
Are all profaned—Remember my requests!—
Now lead me on in triumph, till I gain
Immortal joys, and an immortal reign.

FUGITIVE;

A

COMEDY,

IN FIVE ACTS.

AS PERFORMED AT THE

KING'S THEATRE, HAY-MARKET.

BY

JOSEPH RICHARDSON, Esq.

DRAMATIS PERSONÆ.

LORD DARTFORD,	*Mr Dodd.*
SIR WILLIAM WINGROVE,	*Mr Bensley.*
MR WINGROVE,	*Mr Wroughton.*
OLD MANLY,	*Mr Parsons.*
YOUNG MANLY,	*Mr Palmer.*
ADMIRAL CLEVELAND,	*Mr King.*
MR WELFORD,	*Mr Barrymore.*
JENKINS,	*Mr Maddox.*
LARRON,	*Mr Wewitzer.*
O'DONNEL,	*Mr Phillimore.*
WILLIAM,	*Mr Benson.*
SERVANT,	*Mr Banks.*
MRS MANLY,	*Mrs Hopkins.*
MISS HERBERT,	*Miss Farren.*
MISS JULIA WINGROVE,	*Mrs Jordan.*
MISS MANLY,	*Mrs Kemble.*
MRS LARRON,	*Miss Pope.*
MRS RACHEL CLEVELAND,	*Mrs Ward.*

FUGITIVE.

ACT THE FIRST.

SCENE I.

An Apartment in SIR WILLIAM WINGROVE'S *House.*

Enter SIR WILLIAM *and Miss* JULIA WINGROVE.

Miss J. Win. Let me intreat you, sir, to hear me
—let reason be my advocate.

Sir W. Win. Reason, Julia! You know 'tis my
delight, my glory. What constitutes the pre-eminence of man, but his reason? 'Tis, like the sacred
virtue of high blood, a natural exaltation, of which
we can never lose the advantage, but by voluntary
degradation, or perverse misuse—What but reason
is the foundation of my preference for Lord Dartford? Is he not of a family as ancient even as my
own?

Miss J. Win. Did Lord Dartford inherit any of
the virtues, which probably acquired those highly
valued honours of his ancestry, my father might
have some cause to regret that his daughter's inclinations were at enmity with her duty.

Sir W. Win. And where, madam, have you learnt,
that the splendour of Lord Dartford's family suffers
any diminution in his own person ?

Miss J. Win. Where some of the happiest years
of my life have been passed, sir; at my dear deceased aunt's.

Sir W. Win. Mr Manly, now, I dare say, had
not the least share in producing this aversion to
Lord Dartford.

Miss J. Win. Mr Manly, sir ! Mr Manly would
scorn—nor can it ever be necessary for him to raise
his own character by a useless degradation of Lord
Dartford.

Sir W. Win. Aye, aye, now we have it—I
thought what share the eloquence of your aunt had
had in this apostacy from the faith of your ancestors
—Mr Manly, it seems, has contrived to make so
successful a monopoly of all the virtues, that there
does not remain even the leavings of an accomplishment for any other person. But since I despair of
making you enter into the just views of your family, by dutifully consenting, as you ought, to marry
a man for the revered merit of his blood, your brother shall try, whether your young spark be not
composed of more practicable materials.

Miss J. Win. For heaven's sake, dear sir, forego this—What must be the consequence of their
meeting ?

Sir W. Win. If you have any objection to the interview, you know how to prevent it.

Miss J. Win. O, sir, do not force me to so dreadful an alternative. I will, if you require it, bind

myself by the most solemn engagements to give up all thoughts of Mr Manly, only let me no more be persecuted with the addresses of Lord Dartford.

Sir W. Win. Nay, now I must believe you ; for where has it been recorded that an enamoured damsel ever broke a promise to an old father, when given at the expense of a young lover ? For once, however, you must excuse me, if I am a little disobedient to the authority of precedent, and endeavour to find some better security for the honour of my family, even than your love-sick renunciation of the object of your affections.

Miss J. Win. Yet, sir, hear me.

Sir W. Win. I do hear you—But first tell me why have I preserved you, since the decease of your aunt, from all intercourse with the world, with the single exception of the friendship of Miss Herbert, whose approaching alliance with your brother gives her a common interest in the lustre of our house ?—Why have I, like a fond parent, forbid you society ?—kept you sacred from the arts of our sex and the more dangerous follies of your own ?—locked you up, and guarded you, like the archives of my own family, that you might increase in value as you advanced in years ?—Why, but to secure you from the contagion of a degenerate world—who feel more anxiety about the means of supporting new families, than awful reverence for the names of old ones, and would meanly thrive by plebeian industry, rather than diet on the rich recollection of their immortal ancestry.

Miss J. Win But my dear father, just now, kindly condescended to say he would suffer me to reason with him on this subject. Can birth alone entitle a man to the high distinction you speak of ?
—And surely Lord Dartford—

Sir W. Win. Grant me patience, heaven! Do you call in question the prudence of my choice? Ungrateful Julia, never more will I hear you on this subject—and now attend my final determination—To-morrow you marry Lord Dartford.

Miss J. Win. To-morrow, sir!—You will not?—

Sir W. Win. Positively to-morrow—neither remonstrances nor tears shall sway me from my determined purpose. I leave you now to your reflections, and go to adjust the necessary preliminaries of a ceremony, that will recal you, inconsiderate girl, to duty and to reason. [*Exit.*

Miss J. Win. Is it possible!—Can my father thus shut his heart to the distresses of his Julia?—My brother too, happy in his own affections, not only abandons me to the interested rigour of his cruel ambition, but assists and animates him in the prosecution of his views.—Wretched, friendless Julia!—Whither wilt thou turn?—Ah Manly, that amidst the various excellencies of thy heart there is yet a careless generosity in thy nature—an irregular, though not ungraceful excess in thy very virtues, which, though it neither forbids esteem, nor damps affection, yet gives the alarm to delicacy, and checks the full pleasure of a fearless, unsuspecting confidence—were it not for this, I think I could not deny myself with thee a willing asylum from the severities of this domestic persecution. [*Exit.*

SCENE II.

Sir William's *garden.*

Enter Young Manly.

Young Man. Thus far I have achieved my purpose without discovery—what a devil of a wall have
I had to scramble up to obtain even the chance of
an interview—The sulky grandeur of your ancient
battlements was always the difficulty and the glory
of an enamoured hero—But what can the maddest
of the most venerable lads of chivalry lay claim to,
that does not to the full as reasonably belong to
me ? I have all their hopes with all their apprehensions, all their fears with all their confidence, all
their weakness with all their fortitude—So I think
it cannot be denied but that I possess as many good,
sound contradictions in my character as the best of
them—I have not, indeed, the gift of waiting that
those gentlemen had, for I begin already to feel impatient at Julia's delay.   Would I could gain but a
distant glimpse of her, or hear one strain of her enchanting voice—dear melodious voice ! soft as a
lover's sigh embodied into music, and sweet as the
inspired eloquence of a consenting smile—But soft !
soft ! she approaches, and in tears ! let me endeavour to learn the cause of them, before I make my
appearance ; what must he be composed of, and
what does he not deserve, who has been profane
enough to excite them.   [*Retires behind a tree.*

Enter JULIA, *and seats herself in an alcove.*

Miss J. Win. Here let me rest a while, and endeavour to collect my scattered thoughts. Could it be believed that my father, strict as his general notions of honour are, should think of forcing me to become the wife of a man whom my soul abhors!

Young Man. Forcing thee!

Miss J. Win. When, too, he is convinced of my being attached to another.

Young Man. To another!

Miss J. Win. I think he loves me.

Young Man. I am sure he does—that is, if I am he.

Miss J. Win. He is kind and generous, capable of the most ardent and disinterested passion.

Young Man. It must be me.

Miss J. Win. But he has faults, great faults.

Young Man. Now I am sure 'tis me.

Miss J. Win. I dread the levity of his nature— O Manly, Manly, why cannot I trust thee?

Young Man. I am sure I can't tell.

Miss J. Win. How gladly could I owe the relief of my present afflictions to thy kindness, but for the dread of being afterwards exposed to the severer calamity of thy indifference. O why, why, Manly, cannot I confide in thee?

Young Man. (*Comes forward.*) Why, indeed! Dear, generous Julia, banish these apprehensions; I never can injure truth, innocence, and beauty like thine.

Miss J. Win. Mr Manly! How you have alarmed me! What a rash step is this—But fly, I conjure you; if you have any regard for my happiness—fly.

Young Man. Fly, Julia! Yes, swifter than a lover's thought; but you must be the partner of my flight.

Miss J. Win. You cannot surely be serious.

Young Man. So serious that I shall not stir one single step without you—Julia, Julia, this is no time for trifling or for ceremony. To be candid with you, I have overheard you, and if I deserve punishment for the involuntary offence, reserve it till the danger is over that threatens you.

Miss J. Win. Indeed, Mr Manly, your generous concern for me leaves me as little right, as I have inclination, to be severe; but therefore it is I intreat you to quit this scene of danger—You know the fury of my relations.

Young Man. Nay, Julia, I care not how soon I go—As we depart together you cannot reasonably suspect me of being an advocate for delay.

Miss J. Win. What can you mean?

Young Man. Mean! Why to decide my fate on the instant—Either to follow you as your humble slave through the wide world of happiness, for it can have no place in it forbidden to delight while you are with me, or meet with resignation, on the spot, the bitterest resentment of your vindictive family.

Miss J. Win. O Manly! give me not such a fatal proof of your affection—I will consider of your proposal by to-morrow—but go now, I beseech you.

Young Man. Not a step—If I am stubborn, Julia, you are my example. I have not often such authority for my conduct—I will not quit you till I am assured of your deliverance from this unnatural tyranny.

Miss J. Win. Hear me for a moment—I do not wish to conceal from you how much my gratitude is interested in your safety—The embarrassment of my present situation, added to this dangerous evidence of your attachment, will, I hope, in some measure, excuse me for the confession I am about to—But indeed, sir, indeed—what shall I say? A womanish apprehension prevails over my tongue, and sways it from the direction of my heart, in spite of me—Indeed, I cannot go with you—Character, prudence, duty forbid it.

Young Man. I confess, madam, I was prepared to expect more candour, and more decision, from the lips of Miss Wingrove.

Miss J. Win. Dear Manly, I thank you for this rebuke—it brings me back to myself—something must be allowed to the fond agitation of a woman's fears—but they are gone; Love himself, unfriendly as he is to truth, yet smiles propitiously upon a slow obedience to it at last.—Meet me at one, in the avenue before our house, and then with more safety to my Henry, as well as more security to our enterprise, I will resign myself, and all my hopes, to your faithful guidance.

Young Man. Dearest Julia, on my knees I thank you—I am oppressed at once with love and gratitude—It is needless to say with what anxious, vigilant punctuality I will obey your mandate—with what idolatry of submissive affection, I will watch over every rising thought, and half-formed object, of your future life. (*Rises.*) From this moment, then, dismiss all apprehension of your Henry's levity, and be satisfied that——

Miss J. Win. I am satisfied—Surely, I have proved I am so—But interesting as your conversation always is, and on this theme fraught with peculiar endearment, I must deprive myself of it—You must go—pray obey me now—My turn for obedience approaches fast. Remember.

Young Man. Can I forget· the consecrated moment! Adieu, ever dearest, till then.

Miss J. Win. Adieu, dear Manly.   [*Exeunt.*

SCENE III.

LORD DARTFORD's *House.*

Enter LORD DARTFORD, *followed by* JENKINS.

L. Dart. Jenkins, does Sir William know of my arrival here ?

Jen. He does, my Lord.

L. Dart. Well, I suppose I must pay the first visit—But hold, should not I brush up my style a little, to enable me to undergo this encounter of genealogy ? No—I believe there is no occasion; the secret lies in a short compass—Pedigree's the word —and one of your real accurate lovers of historical virtu—will believe any thing—And so, we'll trust to chance, and the assistance of such convenient absurdities as may happen to arise. (*A knocking at the door.*)—But see who's there, Jenkins.

[*Jenkins goes, and introduces* SIR WILLIAM WINGROVE.

Sir W. Win. I hope, my Lord, my presence, thus unannounced, does not interrupt any of your Lordship's weightier concerns.

L. Dart. It is impossible that the favour of Sir William Wingrove's company can ever be felt as an intrusion.

Sir W. Win. Your Lordship is kindness itself— (*They sit down.*) It is a doubtful point with me, my Lord, in the alliance which is upon the eve of accomplishment, by which party the honour will be given or received.

L. Dart. So he's off already—there's but one way for me—I should ill deserve my good fortune,

Sir William, were I not sensible that the honour and the happiness are both eminently mine.

Sir W. Win. Why, my Lord, that is by no means a clear case—I perceive that your Lordship possesses a very competent knowledge of the antiquity of our family; but, to deal candidly with you, I believe yours takes its rise nearly about the same time—pretty nearly, that is to say—I mean within a century of us, or some such trifle—I dare say it does; for the Dartford family may be very clearly traced to the conquest.

L. Dart. The conquest, Sir William, is modern— It is not long since I perused a valuable manuscript, that makes very honourable mention of the Wingroves in one of the remoter reigns of the Saxon heptarchy.

Sir W. Win. Could your Lordship procure me a sight of that manuscript? The favour will be infinite.

L. Dart. Sir William may rely upon it, that if my friend can be prevailed upon to resign the parchment, I shall be happy in promoting his wish. (*Aside.*) And if he does, his politeness must positively be of a most accommodating cast, to enable him to part with what he never had.

Sir W. Win. In one of the remoter reigns of the Saxon heptarchy! Is it possible! But why not possible?—To what times may not the family of the Wingroves be traced by the laudable diligence of learned inquiry? Even up to the dark periods of early nature, of rudeness, ignorance, and barbarity, where knowledge fails us, and History herself is lost in the confusion of her materials.   [*Muses.*

L. Dart. Now will he not be content till he has pursued his high birth to the illustrious parentage of a savage, and drawn the boasted stream of his pure blood from the polluted leavings of the deluge.

Sir W. Win. Now, my Lord, to business.—The fifty thousand pounds which I purpose as my daughter's dower, is but a small, and indeed inadequate compensation for the honour of your dignified alliance—Happy, but too happy, should we all feel ourselves, if her inclinations accorded with our wishes, and acquiesced in the brilliant provision we have made for her—But she is perverse, my Lord, unaccountably perverse—Yet submit she shall, and that without delay—I am fixed, immutably fixed. But if your Lordship will do me the honour to accompany me to my house, I will there explain to your Lordship the difficulties we have to encounter, and the expedients we have provided to overcome them—Nay, my Lord.

[*Contending on the etiquette of precedency.*

L. Dart. Impossible, Sir William! mere title is adventitious, birth inherent.   [*Exeunt.*

SCENE IV.

The Road, with a distant View of SIR WILLIAM WINGROVE's *House.*

Enter Young MANLY, *singing.*

Young Man. Was there ever such a happy, unlucky dog as myself—happy beyond the narrow bounds of mortal imagination in the love of my Julia—but horribly unlucky, that the certainty and near approach of my felicity has quite bereft me of my senses—Just as I had abandoned myself to

despair, to be raised in one delicious half-hour to
the summit of—O! egad there's no bearing it! I
shall run mad—I am mad, that's certain.

[Sings and dances.

Enter ADMIRAL CLEVELAND.

Adm. Cleve. So, so—there's young frolicksome in
his whirligigs—What, 'squire madcap, are you prac-
tising how to make a fool of yourself? Don't take
so much trouble, young man; you can succeed
pretty well without so much pains.

Young Man. Ha! my old man of war—give me
your hand—When shall you and I go upon a voyage
to the—

Adm. Cleve. To the moon, Eh! young fresh-
water? Why, you seem to be in her latitude already; or have you been stowing in a fresh lading
of champagne?

Young Man. Your first conjecture is perhaps a
little near the mark; for my understanding, I believe, is rather upon the go; but as for champagne
—curse champagne.

Adm. Cleve. What then, you have been in a tight
engagement at play, and have brought the enemy
to. A'nt that it, my young shark?

Young Man. No, no, my heart of oak; I defy the
power of gold to disorder my senses. But what do
you think, my noble commander, of gaining the
woman one loves. Can your old weather-beaten
fancy conceive any joy equal to that?

Adm. Cleve. Why, I don't think I can, unless it
be seeing an enemy's ship strike; and that does give
the senses a whirl that none but a seaman can be a
judge of.

Young Man. Why then, as I am a stranger to
naval sensations, the pleasure of being beloved by an
angel, must serve my turn—When conquered beau-

ty prepares to yield—when willing love strikes the
flag—that's the whirl for my money.

Adm. Cleve. Well, that's good natured, however,
to rejoice at the thoughts of an engagement, where
you are sure to have the worst on't.

Young Man. Dear admiral, had I but known you
when I was a boy.

Adm. Cleve. What then?

Young Man. Then? Do you ask me what then?
O, Julia!

    My soul hath her consent so absolute,
    That not another comfort like to this
    Succeeds in unknown fate.

Adm. Cleve. Poor young man—well, my lad, when
your wits are at anchor, though I fear the vessel's
too crazy ever to see port again, you and I may
drink a can together—till then, your servant.

Young Man. Nay, nay, don't go yet.

                         [*Dancing.*

Adm. Cleve. Why, damn you, you vere about so,
one might as well look for anchorage in a whirl-
pool, as think to hold a parley with you.

Young Man. Well, come then, I will be serious
—Do you ever pray at sea, admiral?

Adm. Cleve. Why, what should we pray for? Except, indeed, when there's danger in the wind, and
then, to be sure, that alters the case.

Young Man. Well, now, there lies your error.

Adm. Cleve. Error!—meaning me. You?

Young Man. Aye !—I hold it such an abominable
ignorance of duty.

Adm. Cleve. Ignorance of duty!—why, you pala-
vering whipper-snapper, am I to be taught my duty,
after having had the command of a fleet, by such a
sneaking son of a whore as you?

Young Man. Nay, but why so hot, my good
friend? You cannot think I meant to offend you?

Adm. Cleve. Not mean to offend, when you tell
me I don't know how to command? Ignorance of
duty indeed—out of my way, you live lumber—
damn you, I only thought you were mad, but now
I find you're a fool. [*Exit.*

Young Man. Ha! ha! ha!—At any other time I
should have been a good deal vexed to have offended old True Blue, that's certain; but at this moment my heart's so crowded with sensations of
mirth and joy—with such a confused jumble of contending raptures—with so much delight at what has
already passed, and such a maddening anticipation
of what is yet to come, that no thought of apprehensive care can obtain sanctuary in my bosom.
My dear Julia, my own Julia! O! that idea over-
powers me with transport—Gad so, there's Sir William—if I stay here much longer, playing the fool,
I shall be observed by some of the family, and then
—adieu to all my hopes—What shall I do? I'll
return to the Star Inn, which is just in view of the
house, and deceive the tedious interval with my
companions whom I left there, till my fair day-star
arises, that leads me to new life, to happiness and
love. [*Exit.*

ACT THE SECOND.

SCENE I.

A nearer View of SIR WILLIAM WINGROVE's
House.   (Moonlight.)

Enter JULIA.   *She opens the Door gently ; and after
an appearance of irresolution, shuts it after her.
She then comes forward.*

Miss J. Win. So, now my fate's decided ! What
have I done ?—I dare not think upon it—if Manly
now deceives me, I am undone—shall I go back?
—and consent to be the wife of Lord Dartford—
that must follow—for but too well I know, that tenderness never yet prevailed upon the stern ambition
of my father's nature.   But why should I doubt
my Henry's unstained honour ? Though he is wild,
whom did he ever wrong?   Pardon, dear Manly—
pardon the unjust suspicion of thy Julia—and see
he comes to clear my heart of doubt.
                    [MANLY *sings without.*
O, gracious heaven ! is this the man I've chosen to
be the guardian of my honour—Fly, fly, my feet—
let me but reach my father's—The door is fast ; I
have now no hope left, unless the wild confusion

that wine has made in him, prevent his observing
me. Heaven grant it may.

> [*Conceals herself behind a tree, and draws a
> veil over her face.*

Enter YOUNG MANLY, *singing*.

Heighten every joy to-day, and never mind to-
morrow.

Aye, so say I—the present—the present is the
only time that's worth a wise man's concern—why
should we give ourselves any trouble about to-
morrow, when we don't know that to-morrow will
ever reach us?—or that we shall reach it, which is
pretty nearly the same thing, I take it; and then
there is just so much good care thrown away.
'Fore heaven, the man that wrote that song must
have been a most profound person : that single line
ought to have immortalized him—it shall be my
motto.   [*Sings.*

Why the plague should we be sad,
  Whilst on earth we moulder ;
Whether we're merry, or grave, or mad,
  We every day grow older.

'Sdeath, the ground's full of rocks and quicksands,
I think ; my feet either sink or stumble at every
step : what can be the reason ? I that am so steady
a goer—always, always was—all my life. Egad, I
believe the thickets are going to dance. May be,
they mistake me for Orpheus. Nay, gentlemen, if
you pay such a compliment to my singing, I can do
no less than take a turn with you—I am as frolicsome
as you can be for the soul of you—so now, let me
choose my partner.

> [*Catches at a tree, behind which* JULIA *is con-
> cealed, who shrieks.*

By all the sylvan powers, another Daphne. [*Kneels.*
Madam, behold a swain, not altogether so musical

as Apollo, I grant you, but a good honest fellow for all that—So, madam, so—psha, never mind more words—let us go.

Miss J. Win. O, my hard fortune !

Young Man. What do you say ?—Speak out, my angel—I know that your voice is more tuneful than Philomel's or mine—that your eyes are the sparkling harbingers of love—that your dimples are the chosen hiding-places of all the cupids. And those lips !—but hold—rot it—I had forgot—I can't see e'er a one of them—Never mind—no matter for that—I dare say it's all true ; and if it isn't, why then we must mend the matter with thinking.

Miss J. Win. O heavens ! is it possible !

Young Man. No, certainly—it cannot be possible—it is'n't possible—Come, come, I know you are kind as you are beautiful, and so it is possible—and so, without more waste of time, come to my arms, and——

Miss J. Win. It is in vain to reason with him in this state—I must endeavour to divert his attention, and by that means escape him if I can. If you will permit me to be your guide—

Young Man. Enough, my pretty pilot ; take me where you will. We will never part any more, shall we ? No, never.

Miss J. Win. I dare say not, sir.

Young Man. Not, sir ?—Why to be sure not, sir. —Never, never, never.

Miss J. Win. Let us walk quickly. (*Aside.*) O heaven, assist me !

Young Man. As quick as you please, my angel—I'll fly, if you choose, for I'm very steady, and very loving.   [*Exeunt.*

SCENE II.

A Wood.

Enter JULIA.

Miss J. Win. At length, thank heaven! I have escaped—escaped—but is this a place of safety? What will become of me? Yet 'tis some comfort, that the day appears—O Manly, thou hast made life hateful to me.—Who comes here?—I've surely seen his face, O! I remember I have seen him sometimes at my aunt's, with lace and gauzes—If he should not know me, perhaps I may prevail on him to conceal me—He has a wife, I know. Let me consider what I shall say to him.

Enter LARRON (*with bundles.*)

Dese villain custome-house officers give von honest man no reste—You go to bed late—you rise early—pardie—you sit up all night—it make no difference, dey vil be vid you—Ma foi, I believe dey tink sleep contrabande (*sees Julia.*) Ah! par St Dominique, here be von young ladi en great agitation. Ah! par hazard, her equipage est un peu derangé, and she be retire here till tout soit ajusté—a littel civilité de ma parte me produira peutêtre beaucoup de pratique on de ladis. En verité, de torough bred trader know how to faire son profit de chaque circonstance. Madame, excuse—but you seem beaucoup affligé—si, madame— if I can by de utmost exertion of mine contribuer en de smallest instance to votre accomodation, I shall consider de fortune vich led me dis vay, as de plus grande félicité de ma vie, de greatest happiness of my life.

Miss J. Win. He speaks very civilly; I think I may venture to tell him so much of my unhappy situation, as may let him know how much I need his assistance.

Lar. Madam, you no ansere.—May I beg de faveur to be informé, if I can merite l'honneur de vous rendre le moindre service? Your servants, madame, ave you any littel message to convey to dem? May I hope you vill permit a me de vous escorter a votre carosse?

Miss J. Win. Sir, you mistake the matter entirely. I have neither coach, servants, nor friends at present—The cruelty of one in whom I most confided, has involved me in this calamity; and I must thankfully avail myself of your obliging offers of service, by entreating the shelter of your roof, till I can dispose of myself, so as not to be an incumbrance to any one.

Lar. Eh, my dear—vat you say? You no coche, no servantes, no friend, no house, no home, ou vant to come and live a vid me?—Non, non, ma fille—dat vill not do—non, non—Dere be de vat do you call?—de maison d'industrie, de vorkhouse for de poor girl. Personne go to my house, but such as peut faire une belle depense.

Miss J. Win. (*Aside.*) Mercenary wretch!

(*Going.*)

Lar. Holla! you little girl—you tell me, can you vorke? Suppose dat I vas to take pitie upon your condition, can you pay me vell derefor?

Miss J. Win. What shall I say? I must bear with his low impertinence, to induce him to give me a shelter. (*To Larron.*) I can, sir, embroider neatly, and make lace.

Lar. O pardie, you be von little busy bee! You can make love too. Can you not my dear?

Miss J. Win. Insupportable ! If, sir, you consider the favour you seemed inclined to confer, as
a sanction for your impertinent freedom, I must
beg you to leave me to my misfortunes.

Lar. Comme vous voulez, ma fille—dere not
be many dat vill take you in. You may meet vid
some, if you stay here long, dat vill make you
vorse offer.

Miss J. Win. That's too true ! If I get to his
house, his wife will protect me from his odious familiarity—I must try to make my peace. (*To Larron.*)
Perhaps, sir, I have been too hasty. If you will
conduct me to your house, I shall consider it as an
obligation which I shall endeavour by my utmost
industry to repay.

Lar. Ha, hah ! You say so ?—Vell den I vill tink
about it. (*Aside.*) She poor, she pretty, she vorke.
Mais elle est fierte comme une princesse—Vell, I
vill have her—She be von fille dat know de vorld;
it save so much trouble. She be von pauvre inno-
cente, my glory will be de greater. (*To Julia.*)
You be good girl, and I vill take you. I vill inform
you vat you say to my vife as ve go along.

Miss J. Win. How one rash step has involved me
in a labyrinth of difficulties. I see no end to it ;
yet dare not tread back the way I've gone. (*To Larron.*) Very well, sir.

Lar. Vell, you hold up your head.—You not be
so cast down. Tenez—you carry dis bondel—you
valk first—If you see an homme dat look like von
officer des custome, you run straight forward till
you come to de stile, and vait dere for me.

Miss J. Win. Excuse me, sir ; I cannot consent
to be employed in any unfair transaction.

Lar. Vat you not smogel for me, petite ingrate ?—Must I not smogel for you ? Must I not
run you upon my vife ? Are you not von littel

piece of contrabande vous meme? You see, my dear, you have to deal vid von bel esprit—but prenez courage, I vill not be too hard vid you. A ça—you vill do ver vell by and by.   [*Exeunt.*

SCENE III.

Sir William Wingrove's *House.*

Enter Mr Wingrove.

Mr Win. How powerful is the influence of pre-judice. My reason convinces me that there is no other just criterion for deciding upon the merits of men, but such as grows out of their own personal good or ill properties. If it were true, that the qualities of the parent were transmitted to the pro-geny, then, indeed, it might be as necessary to esta-blish the genealogy of a man, as to ascertain the pedigree of a horse. But the properties of the mind elude the frail laws of hereditary descent, and own no sort of obedience to their authority— How is it, then, that with this distinct light before me, I cannot help falling into my father's pre-judices?—I feel them to be unjust; I know them to be absurd: and yet, unjust and absurd as they are, they influence my conduct in spite of me—I love my sister—I know her affections are engaged to Young Manly—I am satisfied he is worthy of her. Yet I am adverse to the match, and conspire with my father in throwing every obstacle in the way of its completion—and in favour of whom? Of Lord Dartford—a man void of feeling, senti-ment, or sincerity—uniting in him every contra-diction of depravity; cold, gay, ostentatious, and interested—But he is a man of birth—Despicable distinction!

Enter O'DONNELL.

O'Don. O, sir, sir!—my young master—the house is in an uproar, sir, sir.

Mr Win. Well, sir, what's the matter?

O'Don. O! I don't know what's the matter, sir; my young lady's the matter, sir—we're all undone, sir—She's gone, sir—Nobody knows where, sir.

Mr Win. My sister gone! impossible—Degenerate Julia! Is it thus you reward the kind, the anxious zeal of your friends to place you in a situation worthy the exalted regard they entertained for you; to throw yourself away upon the mean pretensions of a plebeian——But where is my father?—Let me fly to him with the news of this disaster.   [*Exit.*

Enter SIR WILLIAM, *with servants.*

Sir W. Win. I'll not believe that she is gone—gone! What!—my daughter eloped at midnight! Go all of you and search again. I am certain she is hid somewhere.

O'Don. Suppose your honour then was to order the canal and the fish-ponds to be searched, for I am certain if she be hid, it must be at the bottom of one of them.

Sir W. Win. Be dumb, horrible brute. Would you have me think—Did I ever give her cause—Was I not ever the fondest of parents?

O'Don. Sartinly, your honour meant it all for her good. But when a young lady finds nothing to plase her in this world, she is apt sometimes to take a peep into the other to try the difference.

Sir W. Win. Begone, I say—find her, or I'll discharge you all for your negligence in suffering her to escape. (*Exit O'Donnel and servants.*)   The

conjectures of this blundering blockhead terrify
me. I hope Julia has not in a fit of rash perverse-
ness—Yet I think her piety—

Re-enter MR WINGROVE.

Well, William, any news of your sister.

Mr Win. No, sir, no news, but of her dishonour—
disgraceful girl!

Sir W. Win. O'Donnel alarms me exceedingly—
he thinks that in a phrenzy of disappointed passion
she has———

Mr Win. No, my dear sir, Julia is not so weary
of life—The porter tells me he found all the doors
leading to the road unbarred this morning. Would
I could discover whether she had a companion in
her flight—If she be not recovered speedily, the
disgrace will be indelible—Lord Dartford will be
here soon. What shall we say to him? O! shameless Julia.

Sir W. Win. Forbear, my son—these violent
transports distress me even more than your sister's
flight—Consider that it is through you the pure
blood of our family must descend to posterity—
that through you the name of Wingrove must be
transmitted to ages as distant and unknown as those
from whence it sprung. Reflect a little, my son,
bring reason to your aid, and consider how trifling
and insignificant are the misfortunes of your sister,
compared to objects so important and so sacred as
these. Be calm then, William.

Mr Win. I will endeavour it, sir.

Sir W. Win. If you were to go to Miss Herbert's,
her acquaintance is so extensive, you perhaps may
obtain some information of Julia there. Go, go,
my son.

Mr Win. I obey you, sir. [*Exit.*

Enter O'DONNEL.

O'Don. Lord Dartford, your honour.

Sir W. Win. He has not been informed of my daughter's absence?

O'Don. No, your honour; not a syllable has been spoken to him since he entered the house.

Sir W. Win. Where is he now?

O'Don. In the saloon, sir, in arnest discourse with your honour's chaplain.

Sir W. Win. Blockhead! I'll go to him then.

[*Exit.*

O'Don. O! 'tis a pretty blundering piece of business, fait. Devil burn me, but if I didn't tink how it would end. There's nothing so sure to make a young lady run away, as keeping her fast by the heels. O! if I had a wife that I wanted to get rid of, fait, I would keep here safe under lock and key.

[*Exit.*

SCENE IV.

MISS HERBERT'S *House.*

Enter MISS HERBERT, *and* MRS RACHEL CLEVE-
LAND.

Miss Her. Miss Wingrove eloped, aunt? Heaven grant it may be true! and that those to whom she has fled for refuge may be sensible of her merit—though I think I can guess the person.

Mrs R. Cleve. I have heard it supposed that young Mr Manly had a place in her affections—if he is the protector she has made choice of, I fear the lady's character and the young man's life are in equal danger.

Miss Her. The adventure wears a much less formidable aspect to me, I confess, provided she escapes her father's pursuit—O ! how I shall enjoy the vexation of Sir William and his son, at finding all the views of their persecuting ambition thus happily disappointed.

Mrs R. Cleve. Nay, Harriet, now I think you do not speak with your usual sincerity—Mr Wingrove I am persuaded is not indifferent to you.

Miss Her. Dear aunt, you are partly right, and partly wrong. Mr Wingrove has, I acknowledge, touched my heart a little, but the contagion has not yet made its way to my head—for though the little god may have thrown away upon me an idle arrow, or so, he has kept his bandage as an embellishment to his own person : I can see the failings of my swain as well as another.

Mrs R. Cleve. You're a mad girl.

Enter a Servant.

Ser. Mr Wingrove, madam.
Miss Her. Desire him to walk up.

[*Exit Servant.*

Now I must teaze him a little—do not oppose me, my dear aunt. I've a mind to lead him to believe that his sister is under my protection—this will serve her, by stopping further pursuit for a while, and at the same time put him into a most entertaining rage with me.

Enter MR WINGROVE.

But, dear madam, have you been kind enough to see that every avenue to the east wing of the house is secured ?—Has good care been taken that the postern gate at the lower end of the western parterre is properly fastened ?—Are the man traps all ready for snapping ?—Are the spikes new sharpened on the south wall ?—Have orders been given, that if any of the inquisitive family of the Wingroves—O Mr Wingrove !—you come upon one so suddenly—but I am overjoyed to see you, sir.

Mr Win. I am bound in politeness, madam, to return the compliment ; yet, after what I heard at my entrance, there would perhaps have been no great offence to truth, if the joy had been suppressed on both sides.

Miss Her. You do well, sir, not to express more than you feel.

Mr Win. If I did, madam, it appears I should not want a precedent for my justification.

Miss Her. But why, Mr Wingrove, if, as you are constantly telling one, I use you so very, very ill, why will you throw yourself perpetually in my way ?—I don't recollect that I sent for you—Did I, aunt ? Did any body go to desire dear Mr Wingrove to come to us ?—I forget, I vow.—And yet perhaps I might—for I know it does him a world of good, poor dear man !—He is fond of primitive times, and, like all your good people of those days, loves to throw himself in the way of a little wholesome persecution—But now, sir, answer me this, you unjust—you ungrateful man, you—Did I ever disappoint you whenever you came here for a little healthful mortification in a morning ?—Was I ever the person to send you away without your errand ? No, sir, with all your malice, I defy you to lay that to my charge.

Mr Win. Madam, I have many obligations to be sure to the gentleness of your nature ; but I entreat you not to add one more to the many kindnesses I do owe it, that of driving me to distraction—Will you have the goodness to answer me, madam—Is not my sister here?

Miss Her. Bless me, sir, and suppose she is— But it is all of a piece—You set out with informing me you were very sorry to see me, and now you would forbid me all intercourse with the only part of your family I have any desire to be acquainted with.

Mr Win. Let me conjure you, my dear lovely tyrant, not to play with my anxiety—suspend a while the triumphs of your sarcasm, you cannot misunderstand the agitations of my heart at this moment—you know the cause of them—if you have given my sister an asylum——

Miss Her. Then, sir, with equal solemnity, I desire you to believe, that if I have given your sister the shelter you imagine, I shall not withdraw it to gratify the prejudices of any of her relations; besides, sir, were your sister assured she should be secure from the odious danger that threatens her from a man she detests, she would, I am convinced, be happy to throw herself at her father's feet, and on that condition———

Mr Win. It is a condition, however, that will not be granted her, madam. What, when our honour, when the dignity of our house, are committed—shall all be sacrificed to the frivolous partiality of a disobedient girl.

Miss Her. Give me leave, sir, to tell you that you seem to me to mistake this honour for which you declaim so warmly; honour holds no society with injustice.

Mr Win. Injustice, madam!

Miss Her. Yes, sir, there can be no injustice equal to that of compelling a woman to so sacred a connection as a married union against the known and settled preference of her heart. It is, besides,

sir, acting a very ungenerous part towards Lord
Dartford himself.

Mr. Win. Not at all, madam ; Lord Dartford
knows of her aversion, and has spirit enough to disregard it.

Miss Her. Does he, sir ; then indeed there can
be no doubt, with all due deference to his spirit,
but he merits it.   But in the meantime, Mr Wingrove, permit me to embrace the very earliest opportunity of expressing my gratitude for this new
philosophy you have been kind enough to teach us.
You are the first lover, I believe, that ever told his
mistress to her face, that a union of the affections
was a superfluous ingredient in the composition of
matrimony—You made the discovery, sir—You
will leave it to me to make the proper use of it.

Mr Win. Nay, madam, if you are determined to
make no other use of what I say, but to pervert it
into ridicule or injury, I know nothing that's left
me, but to use the only privilege, which I think you
will not deny me, that of making a speedy departure.   I have long despaired of exciting any sympathy in you towards myself ; yet the distresses of
an afflicted brother, I had fondly believed, would
have inclined you to forbearance at least, if they
had failed to produce any more active effect upon
your humanity.   [*Exit.*

Miss Her. Haughty to the last—Well, thank
heaven ! this interview is over.   Julia, I have fought
hard for you.

Mrs R. Clev. Indeed, my dear niece, you carry
matters too far ; you will certainly lose Mr Wingrove some of these days, if you persevere in your
present treatment of him.

Miss Her. No, my dear madam—certainly no—
The symptoms of love vary with the difference of
constitution, and in a lively nature there is no surer

proof of it, than a little playful malignity—and that the man ought to have sense enough to understand; or, wanting that, I am sure he has too little to entitle him to become the lord and master of a young woman of my spirit and pretensions.

Mrs R. Clev. Aye, but have a care, Harriet.

Miss Her. Well, madam, I'll do my best—but, indeed, if I cannot laugh and teaze him out of some of his faults, we shall make a miserable couple. I can be a willing slave to a gentle master, but I should prove a most rebellious subject to a tyrant, I am certain.   [*Exeunt.*

SCENE V.

Mr Manly's.

Enter Young Manly.

Young Man. Heigho! What is't o'clock, I wonder? My head aches horridly—perhaps a little tea timely administered will set all to rights; we'll try.

Enter William.

William, how came I to have no better accommodation than the sopha last night?—I suppose I was a little gone, but you might have put me to bed, sirrah.

Will. Sir, you know I was'nt at home, you employed me elsewhere.

Young Man. Elsewhere? Hang me, if I remember—why, how did I employ you?

Will. You know, sir, when I called upon you at the Star Inn, you sent me to hire a little vessel to carry you and Miss Wingrove to France.

Young Man. Miss Wingrove and me to France!
—peace, you profane rascal.

Will. Dear sir, I wonder you should forget—
You know you was almost beside yourself for joy
yesterday, and told me that Miss had consented to
be yours, and that you should marry her in France
first, for fear of accidents; and then you bid me hire
a good tight vessel, and to tell the master, that if
he would bring to, in the west creek, and put to
sea directly upon your getting on board, you would
give him a hundred guineas as soon as he had landed you upon the coast of France.

Young Man. Eh!—how?—Miss Wingrove—
coast of France!

Will. But it growing day-light, and the captain
getting sulky, thinking as I had made a fool of him,
I made the best of my way home to see what was
the matter, and now it's all the talk this morning
that Miss Wingrove is run away.

Young Man. What's that? Julia left her father's!
—And where is she? Tell me this instant.

Will. Dear heart, sir! why, how should I know?
I thought she had been with you.

Young Man. This is most unintelligible—William,
are you sure I am awake now? Don't laugh, you
rascal—Speak, fool, are you certain I am awake, I
say—I believe I had better convince myself by
beating the fellow handsomely—what say you, sir?

Will. Why, sir, only—that if it be the same thing
to your honour, I would as lieve you would be so
good as try some other experiment.

Young Man. Heavens! what a confusion of horrors breaks in upon my mind—My Julia fled, and
I not the partner of her flight! O! I dare not
speak my apprehensions even to myself! If they
are true, I am undone—Wretch that I am, were
that all, it would be a trifle; but, Julia, my life, my

soul, my love, I have ruined thee. I feel it all come rushing o'er my mind; yet still it has the wildness of a dream—I recollect something of a fair creature weeping and entreating me to let her go—Was it possible, that in any state I could let her sue in vain!

Will. I hope, sir, you'll forgive me for being so bold, but I am afraid Miss and you have had some difference.

Young Man. What's that to you, sir?—Contemptible villain that I am, I blush that my own servant should guess at my conduct—Yet she has escaped Lord Dartford—How know I what she has escaped, or what endured? Those heavenly charms of hers may have exposed her to worse than robbery! Yet surely her melodious tongue would subdue a tiger!—Did it soften thee, thou more obdurate far than any other of thy kindred savages in the forest?—And yet 'tis hard—'Twas to her own dear health I sacrificed my reason—O Julia!—if I had loved thee less, I had not deserved to have lost thee—Perhaps William might get some intelligence—I cannot let him know how I have acted—Selfish wretch, dost thou start at shame?—May he not bring word where she has taken refuge—Possibly I can serve her—not for myself—I renounce all hope—Yet if I can but serve her—William.

Will. Sir.

Young Man. I have behaved like a scoundrel, William—worse than a brute. I went to meet Miss Wingrove, and you find how I qualified myself to be her protector. Where she is, I know not—Go, inquire, good William—and be speedy—Go to her father's—everywhere—and bring me word before I'm quite distracted—Stay, I'll go too—we'll divide, and meet at the post-house an hour hence.

Will. Sir, you're so much flurried, you had better stay here till I come back.

Young Man. Don't talk, sir,—And do you hear?
—Take care you don't get drunk, sir—I know your
failing, rascal; but when matters of importance are
in agitation, none—no, none but a scoundrel like
myself would degrade his nature by basely unfitting
it for all the functions which render it either useful
or respectable.   [*Exeunt.*

ACT THE THIRD..

SCENE I.

LARRON's *House.*

Enter Mrs LARRON *and* JULIA.

Mrs Lar. So, my pretty young madam, I have found you out, have I ? But I guessed how it was from the first, hussey.

Miss J. Win. Is there any thing I can say that will convince you ?

Mrs Lar. Why no, to be sure there an't—Don't you think as all you says must go for nothing, after all that fine masquerading story trumped up between my husband and you ? He said you was just com'd out of a nunnery. What sort of a nunnery was it, I wonder ?

Miss J. Win. Good madam, let me prevail on you to listen to my unhappy story.

Mrs Lar. Well, child, you may go on, I hears you.

Miss J. Win. Your husband found me this morning, deprived (by a most unlooked-for accident) of friends, of home, of every thing.

Mrs Lar. You must be a good un by that—Well, let's hear—go on, child.

Miss J. Win. I made him acquainted with my distress, and he agreed to afford me shelter, till I could form some plan, adapted to my melancholy situation.

Mrs Lar. And so you'd have me believe, as you and my husband knowed nothing of one another before this morning? Hey!

Miss J. Win. I can solemnly assure you, that this morning was the first of our acquaintance.

Mrs Lar. Well, have a care that you doesn't equiviokit now—If I finds you equivikiting, you shall dearly repent it, I promise you—And so you says as you wants work—Why, if I thought you would behave yourself as you should do, may be I'd find you a friend myself, that wou'dn't require much of you; and I suppose you don't care how little you does—But I should like to know how you lost your last friend.

Miss J. Win. Let me entreat you, madam, to spare me upon that point.

Mrs Lor. Aye, you none on you likes to tell—I suppose it wa'n't for no good as he turned you off. (JULIA *turns aside and weeps.*) What a poor little whimpering thing it is—I wonders where she can have been, as I have never seen her afore—If I can get her off to old 'Squire Manly, who is a little like my husband for goodness, it will be putting her out of Larron's way, and be something into my pocket—Well, well, adone crying, do—I suppose you're not so dilliket as to object to a middle-aged gentleman.

Miss J. Win. Has he any family, madam?

Mrs Lar. O, yes—he's a son and a daughter, and a wife into the bargain—but you know that's no hobsticle to the likes of you.

Miss J. Win. Quite the contrary, madam; I am glad to hear it.

Mrs Lar. Well, that's as much as ever I hard—But that's none of my business.

Miss J. Win. Is the gentleman an embroiderer, madam, or what?

Mrs Lar. Embroiderer? No; the gentleman's a gentleman.

Miss J. Win. Then, madam, I should prefer going into a family where I might be useful, rather than to become an idle dependant on any one.

Mrs Lor. What the deuce is in the wind now, I wonders? Well, the gentleman is an embroiderer; so let's have no more of your hums and haws, but get up to your own room, and be sure you doesn't stir till I calls you.   [*Exit* JULIA.
If I can tell what to make of her, she's so full of her fine words, and things—As I lives, there's the old squire going by; I'll bring him back. Mr Manly, Mr Manly—It's a pity he's so old; for he has faults enough to make him agreeable to any woman.

Enter OLD MR MANLY.

So you forgets your old acquaintance, sir; I warn't worth thinking on; you goes by the door, without ever axing how one does.

Old Man. What, do you think I can ever forget my durable blossom of five-and-forty.

Mrs Lar. Forty! Lord, sir, why you reckons every body's years by your own lady's—I shan't be the age you mention these five years.

Old Man. You mean you hav'n't been the age I mention these five years—The register can add nothing to the evidence of your face—which proclaims fifty as strongly as if it was in black and white in the parish books.

Mrs Lar. Ah ! you're a merry man.   No wonder madam is so jealous of you.

Old Man. To tell you the truth, Mrs Larron, I never thought of roving till she put it in my head by her doubts of my constancy.

Mrs Lar. Why, sir, contradiction's as natural to gentlemen as to ladies, for any thing as I see —— Now there is up stairs——

Old Man. What, what is there up stairs ?

Mrs Lar. As pretty a young creter as ever you set eyes on.

Old Man. Let me go and look at her directly.

Mrs Lar. Nay, but stay—She's as full of freaks as she can hold.   I hardly knows how to deal with her—She says she wants to work at embroidering—But that's all a pertence—Howsoever, I must tell her at first you wants to employ her that way.——I'll bring her down in a minute.   [*Exit.*

Old Man. Hang her—I wish she had not called me in.   I begin to be too old for these follies; I have half a mind to be off—But when a man has continued in a bad practice for a length of time, it almost costs him as much shame to make good a reformation, as it did at first to venture on the transgression—But I hear a lighter foot on the stair-case than Dame Larron's ; and so for the present, good-bye morality—We'll call upon you another time.

Enter Miss Julia Wingrove *and* Mrs Larron.

Old Man. By all that's lovely, an angel ! (*starts.*) Miss Wingrove.

Miss J. Win. Mr Manly !

Old Man. Madam, you must think it very odd —very strange, I say, and very odd—to see me here upon such an occasion—Appearances, I confess, make against me.—Yet upon a proper explanation, madam, I don't fear being able to set all to rights.

Miss J. Win. Sir, to see you here was what indeed I did not expect—By some means, I find the place of my concealment is discovered—But, sir, though I cannot deem it otherwise than amiable in you, to attempt some apology for the conduct of your son, yet I must tell you, in the anguish of my heart, that I would sooner become the wife of the man I once most abhorred, than unite myself to him, or even listen to the smallest palliation of his perfidy—And now, sir, excuse my abrupt departure.
[*Exit.*

Old Man. Why, Mrs Larron, are we awake here?——Is there nothing of enchantment in all this? Egad, I hope it's no trick of yours, mistress.

Mrs Lar. Trick?—Deuce take me if I knows of any; I hav'n't been able to find what you and she meant, for my part.

Old Man. As to what she meant, that does not appear so difficult to unravel—How she came here is what puzzles me.

Mrs Lar. Why, my husband brought her—He found her like a strayed sheep, and so seized her for his own.

Old Man. Your husband must be a courageous sort of a man, I think, to steal a young lady of her pretensions—And you're a pretty gentlewoman, to come and draw a man in to make a fool of himself—Here did I expect to find a pretty little good-humoured, good-natured, insignificant sort of a good-for-nothing play-thing; when, instead of that, I am exposed to encounter the reproachful glances of Miss Julia Wingrove.

Mrs Lar. Miss Wingrove! my stars! Why, is

she the runaway lady that all the country's up in
arms about? (*Aside.*) I am glad to hear this.
Well, sir, I'm a little in a hurry, and so I knows
you'll excuse me.

Old Man. O, with all my soul—I can find excuses enough for going away: the only difficulty is,
how to discover an apology for coming in.   [*Exit.*

Mrs Lar. Well, sure some luck'll come of this at
last.   Who'd have thought she'd been such a proud
man's daughter, so as she be-humbled herself to me.
I hope she ha'n't given me the slip, though—if
she is fairly out of the house, I dares not follow her.
But I warrant she's gone back to the room—she's
too genteel to have sense enough to take care of
herself.   [*Exit.*

SCENE II.

MANLY'S *House.*

Enter MRS *and* MISS MANLY.

Mrs Man. Surely, Emma, it was very indiscreet
to give Mr Welford permission to wait on you, at a
time when your brother and he are at variance.

Miss Man. Well, madam, let him be refused admittance.   I find every caprice of Henry's is to be
complied with, however it may interfere with any
prospects of mine.   But I dare say he will have the
goodness to repay your tenderness with his usual
gratitude ; for, if I mistake not, there is some new
adventure in agitation.

Mrs Man. Don't speak with so much asperity of
your brother, Emma: if I seem to feel a particular
interest about him, it is not that I entertain a great-

er affection for Henry than I do for you; but where
a young man's imprudences are constantly exposing
him to danger, there the anxiety of common humanity is added to the apprehension of motherly affection; so that it is only the same regard more
powerfully awakened, and pity taking part with duty.
But what makes you imagine that he is at present
engaged in some new adventure?

Miss Man. Indeed, my dear madam, I am sorry
I spoke so harshly; but my reason for apprehending
that he has some wild scheme on foot, is, that yesterday evening his servant told my maid, that his
master would soon be a happy man. William staid
out all night; and this morning they went abroad
with a sort of mystery together, when William told
my woman, that his young master had, according
to custom, been cutting out vexation for himself.

Mrs Man. Never, sure, had any woman so much
to disturb her peace as I have! What with Harry's
imprudence, and Mr Manly's neglect of me, it is a
miracle how I support it.

Miss Man. Dear madam, your own apprehensions
create all your affliction in that quarter. Indeed, I
have heard my father say as much.

Mrs Man. What, could he not be satisfied with
disregarding me himself, but he must endeavour to
prejudice your mind against me?

Miss Man. O, you mistake my father's meaning
entirely, madam. He was only lamenting your
want of confidence in him, and saying, that had he
never been causelessly suspected, he should never
have given you cause of suspicion.

Mrs Man. So, then, he owns he has wronged
me? He confesses his infidelity, and makes no
scruple of avowing it to you too. This is beyond
even what I ever supposed. I did, indeed, think
there was a little inconstancy in his nature. I

confess I had some slight suspicions of that sort.
Now I find I am justified in all my conjectures.
O Mr Manly, you have much to answer for on my
account.

Miss Man. I hope not, my dear mother—I am
sure he always speaks of you with great tenderness.

Mrs Man. Does he, my dear Emma? Well, and
what does he say?

Miss Man. I have heard him say, madam, that
could you but confide in him, you would be one of
the happiest couples in the world.

Mrs Man. And did he, indeed, my dear girl, say
this? Don't you flatter me now, my child?

Miss Man. Be assured, madam, that he said every
syllable I have related to you.

Mrs Man. How could I ever make him uneasy?

Enter OLD MANLY.

Old Man. Mrs Manly, my dear—Emma, my
child, have you heard—

Miss Man. O yes, sir, that Miss Wingrove has
left her father's, and my mother is alarmed, lest my
brother—

Old Man. No, no, my dear, I can ease you of
your apprehensions respecting Henry: Miss Wingrove is not with him, I can assure you.

Mrs Man. How do you know that, my dear Mr
Manly?

Old Man. Why, I saw her about an hour ago.

Mrs Man. You saw Miss Wingrove! you surprise me! Where?

Old Man. At Mr Larron's.

Mrs Man. And pray, Mr Manly, what business
carried you there?

Old Man. No, 'twas not at Mr Larron's neither
—yes, now I recollect, it was there too.

Mrs Man. 'Tis very strange, Mr Manly, that
you should be at such a loss to know where it was
you saw her.

Old Man. Why, I remember now very well, it
was at Mrs Larron's ; I happened to be there, and
she came in—psha !—how I blunder—I mean she
went in there, and—

Mrs Man. You followed her—yes, I begin to
guess how it was.

Old Man. This is ever the way ! Perpetually
cross-examined, and contradicted.

Mrs Man. It is you that contradict yourself, Mr
Manly.

Old Man. Why, will you give me leave to tell
my own story my own way ?

Mrs Man. Another time, sir ; it will be better
policy to determine what way you choose to tell
your stories, before you begin to relate them : you
will be less perplexed—less puzzled with the variety of your inventions. But, pray, let us hear
the sequel.

Old Man. Nay, you may guess the remainder ;
if you will not listen to the beginning of my story,
I'll be cursed if you shall·hear the conclusion of it.
[*Exit.*

Mrs Man. O Emma, child ! what a life is mine,
just to be relieved from one apprehension, by being
plunged into another ! Who could have believed
your father would so forget himself as to seduce—

Miss Man. Dear madam, 'tis impossible your
fears should be true. If you will give me leave, I'll
follow my father—I dare say he will acquaint me
with the whole affair.

Mrs Man. Go, my dear Emma, go.   [*Exeunt.*

SCENE III.

An Inn.

Enter YOUNG MANLY.

Young Man. No tidings to be gained of my Julia: where can she be? wandering perhaps—perhaps—O, I dare not trust myself with the suggestions of my own thoughts! How shall I avoid them. O Manly! thou wert to have met a trembling angel, kindly ready to have thrown herself into thy arms for ever—and—

Enter WILLIAM.

Will, what news? does she live? where is she? is she married?

Will. Sir, I hope at last to bring some comfort.

Young Man. Honest William! well, your news, my good friend.

Will. About half an hour ago I began to be quite out of hope; but, thinks I, I'll not return to master till I've got some account to carry him, come on it what will.

Young Man. That's a good fellow; well.

Will. And so I went from barbers to barbers, and from bakers to bakers, and from inn to inn, and from alehouse to alehouse.

Young Man. Are you sure you have not been drinking, Will? If you have, you know it's what I've sworn never to forgive.

Will. Lord, sir, drinking? No, sir, no more than

in a reasonable way—not to disguise myself, an like
your honour.

Young Man. Tell me of my Julia, you blockhead.

Will. Why, your honour's so touchy, you see ; if
you'd ha' been pleased to have heard me.

Young Man. Well, well, that's a good Will—go
on—go on.

Will. Well, pray, sir, be pacified.   Well, and so,
sir, as I was sitting at the Fox and Gridiron in
West-lane, who should come in promiscuously, but
Larron the smuggler, as conceited as you please—
so I never much cared for having any talk with the
fellow, being as he's a foreigner, and a great rogue.
However, thinks I, all your French folk have woundy
long tongues, and if he knows any thing, fifty to one
but he pops it out.

Young Man. Psha ! Curse your tedious introduc-
tions.

Will. So says I—Mr Larron, have you heard
what a stir there is in our village—such-a-to-do—

Young Man. Pish—go on—I say—go on.

Will. There—there's a young lady lost, says I—
Wee, says he, and there be young one ladi found
too.

Young Man. What's that !—go on, good William.

Will. What, says I, have you had the luck to find
her then, says I—Wee, says he again, splutter-
ing out a French oath, and she have the luck to
find me as well—Oh ho, says I, you'd make me believe that she run away for your sake, would you ?
Make a believe, says he, she not be the first young
ladi that run away for my sake.   Young ladies have
droll fancies then, says I.   But mayhap she may'nt
be the same that all the rout is about—she that I
mean is a raw-boned gawky girl, pretty round

shouldered (just to sift him you see, sir,)—Round
shoulder, says he, round shoulder. More blue—
She one model—she von Venus.—So then I knew
we were right, for I've heard your honour say Miss
was as like Venus as two pease.

Young Man. Will, you have conducted the
whole affair like a complete orator, and profound
politician.

Will. Very like, sir; but had'nt we better go
after Miss for fear of her father's getting her back
again.

Young Man. Certainly—yet now that my fears
for her safety are somewhat abated, the recollection of my offence places itself between us as an insurmountable obstacle to our ever meeting again.

Will. Lord, sir, why to my thinking you had better go and ask her pardon, and then there'll be an
end on't.

Young Man. Never—I can never think of asking her to pardon me.

Will. Why, dear sir, how hard-hearted you are.

Young Man. (*Speaking to himself without regarding the presence of his servant.*) I have given her
such cause of resentment, that it would be an affront to her justice, as well as her delicacy, even to
supplicate forgiveness.

Will. Aye, aye, see what good'll come of these
megrims.

Young Man. Any common penitent may look
with a rational confidence for pardon; but he who
has sinned against the sanctity of beauty, and the
religion of a sworn and plighted affection, cannot,
ought not, to expect forgiveness——

Will. Nay sure, sir, do listen to a——

Young Man. But come—Though I must now for
ever forego the dear hope of calling Julia mine,
yet if she will but suffer me to possess the soothing

reflection of having rescued her from the persecutions of her family, I will bear my loss without a murmur, and resign my future days to patient suffering and unavailing regret—Follow me, sirrah!
                                        [*Exit.*

Will. Certainly, sir—how difficult it is to make two people think alike in this world—I cannot bring myself to be of my master's mind for the soul of me.   [*Exit.*

SCENE IV.

A Wood.

Enter MR WELFORD.

Wel. What an unlucky fellow thou art, Welford— Here have I, by my Emma's order, been wandering this hour in pursuit of Manly—One would think that he knew my intentions, and had hid himself to avoid me—Ha! who can this be whose looks betray so much agitation and distress? The grief must be of magnitude indeed that thus presents itself to the licentious comment of every unfeeling passenger— What can be the cause that has reduced loveliness like this (*retires*) to so cruel an affliction?

Enter JULIA.

Miss J. Win. Whither shall I fly?—What refuge is there left me—injured—insulted—pursued—persecuted every way—what more could vice itself endure? And what indeed have I not sustained of its torments, saving only the pang of consciousness. Yet that's something—Whither shall I now direct-my trembling feet? Where, where hope to meet a friend?

Wel. That friend is made, madam, if he's happy enough to be accepted—Pardon me for thus intruding on your griefs, and only rejoice me by saying in what way I can be accessary to your service.

Miss J. Win. May I believe you, sir? I have of late been so much the sport of cruelty, that I dare hardly think any one sincere that approaches me with the voice of kindness—Yet your countenance indicates compassion.

Wel. It would be false to my nature, madam, if it indicated any thing less on the present occasion. But, madam, you talked of being pursued—If so— permit me for the present to conduct you to my house—I have some female relations there, with whom a temporary residence can reflect no disgrace to your reputation—May I, madam, be favoured by your compliance.

Miss J. Win. My tears must thank you, sir—I have no words to do it.

Wel. This way if you please, madam.   [*Exeunt.*

SCENE V.

LARRON'S *House.*

Enter MR LARRON, *and* YOUNG MANLY.

Lar. Sir, vat you vant? Pardie vat you make noise at my house—de house in England you call de chateau, de castel—vat you mean, you besiege my castel, sir?—Vat you vant, hey?

Young Manly. Want!—must I repeat it to you

a hundred times, you blockhead? I want Miss
Wingrove—where is she? Miss Wingrove, sir, Miss
Wingrove, is the fellow dumb? Produce Miss Wingrove—produce the young lady you brought home
this morning—let me see her instantly.

Lar. De young ladi, qui m'acompagnoit ce matin,
vât right have you to make question of me, sir? I
know noting of de young ladi—I no lock de ladi up,
Monsieur—You say she Miss Wingrove. If Miss
Wingrove shose rader to come to my house den
go to her fader's, ce n'est pas ma faute ; if she take
into her head to go away again, ce n'est pas ma
faute neider.

Young Man. I would advise you, sir, not to be
altogether so indifferent upon this occasion—You
may not perhaps be aware that I possess a most
excellent remedy for a certain complaint, called in
your country *sang froid*—and if your symptoms
should continue so very alarming, I fancy I shall
feel myself under the necessity of applying it.

[*Showing his cane.*

Lar. Monsieur! you not take a me right—my
deficience of de langue Angloise must, s'il vous
plait, be mon excuse—Veritablement, I not know
vere de young ladi be more den yourself, sir. Vous
plait-il, you please to make demande of my vife.

Enter MRS LARRON.

Monsieur, elle aura peutetre so much complaisance
for you to inform of de cause of de ladi's departure,
but pour moi, she vil not have de condescension de
m'instruire pas un seul syllable.

Young Man. Well, Mrs Larron, you hear I am
referred to you, will you favour me with some account of Miss Wingrove?

Mrs Lar. Dear heart a day—Here's a racket

and a fuss indeed ! I wishes she'd been fur enough
before she set her foot within my doors, I knows.

Young Man. Nay, but Mrs Larron, I must know
immediately where she is.

Mrs Lar. Must you; sir ?—Why then you must
know more than I can tell you—Your father came
to visit her.

Young Man. My father !

Mrs Lar. Yes, sir—and so she went away—
that's all I knows.

Young Man. Did she go with him ?

Mrs Lar. Why, yes, sir—I suppose so—Lord,
you axes one so many questions.

Young Man. My dear Mrs Larron, why wouldn't
you make me happy sooner by saying so at once.

Mrs Lar. Lord, one should have a fine life on't,
indeed, if one was to do nothing but make every
body happy.

Young Man. Your economy in that respect,
madam, is at least good natured to your visitors,
and as I have no inclination to disturb so laudable
a cruelty, I will wish you a good morning.   [*Exit.*

Mrs Lar. And a good riddance of you then, if
you goes to that. This comes all along with you,
Larron, I'm sure I may say it's a judgment upon
you for thinking to serve me so.

Lar. It be von judgment done upon ma follie to
keep in de house von termagant like yourself—De
young ladi like ver well to come to my house—She
beg, she pray to come—I bring her to you—I leave
her vid you—Vat she do den ? Ma foi, she run
away directiment.

Mrs Lar. Was it so indeed ? And so I was in
madam's way, was I ? O, this is pretty usage, indeed !
to me who have been the making of you.

Lar. You not hold your tongue, begar, I tourne
you of doors, tout de suite.

Mrs Lar. You turn me out of doors, Larron? I dares you to do it—You knows as I knows enough to hang you if I pleases—You forgets who broke open———

Lar. Vat you keep quarrel, quarrel for? You know I not like the quarrel—You and I be good friend—A ça—Give me your hand—pardie—I vill set all right—I vill make you my vife.

Mrs. Lar. Will you? But I am grown a little too wise for that now; I sees your aim well enough, you only wants to get clear of my evidence, and to have the law of your side, for using me ill—No, no, Lewis, I am not such a fool as you thinks me.

Lar. Vill any ting please you? You juste now complain———

Mrs Lar. Aye, but now, d'ye see, I will keep my freedom as security for your good behaviour—You are in my power now, and so I will keep you —I knows you have no love for me, but I will make you fear me.

Lar. Eh bien, my dear, we understand von anoder now—you now be ma maistresse en toutes choses et pour toujours.

Mrs Lar. What's that you are jabbering?

Lar. I say, my dear, dat you are so convince me of your great discretion dat you now be my mistress in all tings, and for ever.

Mrs Lar. O! why that's very well—come into dinner then like a good creter as you are, and never, my dear Lewis, never, never forget, that it is in my power to hang you.   [*Exeunt.*

ACT THE FOURTH.

SCENE I.

MISS HERBERT'S *House.*

Enter MISS HERBERT *and* LORD DARTFORD.

Miss Her. I am happy to see your Lordship—I hope you bring good tidings of Miss Wingrove.

L. Dart. Indeed, my dear madam, you flatter yourself and me. I was sent here in pursuit of good tidings, or of any tidings—for after the most prodigal expense of bodily fatigue, we are just as much in the dark as ever.

Miss Her. What, no intelligence?

L. Dart. None—none—I have just left her fantastic father, and her imperious brother, almost as anxiously on the hunt for this modern relation, as if they were persecuting an old parchment, to bring forth a lurking morsel of ancient kindred in the reign of king Lud, or queen Boadicea. It is very unaccountable.

Miss Her. Unaccountable indeed!

L. Dart. I mean every way unaccountable—the motives that could have led to her escape, as well as the success with which she has accomplished it.

Women are not apt to misunderstand their happiness in these matters—I cannot lay th t to their charge, positively.

Miss Her. (*Aside.*) Coxcomb !—a thought occurs to me, by which if I succeed I shall be better enabled to reconcile matters with my haughty lover, and rescue Julia from her embarrassments, should she be discovered—I'll make him believe I have a fancy for him myself. (*To Lord Dartford.*) Indeed, my Lord, as your Lordship very justly observes, women are but seldom guilty of such extravagant inattention to their own interests—giddy girl !—what would she have aspired to ?—such rank —such accomplishments.

L. Dart. Yes—and such a rooted, such a disinterested, such an inviolable attachment.

Miss Her. To be sure, my Lord. Obdurate Julia ! Where were your eyes ? Where was your sensibility ? Where had you mislaid your understanding ?

L. Dart. Very true ! Where indeed ? I that lived but for her.

Miss Her. That an affection so ardent—a constancy so noble, should receive so ill a return—unkind Miss Wingrove.   [*Sighs heavily.*

L. Dart. Eh ! What's this ?—I begin to perceive something here, and the best on it is, she has a better fortune than the other—I wish I had not talked so much of my constancy. I must wheel about though. (*To Miss Herbert.*) And yet, Miss Herbert, I cannot help thinking, that latterly Miss Wingrove hardly appeared to me to preserve that——

Miss Her. No, indeed, my Lord—I have partly thought so too.

L. Dart. That kind of suavity, as it were—that inexpressible something.

Miss Her. That plaintive delicacy—that depre

cating eye—those imploring smiles—that persuasion which carried with it the authority of conquest, and that gentle command which turned enforced captivity into voluntary submission. (*Aside.*) Dear girl, I cannot help doing her justice in the very heat of this feigned hostility.

L. Dart. And then her spirits—have somehow or other——

Miss Her. Yes, her spirits too have lost that elegant dejection, that pensive apathy—that graceful mope—if one may so express it, that used to shed the soft benignant influence of an autumn evening over every thing around her. How blind have I been! now that your Lordship suggests it, I see it all. (*Aside.*) I am obliged to help him out in his very abuse, for he knows too little of love's rhetoric, even to hate with eloquence.

L. Dart. Now there is a person, in whose radiant eyes, and sparkling decorums, the majesty of imperial cupid sits in state, and dispenses innocuous glories with the careless profusion of a city feast, or the dazzling splendor of a courtly gala.—There is a person——

Miss Her. Your Lordship means Miss Manly!—Yes, indeed, she is a fine young woman enough——

L. Dart. Miss Manly! Miss Manly, madam, is as a scintillating link to the gorgeous orb of day, compared to the ineffable divinity of my prostrate adoration.

Miss Her. Whom can your Lordship mean?

L. Dart. Mean! whom should I mean—whom must I mean, whom can I mean, but the celestial Phœnix of her sex, the divine Miss Herbert?

Miss Her. Me, my Lord!—Good heaven!—I am so confused all on a sudden—Did your Lordship say me?

L. Dart. Yes, yes, your adorable everlasting self.

Miss Her. If your Lordship really entertains—If

your Lordship has indeed done me the honour to have conceived a passion——

L. Dart. A passion !—a flame—a conflagration—a volcano !.

Miss Her. Nay now, my Lord, I can no longer doubt the plain sincerity of your professions—but as it is a fixed rule with me, rather to follow than to lead, in events of this awful importance, I should wish to avoid any further communication with a person of your Lordship's dangerous eloquence, till the proper sanction of my relations has been previously obtained ; my aunt would be too happy to receive any proposals of your Lordship's ; till then permit me to take my leave.——Successful even beyond my hopes.   [*Aside.*
                                                    [*Exit.*

L. Dart. Hah, hah.   Now this I call being in luck—just as one had lost scent in one quarter, to have a nobler game started in another.—Now, gad take me, 'tis very odd, but what a blunderbuss I am at a speech—I mean in the love way—for on other subjects I can deliver myself with a becoming intelligibility enough ; but we higher order of beings, that have sense enough, never to be more than merely artificial lovers, as we never understand the real orthodox gibberish of the passion, so when we once get to talk upon it, we never know when to stop —Now that scintillating link—gorgeous orb—conflagration, and volcano, were not at all to my liking, but what could I do ? I must say something—but above all, what had I to do with an allusion to a city feast ? What has a city feast to do among the delicacies of a lover's commons? Well, I must read for it—at least till I am married ; and then, indeed, it will be full time to discard both the passion and the language of it in amicable indifference together. Well, I will lose no time in preparing my proposals.
                                                    [*Exit.*

SCENE II.

MR MANLY'S.

Enter MISS MANLY.

Miss Man. Could I have suspected Welford of infidelity! Happy, happy Miss Wingrove. So vanish all my hopes!

Enter YOUNG MANLY.

Young Man. Emma, what means this agitation? Whence these tears? Is my mother well? Where is my father? Speak, dear Emma.

Enter MRS MANLY.

Mrs Man. O Harry! what uneasiness has your absence occasioned?—why will you pay so little attention to your family?

Young Man. Dear madam, I deserve more reprehension than I ever meet with, yet let me entreat your present forbearance. My heart, since last I saw you, has been torn by such a variety of anguish, that I have not yet been master of my conduct—But why is Emma thus uneasy?

Mrs Man. Dear girl, I believe her uneasiness results from mine—could you have thought it, Harry? I scarce know how to tell you, but your father has seduced Miss Wingrove from her friends —where he has placed her I know not—but——

Young Man. Thank heaven, then, I have been truly informed, and she is with my father.

Mrs Man. Thank heaven, Henry! Do you thank heaven that your father wrongs me? Your behaviour shocks me, Harry—It is even worse than his.

Young Man. Dear mother, don't indulge such suspicions—my father steal Miss Wingrove from her friends!—No, no, indeed he did not: that she is with him truly rejoices me?

Enter OLD MANLY.

Young Man. Dear sir, where is Miss Wingrove? Where is my lovely Julia. Will she permit me to behold her face again? Yet how dare I hope it?

Old Man. Ought I to permit you to behold my face again, sir; how dare you hope that? Instead of asking impertinent questions about what does not concern you, have the goodness to account for your own conduct, sir—you leave your family— fill them with apprehensions for your safety, and at your return, instead of meeting us with proper submission, you begin by hectoring your poor innocent father, and bullying him with a long string of saucy inquiries—Where is Miss Wingrove?— Where is my Julia? (*Mimicking him.*) What have you to do with Miss Wingrove? Who made her your Julia?

Mrs Man. Who, indeed? She is differently disposed of.

Young Man. Dear sir, how could I possibly imagine that what I said would give the slightest ground of offence? The Larrons assured me she went away with you.

Mrs Man. There, Mr Manly, there! I am jealous now without a cause! I have no foundation for my suspicions!

Miss Man. Dear madam, dear sir! hear me one moment, I can too certainly assure you where Miss Wingrove is.

Mrs Man. Where, Emma, where? ⎫
Young Man. Dear, dear Emma, tell ⎪
me instantly.   ⎬ *All at once.*
Old Man. Aye, let us hear, child— ⎪
let us hear it.   ⎭

Miss Man. The report we heard, madam, was
too well founded; Miss Wingrove is indeed with
Mr Welford.

Young Man. With Welford!

Mrs Man. Ridiculous, child! mere jealous apprehension!

Young Man. Madam!

Mrs Man. Ask your father whose supicions are
the wildest, hers or mine—he can set you right at
once if he chooses it—but I'll stay no longer to endure such treatment.

Old Man. Don't, my dear, don't.

Mrs Man. Your indifference, Mr Manly, is even
more injurious than your infidelity.   [*Exit.*

Old Man. Before I go to appease your mother,
who is as absurd as you are profligate, let me caution you, young man, how you practise such another
frolic in a hurry—the wicked story that you have
so ingeniously trumped up about my being at such
a place as Larron's—this excellent joke, I say, sir,
which owes all its genius to its being a falsehood,
and its wit to the certain mischief it was sure to
produce in your family, won't be passed over un-
punished, I assure you—have you no duty?—no
regard for truth?—But it was ever thus with you,
you prodigal—The best example I have ever been
able to set you, either for truth or modesty, never
produced the slightest effect upon your vile, impenetrable nature, and the mildest language, you
rascal, was always thrown away upon you. [*Retires.*

Young Man. Dear Emma, unravel, if you can,
this knot of perplexities; my father answers me

with anger, my mother with tears, and you, my dear sister, start an idea, which is one of the last that would have entered my imagination; yet, being once presented, love will not suffer it to repose in idleness—Tell me, my Emma—Can Julia be with Welford? Can she—can he!—can both be so inconstant?

Miss Man. O Harry, why did I mention it— This may be the source of fresh affliction—Think, if it is so, that I endure enough, and do not increase my misery—You know my fears.

Young Man. Lay them aside, dear Emma! be assured I shall act with moderation—I know I shall —O Julia!—But you must tell me all you know respecting her, and the villain—I will not name him—that has stolen her from me. Come to my study, Emma; nay, dry your eyes—you shall see what an example of patience I will exhibit—I shall quarrel with no one but myself, for in myself alone is the foundation of all the miseries I am exposed to.   [*Exeunt* YOUNG MANLY *and* EMMA.

Enter Servant to OLD MANLY.

Ser. Miss Herbert, sir, desires to know if she can have the pleasure of half a minute's conversation with you.

Old Man. Show her in.   [*Exit Servant.*

Enter MISS HERBERT.

Old Man. This is indeed a kindness, my dear Miss Herbert; your visits are valuable in proportion to their rarity, like winter's suns—or—or— no—like—

Miss Her. Never mind, my dear Mr Manly, what they are like, we will settle the impromptu upon more mature deliberation another time.

Old Man. Egad, and so we will, for nothing requires so much time as an off-hand speech.

Miss Her. Now, sir, to the object of my visit—Report says that you have seen Miss Wingrove, and I am anxious to hear how the charming creature endures her misfortunes.

Old Man. Very true, madam; but where should I see Miss Wingrove?

Miss Her. Why, report does say, sir, that you met her at a place where it would have been equally for her happiness, and your reputation, that you had never met at all—at Mrs Larron's.

Old Man. It's a falsehood—a confounded falsehood—I go to Mrs Larron's! but, dear Miss Herbert, how can a young lady of your candour and good sense give credit to such a thing, particularly when you had such good reason for disbelieving it, as its being the general report.

Miss Her. Why, indeed, Mr Manly, as you say, what should you do at such places? You know you are subsiding into the calm evening of life, when the tempestuous passions gently sink into a soft undisturbed repose—I dare say now you feel this sweet cheerful twilight of your days to be attended with more substantial comfort, and much more real happiness, than the gaudier scenes of your meridian life, when every thing was brilliant, and nothing solid; every thing gay, but nothing rational.

Old Man. Twilight! Gadso!—None of your twilights neither, Miss—This is the way—There is no such thing as purchasing impunity in this world for one offence, but by pleading guilty to a worse—Well, Miss; and suppose I was at Mrs Larron's.

Miss Her. (*Aside.*) O ho! I thought I should bring him to a confession; he will acknowledge any vice but age. So, sir, you were there, then, after all.

Old Man. Gad's life, ma'am, don't ask so many questions; I understand you well enough, Miss— You would insinuate that I am a helpless old fellow —that you can see no great use in my living, and that the sooner I am hanged out of the way the better; but give me leave to tell you, madam—

Enter Admiral CLEVELAND.

Adm. Cleve. Hey day! What storm's a-brewing now? Why, neighbour Manly, this is a rough gale upon so fair a coast—what, quarrelling with my niece?

Miss Her. Dear uncle, I'm quite rejoiced to see you, you never came so seasonably to the rescue of a poor little disabled frigate in your life—Mr Manly here——

Old Man. Your niece is an impertinent, forward, malicious young woman, Mr Cleveland, and I desire never to see her face again—I'll never, never forgive her—No, if I were to live till I was sixty.

Miss Her. What a formidable resentment! Why, the period of it has expired these five years.

Adm. Cleve. (*Aside.*) Leave him to me, I'll teaze the old fellow—I came on purpose.

Miss Her. I will.

Adm. Cleve. But how did the brush happen? What is the cause of it?

Miss Her. Why, sir, I spoke, I am afraid, somewhat too justly of your friend's age, and appeared to entertain too favourable an opinion of his morality—offences which a lively, determined rover, in his climacteric, can never reconcile to his forgiveness.

Adm. Cleve. O, is that all?

Miss Her. So, good Mr gallant, gay Lothario of sixty-five, a good morning to you.

[*Exit Miss* HERBERT.

Old Man. A saucy minx.

Adm. Cleve. Come, Manly, you have too many of the substantial afflictions of life to contend with at present to be ruffled by little breezes of this sort— But I am your friend, and I thought it my duty, as such, to call upon you, and to do what a friend ought to comfort you.

Old Man. Why, that was very kind, my old neighbour, very kind indeed—be seated, I beseech you —Yes, indeed, 'tis very true, as you say, Admiral, I am a wretched, miserable, unhappy man, oppressed with sorrows, laden with affliction—overtaken, before my time, by many cares. Yet 'tis something, my worthy neighbour, to have a trusty friend to take a kind interest in one's misfortunes— to share, as it were, the sad load of life—to ride and tie with one in the weary pilgrimage—O, 'tis a charming thing to have a friend !

Adm. Cleve. I think so indeed, and hope to prove as much—I have no other object but to comfort you—None, none. You are indeed very unhappy.

Old Man. Very, very !

Adm. Cleve. Why, there's your wife, now.

Old Man. Aye—my wife—O ! O !

[*A long sigh.*

Adm. Cleve. Nay be comforted, my friend—be comforted—Why she is of herself a sufficient load of misery for any one poor pair of mortal shoulders. Always fretful, her suspicions never asleep—and her tongue always awake—constantly making her observations, like a vessel sent out upon discovery —ever on the watch, like an armed cutter, to cut off any little contraband toy, and to intercept any harmless piece of smuggled amusement.

Old Man. O ! 'tis dreadful, neighbour, quite dreadful indeed.

Adm. Cleve. Take comfort, my friend—What did I come here for ? Take comfort, I say—There is your son too.

Old Man. Yes, my son too, an abandoned profligate.

Adm. Cleve. Nay, if that were all, there might be hopes—the early little irregularities that grow out of the honest passions of our nature are sometimes an advantage to the ripened man ; they carry their own remedy along with them, and when remedied, they generally leave the person wiser and better than they found him—wiser for his experience, and better for the indulgence which they give him towards the infirmities of others—but a canting, whining, preaching profligate—a sermon-maker at twenty—a fellow that becomes a saint before he's a man—a beardless hypocrite—a scoundrel that cannot be content with common homely sinning, but must give it a relish by joining a prayer with it in his mouth—of such a fellow there can be no hopes—no hopes indeed.

Old Man. None, none. O miserable that I am, where will my affliction end ? Where shall I find consolation ?

Adm. Cleve. Consolation !—In me to be sure !—What else was the purpose of my visit ? I forbear to say any thing of your daughter, poor unhappy girl.

Old Man. Conceal nothing from me. What has happened to my poor child?—what has happened to her ? She was my favourite. Miserable man ! O miserable man !

Adm. Cleve. Nay, if it will give you any comfort, I will tell you. It is my duty to do so—why, she, you know, was desperately in love with Charles

Welford. He has turned her off, I find—discharged her the service, and has fallen in with somebody else; so that I suppose by to-morrow morning we may look for her birth, poor girl, in the ambush of a willow, or the retirement of a fishpond.

Old Man. Now the sum of my calamities is complete. (*Weeps.*) Now, indeed, the cup is full—poor undone man!—miserable husband!—wretched father!

Adm. Cleve. Aye, and all to come upon you at your time of life too—Had your misfortunes reached you when you were in the vigour of your days—(OLD MANLY *dries his eyes, and looks resentfully*) when you retained enough of bodily strength and force of mind to cope with them—but—at your time of day, when the timbers are approaching fast towards decay, when the lights of the understanding are upon the glimmer, and the reckoning of life is pretty nearly out—O! 'tis too horrible. Faith, after all, I don't know how to comfort you.

Old Man. (*In a rage.*) (*Both rising.*) I believe not, indeed; you fusty, musty, old, foul-mouthed, weather-beaten coxcomb—timbers approaching fast to decay! Whose timbers do you mean, old jurymast? look at your own crazy hulk—do—and don't keep quoting your damn'd log-book criticisms upon your juniors and your betters.

Adm. Cleve. Nay, my good friend.

Old Man. Damn your friendship and your goodness too. I don't like friendship that only wants me to hate myself—and goodness that only goes to prove every thing bad about me. So, good Mr Yellow Admiral, sheer off—do—and till you can stuff your old vessel with a cargo of more commoditable merchandise, don't let me see you in my latitude again.

Adm. Cleve. Sir, let me tell you, you may repent of this language ; and were it not for pity of your age and your misfortunes——

Old Man. O curse your pity ; and as for misfortunes, I know of none equal to your consolation.

Adm. Cleve. You shall hear more of this, Mr Manly.

Old Man. Not for the present, if you please—if you want my life, take it—take any thing—only take yourself off.

Adm. Cleve. Very well, sir. You shall hear from me at a proper time. (*Aside.*) I have made the old fool nobly miserable ; that's some comfort, however.

Old Man. (*Solus.*) What an ass was I, to listen so long to the hollow croakings of this melancholy sea monster—a rusty old weather-cock ; always pointing one way, and that to the quarter of misfortune—I miserable !—What should make me so ?—Is not my wife kind and faithful, and only a little troublesome now and then for my good ?—Is not my son generous and gay—and—and like his father, as a son should be ?—and a'n't I stout in body, and sound in mind ?—And is not every thing as I would have it ?—A dismal old !—now has he given me a sample of the view with which advice is always bestowed, and I him a proof of the effects with which it is always taken—he came to me to increase my distresses by consolation, and I have made use of his counsel as a new argument for pleasing myself. [*Exit.*

SCENE III.

MISS HERBERT'S.

Enter Miss HERBERT *and Mrs* RACHEL.

Miss Her. Well, my dear aunt, have you been more successful in your inquiries after the unfortunate Miss Wingrove than I have been?

Mrs R. Cleve. I don't know how to say I have been more successful—but from your account, I have collected more particulars—I understand she was accidentally encountered by Mr Welford, who kindly offered her the asylum of his house, which she accepted—but learning, by conversation with his relations, that her reception there had produced a quarrel between him and his mistress, the generous girl scorned to consult her own comfort at the expense of her protector, and having contrived to change her own clothes for those of a younger brother of Mr Welford's, she accomplished her escape.

Enter Servant.

Serv. Mr Wingrove, madam.

Miss Her. Admit him. O, he shall receive no mercy at my hands whilst he continues the persecutor of his sister—Will you give me leave, madam, to receive him alone?

Mrs R. Cleve. Certainly, my dear. [*Exit.*

Enter Mr WINGROVE

Mr Win. Will Miss Herbert permit a penitent to approach her?

Miss Her. O! by all means—a real penitent—but are you quite sure that you come under that description, or is yours like the common repentance of the world, which consists rather in a prejudice against punishment, than a sincere contrition for the offence?

Mr Win. Dear, charming Harriet, how can you question it?—I am ashamed of the violence of my behaviour at our last interview; yet you must acknowledge that you drew me into that suspicion by your ambiguous deportment. Surely my Harriet could not find entertainment in the uneasiness of the man who adores her.

Miss Her. (*Aside.*) Bless me, if he continues in this strain of humility, I shall never be able to punish him as he deserves—yet I must.

Mr Win. What's that, my Harriet? You cannot doubt the sincerity and devotion of my love.

Miss Her. A-propos—Was it you that fell in love with me, or your father?

Mr Win. My father! Harriet?

Miss Her. Aye, you or your father; which of you is it that I have had the good fortune to inspire with so favourable an opinion of me? I am inclined to think it is to the elder gentleman I owe the obligation.

Mr Win. Nay, now, madam, I don't understand you.

Miss Her. In plain English, then, had you your instructions from your father to undergo the labour of wooing, or did you come of your own accord?

Mr Win. Can my Harriet entertain so humiliating an opinion of me, as to suppose I would be actuated, in so dear a concern as that, by any influence but the impulse of my own affection?

Miss Her. Take care, Mr Wingrove—take care

—there is nothing so tempting, I admit you, as those pretty words that fall gracefully in to close the procession of an ambitious sentence; but let me ask you plainly, sir, Whether, if your father should now, even now, lay his commands upon you to relinquish the passion with which you affect to regard me, you would not instantly obey him, and leave me forsaken and forlorn, to transfer your obedient ardours to any new lady of his choice?

Mr Win. 'Tis true, I feel the most sincere respect for my father; yet had he thought proper to interpose his influence in a case where nature claims a paramount authority, I had renounced a submission which I should have held to have been unjustly exacted.

Miss Her. Are you sure of it?

Mr Win. Quite sure.

Miss Her. Dear Mr Wingrove. (*Taking his hand.*)

Mr Win. (*Kissing it.*) My lovely, my adorable Harriet!—Sure of it! am I sure of my existence? Am I sure of your being the most lovely of your own sex—or I the happiest of mine? (*Kisses her hand*). Am I sure that we shall never exchange another harsh word, or another unkind look? Am I sure——

Miss Her. Nay, now, sir, you are fairly caught.

Mr Win. Hey-day! What frolic is in the wind now?

Miss Her. If all this be true, Mr Wingrove, tell me, sir, what it is that constitutes the offence of your sister? Why is she driven out a disgraced wanderer to encounter all the unknown hazards of a merciless world, when one of her persecutors not only aknowledges that he shares in all her guilt—if guilt it be—but glories in the sympathy he feels in her disobedience, because he considers it as a just tribute to the object of his affections, and a proof of his independence?

Mr Win. My sister, ma'am, is a woman—and— and—

Miss Her. My sister, ma'am, is a woman!—and —and—that is, my sister is an interdicted being— disinherited by Nature of her common bounties—a creature, with regard to whom, engagements lose their faith, and contracts their obligations. In your fictitious characters as lovers, you endeavour to make us believe that we are exalted above human weaknesses; but in your real characters, as men, you more honestly demonstrate to us, that you place us even below your own level, and deny us the equal truth and justice that belongs alike to all intelligent beings. This language, sir, is new, at least in the vocabulary of love; I wish I could say the senti- ments it conveys were equally so in the hearts of your most imperious sex.

Mr Win. Before I was interrupted, madam, by this torrent of modest rhetoric on the merits of your most unimperious sex—for so, in particular, I am bound to think them, I meant merely to have said, that I can aggrandize the woman with whom it may be my fate to be united—whereas, if my sister joined herself with an inferior, she would have be- come necessarily degraded to the rank of her hus- band. But I find, madam, these insults are cal- culated merely to gratify your pride, by proving to what extremity of meanness your power can re- duce me. I blush at the servilities to which it has already exposed me, and now throw off the yoke for ever.   [*Going.*

Miss Her. Stay, sir; before you go, let me beg you to favour this letter with a perusal. Read it at your leisure; and now—a long farewell to all my greatness.

Mr Win. Damnation! laughed at too—Farewell, madam, and I swear——

Miss Her. Nay, sir, don't swear; or if thou wilt swear—swear by thy gracious self!

Mr Win. (*In a fury of passion.*) Madam, I go —for ever. [*Exit.*

Miss Her. To have convinced me of that, your congé, my rebellious captive, should have been taken with somewhat less disturbance. I am glad I had recollection enough to give him Lord Dartford's letter of proposals before he went. He was in a terrible rage, to be sure—so much the better —while a woman retains power enough over a man to make him lose his temper, he is not yet in that state of healthy indifference that entitles him to bid defiance to a relapse of affection. [*Exit.*

ACT THE FIFTH.

SCENE I.

The ADMIRAL's *Garden.*

Enter JULIA (*in boy's clothes, looking back.*)

Miss J. Win. Yonder is my brother, and his servant, as I live; perhaps in pursuit of me! I dare
not meet them—Yet sure they could not know me
—I hardly know myself—Their eyes seem directed
this way—I'll shut the gate till they have passed.
Ha! who comes here? perhaps the owner of this
place. From my long residence with my aunt, I
am almost a stranger in my native village—Bless
me, he has a stern countenance! I had best conceal myself till he quits the garden.   [*Retires.*

Enter ADMIRAL.

Adm. Cleve. Why, what a pack of idle fellows I
keep about me! When I'm laid up with the gout,
these rascals do nothing—See what a fine jessamine
here is almost spoilt for want of tying up—let's try
what I can do. (*Goes to tie it,* JULIA *shifts her
place.*) What's that shakes the leaves so?—Hey, is
not that a man? O! O! there's the way my nec-
tarines fall so short. (*Goes and brings* JULIA *forward.*) Here! here! no resistance—Come out, and

let us see what we can make of you. Well, young graceless, and what do you do here? Come, let's hear what account you can give of yourself.

Miss J. Win. I do assure you, sir, I came in by accident.

Adm. Cleve. By accident! Well that's a good beginning enough; what, do you shut your eyes as you go along, that you can't tell the highway from an enclosure?

Miss J. Win. I mean, sir, I just stepped in to avoid a person I wished not to see me.

Adm. Cleve. Very like, sir; but pray, sir, will you have the goodness to tell us who you may happen to be, sir?

Miss J. Win. Pray, sir, excuse me.

Adm. Cleve. Indeed, sir, I shall do no such thing —Come, sir, who's your father?

Miss J. Win. I cannot tell you, indeed, sir.

Adm. Cleve. Indeed, sir—Well, after all, it might puzzle a wiser head than yours to do that; but possibly you may have better luck with regard to your mother—who is she?

Miss J. Win. My mother, sir, is dead.

Adm. Cleve. Dead, is she? But had she no name when she was alive? Egad you shuffle so, that I fancy you've been longer at the trade than I at first imagined. You're a gay spark for the profession too—If Rachel had been a young woman, I should have suspected something else; but perhaps the coat may have been stolen too; these gentry now-a-days think nothing they can get too good for them, and the finger is only an accomplice to the felonious pride of the back—" win gold and wear it." —Hey, is that your maxim, my young poacher? Gadso, now I remember, I have seen Sam Welford in those very clothes—I shall secure you, my lad; you shall answer all this.

Miss J. Win. I beseech you, sir, not to expose
me.

Adm. Cleve. Not expose you—What ! do you
think I shall connive at felony ? Here, Tom, Si-
mon, Ralph—attempt to move, and you're a dead
man. Here, will nobody help me to secure this
villain ?

Enter Mrs RACHEL *and Servants.*

Adm. Cleve. Here, seize that fellow, and tie his
hands behind him—Keep off, Rachel, I dare say he
has got pistols in his pockets—Lead him directly to
a magistrate, I'll follow.

Miss J. Win. Dear madam, I implore you to plead
for me to that gentleman—your looks speak benevolence—I entreat you, madam, to have pity on
me.

Adm. Cleve. There's a young artful dog now, beginning to coax and flatter Rachel about her good
looks ; aye, that's the way with these handsomer
sprigs of the fraternity, they are sure to attack the
women ; but 'tis such a snivelling puppy—why
hang it, my lad, you must expect these rubs in the
way of your business, it's only a misfortune in trade
—Come, man, behave yourself a little more like a
rascal of spirit.

Mrs R. Cleve. Brother, I entreat you to send
your servants in.

Adm. Cleve. Send 'em in, Rachel ! why—how's
this ? Do you want him to make his escape ? Has he
softened you with his whimpering ? You know if he
takes to his heels, I can't follow him.

Mrs R. Cleve. I have particular reasons for my
request.

Adm. Cleve. Well, be it so then—wait in the house
till I call you. (*Exeunt servants.*) Don't you think to
get off though—if you attempt to stir——

Miss J. Win. You may rely upon it, sir, I will
not move. O madam, may I hope that you will
befriend me in this dreadful exigency?

Adm. Cleve. No, no, my lad, You are dipping into
the wrong pocket there; Rachel is not, like most of
her sex, to be won over by wheedling, you do but
fling away your skill. But why was I to dismiss
those fellows, Rachel?

Mrs R. Cleve. Brother, if what I've already said
has surprised you, I shall increase your astonishment still farther, by desiring to have a short conversation with this stranger, while you walk aside.

Adm. Cleve. What, leave you alone with a pick-
pocket, a house-breaker? I tell you, he has pistols
in his pockets, or a swashing cutlass in his coat-
lining! Rachel, Rachel, you are a poor ignorant
woman, you can't tell what instruments these fellows may have about them.

Mrs R. Cleve. You are mistaken, brother, this is
no robber, I am persuaded.

Adm. Cleve. O Rachel, Rachel, is it come to this
after all!—I did think, for your sake, that there
might be such a thing as a woman without folly or
frailty; but you are determined that I shall not die
with too favourable an opinion of your sex—for
shame, Rachel, for shame—'tis too bad—too bad
indeed.

Mrs R. Cleve. A few minutes will convince you,
brother, that if I merited your good opinion before,
I shall not be likely to forfeit it on the present occasion.

Adm. Cleve. May be so, may be so, Rachel, it has
an odd look however; have a care of yourself,
old girl; if you should do a foolish thing, it won't
be taken as if one of your prudes had been guilty
of a little trespass, who prepare people for their
fall by the fuss they make about their virtue.

You'll have a hot birth on't, my old lass, you will
—but, however, mind I give you fair warning.

[Retires.

Miss J. Win. Dear madam, vouchsafe to hear my
wretched story.

Mrs R. Cleve. As I know not what impression
my brother's strange conjectures may have made
on your opinion, suffer me to gain a little credit, by
sparing you the trouble of informing me that you
are Miss Wingrove.

Miss J. Win. Madam!

Mrs R. Cleve. Dear young lady, be not alarmed
at this discovery, for never was there more sincere
commiseration than what your sufferings have produced in me.

Miss J. Win. O madam, how has my wretched
situation been made known to you? and by what
means may I obtain your friendship?

Mrs R. Cleve. I have but one condition to propose, and that is an unreserved communication of
the circumstances that have involved you in this distress—that made, for I cannot admit an idea of criminality in you, I can assure you not only of my
own protection, but my brother's; who is as warm
in his atachments, as he is rash and hasty in form-
ing conclusions from first appearances; but my brother returns; I would not meet him till I can inform him of the whole.   This way, dear Miss Wingrove.   *[Retire to an alcove.*

Enter ADMIRAL.

Adm. Cleve. What, isn't this tete-a-tete over yet!
what, they retire at the sight of me—O! guilt!
guilt! I'll observe you though—why, she seems to
be courting him! I'll be sunk if it isn't so—Aye,
Rachel, now you have flung aside propriety, decency, I fancy, will soon follow. Women, I find,

never love to do silly things by halves; when once
they slip cable on a voyage of folly, let them bring
them to that can—particularly your reasoning sort
of sensible, elderly gentlewomen—for when they
have fairly passed the equinox of life, they know
they sail with a trade-wind, and the devil can't stop
them, till they are snug in harbour with a yoke
fellow, after a tedious passage of difficult virginity.
By all that's scandalous she takes his hand—O, sit
down, sit down, my gentle swain—Why he's weeping still—sink me if ever I saw such a watery-ey'd
puppy. Not but there was something in his distress that moved me—if circumstances had not been
so strong against him, I should no more have taken
him for a thief than for a sailor—What, must he
have your smelling bottle too?—why she has left him
in the arbour, and comes this way—she looks as if
she saw me too—can she face me? will she brazen
out her folly? (RACHEL *advances*.) Well, Mrs
Rachel Cleveland.

Mrs R. Cleve. Well, brother, I come to clear up
all your doubts and difficulties.

Adm. Cleve. O, don't take so much trouble, madam, it is sufficiently clear already, I give you my
word.

Mrs R. Cleve. Nay, then I perceive you are under your old mistake, so I shall explain all at once.
This way, my dear. (*To* JULIA.)

Adm. Cleve. My dear! by heaven, that's too
much—what, no shame, Rachel!

Mrs R. Cleve. Now learn your error, brother,
and give me leave to recommend to your protection (JULIA *advances*, RACHEL *takes her hand, the*
ADMIRAL *going out in a rage*) Miss Julia Wingrove.

Adm. Cleve. What's that, Rachel! who did you
say?

Mrs R. Cleve. This young lady, brother, whose misfortunes you have heard in part, is Miss Julia Wingrove; I am convinced she deserves your friendship, and it is evident she is much in need of it.

Adm. Cleve. And she shall have it, cost what it will. Young lady! why, what a fool have I made of myself!—Can you excuse an old fellow, madam, who frequently lets his hasty temper run away with his slow wits?

Miss J. Win. Your present kindness, sir, infinitely overpays the fears occasioned by your misconception.

Adm. Cleve. You must seal my pardon, miss, by a salute, or I sha'nt think we are fairly reconciled. Rachel, I don't apologise to you, as I know your forgiveness is always close in tow of my repentance; but as for you, lady fair, since you have been forced upon my coast, they must fight through fire and water for you that drive you out to sea again.

Miss J. Win. Do not, I beseech you, sir, let your generous compassion for me lead you into danger; the bare idea of such a consequence would compel me to forego the comfort of your hospitable protection.

Adm. Cleve. O, don't let your little fearful heart begin conjuring up vexations, it'll do me a great deal of good—make my blood circulate—I have been too long out of action—a vast while too long —I am mere still water—spoiling for want of motion—a little hurricane or two will shake me clear again—I want a bit of a storm for the quiet of my old days, and a little wholesome danger will promote the safety of my health; so away with your fears, my little light fing—'Sblood I was getting on the old tack again.

Miss J. Win. But, dear sir——

Adm. Cleve. Do, Rachel, tell her what an obstinate old fellow I am, and that it is only wasting her ammunition to oppose me.

Mrs R. Cleve. There is so much generosity, brother, in the substance of what you say, that I have no inclination to dispute about the expression of it. Miss Wingrove, if you please, you shall lay aside this dress.

Miss J. Win. Gladly, madam.

Adm. Cleve. Come, young lady, let me be your conductor, and they that can make prize of British beauty when under the convoy of a British admiral, must have more weight of metal about them than the whole bulk of your lubberly relations, saving your presence, in a body—so cheerly, my little angel—bear up—" Blest isle with beauty, &c." (Singing.)   [*Exeunt.*

SCENE II.

Changes to LORD DARTFORD'S *House.*

LORD DARTFORD *and* JENKINS.

L. Dart. So this triumph of my attractions, as I had so naturally believed, was a sham after all—Death ! how dared this saucy baggage venture to set her pert wits on so hazardous a deception ?—but my turn may come ; and if she should marry this bouncer Wingrove, and grow disgusted with him, which of course must be the case, it will be in vain that she turns her eyes to me, I assure her—But what's to be done in this affair ?

Jen. Can't your Lordship disown having sent any proposal to Miss Herbert?

L. Dart. How can I do that; you delivered the letter, did'nt you?

Jen. Yes, my Lord, but he must be a very indif-ferent servant whose memory cannot fail him a little, for the advantage of his master.

L. Dart. Well, we must consign that difficulty to the ecclaircisement of time and better fortune—but, in the interim, this refusal of Miss Herbert's makes it of importance to recover this wandering nymph as soon as possible. Did Thomas, do you say, trace a young gentleman, resembling Miss Wingrove, to Admiral Cleveland's.

Jen. He did, my Lord, and was almost certain it was herself.

L. Dart. If it should prove so, and she obtains shelter there, I think it might be easy to watch for her in the garden, and steal her thence, but first the Admiral must be watched out though—remember that—there may be danger else.

Jen. That's one of the cases, my Lord, in which my memory never fails me.

L. Dart. Well then, let's about it instantly—if I could meet with the lady, there is no harsh treatment to her that the old Baronet will not interpret into respect for him; and as for the swaggerer, his son, let him know of my attempt upon his mistress, when I am married to his sister, with all my heart—Decency will prevent him from killing me then; and as for his opinion, as that is innocent of any effect upon the body, we must endeavour to endure it.   [*Exeunt.*

SCENE III.

MISS HERBERT'S.

Miss Her. I don't know how it is, but I feel a sort of uneasiness about me, as if something had happened to vex me. What can it be? forgetful creature that I am!—Miss Wingrove's distresses, to be sure. Yet that is not a novelty at the present moment; and then the persevering absurdity of her lofty brother—ha! ha!—Sits the wind in that quarter? Well, I can't help it. I am afraid he is not quite indifferent to me; yet I must tame him out of this unreasonable haughtiness before marriage, that he may be entitled to the just pride of a husband when he becomes one.

Enter WINGROVE.

Bless me, how came you here?—Always stealing upon one?

Mr Win. I am so truly ashamed, madam—I cannot—

Miss Her. Come, sir, there is an eloquent humility in your manner that speaks for you. I have once before to-day construed your meaning; and I begin to flatter myself I shall not be a less faithful interpreter now, when I suppose that you are indeed a penitent for the treatment to which you have exposed your sister.

Mr Win. Indeed, indeed, I am so.

Miss Her. I am rejoiced to hear it. You have read the letter I gave you?

Mr Win. I have, madam.

Miss Her. Well, in all this wide world of caprice and uncertainty, there is but one thing infallible.

Mr Win. What is that?

Miss Her. That!—Why, that a man of rank never violates his plighted honour, and that birth involves in it every human virtue.

Mr Win. Perfidious scoundrel!—I'll tear him piece-meal.

Miss Her. Tear your own prejudices from your heart, Mr Wingrove.

Mr Win. They are gone, madam; and I have no other proof that they ever had an existence in my bosom, but the mortified sensibility which they have left behind them.

Miss Her. Come, sir, keep up your spirits; you will do charmingly, I am convinced.

Mr Win. Nay; I am not now a convert to your opinion, my Harriet.

Miss Her. What!—a relapse?

Mr Win. No, I only mean to say, this is not the first time of my life in which I have thought as you do. Reason has had many ineffectual struggles with prejudice in my mind upon this subject before. But henceforth I disclaim all reverence for such idle superstitions—I despise birth, and all the vanities which attend it.

Miss Her. Now, Mr Wingrove, I do not think so well of your case as I did. I am myself no peevish, morose caviller at birth. It is always graceful, and often useful, when it operates as a motive to a kind and honourable emulation with the illustrious dead; but when those who possess the advantage, endeavour to make it a substitute for every other excellence, then indeed I think the offender is entitled to no gentler sentiment than my contempt, or my pity.

Mr Win. My Harriet shall, from this time, regu-

late my opinions in every thing—and now may I
hope—

Miss Her. Not now! not now—Go home, and
be upon the watch to avail yourself of the first opportunity to reconcile every thing.   Let this be the
first probation of your recovery ; and if, when next
we meet, I should find matters in a way that promises general happiness, perhaps I may not be so
cruel to myself as to deny you the civility of par-
taking in it.

Mr Win. Charming Harriet. [*Exeunt separately.*

SCENE IV.

The ADMIRAL'S *Garden.*

Enter MRS RACHEL, WELFORD, *and* YOUNG
MANLY.

Mrs R. Cleve. Excuse me, Mr Manly, Miss
Wingrove's feelings have been lately too much
agitated for me to suffer her to be exposed to new
conflicts.

Young Man. Madam, I came here to satisfy my
anxious doubts about Miss Wingrove's safety ; being once assured of that, I resign myself to the despair I have so justly merited.   [*Walks off.*

Wel. Nay, but, madam, don't let your generous
compassion for the fair sufferer entirely prevail over
the penitent misery of the offender—let them but
meet, and leave the rest to chance.

Mrs R. Cleve. Well, sir, if I can prevail, Mr
Manly shall see Miss Wingrove—but let him under-

stand I will not have her urged upon any point,
and the length of the interview must be entirely
left to her own pleasure and discretion.

Wel. It shall, madam—I engage for his obedience
in every thing. (*Exit* RACHEL.) Come, Manly,
throw away your despair. Mrs Cleveland is gone
to bring in your Julia.

Young Man. Call her back, I beseech you. I
dare not meet my injured love—Call her back, I
intreat you; though I feel this kindness from you,
Welford, with double force, after my late behaviour to you—how could I suspect you?

Wel. No more of that—here she comes without
my trouble, and with her—shall I send them back?

Enter MRS RACHEL *and* JULIA.

[*As soon as they see each other,* MANLY *kneels, and*
JULIA *reclines on* MRS RACHEL.]

Young Man. O Julia!

Miss J. Win. Mr Manly!

Young Man. O my loved Julia! I dare not approach you; yet let me survey that form, where
every virtue claims its own impression. Let me
see anger aggravated by sweetness, and justice, in
her most awful form, invested in all the terrors of
offended beauty. Look on me but whilst I describe the agonies I have endured for your sufferings,
and the pangs I have undergone for my inexpiable
guilt. I do not expect to be forgiven—only say
you will endeavour not to hate me; and I go, my
Julia—if you will have it so, for ever.

Miss J. Win. Mr Manly, I cannot very easily hate
—nay, sir, I even forgive you—but if your hopes,
which I can hardly suppose, should exceed this
prudent limit, they deceive you.

Wel. Come, Miss Wingrove, let me hope you

will consider this matter. I will not press it now—
but—

Miss J. Win. My obligations to you, sir, have been
important indeed; but this is not a topic even for
the claims of gratitude. Mr Manly, I am sure, will
not oppose the only plan of comfort that is left me
—a quiet, peaceful seclusion.

Young Man. No, my Julia, no—never will I disturb your repose.

Miss J. Win. I beg your pardon, Mrs Cleveland; but indeed I am not well.

Mrs R. Cleve. Be seated, my dear. I entreat
you to take your leave for the present, gentlemen.

Young Man. Rascal that I am !

     [Exeunt MANLY *and* WELFORD.

Mrs R. Cleve. Keep up your spirits. I'll step
into the house, and fetch something for your relief,
my dear.   *[Exit.*

Miss J. Win. I am sorry, madam——

Enter LORD DARTFORD *and* JENKINS, *with Servants behind.*

L. Dart. There she is—and alone, by all that's
lucky. Lose no time. You are sure the admiral
is not at home?

Jen. Quite sure, my Lord.

L. Dart. Very well; lose no time; advance.

       [They seize JULIA.

Miss J. Win. What means this rudeness?—Help !
help ! O help me, or I am lost !

Re-enter MANLY, WELFORD, *and* RACHEL.

Young Man. My Julia's voice !

       *[*JENKINS *runs away.*

L. Dart. Take care, Mr Manly—We are well
armed—take care, I say.

Young Man. Dastardly villain—a pistol.

[*Strikes it out of his hand.*

[*The Dartford party escape.*

How is my Julia ?—Thank heaven, that has afforded me an opportunity of being serviceable to her in any thing.

Wel. How fare you, madam ?

Miss J. Win. Much beholden, gentlemen, to you both ; but weary of this life of alarms and rescues.

Enter ADMIRAL'S *Servant.*

Ser. Your father, Sir William, madam, is within, inquiring for you.

Miss J. Win. I will intrude upon you so much further as to lead me to my father instantly.

Young Man. To your father !—Must it be so, Julia ?

Miss J. Win. Do not oppose my request, Mr Manly ; I am resolved to throw myself upon his mercy.—My misfortunes may have softened him. Will you be kind enough, madam, to accompany me ?   I shall need your friendly offices.

Mrs R. Cleve. Miss Wingrove may command me in any thing.

Young Man. Come then, my Julia, and let me deliver you up to that father from whose capricious cruelty I so lately thought to have given you a happy and a lasting freedom.   [*Exeunt.*

SCENE V.

The ADMIRAL'S *House.*

Enter SIR WILLIAM, MISS JULIA, MRS RACHEL,
YOUNG MANLY, *and* MR WELFORD.

Sir W. Win. I am overjoyed at your safety, Julia;
but yet your leaving me—

Mrs R. Cleve. Nay, Sir William, if the step your
daughter took was imprudent, who forced her to
it ? Who was it that compelled her to seek an un-
certain refuge among strangers ?

Sir W. Win. 'Sdeath, madam, what had my conduct to do with her disobedience ? 'Tis true, Lord
Dartford's proposals to Miss Herbert render him
unworthy my alliance ; but is not this man a plebeian—a fellow of yesterday ?

Wel. Here, sir, you must allow me the liberty of
observing, that Mr Manly's recent services to your
daughter, which you have just heard, merit a more
liberal return.

Sir W. Win. That's very true, indeed—very true—
I am sorry, indeed. I beg you ten thousand pardons, upon my word, sir.

Enter MR WINGROVE.

Mr Win. Where, where is she ? [*Runs to* JULIA.

Sir W. Win. Gad, I must retrieve my dignity in
time, or William will be in a tremendous fury—I
say, sir, for any thing I know, you may be a very
good sort of person, but you will excuse me if I

decline disgracing my family by a connection with one of your condition.

Mr Win. What's that?

Sir W. Win. I say, young gentleman, you have done my family a service—I acknowledge it—I am grateful for it—but ——

Mr Win. Nay, sir, now let me interpose. I have long been sensible of Mr Manly's merits, and have placed myself in the way of the accomplishment of his wishes, from causes which at this moment I feel no delight in contemplating.

Sir. W. Win. Why, what's all this? Why, William, is it you?—Are you sure it is you?

Mr Win. If identity depends upon the mind, sir, I glory in saying it is not—but, permit me to tell you, sir, we have been too long unjust to the merit of Mr Manly, and to the preference of the unhappy Julia—besides, sir, after what has happened, it will be necessary, even to the pride of your house, that an immediate union should take place between Julia and Mr Manly.

Sir W. Win. Well, if the necessity of the case forbids the possibility of a choice, I desire it to be understood—I give my free consent.

Young Man. Do you hear this, my Julia? Pardon me, but can I be blamed if I am astonished into audacious hope.

Miss J. Win. Do not, Mr Manly, renew a solicitation that may tend to plunge me into the guilt of disobedience a second time.

Enter OLD MANLY, MISS MANLY, *and* MISS HERBERT.

Old Man. Mrs Cleveland, you will excuse an impatient set of people who have too much affection for that inconsiderate fellow there; but hearing something of a skirmish here, in which he had

borne a part, we could not resist a kind of curiosity to know the particulars. I would have come
by myself; but though my wife was too much frightened to be able to stir abroad, my daughter was too
much alarmed to be able to stay at home, and so
here we are together.

Mr Win. You are heartily welcome, sir, and I
hope we shall all be better friends before we part.

Wel. (*To Miss Manly.*) Dare I hope now that
my Emma has dismissed her doubts?

Miss Man. Name them not, dear Mr Welford,
I beseech you.

Enter ADMIRAL CLEVELAND.

Adm. Cleve. Why, Hollo Rachel! What's all this?
There was I gone to attend the examination of that
smuggling dog Larron, and the woman he lives
with, for receiving stolen goods, when in comes a hue
and cry after me, with a Canterbury tale of your
being run away with—I confess I did not give much
credit to that part of the story, because, thinks I,
an old maid, whatever may be the value of her
lading, is a sort of neutral vessel, that all nations, to
do them justice, hold very sacred from attack. I
am glad to see you all at my house. Well, Sir
William, may an old seaman, who boasts no larger
store of arms than the short allowance which Nature
gave him, presume to strike hands with a man
whose ancestry bore command while Noah was a
midshipman, eh?

Sir W. Win. I don't very well understand the intention of your speech, Admiral, but your kindness
to my daughter spoke a language that could not be
misinterpreted. I hope you'll excuse our breaking
in upon you in this manner.

Enter O'DONNEL.

Who sent for you, sir.

O'Don. An plase your honour, they have secured the smart little gentleman below, that made such a dirdum about Miss—and we want to know what your honour intends to do wid him. Wheder your honour would give him de liberty to beset in de stocks, or would like better that he should take a pritty little walk in de horse pond, your honour?

Sir W. Win. Who is it the fellow means?

Young Man. Lord Dartford, I suppose.

Mr Win. O, let him go—[*Exit O'Donnel.*] you cannot punish him—he is above your ridicule—for he is below your contempt.

Old Man. But, I say, Admiral——

Adm. Cleve. Well, my friend.

Old Man. I was only going to say, that as this Lord cannot but feel himself at this juncture in a sort of an awkward kind of a taking, it would be good natured in you, and I am sure very agreeable to the company, to go to him and give him a little of your comfort—he's only vexed now at his disappointment—but go to him, worthy Admiral—do —and console him into perfect misery.

Adm. Cleve. Nay, my worthy friend, no more of that, I beseech you, it was only a small splice of forecastle merriment—the last faculty an old seaman parts with is a little sort of a sneaking fondness for a joke—and as it is often the only comfort that sticks to him after a life of service, it would be hard to deprive him of that.

Old Man. So, when you are no longer fit for duty, you kindly turn the hulk into a tender, and make it a crazy receptacle for forced jokes, and pressed witticisms. Well, I forgive you.

Adm. Cleve. (*To Old Man.*) Thank you, thank you—and now, Manly, I give you joy.

Old Man. Eh !—what—joy !—I entreat you my good friend—joy from you—

Adm. Cleve. Nay, I am serious now—I heartily congratulate you on the approaching happiness, I hope, of this wicked, honest fellow of a son of yours —the conduct of this Lord has brought him into the wind of my favour again—well, they may say what they will about the degeneracy of the times, and the falling off of our morals, and all that; but to my thinking, we improve in every thing except in fighting, and in that—though we may equal—damn me, if we can better, the good old model of our forefathers. I remember, in my younger years, there were some few scattered remnants of such chaps as his Lordship—some remains of your old school of beaux, who had been the insects of the former century, and which I had hoped were all extinct by this time; who, like him, were shewy and dangerous, fitter for manœuvring than action, and more gaudy in their tackle, than sound in their bottom—whereas, for ought I see, the striplings of these days, like this pickle Manly, have all the gaiety of their predecessors, with not a quarter of their foppery; and with less vice in their hearts, have more nature in their follies.

[*Miss* WINGROVE *advances.*

Miss J. Win. I can deny nothing, madam, to the kind eloquence of such an advocate, the more so, when, all-powerful as it is, it receives some small assistance, I fear, from the persuasions of my own heart—and now, Manly, may a poor, persecuted fugitive hope at last for a happy asylum from the severities of her fortunes ? Shall I trust myself again to the precarious direction of so fickle a guide —yes, I will trust, most confidently trust thee, for

where there is generosity as the foundation virtue
in a man's nature, the memory of a woman's sorrows will secure her against a repetition of the
cause of them ; nor with such a mind can her affection, fondly bestowed, ever be quite hopeless of a
return.

Young Man. Dearest Julia, I will not injure
either my gratitude or my love, by any attempt to
convey them through the feeble vehicle of words—
let my life speak the sincerity of my repentance, and
the homage of my devoted affection : and as for
that vice in particular which has protracted my
happiness, and, but for the generous kindness of
your brother, might have intercepted it for ever, I
renounce it to the end of my life—I abjure it—no,
never shall I offend by intemperance again—unless——

Miss J. Win. Unless, Manly !

Mr Win. Unless, Mr Manly !

Young Man. Unless one favouring smile from
this company should hurry us all into an unexpected
excess—an intemperance of HONEST GRATITUDE.

HE WOULD BE A SOLDIER;

A

COMEDY

IN FIVE ACTS.

AS PERFORMED AT THE

THEATRE-ROYAL, COVENT-GARDEN.

BY

FREDERIC PHILON.

DRAMATIS PERSONÆ.

COLONEL TALBOT,	*Mr Aicken.*
SIR OLIVER OLDSTOCK,	*Mr Quick.*
CAPTAIN CREVELT,	*Mr Lewis.*
MANDEVILLE,	*Mr Farren.*
COUNT PIERPONT,	*Mr Wewitzer.*
WILKINS,	*Mr Fearon.*
CALEB,	*Mr Edwin.*
AMBER,	*Mr Thomson.*
JOHNSON,	*Mr Brown.*
SERVANT TO COLONEL,	*Mr Helme.*
CHARLOTTE,	*Mrs Pope.*
LADY OLDSTOCK,	*Mrs Webb.*
HARRIET,	*Mrs Wells.*
MRS WILKINS,	*Mrs Brown.*
BETTY,	*Miss Stuart.*
NANCY,	*Miss Rowson.*

HE WOULD BE A SOLDIER.

ACT THE FIRST.

SCENE I.

A Street.

Enter MRS WILKINS, *followed by* JOHNSON.

Mrs Wil. There's no such thing as stirring out of doors for the fellows now-a-days. I beg, sir, you would not follow me any farther.

Johns. I cannot leave you, my sweet, divine, charming girl !

Mrs. Wil. To how many, now, have you repeated the same lesson before you met me this morning ?

Johns. To how many ! Were a dozen such fine women as yourself to appear every day in public, there would be no such thing as walking the street for you ;—a man should have a piece of flint in his breast.

Mrs Wil. He's a good handsome fellow, and don't talk badly.   Then you will persist in following me?

Johns. How can I help it? I follow a fine woman by instinct—Do, my dear, kind, cruel angel, tell me where you live.   [*Takes hold of her hand.*

Mrs Wil. But to what purpose? I can never see you.

Johns. Why not, my love?

Mrs Wil. Lord, I am an old married woman? (*Faintly struggling to disengage her hand.*)   You wicked devil, leave me.   The neighbours will take notice, and I shall get a bad name by you.   Do go—I'm just at home.

Johns. But which is the house you live at?

Mrs Wil. I can't tell you—besides, I think I see my husband talking to the orange woman at the door, in the straw hat and scarlet cloak, with a little curly-pole boy in her hand, eating gingerbread.

Johns. Why, that's the George Inn. 'Sdeath! do you live there?

Mrs Wil. O you devil! I shall be ruined if ever you come after me.

Johns. Zounds! it's the very house I was going to—Isn't it kept by one Jacob Wilkins?

Mrs Wil. Yes, it is.

Johns. We're quite at home now—I suppose you're old Jacob's daughter.

Mrs Wil. I happen to be old Jacob's wife, though.

Johns. Pray, my dear, how long have you been married?

Mrs Wil. A long time, sir.

Johns. Not a long time, I am sure, from your looks.

Mrs Wil. Looks are very deceitful, especially those of married folks.   I was married Candlemas-day, five—long—months.

Johns. Poor creature! you have had a tedious time of it.

Mrs Wil. But what's your business with Jacob Wilkins? Can't I do it?

Johns. Then you do Jacob's business sometimes?

Mrs Wil. To be sure I do, when he's out of the way. Poor man! it's a great relief to him.

Johns. But this is a matter on which I must see himself. Colonel Talbot, a gentleman of whom I think you must have heard, if you be Wilkins' wife, has wrote to him, and desired I would see him in consequence of that letter: were you at home when he received it?

Mrs Wil. No, I was not, sir: but I have often heard of Colonel Talbot; he's an Oxfordshire gentleman; his family, I hear, was the making of Wilkins. Lord! he has been a long time in the Indies, and, I'm told, has made a power of money. But is he come here, sir?

Johns. He is; and since his return has been down in Oxfordshire, in search of Wilkins, where he thought he still lived, and would have come here himself now, only he's very much indisposed.

Mrs Wil. Bless your heart! Jacob Wilkins has been in town, and kept the George Inn these ten years.

Johns. He has made a very ungrateful return to his benefactor Colonel Talbot. My master thought him dead, not having heard from him so many years; a conduct that was unpardonable, considering his obligations to the Colonel, and the great trust reposed in him.

Mrs Wil. Great trust! Lord, sir! what was it?

Johns. Why, Colonel Talbot left a son in his care—but come along, and I'll tell you the whole story by the way.

Mrs Wil. We must not be seen together for the

world; my husband is as jealous as the vengeance.
Take a turn down this next street, and let me go
home alone : follow me in about ten minutes; but
take care you don't speak to me as if you had seen
me before.

Johns. My dear Mrs Wilkins, what do you take
me for ? Do you suppose I never paid a visit to a
married woman in my life ?   [*Exeunt.*

SCENE II.

The Bar of the George Inn.

Enter CALEB, *followed by* WILKINS, *who appears
greatly agitated.*

Ca. What do you knock me about for at this
rate ? Don't I slave like a horse from morning till
night ? I wish I had gone for a soldier as my brother did ?

Wil. Your brother, you dog ! I wish I never had
seen either of your faces. What shall I do, I have
no son to restore him !   [*Bell rings violently.*

Ca. Coming ! coming !—There's a bill wanted in
the General Elliot.

Wil. Let them wait.

Ca. But suppose they won't wait, who'll pay off
the score ?

Wil. Out of my sight, sirrah, or I'll pay off your
score—don't you see my temper is ruffled ?

Ca. Yes, and I feel it too. (*Bell rings.*) Coming !
coming up, sir !

Enter MRS WILKINS.

Mrs Wil. My dear Mr Wilkins, what's the matter? The whole house seems turned topsy-turvy.

Wil. I am ruined.

Mrs Wil. Ruined! O, heaven forbid!

Wil. I say, woman, I'm undone; and the sooner I'm out of England the better.

Mrs Wil. Lord, Lord! you terrify me out of my wits, Jacob!

Wil. Suppose the best friend you had in the world had entrusted an only child to your care, and that through neglect you had lost him, what would you have to say for yourself?

Mrs Wil. And is that case yours, my dear?

Wil. It is.

Mrs Wil. But tell me how it happened.

Wil. You have frequently heard me make mention of Colonel Talbot, in whose family I was brought up?

Mrs Wil. To be sure I have.

Wil. It is a son of his I have lost.

Mrs Wil. You astonish me! But how came so great a man's son to be left in your care?

Wil. Why, you must know that Colonel Talbot, previous to his going abroad, was privately married to a beautiful girl, who waited on his mother: he had a son by this girl; and as the child came into the world, just as he was obliged to embark with the army for Portugal, the war before last, he left him in my care, desiring me to let him pass for my own till his return; and in case he was killed, to continue the deception till the death of his father.

Mrs Wil. And has the Colonel never been in England since?

Wil. Never till within these few days; therefore

his son continued with me till he was twelve years old, when I lost him.

Mrs Wil. In what manner did you lose him?

Wil. I cannot be certain; but as he was a boy of great spirit, and ever prattling of being a soldier, I suspect he was inveigled off by a recruiting party, which at that time was beating up for men in the village.

Mrs Wil. Didn't you acquaint his mother immediately with what happened?

Wil. She was dead.

Mrs Wil. You wrote to the Colonel to be sure.

Wil. There I was to blame. I couldn't summon up resolution sufficient. I thought he would have attributed the child's leaving me to neglect, or cruel treatment.

Mrs Wil. The best advice I can give you is, to tell Colonel Talbot his son is dead.

Wil. But how shall I produce a certificate of that? Should he examine the parish register, and no record of such a child's death be found, I should be taken up, and tried on a suspicion of murder.

Mrs Wil. Then tell him the truth at once.

Wil. Worse and worse!—He'll supppose this a mere invention of my own to screen my villany; else, why was I silent so long? and that I had been bribed by his relations to remove an obstacle to their inheriting both his acquired and paternal fortune.

Enter CALEB.

Ca. There's a gentleman from Colonel Talbot desires to see you.

Wil. What's to be done?—I dare not face him!

Ca. What shall I say to him, father?

Wil. Was there ever any thing so provoking as this fellow?

Mrs Wil. I have it.   Show him into the parlour, my good boy ; and tell him, Mr Wilkins will be with him presently, my good boy!

Ca. My good boy !—Ecod, she good-boys me to some tune this morning ; I hope there's no mischief in the wind ; for I'm sure those are the first good words I have had from her since she was my step-mother.   [*Exit* CALEB.

Mrs Wil. How old is your son Caleb ?

Wil. There's only a week difference between his age and young Talbot's.

Mrs Wil. Pass him on the Colonel for his son.

Wil. How ?

Mrs Wil. Put a good face on the matter, and you'll not only slip your neck out of a halter, but make your fortune.   I can turn Caleb round my finger.   Go and speak to this gentleman, and let him know you'll introduce young Mr Talbot to him immediately.   Do as I bid you, and leave the management of the rest of the business to me.

Wil. But what reason shall I give for not writing to him so long?

Mrs Wil. You must say you never received one of his letters ; and your quitting the country will make it probable enough they might have miscarried.

Wil. Then to give his son no better education !

Mrs Wil. You must say he would not take any better ; and you may find instances enow of as dull heirs to large estates, to give colour to your story.

Wil. And make a drawer of him too !

Mrs Wil. Well, he'll not be the first great man that has cried, Coming up, sir!—What do you stand confounded for ?   Away, away, man ; and let me break the matter to Caleb.

Wil. It goes against my conscience—but self-preservation will have it so.   [*Exit* WILKINS.

Mrs Wil. (*Alone.*) Now have I my gentleman under my thumb—whenever his tongue wags with the sound of jealousy, I'll threaten to discover upon him—and I'll see my dear, sweet fellow, who followed me home to-day as often as I please.—But to prepare this great booby—O! here he comes.

Enter CALEB.

Ca. Here, mother, I have brought you the bill.

Mrs Wil. Well, never mind the bill—I have something very particular to say to you. Do you know, Caleb, that your father is a man of the first character in this town?

Ca. To be sure he is, for selling the best old port and sherry in the kingdom.

Mrs Wil. But come, sit down, and listen to me.
                                                    [*They sit.*

Ca. What signifies hearing so much about father's character—who gets him that character? Why, Caleb, is there one in the house fit to talk to a gentleman but myself?

Mrs Wil. My dear Caleb, let me entreat you to hear me.

Ca. Dear Caleb!——Yes, I'd listen to you all day for such words as these; good words are sugar plums to me: besides, mother, you can't think how pretty folks look when they are pleased.

Mrs Wil. Do you know, Caleb, whose son you are?

Ca. Whose son I am! My father's to be sure.

Mrs Wil. Certainly; but that father is not Jacob Wilkins.

Ca. No!

Mrs Wil. Colonel Talbot, the great nabob just arrived from the Indies, is your father.

Ca. My godfather, I suppose you mean.

Mrs Wil. I tell you he's your own father. You

were given when an infant to my husband, and he
was ordered to bring you up as his son ; it being
necessary, for family reasons, which you'll know another time, to conceal your birth.

Ca. I always thought I was a better man's son
than I appeared to be—But, mother, is'nt this all a
joke?

Mrs Wil. Can my husband convince you th..t I
am in earnest?

Ca. He has often convinced me that he himself
was in earnest, as my shoulders can witness.

Mrs Wil. But, dear sir, I beg ten thousand pardons for keeping my seat so long. (*Geting up and
curtsying very low.* CALEB *keeps his seat, with a
vacant stare, and chuckling laugh of joy.*)

Ca. I thought I'd come to something at last.

Mrs Wil. Your father's gentleman, sir, is now
waiting to see you.

Ca. My father's gentleman!—I suppose I shall
have a gentleman too.

Mrs Wil. O ! no doubt.

Ca. Then there will be a pair of us—But you're
sure now you are in earnest?

Mrs Wil. Will you go and be convinced I am?

Ca. Come along, Mrs Wilkins—I think that's
your name.

Mrs Wil. At your honour's service.

Ca. Great men are apt to forget such trifles—but
I'll call and see you now and then, though I am a
Colonel's son.

Mrs Wil. We'll always think there's nothing too
good at the George Inn for your honour.

Ca. But hark'ee, give old Jacob a hint not to forget himself and make too free.

Mrs Wil. I hope, sir, we shall never forget ourselves in your presence.

Ca. Well, well, I hope not, good woman—Colo-

nel's son !—What a fool I must be, not to have
found out this of my own accord !—But it's a wise
child knows its own father.

⌊*Exeunt. Mrs* WILKINS *ridiculing him.*

SCENE III,

A Drawing Room at the House of SIR OLIVER OLD-
STOCK.

Enter CHARLOTTE *and* HARRIET.

Char. How you teaze me about this all-accom-
plished Sir Charles !—I can't abide him !

Har. Can't abide him !—I don't think it possible
for any woman actually to dislike him.

Char. Yes, he's the last person breathing I should
elect for my *caro sposo ;* the man's well enough as
an acquaintance ; he's lively ; does not want for understanding : but the best of him is, the talent he
possesses for discovering the ridiculous, wherever it
is to be found—then he paints it in colours so high,
and so pleasantly ill-natured, that a woman takes
him in her suite, as the natural appendage of superior understanding, to shew that her wit has raised
her above the power of ridicule, and that she has
the chief laughers in town upon her own side.

Har. What you praise him for is, in my mind,
the only exceptionable part of his character.

Char. Lord ! what harm is there in a little good-
humoured ill-nature ?—Besides, what would you
have people talk of when they meet ? As politics
are to the men, scandal is to our sex—these two
subjects are the vast magazines of the major part of

our ideas; between them the heads of half the nation are furnished.

Har. Have you seen Mandeville to-day?

Char. Poor Harriet! now do I perceive the cause
of all this extraordinary zeal for the interests of the
handsome baronet; you still are apprehensive, if
you don't provide me with a husband, I shall take
your beloved Mandeville from you.

Har. He is sole heir to Colonel Talbot's immense
fortune; I know your father will proceed to the last
extremities.

Char. Dear Harriet, rest perfectly satisfied in my
friendship for you; I never will have him : I don't
know what I would not do to avoid it : My heart is
at present a virgin tablet, on which Love has not
written a single character ; however, should things
come to the worst, you yourself must be my deliverer.

Har. As how?

Char. Even by taking wing, with your beloved
swain, for that blessed spot where law forges no
fetters for the heart ; and Hymen, with a smile upon
his cheek, and his torch burning clear, lights consenting votaries to the temple of real and lasting felicity.   Heaven and a generous uncle be praised,
who bequeath'd me ten thousand pounds independent of my father, I am not obliged to sacrifice my
own, and my friend's happiness !—O glorious Independence !—thou parent of every virtue—no
wonder so many noble hearts emptied their crimson
fountains to preserve thee !

Har. I'm ashamed, Charlotte, to have harboured
a suspicion but for a moment, that a mind like yours
could act unworthy of itself.

Char. Now, to put my theory into practice.—
Here comes Mandeville ; do you step into the next
room, where you may overhear our conversation,

and you shall be entertained with a prologue truly antimatrimonial.

Har. Dear Charlotte, I am already perfectly satisfied.

Char. But I insist on your going : it will entertain you.   [*Exit.* HAR.

Enter MANDEVILLE.

Char. My dear Mandeville, I was just wishing for you ; if you had staid much longer, I should have been insupportably vapoured ; nothing runs in my head but our marriage : But I was thinking, as the fondest couples have certain dull hours that hang heavy upon their hands, how we two shall kill time during those spiritless seasons.

Mand. I suppose we shall follow the example of other people—do all we can to make one another uneasy.

Char. That's one way, to be sure, of killing time : but we shall grow tired of that at last ; don't you think so, Mandeville ?

Mand. When I entertain a good opinion of a lady's wit, it rids me of all apprehension on that score.

Char. Sir, your most obedient.

Mand. I thought your cousin Harriet was here.

Char. My cousin Harriet !—Lord ! what's my cousin Harriet to the purpose ?—I shall grow jealous of you at this rate. I wonder, Mandeville, what star shed its influence when our marriage was first talked of ; no two people breathing agreed better.

Mand. I always thought you the pleasantest companion imaginable.

Char. We were commonly laughing at one body's expense or another.

Man. And as soon as we are married, I fancy every body will be even with us.

Char. Heigho!

Mand. What's that for, madam?

Char. Not for a husband, I assure you; it was only a requiem to friendship, going to be laid in the grave of matrimony. Methinks we two are preparing ourselves for the penance of our future union, as knights-errant of old prepared themselves for the toils of chivalry. I've read somewhere, that those champions of distressed damsels at first wore heavy weights to their armour, which they fancied, on removal, would give a comparative lightness to the galling load with which they were about to tax their shoulders.

Enter HARRIET.

Har. Just now, Mr Mandeville, as I parted from my cousin, a servant came and told me that your uncle, Colonel Talbot, was arrived—Your father, Charlotte, has received a letter from him—But what do you think? It seems he has a son nobody ever heard of before.

Char. A son!—Now, Mandeville, if you can be content with your mistress, and a moderate income, I'm satisfied you may have her; as the bulk of Colonel Talbot's fortune will certainly devolve to his son, depend upon it, my father will no more press my ladyship on your worship.

Mand. Madam, my uncle may dispose of his property as he pleases—I sincerely rejoice at his safe arrival in England; and as he has an heir, I shall be the first to congratulate him on the event; and I hope that heir will prove an heir to his virtues.

Char. You are a generous fellow, Mandeville; and, if it had not cost you so dear, I should congratulate you on the certain prospect you may indulge, that we two shall never be one.

Mand. My dear Harriet—

Char. Now, why don't you say, my dear Mandeville? One as naturally follows the other as the echo does the sound.

Mand. The occasion, ladies, I trust, will apologise for my leaving you thus abruptly.

Char. O, go, go; you have my ample consent— But, Harriet, will you let him go so easily?

Har. How can you be so ill natured?

Char. She says she gives you leave to go: but it's on condition that you do not dedicate a second of your time to any human being but herself, longer than common decency requires it. But, Mandeville, do you and I part as we ought, a betrothed pair?

Mand. Yes, Charlotte; for we part wedded friends again.

Manent HARRIET *and* CHARLOTTE.

Char. Now, Harriet, are all your apprehensions removed?

Har. They are, my friend; Hope sits smiling at my heart, and once more chears it with a prospect of happiness.   [*Exeunt.*

ACT THE SECOND.

SCENE I.

An apartment at SIR OLIVER OLDSTOCK'S.

Enter SIR OLIVER. (*Alone.*)

Sir Ol. This is a devilish lucky hit, the Colonel's having a son ; it enables me to provide for both my niece and daughter—I expect from the latter a good deal of contradiction in this business, but I like that. I shou'dn't love her half so much as I do, if she hadn't spirit enough to contradict me—it shows she has an opinion of her own, and gives me an opportunity to prove that I have one also; but of a much superior kind, and upon occasions of a very coercive quality; it's one time in a hundred I can get any body to contradict me ; but men of large independent fortunes never hear the truth—nobody has spirit enough to oppose them in discourse— Henceforward, I am determined to take no man by the hand, who does not speak and look, when we come to debate, as if he would knock me down in an argument. Well, I think I shall be as happy as a married man can be, when my girls are disposed

of—my wife, to be sure, has a most unaccountable
humour, to suppose I'm jealous of her, now she's
in her fifty-fifth year—to do Lady Lucretia Oldstock justice, she was once a charming woman;
but at present, I think her as plain a piece of goods,
as a man could meet between Temple-Bar and
Whitechapel—Here she comes, brimful of news.

Enter LADY OLDSTOCK.

L. Old. Was ever any thing so wonderful!

Sir Ol. Nothing upon earth! what's the matter,
my love?

L. Old. Why, haven't you heard that Colonel
Talbot has a son?

Sir Ol. A son!—a dozen, I dare be sworn, if he
would but own them; an old soldier has generally
children in all quarters of the globe.

L. Old. Sir Oliver, you're a censorious man, and
judge of every body by yourself.

Sir Ol. Upon my soul, my dear, you allow me
too much credit; I never was a man of all that
gallantry; no, no; I had a domestic magnet that at-
tracted and fixed all my affections; united to such
a woman as Lady Oldstock, who could be a rover?

L. Old. Why, to do you justice, Sir Oliver, you
have, upon the whole, made a very good husband;
and if it was not for the weakness of your temper
in one particular, we might live very happily.

Sir Ol. (*Aside.*) Now she's off.

L. Old. If, indeed, I was one of the giddy flirts
of the day, it would be another thing—but a woman,
of whose truth you have had so many years experience, to be jealous!

Sir Ol. I tell you again and again, I am not
jealous.

L. Old. Ah! Sir Oliver! I wish you would make
your words good; if any man of the least tolerable

appearance pays me a common mark of respect,
don't you immediately sneer and say that fellow has
a design upon me?

Sir Ol. So I do: I always think that person has
a design upon another, to whom he gives their own
way in every thing; no, no; if I am to choose a
friend, and an agreeable companion, give me the
honest fellow who contradicts me.

L. Old. Then you are not jealous!

Sir Ol. No.

L. Old. No?

Sir Ol. No; damme if ever I was jealous of you!

L. Old. You are now more provoking, if possible, than ever; when you find I hold your ridiculous suspicions in contempt, you would wound me
another way, and mortify my pride, by insinuating,
that I never had attractions sufficient to have a civil
thing said to me, like other women.

Sir Ol. Then it seems, my lady, you have had
your civil things said to you, like other women, in
your time?

L. Old. There, there it broke forth! What it is
to be married to a jealous husband!

Sir Ol. Well, all this I can bear, because I like
contradiction—I consider the mind like a spring;
the more you press it, the more vigour you lend
to its elasticity; since I can remember, I always
delighted to be of a different opinion from other
people—There's something wonderfully flattering
to human pride in being singular—but in marriage
it is absolutely necessary—man and wife are like
contending qualities of bitter and sweet; they naturally quarrel, and exist by downright opposition.

Enter CHARLOTTE.

L. Old. I'll submit my cause to the judgment of
Charlotte.

Char. Submit your cause to my judgment: my dear ma'am, by no means; in all cases of matrimonial litigation, the parties should be tried by their peers.

Sir Ol. Right, my girl! now, in order to qualify you to be impannelled on suits of the kind, I was that moment thinking about moving the court of Hymen, to show cause why a rule should not be granted to provide you with a husband.

L. Old. Whenever you marry, Charlotte, if you wish to be happy, above all things avoid a temper like your father's.

Sir Ol. And like your mother's also, if you wish your husband to be happy.

L. Old. I clearly perceive my company is not agreeable.

Sir Ol. Your strange turn of mind, I confess, Lady Oldstock, is not altogether so agreeable; but you see it does not make me angry.

L. Old. It's that that tortures me—if I could vex him, it would be a proof I had some power left; but he treats me like a child.

[*Exit* LADY OLDSTOCK.

Sir Ol. It's a spoilt one if I do.

Char. Dear sir, let me follow her.

Sir Ol. You shan't budge a step after her.— Soothing her in these humours is only adding fuel to fire. Your mother, Charlotte, was born a coquette, and will die one. She was a reigning toast in her youth, and to this hour expects the adulation of those days. She had a whole army of lovers; and what, you'll say, ought to make me set a very high value upon her indeed, either from necessity or choice, she hung like an overblown rose on the virgin thorn, full four and thirty years waiting for me; but come sit down, and let me talk to you. (*They sit.*) I have for some time back observed, Charlotte, that the match I proposed to you with Mandeville does not meet your wishes.

Char. I confess, sir, it never did—besides, I know that gentleman's affections to be engaged elsewhere.

Sir Ol. I understand you; he's fond of my niece Harriet; well, in the name of happiness, let them go together; I'll never mention his name to you again; nor indeed shall I propose any match to you, upon which I may expect rational contradiction.

Char. Now, sir, you speak like my father—O, how my heart springs with gratitude and joy, to hear those generous words from your own lips!

Sir Ol. No, my girl, you shall never be sacrificed at the altar of Plutus—I say, sacrificed—for what is it, in fact, but a sacrifice, to throw away a fine young woman upon a man it is impossible she should like; as many father's do every day, who love money more than their children.

Char. The liberality of these sentiments delight me, they are so exactly in conformity with my own! Dear sir, you have given me such spirits— Do you know, when you asked me to sit down, I expected to have a quite different kind of conversation with you?

Sir Ol. I suppose you thought I had a golden calf to propose to you for a husband?

Char. I own I was so ungenerous.

Sir Ol. A fellow with nothing but gold in his pocket, and lead in his pate; ha, ha, ha!

Char. Ha, ha, ha!

Sir Ol. How liable we are to be mistaken in our surmises of other people's thoughts! No, no, my girl, I have no such match to propose to you—I have a husband for you, it is true, in my eye; and a rich one too—but it is not to riches you object—it is to the man; and provided he be agreeable, I imagine no woman in her senses can suppose a husband may be too rich ?

Char. Provided riches be obtained without leaving a stain upon the principles, it is happiness to possess them, as they give us so much more ample power of distributing felicity. I never was that romantic fool to imagine there can be happiness where there is not independency : grant me that, and all the wealth beside which the earth contains, or the sea devours, should not bring me to sell the free election of my heart, or barter for gold, what gold could never restore me.

Sir Ol. Give me a kiss, you jade ! you are your father's own daughter ; but every body tells me you're the picture of me ; and if the Colonel's son be but as like his father as you are yours, you'll be the handsomest couple in Great Britain.

Char. (*Rising.*) The Colonel's son, sir !

Sir Ol. Yes, my old friend, Colonel Talbot's son ; one of the finest young fellows I am told—but no fop—he has none of the vices and follies of your young butterflies of fashion.

Char. No, sir, nor any of their accomplishments, or I'm misinformed.

Sir Ol. It was an excellent thought of his father's, to have him brought up in a snug private way.

Char. And yet, I'm told he has lived some time in a snug public way.

Sir Ol. What, Charlotte, have you been listening to any scandalous reports of the youth ?

Char. A pretty youth I understand he is for the husband of your daughter—I am told he was actually a waiter at some horrid place near Smithfield.

Sir Ol. O infamous scandal !—He waiter at some horrid place near Smithfield !—The next report, I suppose, will be, that you were bar-maid at the same place ; and that I'm an old tobacconist, who

supplied the house with cut and dry, from the sign
of the Black Boy in a neighbouring alley.

Char. I am petrified at the very thoughts of the
brute!

Sir Ol. Look you there now: she knows I love
contradiction in my heart, and therefore seems
averse to the match, because she thinks it will
please me. But, come; you and your mother and
my niece shall go pay the Colonel and his son a
morning visit.

Char. Sir, as you insist upon it, I will go as I
would to any other great natural curiosity.

Sir Ol. Was ever any thing like this! she has
heard a scandalous report of a man, and she won't
wait to be undeceived by her own eyes and her
own ears: this is downright inconvincible obstinacy, not rational, well-founded contradiction; and
I hate the one as much as I love the other: besides, I ever thought you a girl of too much sense to
lay any kind of stress on a tale of mere rumour.

Char. But if rumour should speak truth?

Sir Ol. He's so great a liar I would not believe
him.   [*Exeunt.*

SCENE II.

An Apartment at MANDEVILLE'S.

Enter JOHNSON *and* COLONEL TALBOT.

Johns. He's a rough diamond, sir; he requires a
little polishing, I must confess.

Col. Good masters may remove his ignorance,
and good company polish his manners; but there is
a meanness in the turn of his person, and the cast

of his features, which is insuperable; but take man in every point of view, and he will be found the creature of habit; his body, like his mind, is subdued by education.

Johns. I wonder, sir, you never wrote to any particular friend in England, to have inquired about him, when you received no letter about this man, to whose care you committed him.

Col. Who could I trust? None of my own family!—Then, what solid friendships do you suppose are contracted at the age I left England? I was then but twenty, all my intimates were young fellows, sunk in pleasure and dissipation : if any thing like friendship had subsisted between us, the many years we were asunder had dissolved the tie—His mother, I knew, was dead; and from Wilkins' silence, I concluded that he also had paid the debt of nature; therefore I desisted from writing, thinking it was in vain to hope for any certainty till I had myself reached England.

Johns. I should not have believed it possible your honour could have had such a son, let his education be what it may.

Col. I own, Johnson, the weakness of a father induced me to believe I should have seen him emerging from the low contracted sphere to which his fate had consigned him, by the native energy of his own powers; and flattered myself with the pleasing dream of surprising a young man with affluence and distinction, who in obscurity had acquired virtue to deserve them.

Johns. I beg your honour's pardon :—but, as I cannot see the least likeness of you in this young gentleman's face, I suppose he resembled his mother.

Col. His mother!—She had the countenance of an angel!

Johns. Then he differs from you both devilishly !
—But, sir, the sooner you provide him with a fen-
cing and a dancing master the better; the latter of
these gentlemen seems indispensibly necessary, if
it's only to teach him to walk; for no raw recruit
on the first day of drilling was ever more pigeon-
toed.

Col. Where is he now ?

Johns. I left him, sir, very busy over his luncheon.

Col. His luncheon !

Johns. Yes, sir ; a small morsel he takes before
dinner, just to stay his stomach, consisting of about
a pound of beef steaks and a tankard of porter.

Col. Send him to me. (*Exit* JOHNSON.)—I fear
he's incorrigibly gone, beyond the power of reformation.

Enter MANDEVILLE.

Col. Dear Mandeville, what course do you advise me to pursue with this untoward boy? With
all his faults, I must consider he is my son, and
pity, whilst he compels me to blush for him.

Mand. Sir, we must endeavour to form him as
well as we can : but I am rather inclined to think
we shall never be able to give him the graces.

Col. He's not three and twenty—that's young :—
we have many began later in life to acquire the ru-
diments of those sciences in which they afterwards
arrived to the highest pitch of eminence.—Have
you been able to discover how the natural bent of
his temper inclines, or if he has any strong propen-
sities ?

Mand. Why, sir, from what I can collect in my
short acquaintance with him, the natural bent of
his temper seems inclined to gallantry; and if he

has any strong propensity, it is to the game of skittles.

Col. No matter how low and vulgar the game be, it shows a spirit of play in him, and it must be crushed: but if he has a turn for gallantry, it gives me the greatest hopes of his reformation. The society of an accomplished and beautiful woman softens and refines the roughest nature ; she imparts, by a secret magic, her elegances and her graces ; and to converse with her is a kind of study that insensibly polishes her admirer.—But what reason have you to suppose he is inclined to gallantry ?

Mand. He has imparted all his amours to me ; but one in particular, which very much diverted me indeed :—After having been successful with barmaids, young milliners, and tailors' daughters, out of number, Cupid shot him from a cheesecake battery, and he fell in love with a pastrycook's daughter ; which, O terrible ! was the cause of his having an affair of honour with an attorney's clerk, in which both parties were bound over ; but in painting this Helen, who bred the contention, how shall I do him justice at second hand ? Teniers lent him his pencil for her waist, and Titian for her head ; for she was shaped like a Dutch cheese, and her locks were as red as a carrot.

Col. I have sent for him ; and as I shall examine him closely, in order to search if there be any latent seeds of ability which culture may bring forth, I wish you, Mandeville, to be present, and that you will also assist me in the inquiry.

Mand. Certainly ; as my cousin, I think it a duty I owe him.—O, here he comes with Johnson.

Enter CALEB *and* JOHNSON.

Ca. (*Speaks as entering.*) You don't know what's

taste; my hair's the nattiest thing in town as it is dressed now.

Col. Don't you know, sir, I sent for you?

Ca. Ah, father!—Cousin! are you there too?

Mand. You don't attend.

Ca. Attend! no: I hope, I shan't attend any more.—Well, father, you sent for me; now, what do you want, my old cock?

Col. (*Turning away with disgust.*) It is in vain to think of cultivating a soil like this!

Mand. His manner is terrible, to be sure: but we must correct him.

Ca. Correct him! Why, what have I done to be corrected? I thought I was corrected enough by my last father.

Col. Would that correction had taught you to speak!

Ca. That it did; and often to squeak too, till you could hear me two streets off.

Col. Speak to him, Mandeville.—There is something so barbarous in every thing he says or does, that I can't bear to look at him.

Mand. You'll excuse me, dear cousin, for giving you a little advice; but as I mean it well, I'm sure you'll not be offended.

Ca. Bless your heart, you can't offend me! I'm one of the best-tempered boys breathing:—but what's the matter with old Firelock? He seems in the sulks.

Man. He's not pleased with your manner and address; it is too rude and abrupt: you should never approach him without evident marks of respect.

Ca. O! I understand you; I should always make a bow when I come into a place where he is.— Ecod, with all my heart: but what set me wrong, was hearing it said, that to have no manners at all was the best of breeding.

Mand. Ceremony is altogether as ridiculous as rudeness is offensive; you must avoid both.

Col. Have you ever read any thing in your life ?

Ca. Why, do you think I can't read ? Then I tell you I can ; and write and cypher too.

Mand. He doesn't doubt that ; he only wishes to know what kind of reading or books you are fond of.

Ca. Then you may tell him, I am fond of histories.

Mand. That's a good hearing, faith ! If he's fond of history, he must possess from nature a strong inquisitive mind under all this unpromising d'abord. Men educated in a low sphere of life, however uncouthly they express themselves, often manifest a strong intellect ; and on being put to the test, discover a fund of knowledge the better-educated man would not expect from a slight acquaintance with them : I consider such minds like rich metals, as yet unpurified from alloy ; but let it once be known that the ore is gold, and the refiner's hand will soon bring forth the bullion.—As you are fond of history, you have no doubt dipt into the histories of Greece and Rome ?

Ca. The best of their histories.

Mand. Whose were they ?

Ca. Why, in the first place, I have read Don Bellianis's History of Greece, and the Seven wise Masters' History of Rome.

Col. Ask him no more questions.

Ca. Then I've read the History of Colonel Jack, and the History of the English Rogue, and the History of Moll Flanders.

Mand. He appears as well read in modern as ancient history.

Col. I don't know any thing more mortifying to human pride, than to pass the better part of a man's life in toil, anxiety, and danger, accumulating wealth, to leave it to a fool at last.

Ca. You can't think, father, how sensible money makes a fool look, and how foolish a wise man looks without it.

Enter Servant.

Serv. Mr Serge, your honour's tailor.

Mand. He's come to take measure of my cousin for his regimentals.

Ca. Regimentals! Why, am I to be a colonel as well as my father?

Col. Sir you're to be a soldier.

Ca. A soldier! Why, what's all this? Am I to go for a soldier, after all?—Has Doll Blouze been with the parish officers?

Col. I have procured you a commission! no son of mine shall waste his youth in ease and indolence, dissipating that wealth I so hardly earned: the greater part, it is true, he shall enjoy; but he shall first prove by his courage, and his services to his country, that he deserves it.

Ca. There's not a boy within the sound of Bow bell of a better spirit; I'll fight any man in England of my weight and inches, with fair fistesses, for a guinea—aye, damme! if I don't, and lay down first.

Mand. Hadn't you better step to the tailor?

Ca. Presently, presently, cousin—But now I think of it, I'll not step to him; let the tailor step to me.—A captain step to a tailor! Impossible! that's bidding a fieldpiece dance the hayes after a thimble.

Col. I insist upon your going this moment.

Ca. Why, the old boy's in his tantrums—Cousin, a word in your ear: there's one thing before I go, I must beg of you.

Mand. What's that?

Ca. Why, as you and I will be hand in glove,

as a body may say, you'll call me Caleb, and I'll call you Tom, Frank, Harry, or—what is your name?

Mand. My name is Frederick.

Ca. Frederick! what a pretty name! I wish my name was Frederick. Can't I be new-christened for one name as well as another?

Mand. (*Aside.*) Till you're new-born, I fancy nothing can be done with you.

Ca. But I was going to tell you—if you call me Caleb, never do it loud, especially in company.

Mand. For heaven's sake, why?

Ca. Why, if you was to cry out, as thus now, Caleb! (*Bawling out.*) I should cry, " Coming up, sir!" though you made a duke of me. [*Exit* CALEB.

Col. Well, Mandeville, what do you think?

Mand. Hope is left us the worst of times; however, I do not despair of making something of him yet: what I dread most, is introducing him to Charlotte.

Col. Why cannot man make over his mind, like his property, to his children? Any distinguishing quality in all other animals survives in the same species by hereditary descent for ever; man continues upon the earth only in his name and his revenues. O, that he should leave behind him his least valuable part, and all that made him good or great should sink into the dust with him!

Enter JOHNSON.

Johns. Good news! good news, sir! the Carnatic is arrived safe.—Captain Crevelt's servant is just come to acquaint you, that his master and Count Pierpont will be here immediately.

Col. Good news, indeed, Johnson; and heavy and afflicted as my heart is, your tidings cheer it. The Count, Mandeville, is an officer of infinite merit; he was my prisoner during the war, and is warmly attached to English manners and our glorious constitution. But, Crevelt.—to know the merit of such a man, you must be acquainted with him.

Mand. Is he an Englishman?

Col. Yes, and you may judge of his merit as a soldier, when I tell you, he has arisen from the ranks, at the age of three-and-twenty, to the commission he now holds of captain. He's the reverse of this ill-fated boy we have been speaking to. He is self-educated; for, with scarcely any advantages but those he derived from a most noble and excellent nature, he is the man of sense, the scholar, and the polished gentleman. His father, old Crevelt, was no more than a serjeant, and served in Germany under Lord Granby; he brought this young man with him to India, whilst yet a boy: the first day he ever was in action, he saw his father fall; and he was found after the battle among the slain, close to his body, apparently lifeless, with loss of blood, as if he had died in the pious office of defending a parent.

Enter Servant.

Serv. Captain Crevelt, sir.

Mand. Let us go and receive him; my heart burns with impatience to call such a man my friend.
[*Exeunt.*

ACT THE THIRD.

SCENE I.

MANDEVILLE'S *House.*

Enter MANDEVILLE, CREVELT, *and* COLONEL
TALBOT.

Crev. I quitted England, Mr Mandeville, when
a boy, and never was in London in my life before.
I am charmed with the appearance of this noble city,
in which the ease, convenience, and safety of its
poorest inhabitant seem consulted.

Col. There is no token seen in the streets of an
exhausted people, drained by a tedious and expen-
sive war, during which Great Britain fought at more
unequal odds than any nation on the earth ever did
before.

Crev. So much the reverse, that I am astonished
at the appearance of opulence and prosperity to be
met with every where ; and the pleasing sensation
I feel, to find my country in that state, is indescri-
bable.

Col. Let gloomy politicians continue to predict
and foresee calamities that exist only in imagination ; whilst the genius of industry continues to

smile upon the labours of the husbandman, the mechanic, and the manufacturer, and whilst strict probity is the character of England in her dealings with all other nations, the resources of this country will be found inexhaustible : and though its glory may be veiled by a momentary cloud, it soon recovers its former splendour.

Enter CALEB *in Regimentals.*

Ca. Here I am, father, in full feather.

Col. What, sir, is your dancing-master gone already?

Ca. Bless your heart !—no master of any kind for me to-day ; I never put on a new suit of clothes in my life, that I did not make holiday.

Man. (Aside to the COLONEL.) We had better, I think, in some degree give way to him : you cannot expect immediately to reform manners so long confirmed by habit.

Col. (Aside.) I believe you're right; so I'll try what effect indulgence may have on him. Well, it shall be as you would have it ; this day shall be devoted to pleasure and amusement. Crevelt, give me leave to introduce you to my son.

Crev. I don't know any circumstance of my life affects me more than the high honour I now enjoy.
[*Introducing himself.*

Ca. Why, look ye, young man, as my father desires it, I'll shake hands with you, with all my heart : but I would not make so free with every old soldier's son.

Col. How dare you, sir, insult a man of his merit with language so gross ?

Ca. Why, isn't he an old soldier's son ?—pretty company truly, to introduce me to !

Crev. Sir, the humility of my birth I acknowledge ; but must tell you, this is the first time it

ever brought a blush into my cheek—I am choked with rage—Unused to insult, I cannot receive it
without indignation even from the son of Colonel
Talbot !

Col. I insist upon your asking that gentleman's
pardon.

Ca. Why, is he a gentleman ?

Col. A man of his worth, his honour, and ability,
is a gentleman, though sprung in the lowest vale of
society.

Ca. Nay, if you say he is a gentleman, I ask his
pardon with all my heart—Nothing so common now-
a-days as one gentleman's asking pardon of another;
it makes up a quarrel in a trice.

Crev. Sir, I accept your apology.

Col. (*To* CALEB.) But, sir, I will go farther with
you—You must ever consider that man with respect : learn to esteem him, and it will do you more
honour than your birth has done.

Enter Servant.

Ser. The gentleman from the India-House, sir,
that was here before to-day, has called again.

Col. Let him know I'll wait on him immediately.
                                        [*Exit Servant.*

(*To* CALEB.) Young man, I wish to undeceive
you in one particular ; seize all those opportunities
of instruction I mean to give you, and redeem the
time you have lost, which, if you neglect, your provision from me shall be merely independence ; my
name you may disgrace, but I think it a crime to
bestow riches on one who would abuse them ; even
that youth, whose birth is so inferior in your eye, I
should consider as united to me by his merit in
nearer ties of kindred.   [*Exit* COLONEL.

Ca. (*Strutting about.*) So then, I am to be disinherited after all, and for an old soldier's son too !

Crev. What's that you say, sir ?

Ca. Say, sir!—Damme ! he looks so fierce, I don't know what to say to him.—These old soldier's sons are so used to cutting of throats, it's the devil to quarrel with them.

Man. I am ashamed of you, cousin—if you proceed in this manner, you must be locked up from all society.

Ca. I'll beg his pardon again : I know that's all he wants.

Crev. I'll spare you, sir, the mortification of descending to so humiliating an act—in respect to your father, I overlook every thing you have hitherto said—I now coolly behold all that hath been past through a different medium ; and rather feel for a youth, who, from his prospect of immense wealth, has been, perhaps from his childhood, surrounded with sycophants, who never let him know what it was to be acquainted with himself, and persuaded him into an opinion, that wealth supplies the absence of every accomplishment and virtue.

Ca. I don't rightly understand you, captain; but I fancy—only you mince the matter—that you meant to say I was much better fed than taught— Well, no matter—Are we good friends again ?

Crev. Very good!

Ca. Then give your hand. (*Aside.*) He, he, he ! I can't help laughing, after all, to think of such a fellow's being a gentleman !—But I say, captain, they tell me you are a devil of a fellow for fighting : now, do you see me, as I am an officer as well as yourself, I'd be glad to know how you generally found yourself before you went into the field of battle.

Crev. Much as I do at present.

Ca. What, no more frightened !

Crev. No, sir.

Ca. Come, come, no tricks upon travellers, captain ; do you think I'm such a fool as to believe you ?

Ca. Sir ! (*Terrified.*) He looks at me like a tiger—I'll ask him no more questions—he has half frightened me out of my commission already—Eh ! (*Looking out.*)—Ecod, yonder I see my father talking to two fine girls—I'll go have a peep at them— Cousin Mandeville, good bye—Captain, your servant—(*Stifling a laugh.*) A gentleman truly !— What a fine thing it is to be born one—it saves a world of trouble in learning.   [*Exit* CALEB.

Mand. The story of this unhappy young man, and how his education came to be so much neglected, is too long to acquaint you of particularly, at present, but you see what he is, and, I hope, estimate an insult from him accordingly.

Crev. I think no more of it—but my heart bleeds for his father.

Mand. You talk of leaving town to-day—why, dear sir, will you so suddenly quit friends, who, of all things, covet your society ? Is the business which calls you from us, of that urgent nature, you cannot postpone it for a few days at least ?

Crev. It is what I ought not to do—for my relations in England (if I have any living) have never heard from me since I quitted the country ; but perhaps it's better to prepare them for the meeting ; so I shall write to them by this night's post, and continue your guest a little longer.

Mand. Now this is truly friendly—I wou'dn't for the world have you leave the town till after my Cousin Talbot's wedding.

Crev. Then he's going to be married ?

Mand. So his father intends, as the only means of reforming him. The lady is one of those two who came here within this half hour, and whom we left

with Count Pierpont, admiring his magnificent presents from the different princes of the East, at whose
courts he has been occasionally envoy.

Crev. But which of the ladies is intended for Mr
Talbot?

Mand. Charlotte—she whom you so much admired: and, short as the Count's acquaintance with
them is, he appears already smitten with her cousin Harriet.—Unluckily for him, she happens to be
engaged.

Crev. But, Charlotte '—It is she, then, who is intended for Mr Talbot?—I think I never saw a finer
girl.

Mand. She's a divine creature! and though her
Adonis is so near a relation, I confess I wish her a
better husband;—but I don't know how matters
may terminate.—She's a girl of great spirit—has a
very fine independency; and such is her disposition, that I'm confident there is no temptation in
wealth could induce her to marry any man whom
she did not like.

Enter HARRIET.

Har. Ha, ha, ha! I beg your pardon, Mr Mandeville, for laughing so much at the expense of
your cousin Talbot; but his manner, person, and
conversation, are all so truly original, that gravity
itself must be provoked to laughter in his company.

Mand. It's very true, Harriet; he is a most extraordinary being, I must confess.

Har. He introduced himself to Charlotte this
moment; and such a figure does he cut! He can
neither walk, sit, nor stand still, with gazing at
his person. Charlotte and he are together; she
seems delighted with him.

Crev. Then, ma'am, she likes him.

Har. She likes to laugh at him, sir—Do, Mandeville, come, and take a look at him.

Mand. Will you go, Crevelt?

Crev. I'll just speak to Johnson, sir, and follow you. (*Exeunt* MAND. *and* HAR.)—I never saw that woman in my life before, who, in a moment, has had such a power over me.—She will not marry him, they say—but what then? Does it follow, of course, that she must like me?

Enter JOHNSON.

Johns. I understand your honour wished to see me.

Crev. Yes, Johnson; as you came to London before me, I wished to ask you, if you knew any thing of the family of this young lady your master intends his son shall marry?

Johns. Why, sir, I understand she is the daughter of a Sir Oliver Oldstock; an old acquaintance of the Colonel's—her father, I hear, meant she should marry Mr Mandeville, supposing he would be my master's heir; but when a son made his appearance, like all other worldly men, Sir Oliver changed his note; and the poor young lady is to become a sacrifice to this—I wish he wasn't my master's son.

Crev. But she won't, Johnson, be made a sacrifice.

Johns. I hope not, sir;—but, Lord! what won't money do? Don't we see money, every day, couple age and deformity to youth and beauty; a young creature, like an angel, linked to an old skeleton of dry bones!—as if the dæmon of avarice and sin had acquired such ascendancy in the world, as to bring about an union betwixt death and immortality!

Crev. Why, Johnson, you speak with great feeling and spirit on the subject.

Johns. Ah, Captain Crevelt? what a charming couple you two would make—I, who have seen your honour in the field, would expect a Granby, or a Marlborough, from such a marriage.

Crev. (*Musing.*) I promised to follow them ; but the less I see her, the better for my peace ; it's only feeding a passion I should banish from my heart for ever. Johnson, take no notice that I have asked you any questions concerning Miss Oldstock : should I be inquired for, I am gone to the library. Books, or my own thoughts, are the only society I am fit for.   [*Exit* CREV.

Johns. Well, as long as I live, I never will think there is any thing in great blood again.   Here is a son of one of the best families in the kingdom, with neither person nor mind superior to one of his father's domestics ; and if we turn our eyes to the other side, we behold the offspring of an old soldier with the soul of a prince, and the head of a prime minister.

Enter NANCY, *running.*

Nan. Mr Johnson, Mr Johnson, here's a letter for you, brought by the penny-post ; (*gives it*) and short a time as you have been in London, I'm sure it's a love-letter.

Johns. Aye ; pray, Nancy, how have you made that discovery : Is it by the elegant penmanship of its pot-hook and hanger superscription, or by the god of love's own broad seal stamped upon it by a wafer and thimble ?

Nan. Ecod, Mr Johnson, you're a knowing hand ; I'll engage you have hooked in many a poor girl in your time.

Johns. But I haven't paid the postage.

Nan. That's always paid beforehand into the office with the letter.

Johns. But you know, Nancy, letters are conveyed now upon a new establishment, and for fear of mistakes, I'll even pay double postage.

[*Kisses her.*

Nan. It's mighty well! I suppose when you find this is a mistake, you'll be for having the overcharge back again.   [*Exit* NANCY.

Johns. Now for my letter.—'Sdeath! it's from my sweet little Mrs Wilkins! (*Reads.*) "Mrs Wilkins's compliments to Mr Johnson; will be glad of his company this evening to tea, as she wishes to treat with him about those little matters he brought with him from India: if the two sets of china be as handsome as he said they were, she will take them both off his hands; she'll take, besides, some chintz and muslins for gowns, and half-a-dozen shawls; he need not send her any mandarins; she has more old figures than are worth house-room.

" P. S. Mr Wilkins is very sorry he can't be at home the whole evening, very particular business calling him to Hogsden."

I was afraid I should have had no postscript; but all's right I find—Yes, my sweet Mrs Wilkins I will go and talk to you about those trifles I brought with me from India; but you shall have no mandarins :—indeed, I thought you had one too many of these old figures.   [*Exit.*

Enter CALEB, *followed by* CHARLOTTE.

Ca. Well, Miss; how do you like me! Don't you think I look like a captain?

Char. Like a captain! It would be doing you injustice to compare you to any one officer under his majesty: I am really at a loss for a comparison to match you with—Come, turn about, and let me see your shapes.   Mercy! what a long sword they have tied you to !

Ca. That was all my own thought: I haven't learnt to fence yet ; and as I am told a gentleman is no-body till he has fought about a score duels, I was determined the first time I fought not to be over-reached by any body.

Char. A very prudent resolution, I must confess! valour is by no means incompatible with discretion; but pray, sir, are you so very quarrelsome, that you expect to have all these duels upon your hands?

Ca. Me quarrelsome !—Bless your heart, I'm as quiet as a lamb.

Char. Then why do you expect to fight so much?

Ca. Because it's the fashion ; and you know a man had better be out of the world than out of the fashion.

Char. Then I think you are taking an excellent method to have your choice.

Ca. Yes; fighting's quite a gentleman-like amuse-ment : besides, it will be put in the newspapers ; and I shall read my own name in print, along with the debates of Lords and Commons : and that's the cause, I suppose, of all duels.

Char. I believe duels have been fought more than once—and, O fatal delusion! perhaps a valuable life lost for a cause altogether as frivolous !

Ca. But now I am dressed, do you see me, I wish to show myself to some of my old acquaintances : therefore, suppose you and I go this evening to Bag-nigge-Wells, and drink tea—the hot rolls are so nice there, you can't think !

Char. Some other time ; I can't possibly go this evening.

Ca. Mayhap you think I won't pay for the tea, but I will ; and moreover than that, I'll treat you to the half-play afterwards.

Char. You must, indeed, excuse me, sir. (*Aside.*) I wish I could get rid of him.—This moment poor Crevelt passed me with a dejected air—I followed him with a stolen glance, till I traced him into the library—I wish I knew what was the matter with him ; I never saw a man in my life I pity so much.

Ca. (*Looking at himself.*) How they will stare at our hop, to see me in this dress !

Char. This fellow takes no notice of me ; his regimentals have actually rivalled me !

Ca. (*With great delight.*) Dress I see is every thing ; such a suit of regimentals would make any man a great officer. How this world goes ! fine fellows are made by tailors, and tailors undone by fine fellows !

Char. My Narcissus is so engaged with his person, it would be foolish to lose this opportunity of getting rid of him ; I'll drop carelessly into the library—I never saw so sudden an alteration in man's looks as in poor Crevelt's—I hope he's not in love —poor Charlotte, if the object be not in England !

[*Exit* CHARLOTTE.

Ca. (*To himself.*) To be sure, Caleb, you haven't a pair of legs ?—It is not every captain who can beat a march with such a pair of drumsticks—I wonder how my legs would look in a pair of new boots —I never rode of a Sunday, but in a pair of my father's old ones—most smart captains, I observe, foot as well as horse, mount the streets in boots. So you wont go to Bagnigge-Wells ! (*Looking up.*) Eh ! why, she's gone !—I'm glad of it !—and now the coast is clear !—Ecod, I'll have a ramble—what signifies my being dressed, if nobody sees me ?—I'll call over to Jacob Wilkins's, and take a glass with him—who knows, but one of these days, when I return from abroad a great warrior, but old Jacob may take down his sign, and hang me up over his door.
[*Exit.*

Enter LADY OLDSTOCK *and* COUNT PIERPONT.

L. Old. Really, my Lord, I tremble for the consequences of this interview ; if Sir Oliver should
meet us, and happen to be in one of his jealous
moods, it is in vain to tell him of the innocency of
our conversation ; he will interpret my very looks ;
and draw the strangest inferences from even the
tone of voice with which I utter the most good-
natured sentence.

Count. Il est bien extraordinaire ; appears to me
very strange, madame, dat people of fashion en
Angleterre can be so bourgeois.   Mon Dieu ! en
France, quand un homme est marie, ven ve marry,
by gar, our friends cannot nous oblige more dan by
take care of our vives.

L. Old. O my Lord, you're a refined people ! we
are at least a century behind you in point of civi-
lization.

Count. But on my vord, you improve every day ;
people de fashion in both countries vil be ver soon
les memes ; a voile le difference—at present, see the
difference between France and England—Un Anglois
est trop brusque, too rough ; un François, peutetre
trop poli ; but dat be fault sur cote droit, on de
right side—suppose nous avons—suppose we have
von traité de commerce, pour un exchange des ma-
niers ; Jack Bull is von guinea too heavy ; and un
Frenchman, entre nous, peutetre un louis-d'or too
light : now to make a de balance even, scrape de
Englis, or vat you call sweat a de Englis guinea,
and augmentez le louis-d'or, and you give de polish to de one, and de proper weight to the other.

L. Old. I blush, my Lord, to think my education
was so cruelly neglected, that I cannot hold a conversation with you in your own language—People
of condition should always speak French.

Count. Mais j'espere—me hope you understand?

L. Old. O perfectly, my Lord; you speak the language of the graces; and that our sex understand in every country.

Count. Si j'entends vous, ma belle ange! If I understand, it is you have give me the instructions.

L. Old. How well he makes himself understood! I never heard such sweet broken English in my life before.

Count. Mais, madame! may I beg leave to solicit—   [*Taking her by the hand.*

L. Old. My Lord! Dear Count!

                                        [*Seemingly confused.*

Count. Madame, may I solicit votre pitié, pour un passion qui brule mon ame—my passion burn a my heart.

L. Old. O heavens, what a discovery is here? How fatal to the happiness of—I hope, my Lord, you will exert your philosophy on this occasion, and consider the insurmountable obstacle.

Count. Obstacle, madame! quelle obstacle to a man of my rank and fortune?

L. Old. O, fie, fie, my Lord! can a man of your delicacy talk in this strain?

Count. Ah, si vous pouviez lire—if you could read a my heart—

L. Old. Go, unhappy youth! and endeavour to extinguish a fruitless flame; that, if it continue to burn, must only prove a source of disquietude to us both: go, too-pleasing seducer! and like the faithful, but honourable Werter, leave your ill-starred sympathising Charlotte in tears! [*Affecting to weep.*

Count. My Charlotte!—No, it is my Harriet.

L. Old. Harriet!—What Harriet?

Count. Your niece, madame; that petite ange—

L. Old. My niece! Was my niece the object of all this adoration?

Count. Is there one else living deserve so much ?

L. Old. Yes, a hundred, if you had eyes to see.

Count. Eh bien!   Madame, what you say to my proposal?

L. Old. My niece is engaged; or, if she wasn't, you should not have her.

Count. Mais le chevalier Oldstock dit le contraire—Sir Oliver say quite different.

L. Old. Sir Oliver's an old fool, and suppose didn't understand you, for you speak terrible English. [*Exit.*

Count. I speak terrible Englis !—Mon Dieu—il est bien etrange!—just now I speak ver sweet broke Englis !

Enter SIR OLIVER.

Sir Ol. Well, Count, what says my wife ?

Count. She does refuse—she vil not consent.

Sir Ol. I am glad of it.

Count. Diable ! pourquoi you glad of it ?

Sir Ol. Because now I shall have an opportunity of showing my authority, and letting her know you shall have my niece in spite of her.—She's my own brother's daughter ; he left her an orphan to my care, and I'll dispose of her as I like; I asked Lady Oldstock's approbation, only for the pleasure of being refused it—I love contradiction.

Count. Mon cher Chevalier—you transport me.

Sir Ol. Yes, Count; contradiction's my hobby-horse ; I mount him every hour of the day ; and the more he kicks and flings, the greater delight I take in riding him ;—I know you think me a whimsical old fellow ; but you are new to our clime and our manners—we delight in thinking for ourselves—opposition is the very soul of an Englishman—he likes it in himself, and in others also; peace and prosperity, with good eating and drinking, would throw him into a lethargy, if imagination didn't supply that spur to goad him on constantly to action.

Count. Now, mon chere pere, me vill settle—

Sir Ol. Odso, that's right—mind, the foundation-stone of our agreement is, that you settle in England :—a niece of mine shall never breed subjects to fight against her king and country !

Count. Monsieur, you have my vord of honour: and now I vill go visit my pretty miss, vat you call Harriet ;—mais, monsieur, rest assure me vill die and live in England.   [*Exit* COUNT.

Sir Ol. Well said, monsieur ! cart before the horse. But now I am alone, let me see how my accounts stand :—I have secured the French nabob for my niece ; now it would be a master-stroke if I could obtain the English one for my daughter, and thus centre the two nabobs in my own family : This son of the colonel's is a downright savage—Charlotte never could like him ; or, if she could, interest tells me I should not : therefore her liking's out of the question : there's to be a division of the colonel's property between the son and Mandeville : I want the whole, if possible. The colonel's not fifty, and in my mind he's a better looking man than either his son or his nephew. Charlotte's having ten thousand pounds independent of me, makes her very obstinate ; debates will run high, I fear ; as, indeed, they very often do in my family ; where, though I'm constantly left in a minority, I never lose a question ;—it's true, I have open mouths upon me from all sides, till, like greater men, I'm fairly badgered ; but it's only waiting till the strangers are all out, and I tell the house as I please afterwards.—Zounds ! here comes Mandeville : I wish I could get decently out of his way.

Enter MANDEVILLE.

Mand. I have been in search of you, Sir Oliver.

Sir Ol. I wish I had known that, I'd have saved you a good deal of trouble. Well, my good sir, had you any thing particular to say to me?

Mand. Is your conduct towards me consistent with honour?

Sir Ol. I don't understand you.

Mand. How convenient it is to assume ignorance of a subject on which it is painful to hear the truth, even to the man incapable of respecting it! Honour, though shut out from the heart, will still knock at its gates, and tell the guilty, there is a register kept in the avenging court of remorse for every act of injustice.

Sir Ol. Upon my word, Mr Mandeville, you speak to me in a very strange style; this is not a manner in which I am accustomed to be addressed. You bounce in all of a sudden, transported with rage, for what cause is best known to yourself, and with a knock-me-down countenance, treat me as if my age and my rank had no kind of respect due to them.

Mand. Sir, no man honours age more than I, or more readily yields rank every respect it can claim, when that rank does not forfeit its title to esteem, by meanly sinking and degrading itself;—but, when men in superior stations behave, as if their actions were above all censure and controul, they must be told, that they are deceiving themselves, as well as the world, and that no man is suffered to injure another with impunity.

Sir Ol. Well, sir, in what particular have I injured you, to provoke the thunder of this terrible Philippic?

Mand. Can you seriously ask me that question,

when you sanction the addresses of Count Pierpont to your niece?

Sir Ol. Well, and what then?

Mand. Have you forgot your prior engagement to me?

Sir Ol. Mr Mandeville, the poet says, that " Every day's a satire on the last;" as circumstances vary, or events fall out, we are compelled by necessity to change our minds. As to my niece, whom I consider in the light of a daughter, I think it my duty, in providing her with a husband, to make the best bargain I can for her.

Mand. Sir, have you no regard to what the world will say on this occasion? The world, sir; that harsh, blind, misjudging multitude; whose slander, i*f* it soil the ermine purity of virtue, what will it say when it has justice upon its side?

Sir Ol. Nothing that I value. Young man, when you have lived as many years with the world as I have, you'll learn to make your happiness independent of its opinion. Don't you see knaves and fools every day rise into consequence, and all from the opinion of the world—the opinion of the world, sir!—It's a mouthful of moonshine!

Mand. I believe with you, that the world is too indolent—too much occupied with its pleasures, or its miseries, to take up the business of a censor:— I fear it never examines thoroughly any man's pretensions to its favour; the more he asks, the more he generally obtains from the world; hence, folly, confidence, and vice, revel in the arms of luxury, whilst merit, proud, and retiring from the conscious dignity of genius and virtue, is suffered to perish for want of bread!—But, sir—

Sir Ol. But, no more of this debate, Mr Mandeville—the question is put, and I am going. Partial as I am to a polemical mode of discourse, I find

that there may be sometimes even too much contradiction.   [*Exit.*

Mand. What shall I do with this deceitful, unfeeling man? But can I hesitate whilst I have a
particle of spirit left? I'll go this moment, state the
matter to Count Pierpont, and he shall resign, or
fight for his mistress!

Enter HARRIET.

Har. Dear Mandeville, what is the matter?—My
uncle has just parted from you, seemingly much out
of temper, and the wildness and disorder of your
looks terrify me?

Mand. My heart is torn to pieces, Harriet!—Indignation at the ungenerous treatment I have met
with from your uncle, added to my fears of losing
you, distract me.

Har. But can you doubt your Harriet? There is
no power upon earth shall force me to be another's;
do then, dear Mandeville! strive to calm this tumult
in your mind—Betrayed by the violence of your
passion, you talked of going in search of Count
Pierpont—let me beseech you, not.

Mand. You were deceived, Harriet, in what you
heard me say—do not prevent my going—I have
business of a most particular nature calls me.

Har. I know perfectly the business that calls you
—but let me conjure you, by all that regard you
ever professed for me, not to think of it. You say,
your fears of losing me distract you—judge, then, of
the state of my heart by your own. Has Harriet
no fears for her Mandeville, at a moment she sees
him eat up with an ungovernable rage—about, perhaps, to hurry himself, or a fellow-creature, into
eternity?

Mand. Your apprehensions, Harriet, are ground-
less—from what I learn of the Count's character,

I believe him to be a man of too nice honour, too equitable, too generous, to reduce me to the necessity of proceeding to extremities; I only wish to explain matters to him.

Har. I can recommend a much better course to you, and one much more likely to succeed—Go to your uncle, that good, that noble-hearted man :— tell him your story ;—if any body has weight with Sir Oliver, it is Colonel Talbot.

Man. Nobody has weight with him when avarice claims his ear.

Har. You are mistaken : he is not so great a slave to avarice as you suppose him.

Mand. He is your uncle, Harriet, and I cannot speak of him with harshness.

Har. I know by your eyes, you are not so angry as you were.

Mand. I will be guided by you in every thing.— There is a fascinating power, Harriet, in your looks and accents, when you would persuade, that cannot be resisted ; a melting softness clings about my heart, as I listen and behold you ; there is a sure divinity in angel-beauty ! You caused the tempest in my soul, and have calmed it.   [*Exeunt.*

ACT THE FOURTH.

SCENE I.

An Apartment at MANDEVILLE'S.

CALEB *and* JOHNSON *discovered over a Bottle.*

Ca. Come, my boy, since you won't go to Jacob Wilkins's with me, we'll tope a little here—fill your glass higher—higher yet; I'll have no sky-lights—this is a bumper-toast.

Johns. Well, what is it?

Ca. Our noble selves.   [*Drinks.*

Johns. I find that you think a sentiment, like charity, should begin at home.

Ca. I do, to be sure.

Johns. We should have begun with the king and constitution.

Ca. Then here it goes;—and though it's the second toast now, it shall be the first next bottle.

Johns. Next bottle!—but, Mr Talbot, I have a particular engagement upon my hands this evening. I hope you'll excuse my leaving you.

Ca. You shan't stir a foot. [*Pushes him to his chair.* Your wine's so good—I wonder how any body can quit such liquor.

Johns. But, suppose there's a lady in the case—— you won't press me to stay surely, after I tell you that ?

Ca. Damn it !—take me with you !

Johns. Impossible !

Ca. Then sit down and drink with me, for I won't, part with you.

Johns. What the devil shall I do. (*Looking on his watch.*) It wants but a quarter to six, and Mrs Wilkins will be waiting tea for me.   [*Aside.*

Ca. Come, to the charge again, and a brimmer it shall be.

Johns. (*Aside.*) I shall get fuddled too; I have often in a frolic assumed drunkenness; suppose I practise that stratagem now to get away from him.
                                    [*Hiccups,* &c.

Ca. Why, now I look at you, I think you are getting a little forward.

Johns. But I am not quite so bad as you think ; do let me go, Mr Talbot.

Ca. Do you think I have no more regard for you? I tell you, you must go to bed ;—now do, go to bed.

Johns. How the devil shall I get away from him? Zounds, sir, I am not drunk. [*Appearing to be sober.*

Ca. Poor fellow ! I am sorry to see you so far gone ;—but I'll take care of you for this night—no, no ; no going out for this night.   [*Impeding him.*

Johns. 'Sdeath and fire ! Will this convince you that I am sober.   [*Walking firmly up the stage.*

Ca. Take another turn, and I'll tell you.

Johns. But will you let me go then ?

Ca. After we have had another bottle !

Johns. Zounds ! another bottle !—Well, I'll go down to the cellar for it.   [*Crosses.*

Ca. Mind you don't stay.

Johns. No, no ; shan't stay—(*aside*) long in this

house, now I have got out of your clutches, young
gentleman.   [*Exit.*

Ca. This is a devilish honest bottle—there is half
a pint in it yet.—Well, my friend is gone, so here
goes his health, (*Drinks.*) Poor fellow!—I never
saw a man so soon drunk and sober.—Damn it,
how he stays!—I long for a glass of wine; though
he's not here, ecod, I'll fill my glass—a good bottle
of wine is excellent company.   [*Drinks.*

Enter MANDEVILLE.

Mand. What, sir, drinking by yourself?

Ca. I'm sure that's not my my fault—I shall be very
glad if you'll sit down and keep me company: I
expect Johnson every minute with the other bottle.

Mand. I suppose, sir, Johnson has been your
companion?

Ca. Yes; and a choice companion he is; only
apt to get muzzed too soon.—Come, come, let me
fill you a glass.

Mand. I'll drink none, sir; nor shall you drink
any more; your father desires to see you instantly.

Ca. You'll let me finish the bottle.

Mand. You must drink no more! He puts me
beyond all patience.   [*Aside.*

Ca. Ecod, then I'll take it with me. [*Takes it up.*

Mand. Set it down, sir. [*Lays hold on him violently. Caleb, in a fright, drops and breaks the bottle.*

Ca. There. (*Looking at it.*) I have set it down,
and am ready to go with you; we must be good
friends again now we have cracked a bottle together.
                                         [*Exeunt.*

SCENE II.

A Library.

CREVELT, *seated, with a Book.*

Crev. (*Throws the book down.*) It is to no purpose—I cannot read—This adorable girl has taken
such entire possession of my mind, it has'nt room
for any other object: when Mr Mandeville told me
she was going to be married, and to whom, my heart
died within me, for then I knew all hope was lost;
but grant there was no dishonour, no ingratitude
in harbouring a passion for a woman intended for
the son of my benefactor, how should a low-born,
abject thing, like me, aspire to one so much above
him! Would not my birth be an insurmountable
bar to my hopes? She comes this way.——I would
avoid her, but have not the power.

Enter CHARLOTTE, *with a volume of Shakespeare in
her hand.*

Char. (*Reading.*)
—— " She never told her love;
" But let concealment, like a worm i' th' bud,
" Feed on her damask cheek : she pin'd in thought,
" And, with a green and yellow melancholy,
" She sat like Patience on a monument,
" Smiling at Grief."——

Bless me! Captain Crevelt (*starting.*) I did'nt see
you—I was quite absorbed in poor Viola's melancholy relation of undivulged love; this little picture

is so higly finished, so delicately coloured with
touches of the true pathetic, that I never read it
without being wonderfully affected—Don't you
think it one of the finest passages in all Shakespeare?

Crev. I so much admire it, madam, that I would
give the world this moment for the pencil of its
immortal writer, to paint one of our sex in the same
state of uncomplaining despondency.

Char. I protest you spoke those last words with
so serious an air, that I'm half inclined to think
you're in love yourself: if that be the case, come,
make me your confidante; I'll be as secret and as
silent as Shakespeare's own marble Grief and Patience: I have the music of the Avon swan this
moment at my heart, and could hear a lover whisper his tale under a tree in which the nightingale
sung, and the moon tipt its boughs with silver.

Crev. You speak, madam, like one well versed in
the passion.

Char. And is that strange, sir, when I come
with Shakespeare in my hand; a master who teaches
the whole history of the passions? His keen and
ardent eye, in a fine frenzy rolling, pierced into the
secret chambers of the heart where the passions
slumber; and woke them, as he swept his lyre
divine, to all their changeful moods of pain and joy,
till kindled up to madness, or to ecstasy; but when
he touches upon love, though the flash be momentary,
it resembles lightning, suddenly rifting the surface
of the earth, and disclosing the radiant portal of a
diamond quarry.

Crev. Were I to wish for another laurel on the
grave of Shakespeare, it should be planted by the
hand of so charming a commentator.

Char. Sir, there is a laurel already planted on his
grave by one of our sex, which will flourish till the

spirit of his genius, and his writings, are no more remembered—but to the point—I have pronounced you in love ; now let me know who your mistress is?

Crev. Madam, I dare not.

Char. Dare not ! Is that a soldier's phrase ? Courage, man ; there is nothing impossible to spirit and perseverance ; besides, the more difficulties lay in the road to your mistress, the better she'll like you for surmounting them.

Crev. But suppose there was a difficulty not to be surmounted !

Char. If your mistress does not dislike you, I know of no other difficulty which is not to be surmounted.

Crev. But even presuming that were the case, which I have by no means reason to imagine, I cannot think of her without condemning myself.

Char. Is she so much beneath you ?

Crev. She's above my praise, and above my hopes.

Char. If she deserves all this adoration, she never will think herself above a man of merit.

Crev. Then, madam, you don't think marrying for love entirely out of fashion ?

Char. I never would marry for any thing else.

Crev. (*Aside.*) Then I am undone ; she loves the man for whom she is intended ; and the assurance of it that I have now received from her own lips, was meant as a reproach to a passion she has discovered, in spite of all my efforts to conceal it.

Char. (*Seeing his disorder.*) What's the matter, sir ?

Crev. I fear, madam, I only interrupt your studies.
[*Going.*

Char. How can you talk so? I don't know any one whose conversation, on so short an acquaintance, is so agreeable to me; this last has been particularly interesting.

Crev. It is plain, from the sarcasm of that reply, that she understands me—but I am justly punished, for my apostacy to honour, in daring to think of her.
                                                    [*Aside.*

Char. He appears confused and embarrassed all of a sudden ; I fear my vanity has betrayed me too far, and that I have been mistaken in the object of his affections.   [*Aside.*

Crev. I have not power to speak to her.   [*Aside.*
Char. No, no ; I'm not the object.   [*Aside.*

Enter a Servant.

Ser. Sir, the Colonel wishes to see you immediately.

Crev. What a release from torture ! (*Aside.*) I shall wait on him. (*Exit Servant.*) Madam, your most obedient.   [*Exit.*

Manet CHARLOTTE.

Char. So I have as good as told a man I like him, who, it is plain, is in love with another woman : unhappy Charlotte !

Enter SIR OLIVER. (*Speaks as he comes in.*)

Sir Ol. Charlotte !
Char. Sir.
Sir Ol. Sir !—how melancholy a monosyllable comes from a woman's mouth ; it sounds as dismal as a single bell after a full peal.   But, Charlotte, what's the matter ? I never saw you so thoughtful before : I hope it is not your intended marriage that makes you uneasy.

Char. It never gave me an uneasy moment.   I had made up my mind on the subject.

Sir Ol. Well ; well ; let the matter rest then : however, I must confess, I should like to see my girl well married and settled before I left the world.

Char. I don't think I shall ever marry.

Sir Ol. Never marry!

Char. No.

Sir Ol. Confound those monosyllables! Charlotte, let me have no more of them; the laconic style does not become you: I wonder from whom you take it; for my part, I'm fond of the figure of amplification in discourse; and I'm sure your mother deals in an eloquence, copious at times, even to redundancy.

Char. Sir, I have not spirits for conversation.

Sir Ol. I am surprised at that, when you have every thing your own way: you won't marry this body, nor you won't marry t'other; and I, like an easy, indulgent old soul, humour you in every thing, fond as I am of contradiction.

Char. Hav'nt you all's one as held me up to sale to the highest bidder?—I was first intended for Mr Mandeville, next destined to Colonel Talbot's new-found heir.

Sir Ol. His new-found bear you should say; but, Charlotte, Charlotte, how uncandid you are! when I proposed the last match I had not seen the man.

Char. Sir, you change your mind so often, and bandy me about in so extraordinary a manner, that I shall become a topic for public ridicule.

Sir Ol. Well, and if I do change my mind often, isn't it for your good? As one project starts up in my mind better than another, in order to take advantage of that, I must naturally contradict myself. The Spanish proverb says, a wise man often changes his mind, a fool never.

Char. According to that proverb, you should be a second Solomon: who you intend for me next I cannot possibly guess; but as I never will marry without your consent, I trust it will not be deemed undutiful, if I always retain a negative to myself, in a matter which so nearly concerns my happiness as the choice of a husband.   [*Exit.*

Sir Ol. I fear, like all great projectors and politicians, I refine too much; I spin the wires that compose my nets so fine, that though they answer the purpose of deceiving the eye, when their strength is tried, a touch breaks them—What's to be done? she actually sets my authority at defiance; but this comes of rich uncles leaving fat legacies to their nieces; it converts a father into a cypher.

Enter LADY OLDSTOCK *and* HARRIET.

Lady Old. Sir Oliver, Sir Oliver, the whole world is condemning you.

Sir Ol. So much the better; a quarter of the world never was right, but the whole is always wrong; you have brought me this good news, I suppose, knowing I was out of spirits.

Har. To contract for me, without my knowledge, and with an utter stranger too! as if I had not the common privilege of a thinking rational creature!

Sir Ol. Ecod, I think you have too much of that privilege: why, you ungrateful minx, do you fly in my face for endeavouring to get a count for you.

L. Old. A count! A strange kind of count!—the fellow made love to me.

Sir Ol. Then indeed must he be a strange kind of count.

L. Old. I shall sue for a separate maintenance.

Har. And I shall sue for the little property my father left in his hands.

Sir Ol. Damn it, since you have begun, come, fire away from both sides, volley after volley; don't spare me, I'll make you raise the siege at last; contradiction's my element, as fire is the Salamander's.   I can't have too much of it; my opinion is impregnable.

Har. It's in vain to speak to him.

L. Ol. Speak to him,   child!   now he's in all his g ory.

Sir Ol. Hobbes maintains that the whole world is in a state of warfare, and I believe him.

         [Speaking to himself.

L. Ol. I say, Sir Oliver, are you deaf?

Sir Ol. But it is a wise law in nature.

Har. Dear uncle, will you listen to me?

Sir Ol. Opposition calls forth the latent powers of the mind.

L. Ol. Was there ever any thing so provoking?

Sir Ol. Your greatest men have been formed by difficulties.

Har. Every moment is big with danger to my happiness.

Sir Ol. Methinks I now resemble the memorable column of English infantry at Fontenoy, marching down between two forts, with all their batteries playing upon it: whiz fly the small shot from the left; and bang go the great guns from the right; but on we march, firm as a wedge, without confusion, without disorder, without dismay; and quit the field of battle with honour.   [*Exit.*

Har. My principal fear is a quarrel between Count Pierpont and Mr Mandeville.

L. Ol. You had better speak to his friend, Captain Crevelt; for my part, I have no influence with the Count.

Har. Dear aunt, how can you talk thus? So fine a woman will never lose her influence.

L. Ol. Pray, Harriet, have you ever read that elegant fellow St Evremond's account of the lovely Ninon; she who retained her beauty and power of fascination to the age of eighty?

Har. I have never read St Evremond, madam.

L. Old. Then you have read nothing: he was the intimate friend of Fontaine, Racine, and Corneille; all the great men of his time valued his friendship: but what most endears him to me, was his esteem for the lovely Ninon—I shall never forget one of her letters, in which she mentions her first wearing spectacles; but, said that charming woman, as I had always a grave look, spectacles become me.

Har. I declare, aunt, I have always thought the same of you, when I have seen you with your spectacles on.

L. Old. But you're mistaken, Harriet, if you suppose I wear spectacles from any necessity I have for them—I wear them by way of prevention.

Har. As I hope to live, here comes the Count; he'll teaze me to death if I stay—I never saw you look so well, aunt.

L. Old. You may go, Harriet, and find Captain Crevelt—I'll once more try my influence with this Frenchman. [*Exit* HARRIET.

Enter COUNT PIERPONT.

L. Old. Well, Count: I hope you have changed your opinion since our last conversation, and that you're become a little more Anglicised.

Count. Eh bien! Madame, je ne puis pas comprendre, I no understand.

L. Old. Why, we have changed characters; you can't understand me now, and I coudn't understand you before: but, Count, I'd advise you to consider you are in England; and though it may be the etiquette in France to treat a married lady with as much attention as a single, it is in this country of jealous circumspection very dangerous: it is almost sufficient to cause a separation.

Count. Ah, Madame ! have a some pity on those whom your charms enslave, quand l'amour est dans le cœur ? il ait l'esprit comme lui meme ? dat is, ven love is in de heart, he make a dey understand blind as himself, by gar.

L. Old. The French are certainly the most agreeable people in the world; if they transgress, they make reparation with so good a grace, that it's delightful to be on good or bad terms with them.

Count. I made von grand faux pas ; but like good general, me vil profit by my loss. (*Aside.*)— Madam Oldstock is vat you call von grand bastion, or outwork : I will take a that first, and la petite citadel, mademoiselle Harriet, follow of course, by gar.

L. Old. Well, Count, I forgive you; but it's on condition that you are more circumspect in future.

Enter Sir Oliver *at the back of the Stage.*

Sir Ol. If I could lay my hand on Burn's justice in the library, that would set me right : but I think t's a question for gentlemen of the common law.— Eh ! what's all this ?

[*Seeing the* Count *and* Lady Oldstock.

Count. Madame, permettez moi baiser votre main; I must kiss a your von pretty hand in sign of reconciliation.   [*Kissing her hand.*

Sir Ol. I was thinking of the common law ; but here promises to arise a question for gentlemen of the civil law.

L. Old. Jealousy, Count, is a tree of English growth.

Sir. Ol. It may be a tree of English growth ; but it's a tree would never flourish, if a taste for French gardening did not so often make the branches sprout.

Count. Mon Dieu! quelle grand disproportion in your age and the chevalier Oldstock!

L. Old. When a woman marries very young, my Lord, a dozen years difference is nothing in the age of a husband.

Sir Ol. A dozen years! Damme, if there's a dozen months between us.

L. Old. That's a most beautiful brilliant, Count, on your finger—I think I never saw so large a one: the rich cluster of its rays cast a light actually celestial.

Sir Ol. If that poor diamond could speak now, perhaps we'd find it was not very celestially come by.

Count. To reconcile me complete, permettez moi to make you von present.

L. Old. Dear Count, I cannot think of accepting a ring of such immense value—No, no, Count, I am not such an infant as to wish to possess every thing that I admire.

Sir Ol. No, to be sure, you an't.—Why, Count, how is all this?　　　　　　*[Coming forward.*

L. Old. O heaven's! Sir Oliver!

Sir Ol. Yes, my Lady; does the great disproportion of our years frighten you?

Count. Upon my vord, Monsieur Oldstock, this is not behave with your usual politesse.

Sir Ol. Why, what the devil, man!—aren't you content with one of my chickens, but you must have my old hen to the bargain?

L. Old. Old hen!

Sir Ol. Yes, my Lady; when I had you first you were no pullet.

L. Old. Now there will be no end to his suspicions.

Sir Ol. Ecod, I think this is putting suspicion out of the question.—Well, my Lady, what have you to say for yourself? You asked me if I wasn't deaf; now, are you dumb?—Damn it, say something, if it's only to contradict me.

Count. Monsieur Oldstock, je suis—I am your very good friend.

Sir Ol. You are, Count; and what's more, I find you're my wife's friend.

L. Old. Sir Oliver, conscious as I am of the purity of my thoughts, I could look down with contempt on every extravagance to which your jealous temper hurries you: but when I consider how the fairest reputations are every day injured from the slightest foundations—if it should creep into the public prints—

Sir Ol. Then I'll give you a little comfort—nobody will believe it.

L. Old. The cool malignity of his temper is even more provoking than his jealousy—I can't bear to have been all my life reproached for nothing. [*Exit.*

Count. Monsieur Oldstock—

Sir Ol. Count Pierpont, no apologies: I am not at all angry with you, nor do I entertain any suspicion of my wife—Love of admiration is her ruling passion; and as long as she lives, she'll fancy herself an object of that admiration.

Count. Vous savez très bien my passion pour Mademoiselle Harriet.

Sir Ol. I know every thing—I now see your view in all this attention to Lady Oldstock: you imprudently made her your enemy, not knowing her character; but you have very wisely rectified your mistake—You see, Count, I'm a keen old fellow: I haven't lived for nothing so many years in the world.

Count. Mon Dieu! vous etes un Machiavel.

Sir Ol. Come along, Count. But, before you go, how do you think your friend Colonel Talbot stands affected as to matrimony? Do you imagine, if a fine girl was thrown in his way, that he'd marry her?

Count. Nothing more like, on my vord; il est un homme de gallantrie ? sans doute he has a de son, if that be no objection.

Sir Ol. Objection !—he should marry for that very reason, and get more sons, if it was only to convince the world that he has mended his hand in the business.   [*Exeunt.*

ACT THE FIFTH.

SCENE I.

Continues at MANDEVILLE'S.

Enter HARRIET *and* CHARLOTTE.

Har. I am half in love with Count Pierpont for his noble behaviour—The moment matters were properly explained to him, he withdrew his claim instantly—Well, I never more will hear the French spoken ill of; they carry the point of honour to a pitch of heroism—but, Charlotte, what is the matter? Your spirits are intolerably depressed!

Char. You only fancy so from the unusual gaiety of your own.

Har. I have a great mind to send Captain Crevelt to you; you are just fit company for each other: two moping, melancholy fools.

Char. From some conversation I have had with him, I take it that he is in love.

Har. And I fancy I have a fair friend much in the same situation.

Char. He leaves town to-day.

Har. Unless you issue your sovereign commands to the contrary.

Char. My sovereign commands! How you trifle! What influence have I over him?

Har. That influence which a beautiful woman will always have over a man of exquisite sensibility —Mandeville told me he was eternally talking of you.

Char. Talking of me! Lord, I wonder what the man can have to say about me!

Har. O! a thousand handsome things, I dare say: but if you wish to be satisfied as to the particulars, you may have them from the gentleman's own mouth, for here he comes; so I'll leave you together.

Char. Then you will be so ill-natured?

Har. Good-natured, sweet cousin.　　[*Exit.*

Char. Eternally talking of me! Whence, then, arose his sudden coldness and reserve, when I but too plainly discovered my partiality for him? Yet I may have been mistaken; a mind possessed of so much delicacy as his, might have deemed it criminal to address me on the score of love, at a time he thought I was intended for the son of his friend, Colonel Talbot—it is, it must be so—the pulses of my heart quicken at the thought—but he's here.

Enter CREVELT.

Crev. Miss Oldstock, as I mean to quit town this evening, and possibly may never see you again, I am come to solicit the honour of a few minutes conversation.

Char. Never see me again! I hope you are not going back again to India.

Crev. No, madam, that is not my intention.

Char. O! then I understand you; it is that compound of every female excellence, of whom you spoke to me in such raptures, who is the cause of your leaving us.

Crev. I own it, madam.

Char. But you talked of never seeing me again; is your mistress that jealous creature as to exact such a promise from you?

Crev. No, madam; that is a punishment I voluntarily inflict upon myself.

Char. You do say the most gallant things with the most sombre countenance; your wit and face, Captain Crevelt, are the diamond and its foil; the dark shade of the one lends a more vivid glow to the other's sparkling brilliancy:—what an alteration the presence of your mistress would make in your looks!—could you look thus in her presence?

Crev. In the present state of my heart, I could not look otherwise.

Char. No! not if she smiled upon you?

Crev. A smile from her would raise me from despair: but that, madam——Confusion! yonder I see Colonel Talbot; this is the second time to-day he has found me in earnest conversation with her.

Char. I didn't think it possible, till now, Colonel Talbot could put me out of temper.

Crev. Will he not suspect that I am meanly stealing myself upon her affections, and attribute her dislike of his son to me?—But he comes; I cannot meet his eye in the present state of my feelings— Adieu, dear Miss Oldstock!

Char. But are we never to meet again?

Crev. It is a sacrifice, madam, that pierces, and widows my heart for ever; but honour and gratitude demand it.   [*Exit.*

Enter COLONEL TALBOT.

Col. Wasn't that Captain Crevelt, Miss Oldstock, that parted from you?

Char. Yes, sir; he has just taken his leave of me, and said I shall never see him again.

Col. There is a refinement in Crevelt's temper, that to strangers makes his conduct at times appear very unaccountable; but I fancy I have discovered the cause of this extraordinary resolution.

Char. And sure, sir, you can prevail upon him to alter it?

Col. Then my lovely girl wishes he should alter his resolution?

Char. O, sir! is it possible to be acquainted with so noble, so accomplished, so brave a youth, and not esteem him? Never see me more!—

Col. It is as I suspected; and, indeed, as I wish; for who but Crevelt is worthy of such a woman? (*Aside.*) I hope, Miss Oldstock, you are now perfectly convinced that I would not purchase the greatest earthly happiness at the price of your peace of mind. Highly as my pride and natural affection would be gratified to call you daughter, I trust I can turn my eye with manly firmness from the bright, the flattering prospect; and, resigned to the dispensations of a Power who never afflicts his creatures but for wise and good purposes, point out a man in every respect, but birth and fortune, deserving of you.

Char. Birth and fortune, Colonel! despicable distinctions! When Nature asserts her superior claims to reverence, by ennobling the spirit, how low it lays the insolence of ancestry, and humbles the vanity of wealth!

Col. Madam, your words penetrate my very soul; with an aching, joyless heart, I look back to those imaginary scenes of happiness Fancy had painted in meeting with a son; the only pledge of love from the first object of my affections, and whose image still warms this desolated bosom—Birth! when I survey my own offspring, and behold poor Crevelt,

I am ashamed to think so empty a thing as family pride had ever any influence over me.

Char. But you will prevail upon him to alter his resolution?

Col. On one condition, madam.

Char. What is that, Colonel?

Col. That you will receive him as my adopted son—Your father's objections I will remove, by making him your equal in fortune.

Char. I don't know how to thank you, Colonel; but, perhaps, he's already gone.

Col. Gone, without seeing me first—impossible! But what says my sweet girl to the proposal I have made her?

Char. You are so good, so disinterested, and so generous, that it is impossible not to acquiesce in any proposal of yours: but yet I will not make you an absolute promise—mind that, Colonel—till I find you have effectually accomplished my request, and induced Captain Crevelt to alter his resolution.
                                                            [*Exit.*

Col. Luckily Sir Oliver has taken a very great liking to him; and told me that he would insist upon his passing a few days at his house, previous to visiting his relations.—Though Crevelt possesses the spirit of a lion, there is a gentleness and flexibility in his nature, which cannot resist solicitation from a friend.—O my heart, be still! though I am denied happiness in that quarter whence I fondly expected it, let me enjoy it as heaven thinks proper to bestow the boon, by exerting my best efforts to impart it to the truly deserving.

Enter COUNT *and* MANDEVILLE.

Count. J'espere, Monsieur Mandeville, you are perfectly satisfy—sur mon honneur, had I known

Mademoiselle Harriet was engage, I never would pay l'addresse.

Mand. I believe it, Count; and hope you will forgive the warmth I was at first betrayed into.

Count. Mon Dieu! il est l'effervescence d'une grande ame; no brave man ever resign sa maitresse avec sang froid.

Col. Now, Mandeville, to completely remove your fears in regard to Harriet, know, I have made your peace with her uncle—would you believe it? he actually proposed his daughter to me—however, by the dint of argument, added to the influence of an old friendship, I at last brought him to reason.

Enter SIR OLIVER.

Sir Ol. Colonel, colonel, is this strict observance of treaty? the carriages are waiting for us at the door—were we not all to set off for my house immediately? did you not promise to pass ten days with me when you had contradicted me into consent at last?

Count. Monsieur Oldstock, your niece was very pretty to be sure; mais, mon Dieu! votre fille be very pretty aussi; me understand she vill not marry young Monsieur Talbot, and mon ami the Colonel vill not have her—eh bien, vat you say to me for von husband?

Sir Old. With all my heart and soul, Count—I don't know a French gentleman of a long time I have taken such a liking to—damn me! if you have not a fine roast-beef countenance.

Col. I fancy, Count, that lady's affections are also engaged.

Count. Je suis tres malheureux! all de English lady be engaged! but me be not surprised; for if de foreigner set so much value on de English lady, vat must their own countrymen, who know them better, do?

Sir. Ol. Why, what the deuce, Colonel, is all this? You won't marry my daughter yourself;— you won't suffer your son, whatever her inclinations may be, to marry her;—and now you put the Count against her.

Col. Will you leave the lady to her own choice?

Sir Ol. The worst of it is, I must do that.— Count, a word in your ear—to her yourself—you're a devilish straight, well-looking fellow; no appearance of frogs about you, except upon your coat.— I should like to see an union between France and England, if it were only because it has been so long thought a contradiction in politics.

Count. I wish it vid all my heart.   [*Exit.*

Col. How unsubstantial are all the projects of man, in whatever hope flatters him with happiness —this unhappy boy distracts me!

Sir Ol. Damn me! if I wouldn't send him down into Wales or Yorkshire—for about fifteen pounds a-year, you may get him decently boarded and clad, and educated into the bargain.

Enter a SERVANT.

Serv. I have been in search of Mr Talbot, sir, since you spoke to me; and have just heard that he is gone to one Jacob Wilkins's, an innkeeper near Smithfield.

Col. I am exposed, you see, already.

Sir Ol. It's your own fault if you continue to be exposed; come along, Colonel; yonder I see Captain Crevelt putting the women into the carriages: We'll drive round by this Wilkins's, and take this young mohawk by surprise; the moment you get possession of him, banish him into Wales.

Col. I will myself go in person to Wilkins's ; and from his own lips learn every particular respecting this unhappy youth, from the hour I left him in his care ; and as you propose going home that way, Sir Oliver, I will trespass so far upon your patience as to request you will wait for me whilst I make this inquiry.

Mand. Dear sir, don't make yourself so unhappy.

Col. What is there wealth can purchase I cannot possess ; my feelings are at once a satire and a lesson to avarice.   [*Exeunt.*

SCENE II.

A Room at JACOB WILKINS'S.

JOHNSON *and* MRS WILKINS *discovered at Tea.*

Mrs Wil. I'm sure I shall never forget the first time I was in this room ; where you see Mr Wilkins has his honour the Colonel's picture up—dear heart, what a handsome man he is ! it's a great pity he does not marry.

Johns. He's very much altered—consider, it's many years since that picture was painted ; his face is parched to the complexion of an old drum-head, and his hair is perfectly silver.

Mrs Wil. What effect silver hair may have upon your great ladies, I will not pretend to say ; but this I'll swear to ; bait your hook properly with gold, and a poor girl is a trout you may take with a single hair of any colour.   If it was not for his money, do you think I'd ever have married old Jacob Wilkins ?

Johns. Why, no, I hardly think you would ; but

why, my dear creature, has his name escaped your
lips? should he possess such a treasure? the man
worthy of you should always meet you with the ardour of a lover, and dart, as I do, with transport into your arms.

Enter BETTY.

Bet. O madam! madam! my master is come
home, and is raving like mad at your leaving the
bar, and drinking tea up stairs.

Mrs Wil. He doesn't know I have any body with
me?

Bet. Lord, ma'am, to be sure he doesn't; I told
him you were not well, and that you found the bar
too cold for you.

Mrs Wil. You're an excellent girl.

Johns. How the devil will you get me out?

Bet. I hear his cough at the foot of the stairs—
dear madam, he's coming up.

Johns. 'Sdeath, I'll run and shut myself up in
that little room yonder.

Mrs Wil. By no means! that's our own bed-
chamber; his bureau is in it; and as he pays his
brewer to-day, perhaps it's there he's going now for
money.

Bet. I have it, madam; I'll let down this window
curtain, and the gentleman may get behind it; if
my master asks why it is down, you may say you
were so ill, the light was too much for you.

        [*Drops the window curtain before* JOHNSON.

Mrs Wil. Such a servant is worth her weight in
gold.

Bet. Here, madam; tie this handkerchief about
your head; appear very bad indeed—there, madam
—let him come now when he pleases, we are ready
for him.   [*Exit.*

Enter WILKINS *and* AMBER.

Wil. So, Mr Amber, you have a curiosity to see the upper part of my house; you can't think how pleasant it is; my wife can tell you what a prospect there is on my upper story.

Am. Poor Mrs Wilkins is quite muffled up; she's very bad, poor woman; I'm sorry we disturb her.

Wil. Why, Fanny, my love, what's the matter? you were very well when I went out.

Mrs Wil. I have been seized, all of a sudden, with such a terrible pain in one side of my face I can hardly get my words out.

Wil. I am sorry for this, Fanny—but what wiseacre has let this curtain down? I can't bear to shut out the light of a fine day.

Mrs Wil. Has the brute a mind to be the death of me?   [*Seizing him by the arm.*

Wil. Will it do you any good to keep me in the dark?

Mrs Wil. To be sure it will, when I can't bear the light.

Am. Friend Wilkins, friend Wilkins, the light is too much for her.

Mrs Wil. You're a considerate man, Mr Amber, and I dare say make an excellent husband.

Wil. Well, well, then let the curtain remain down —come, Fanny, give your old Jacob a kiss.

Mrs Wil. I'm too fond of you, Jacob, and you take advantage of that.

Wil. No, but I don't—kiss me again, you fond fool, it will do you good.

Am. Ah! you're a happy couple; but you take the right method to be so, by giving way to one another.

Wil. But now we are up stairs, friend Amber, sit

down, and I'll go bring some money out of the next
room and pay you.

Mrs Wil. I beg of you, Jacob, to take him down
stairs and pay him: even your talking sets my head
distracted.

Wil. My dear, I sha'nt be two minutes settling
with him; it will affront him if you turn him out of
the room; you shall have the place to yourself immediately.   [*Exit.*

Re-enter BETTY.

Bet. Madam, you're undone, if you don't come
down stairs immediately: Ned, the new waiter,
saw Mr Johnson, and he as good as told me he'd
acquaint my master.

Mrs Wil. What shall I do? I'm afraid to leave
the room.

Bet. You needn't stop a minute; it's only squeezing Ned's hand, and slipping a sly half-guinea into
it, and all will be right.

Mrs Wil. O Betty, I wish he was well out of the
house—you'll excuse me, Mr Amber, a little; I'm
wanted down stairs.

                [*Exeunt* MRS WILKINS *and* BETTY.

Am. Don't notice me, child; business must be
minded—but let me see—suppose I sign my receipt,
and have it ready for him.

        [*Taking out his pocket-book and ink-horn.*

Enter WILKINS.

Wil. Here is the money, my old boy;—have you
got your receipt ready?

Am. I was going to sign it; but my eyes are so
dim, I can't see with that curtain down.

Wil. As my wife's not here to complain of the
light, I'll draw it up for you. [*Draws up the curtain.*

Am. That will do, I see plain enough now.

Wil. And so do I too—O the Jezebel.

Enter MRS WILKINS.

Mrs Wil. Ruined!

Am. My dear Mrs Wilkins, I beg ten thousand pardons for letting so much light into the room, but I declare I could not see to write my receipt.

Wil. Well, Mr Johnson, what brought you here? —what have you to say for yourself—are you come to rob my house?

Am. O! O! I fear the dimness of my eyes have made others too clear-sighted—but, friend Wilkins, don't be too hasty in judging.

Wil. 'Sdeath and fire, man, shan't I believe my own eyes?

Am. Not always—we are all apt to be suspicious at times—I'll wish you a good evening—there is my receipt:—the fondest couples will spar now and then —but I never like to meddle in family quarrels.— Wilkins, you certainly have a fine prospect on your upper story—good evening, good Mrs Wilkins.

[*Exit.*

Wil. Go, madam; pack up your alls, and leave my house immediately—if you are in want of a morsel of bread, it would give me pleasure to refuse it to you. As for you, sir, I'll take care your business shall be done with Colonel Talbot—I'll see you both beggars, and that will be some satisfaction to me.

Enter SERVANT.

Serv. Colonel Talbot is coming up stairs, sir, to speak to you.

Johns. Confusion! I'm undone.

Enter COLONEL TALBOT.

Col. Johnson here!

Wil. Yes, sir, Johnson; your worthy gentleman is here on a visit to that wretch, my wife.

Mrs Wil. Wretch, Mr Wilkins!

Wil. Yes, madam, an ungrateful wretch.

Col. I'm sorry, Johnson, for this; I was given to understand you were come in search of my son.

Mrs Wil. Wretch! I'll discover all, if I'm ruined for ever. (*Aside.*)   He's not your son, sir—
                                    [*Going up to the* COLONEL.

Wil. Devil! devil! what is she going to say?

Col. Not my son! speak again, woman.

Wil. But, dear Colonel, sure you won't believe what this wicked woman will say?

Col. Away, villain, and let me hear her—alarmed Nature starts up in my heart, and opens a thousand ears to listen to her.

Mrs Wil. He lost your son, sir, when he was a boy of twelve years old; and you may be sure, sir, it wasn't the kindest usage made the child leave him; the booby he palmed upon you is his own. What a terrible thing it is to lose my character, when I sent for Mr Johnson for no other reason, I'm sure, but to tell him every thing; and for fear he might not believe me, I hid him behind that curtain, that he might hear my husband himself confess it.   [*Sobs and cries.*

Johns. (*Coming forward.*) This is the real state of circumstances, I assure your honour.

Col. Unprincipled, inhuman villain! let me hear the whole truth from your own lips, or by every power that's sacred and divine, this moment is your last.

Wil. Dear sir, put up your sword, and I'll tell you every thing.—What she says is partly true; your son strayed from me when he was about twelve years old; but had he been my own, I couldn't have used him better: as a proof of it, his mother, in her last illness, came, as she often did, privately to see him, and was so well pleased with my wife's and my treatment of her son, that she gave me a fifty pound bank-note—I shall never forget the day; it was the last time I ever saw her; she hung a small picture of herself, set in gold, about the child's neck, and wept bitterly over him.

Col. Can you produce that picture?

Wil. Your son took it with him—he was so fond of it, I could never keep it out of his hands but by locking it up, which I sometimes did, as the severest of all punishments I could inflict upon him.

Col. I must have better proof, if this tale is true, before I let you escape that justice I fear is due to your wickedness.   Johnson, take him from my sight, and let him be secured—I cannot bear to look at him.   Tell the company waiting for me, in carriages at the door, to come in : for I am so agitated, and anxious for more particulars, I cannot quit this detested spot.

Johns. They are here, sir.

[*Exeunt* JOHNSON, WILKINS, *and wife.*

Enter CREVELT, MANDEVILLE, CHARLOTTE, HARRIET, SIR OLIVER, LADY OLDSTOCK, *and* COUNT.

Crev. Dear sir, what is the matter?   Observing a confusion in the house immediately after you went in, we were alarmed for your safety.

Col. O Crevelt! I am the unhappiest of fathers; that creature whom you all suppose my son is not so.

Char. Good fortune be praised !

Col. He's son to the fellow who keeps this house. He says, my poor child strayed from him when a boy :—but this tale is so improbable, that I rather fear he has fallen a victim to this fellow's villany and avarice.

Crev. Dear sir, compose yourself, and hope human nature cannot be so depraved; it wrings my heart to see you in this distress. But who is this villain?

Col. His name is Wilkins. When I committed my child to his care, he lived at Henly: he pretends he lost him at twelve years old; and, O agony to think! if he indeed be living, he is at this moment a wandering outcast, and a beggar.

Crev. Merciful heaven! What do I hear? Can it be possible! Shall I, in my loved and honoured patron, find a fond and living father! Sir, did that man lose a son of yours at twelve years of age?

Col. Yes, Crevelt; I have no son but you now.

Crev. I am your son, sir—your happy son! that son you lost.

Col. You! You, Crevelt!

Crev. Yes, sir, the veteran whose name I bear took me with him at the age you mention from Henly, where I lived with the man you have just named, whom I always thought my father; it was the pride of poor Crevelt's heart to have me believed his son: I bore his name, and publicly acknowledged him as my father; for you, sir, could not have loved me better; his dying request to me was, still to retain the name of Crevelt, and never forget the man who made me a soldier.

Char. O Harriet! there is a chord of delight in my heart never touched before: and sure, he who made that heart now moves its springs to ecstasy by the finger of an angel.

Col. He talked of your taking with you a picture of your mother—had you ever any such thing?

Crev. I have it still, sir, and ever wore it next my heart. (*Producing the picture from his bosom.*) You see the frame is shattered:—it was by a musket-ball the day every body thought I was killed.

Col. It is indeed your mother; and see here those specks under the eye ; are they my child's blood, or the tears of a fond parent ?

Johnson to Caleb without. You must not come in : I have already explained every thing sufficiently.

Enter CALEB (*very abruptly*) *and* JOHNSON.

Ca. I tell you I will come in : Zounds ! will nobody father me ?

Col. Young man, you have been deceived ; you are Wilkins's son, not mine.

Ca. Pho, pho ! Father, do you think I know no better !

Johns. If you don't come out this moment, and no longer disturb my master, I'll take you by the shoulder.

Ca. Why, here's a fellow for you—forgets he is talking to a captain !

Col. That is a rank you are so utterly unfit for, that it would only expose you to unhappiness and ridicule ; therefore your commission shall be sold ; and for being one day my son, the purchase-money shall be appropriated to setting you up in business.

Johns. Well, what keeps you now ?

Ca. You are in a devil of a hurry, Mr Johnson : I find I must put up with old Jacob again ; but let me ask you one question, an't I to be entitled to half-pay for my services.

Johns. You shall have full-pay if you don't go about your business.   [*Shakes his cane at him.*

Ca. Well, if I can't be a half-pay captain, I'll be a no-pay captain—for, once a captain and always a captain.   [*Exit* CALEB.

Sir Ol. Captain Crevelt—I beg your pardon, Captain Talbot, give me your hand ; you want nothing now but a wife, and if my daughter Charlotte—

Count. Eh bien ! Monsieur Chevalier, you have forgot—

Sir Ol. Why, no, Count, I have not forgot; but you must know, that whatever my respect for you may be, there is not that man living whose alliance I so much desire as Colonel Talbot's ; besides, I understand there is another branch of the family of my mind.

Count. Chevalier, I love and I respect the English, and by gar, me will have a wife among you.

Mand. It is not in words to express my pleasure —To make a bosom friend, and find a near relation, in less time than others form a common acquaintance, overflows my heart with transport.

Lady Olds. I could wish also to show how this affecting discovery touches me, if I was not apprehensive, Sir Oliver, of your unfortunate suspicious temper.

Sir Ol. Captain Talbot, be so good as to step this way—do give my wife a kiss ; I know, my dear, your lips itch for it ; and with all her faults, believe me, she has a heart that beats in unison to the feelings of all present, and a tear for misery and friendship.

Col. Miss Oldstock, it is your father's wish and mine to unite our families—now that I have a son I can propose to you, there is only your acceptance of him necessary to make me happy.

Char. Why, sir, if the gentleman has but courage to speak for himself—

Sir Ol. As I don't expect the pleasure of contradiction from either party on this occasion, I'll join their hands, (*joining their hands*) without waiting for an answer——there—Colonel, you are now one of my family.

Col. That assurance, Sir Oliver, seals and com-

pletes my happiness—You, Mandeville, shall share
a portion of my fortune as a son; and may happiness
still wait on you and your lovely Harriet—And
now (*addressing the audience*), if this court-mar-
tial, to whom we appeal, acquit us with honour, I
shall bless the hour my boy said, *He would be a
Soldier.*

ENGLAND PRESERVED;

A

TRAGEDY.

IN FIVE ACTS.

AS PERFORMED AT THE

THEATRE-ROYAL, COVENT-GARDEN.

BY

GEORGE WATSON, Esq.

DRAMATIS PERSONÆ.

EARL OF PEMBROKE,	*Mr Pope.*
BISHOP OF WINCHESTER,	*Mr Hull.*
EARL OF CHESTER,	*Mr Farren.*
EARL WILLIAM,	*Mr Middleton.*
EARL OF SURREY,	*Mr Holman.*
JOHN DE WARRENE,	*Mr Curties.*
EARL OF LINCOLN,	*Mr Davies.*
ROBERT FITZWALTER,	*Mr Richardson.*
FRENCH PRINCE,	*Mr M'Cready.*
COUNT DE NEVERS,	*Mr Haymes.*
VISCOMTE DE BEAUMONT,	*Mr Claremont.*
ENGLISH SQUIRE,	*Mr M'Cready.*
FRENCH GUARD,	*Mr Powell.*
HERALD,	*Mr Thompson.*
MESSENGER,	*Mr Williamson.*
LADY SURREY,	*Miss Wallis.*

ENGLAND PRESERVED.

ACT THE FIRST.

SCENE I.

Gloucester.   A Hall.   Flourish.

Enter the LORD PROTECTOR *and* CHESTER.

Prot. Thus far, 'tis well.   Gloucester hath op'd
        her gates
Most opportunely for the prince.   We here
May find a present safety and retreat,
A momentary calm—but such as comes,
Awful and deep, foreboder of a storm—
    Ches. Let the storm burst; we'll brave it's fullest
        rage,
My Lord Protector—still I cry to arms !
Nursed in the lap of war, and trained from youth
To deeds of daring, with great Cœur-de-lion,
In France, in Sicily, in Palestine,

To scourge the infidels, contemn the French,
I cannot stoop to parley where I hate.
Old Chester's blood revolts against these Franks,
Against their slaves, our shameless traitor Lords.

 Prot., Since thus defection triumphs through the
   state,
Thou might'st as well command the lonely pine,
Standing defenceless on the rocky steep,
To stop the blast, and roll it back to heaven,
As to oppose our small and wearied band
Against our barons, while thus leagued with France.

 Ches. Are we submissive, then, to hug our chains?

 Prot. No. Let us try conciliation's power,
Strive to subdue our restless brethren's minds:
The lenient voice of peace may call them home,
And melt the hearts that war could never tame.

 Ches. England, too long by scenes of blood de-
   based,
Too long to riot and rebellion loosed,
Hath lost for ever all her ancient pride.

 Prot. And yet to England's pride shall Pembroke
   trust.
If that should fail me, welcome then despair;
Then death be glory: But, O native land!
I love thee so, with all thy failings love,
I still must trust thee when thou'rt least thyself.

 Ches. But should'st thou, in those treacherous
   bosoms, plant
Remorse——

 Prot. Why then our happy isle is saved,
And foreign tyrants ne'er shall vex it more.
Were all united in one common cause,
Soon should we sweep their rabble down our cliffs,
To court the angry waters for retreat;
Then, as the rocky bulwark of our isle,
Unshaken, beats the assailing billows back,

Should we, one people, owning but one cause,
Mock their vain efforts to regain our shore.

    Ches. By heaven's own light! I venerate thy
        zeal.
I'll take the hazard of such goodly plans.
                         [*Distant shouts.*

    Prot. Ha!—Busy are the times, each moment
        claims
Exertion.   To my sacred charge, the prince—

    Ches. First let me fly, and learn whence this
        alarm.   [*Exit.*

    Prot. (*Alone.*) What more than mortal powers
        my station claims!
Shaken by age, I totter with its weight;
Yet, while my country calls on me for aid,
I still must serve her, till death close the scene.
O! could the censuring multitude but know
The ceaseless cares that wait on him who rules,
Forbearance would they give, for rash reproach,
Making an undisguised abuse of power,
And not misfortune, cause of discontent.
But thou, all-wise Disposer of our fate,
If these my labours be for England's good,
Grant them success for thy once-favoured isle,
That peace and union guard her cliffs again!
So may her name to distant times descend,
Revered by mortals, and approved by thee!
How sweet this converse!—My old heart feels
    now—

Re-enter CHESTER.

    Ches. Arms are abroad. Descending to the plain,
A force is spied along the neighbouring heights,
With many a banner streaming to the wind,
Whose bearings cannot yet be justly traced.

    Prot. The strength of France is now at Dover
        Castle,

Another army cannot spring at once,
To meet us in the west.

   Ches. O! let it come :
Our walls are fully manned.

   Prot. I think each post
Sufficient for a desperate defence.

   Ches. Lo! from our widowed queen, in sorrow,
     comes
The prelate Winchester.

Enter WINCHESTER.

   Prot. My reverend Lord,
Has this alarm renewed her highness' fears?

   Win. Exhausted by the horrors of the times,
Even in the sanctuary she dreads the worst :
For there, even there, the sounds of battle spread,
And, as the trumpet broke the peaceful prayer,
She wildly to her bosom caught her son,
And cried, the murderers' daggers were undrawn.

   Prot. O! bid her not despair, but still believe
Our arms may triumph, and (her power restored)
She long may hold a loyal people's love !

   Win. It is the parent, not the queen, that mourns.
She'll often gaze with anguish on the prince,
And bless the houseless beggar, that can strain
Her naked babe, in safety, on her breast ;
But she with fearful love surveys her son,
While thus, a thorn, rankling in faction's side,
That they will pluck, or perish in the attempt.

   Ches. Then they shall perish, or their passage
     force
Through these our bodies, e'er they reach the king.
                   [*Shouts increase.*

   Prot. The ferment swells without. Good Win-
     chester,
Attend, and bear the tidings to the queen.

Enter a Messenger.

Mes. My Lord Protector, joy!
The host without are of your kindred, friends,
Who, flying from the tyranny of France,
Yield up their swords, confiding in thy truth,
And hail prince Henry their liege lord and king.

Win. High heaven be praised!

Prot. Submission so well-timed
Must make atonement for their past misdeeds.
Admit the chiefs. But say, who leads them on?

Mes. I caught the tidings from the general voice.
But all, my Lord, cry out Earl William's name.
                              [*Retires.*

Prot. My son, my eldest hope, my hero, come!
Then Pembroke's heart is whole. My spirits flow
One way. The ruler's duties press not now
Against the parent's. I am doubly strong.
Yet for a while these feelings must I check,
And probe his spirit to the very quick.
My soul yearns on the boy. Good friends, forgive
These strong emotions.

Ches. We partake thy joy.

Win. Thus may just heaven lead every subject
          home,
In peace and love, to form one flock again!

Re-enter the Messenger, introducing EARL WIL-
  LIAM *and Knights, who make submission to* PEM-
  BROKE.

Mes. Behold, my Lord, the barons here attend.

Prot. Earl William Mareschal, and ye knights,
          arise.

Will. O! my father. [*Approaching with eager-
          ness.*

Prot. My Lord, as Mareschal (*coldly*)
Of England, 'tis my duty bids accept,

And prize thy services.   A father, sir,
Knows not of state necessities; he feels
As well as judges, keenly feels : and when
A son pulls down that image of respect
That Nature hath infixed on filial breasts,
The father bears a sting so sharp, a wound
So deep indeed, that words of penitence
Must long, long vibrate on his deadened sense,
Ere they can touch his soul, and pour the balm
That filial tenderness alone can give.
Five sons I have, and thou, of all the five,
Hast been the one to wound my aged heart,
Cancelling the peace thy brethren's love bestowed.
   Wil. O sir, these words are worse to me than
          death.
Heaven knows how much I venerate my sire.
That life thou gav'st, for thee I'd yield with joy.
   Prot. Thy deeds have greatly proved this solemn
          truth.
'Twas filial love that tore thee from my side,
Sent thee to league thyself with England's foes,
And guide the battle's blind, impetuous rage,
Though I stood victim of the doubtful strife !
   Will. Blot out remembrance of such dire events.
With John, oppression's lawless reign hath ceased,
And all resentment's buried in his grave.
But when he broke the charter we obtained,
When forth to war he led his hireling bands,
Marked every footstep in his subjects' blood,
While desolation followed where he went,
Our castles smoked, our wives and children bled,
And suppliant Misery knelt and wept in vain—
What medium could a free-born spirit keep ?
   Prot. He might have died to guard his native
          rights,
And not have sold them to a foreign lord.
I knelt, no minion of despotic power.

Deep in my heart our liberties I held,
But saw, with shame, this isle betrayed to France,
And trembling stood aloof, to catch the time
When I might act, and save our sacred cause.
    Will. But my impatient nature—
    Prot. What! impatient!
In private strifes, men may be testy now,
And now be calm. A nation's welfare rests
Not on a temper's turn.—Thou show'st thine age.
    Will. Father, I stand in conflict with thy words,
Like the slight reed against the northern blast.
Yet, by the blood I'm ready now to shed
In Henry's cause, I firmly swear to heaven,
I meant my country's good in all my deeds.
    Win. Nay, look, young man, through fields where
            freedom dwelt,
And independence scorned all foreign yokes,
Ere yet thy rashness threw our all at stake,
And see the sad reverse of former times!
See, where the stranger o'er our fruitful fields—
    Will. In pity stop, thou strik'st upon a string
That vibrates to despair. Disgraceful day,
That saw us leagued with France! 'Twas madness
            all.
For, as the eaglet gazes on the sun
Till every object shows to him in fire,
My fancy, warmed by Freedom's fiercest flame,
Imaged her form, where she, alas! was not.
I've waked from faithless dreams to horrid truths,
To curse delusions that have damned my fame.
    Prot. My son, my son! and hast thou found the
            faith
Of France, the tainted Herculean robe,
A pledge of peace—to torture, and destroy?
    Will. O father, trust thy blood that fills my veins.
Believe me true, by these a soldier's tears.
Thus let me hide my face upon thy breast.

Prot. My boy, my hero! thou once more art
       mine,
Thy nature pure, ingenuous as before,
Too fixed in honour for deceitful times.
Be thus, my William, ever next my heart,
My prop, my comfort. Hadst thou known the force
Of love parental, thou hadst never left
These aged arms—but well, well, well—my griefs
Are o'er, and now they will but heighten joy.

    Will. My father, and my own true countrymen!
O! blest exchange for false unnatural friends!
I would not yield these feelings for all France.
Away, seditious spirits! who shall dare
Again exhaust this cup of kindred peace,
And plant dissension in our happy isle?

    Prot. Now to our stations, Lords. The crisis comes,
The awful crisis of our England's fate.
Ye, whose hearts beat but for your native land,
Be firm, repress vain boasts, delusive hopes,
And let us rather contemplate misfortune;
Not thence to sicken, and make cause of fear,
But to attune our spirits to the times,
And fix at that sublimity of courage
That can admit no conqueror—but death.

    Ches. This patriot energy will force success,
Though host on host oppose.

    Prot. Be patient still.
We must advance, in one united tide,
Slow and impressive, like the general swell
Of ocean, rolling to its boundary cliffs,
And not, like torents of dissolving snow,
Destructive, but exhausted, as they fall.
All then to arms! Hence, banished be repose,
Hence, be our mansion on the tented field,
And all our business war; till that great day,
When England's rescued from a foreign yoke!
                [*Flourish.—Exeunt.*

ACT THE SECOND.

SCENE I.

*The French Camp before Dover, with a distant
View of the Castle.*

Rejoicing.—Enter the FRENCH PRINCE, NEVERS,
and BEAUMONT, *from the* PRINCE'S *tent.*

 Fr. Pr. Hail to this day, this proud, auspicious
   day,
That sees us peerless lord of England's throne !
Our rival John sleeps safely with his sires,
And leaves a baby to resist our might.
All then is ours. Proclaim a public feast,
That full festivity through all the camp
Speak the large measure of the general joy.
 Nev. Health and prosperity to England's lord !
 Fr. Pr. Yes, now methinks this island part of
   France,
And much we glory, thus to have acquired
Such bright appendage to our father's crown.
Hence, shall one law the rival lands unite,
This fertile isle the store-house be to France,
These cultured fields for her their grain produce,

These venturous merchants brave for her the seas,
And severing waters be but as the streams,
Designed to waft these treasures to her shores.

 Beau. Vast is the work your sword hath here
   achieved:
Yet think, O prince, whereon your triumph stands.
We cannot hold this country at our feet,
Unless her rebel children bind her down.
You've sworn to keep their antiquated laws,
And should you swerve from such fair promise now,
They may desert, nay, 'gainst us turn their arms.

 Fr. Pr. We cannot keep the conquest we have
   gained !
I say, we can, we will.   The lion's bound
In chains ; and though he roar, and threat and rage,
He cannot harm his master through the toils.
We know these barons swell with bitter gall,
That we neglect to bend us to their will,
And make us minister to their caprice.
But do they think, for them we've crossed the seas,
For them we've spent the treasure and the blood
Of our own kingdom ? O impolitic
And shallow men ! to think we would refuse
An empty oath, to win so fair a realm !

 Nev. Sire ! hither come the leaders of the tribe.

  Enter SURREY, LINCOLN, *and* FITZWALTER.

 Fr. Pr. Most valiant sirs, a gracious welcome, all.
Why so long absent in these times of joy ?

 Lin. Prince, we've been watching Dover tower,
   in hopes
Thereon to see the flag of truce displayed.

 Fitz. Lincoln saith true, and I, sir, will say true.
The English scorn those councils to attend,
Whereat their voices with contempt are heard.

 Fr. Pr. Fitzwalter, whence this lack of courtesy ?

Ye share our bosom's secrets, noble friends.
                              [*Trumpets.*
Our herald comes. Brave English, now attend.

Enter a French HERALD.

Well, man, doth Hubert own our clemency,
And yield this fortress, to save loss of blood?
    Her. Dread prince! he scoffs at all your terms
        proposed.
    Fr. Pr. The fool! did'st thou not say, his master,
        John,
Was dead, and threaten, should he cross our will,
His captive brother should, beneath his eyes,
Be tortured unto death?
    Her. My liege, I used
Each art persuasive, and each threat, in vain.
He said, if John were dead, his children still
Survived, to whom the same allegiance fell;
And for his brother—though his heart grew sick
At those my words, yet as he held yon towers
In trust but for his king, he had not power
To bend the public to his private cares.
    Sur. My generous countryman!   [*Aside.*
    Fr. Pr. Most insolent!
But will the garrison support the slave?
    Her. He spoke, my Lord, the general sentiment.
The people swore to dash their children down—
Their wives, themselves—down yonder steep to
        death,
Ere they betray their king, and yield to France.
And as they saw me from the hill descend,
They sent a sort of frantic shout on high,
Confirming their decree.
    Fr. Pr. Regard we not
This castle-crowned cliff, whose height alone
Withstands our conquering arms: but let us march
Against the northern lands; and when we've stormed

The very temple of the state itself,
Soon shall this altar, to its idol pledged,
Its idol, Independence, prove our prize,
And France's genius seize it for her shrine.

    Sur. Never ; no, never shall thy country's genius
Pluck down our independence ? Sir, thou dream'st ;
Thou hast infringed thine honour in the thought.

      Fr. Pr. (*Aside.*) Such touchy fools !—Why,
        Surrey, so severe !
'Tis not for friends to peer about for words,
Thence to extract some semblance of offence.
Thou dost forerun my thought of injury.

    Nev. Ye testy men, so national, so proud,
Will ye for ever thus mistrust our lord ?
Who rescued you from out oppression's gripe,
Who gave you treasures in your time of need,
Who clothed your fields with troops, your seas with
        ships,
And set his life at hazard, for your sakes ?
This gracious prince !—and now you doubt his
        truth,
And now you thank him with contracted brows,
And taunting words, and still more taunting looks.

    Lin. Nay, good Nevers, thou wrong'st our gra-
        titude.
We owe the very being of our cause
To his support, and feel the debt we owe.

    Fr. Pr. Your cause is ours ; we have one cause.
      We claim
No recompense but faith and truth.

    Sur. If faith
Be kept with us, faith will be kept with thee.
But do thy deeds, nay, even thy very words,
Accord with that same oath thou once hast sworn,
The oath to keep our liberties entire ?
We're firm to that great comprehensive bond.

This sword hath sent one tyrant to the dust ;
It knows its duty for the next.   No more.
  Nev. Unruly man, that dares insult his lord,
All gentle as he is, with such foul threat !
I know thy treachery, know thy changeling mind,
Thy love-sick bosom, thy insidious tricks—
Thou art a traitor, Surrey.
  Sur. Ha ! by heaven !
Thou answer'st for that word.
    [SURREY *attempts to draw his sword;* FITZWAL-
    TER *and* LINCOLN *interfere.*
  Nev. Nay, nay, thy hand
Lay not upon thy sword; burst not with spleen,
Thou froward man, I've proof—
  Sur. Monster, of what ?
Ah ! ha ! a death-like freezing through my veins—
My wife !—my child !—peace—(*Aside.*) Proof of
    what ?
  Fr. Pr. O friends,
Compose this strife : keep your high mettle for
The common foe.   Nevers, thou art too warm ;
Our trusty Surrey spoke a solemn truth.
May every tyrant fall beneath his sword !
We know no tyrant here.   (Sawest thou his look ?
    (*Aside to* BEAUMONT.)
Watch Surrey through these times, there's danger
    in him.)
Come, Lords of either kingdom, cousins all,
Hence, on for Lincoln; which will soon be ours,
And with it all the empire of the north.
  Beau. These unconnected castles soon will fall,
And then our sovereign may enjoy the fruits
Of these his labours—dignity and ease.
  Fr. Pr. Our present fortunes are most pleasing
    too.
Sweet is occasional suspense we deem,
When much to hope, and little's left to fear,

Cousin Nevers, associate with our English friends,
Lead on to Lincoln our victorious bands;
While we to London, there to hold our state,
As lord of England, with more show of pomp
Than that famed city hath e'er yet beheld.

[*Flourish.—Exeunt the* FRENCH PRINCE, NE-
VERS, *and* BEAUMONT.

SURREY, LINCOLN, *and* FITZWALTER (*who walks
wrapt in musing.*)

Sur. Are we awake? are we on English ground?
Nay, are we Englismen? we're not, we're not—
I had forgotten—we're the slaves of France.
Good powers! there was a time—there was! O
      shame!
When, had a miscreant Frenchman raised his breath
Against mine honour, though destruction stood
His champion, this good sword had sent an answer.

Lin. Thy passion, Surrey, hurried thee too far—

Sur. Too far, when that insulting slave, Nevers—
Wretch that I am, I'd felled him to the earth,
Had not the thoughts of those, beyond myself,
Rushed on my heart, and tempered my hot blood.
O thou sole object of my every care,
Thou, sister-being, dearer than my own,
My best beloved Matilda! and thou, boy,
Sweet pledge, confirming this our bond on earth,
And lengthening all our loves beyond the grave!
Ye make the warrior the soft son of peace:
O! but for thee, I'd stop this tyrant's flight,
And fall a martyr, thus to save our cause.

Lin. Surrey, for shame! shake off this tender
      mood;
Thus to be melted by domestic thoughts,
Is soldier-like!

Sur. Yea, on my faith! it is.
He feels not as a soldier ought, who feels

Not as a man , for these same tender ties
Of love domestic, multiplied and mixed,
Through numberless sweet mazes, form the chain
Of this life's interest, and mark the way
To public duties, and to public praise,
As soldier, subject, citizen, and man.

 Lin. These melting, these prevailing arguments,
Struck not thy fancy, when thy wife was left,
Thy child, thy castle, thy paternal seats,
To wage the battle 'gainst the faithless John !

 Sur. 'Twas love for them that led me first to war.
For private happiness must ever wait
On public fortune : and, when John assailed
Our chartered liberties, I flew to arms
To guard the sacred treasure, and therein
To guard each sweet endearment of my hearth
At home.   But since our cause of war hath ceased,
In place of one a thousand tyrants rise,
Ruin on ruin hurries, all's despair—
Panting, aghast, distracted, I recede,
And yield me up to tenderness for those
Whose safety bade me throw mine own away.

 Lin. Whence all this rhapsody ?——Say, what
   do'st thou ?—

 Sur. I'll seek my lovely dame, my helpless babe,
And, rooted at their side, shake hands with Fate.
What ! not a word, Fitzwalter ? Fare thee well.
Fare thee well, Lincoln, too.   I dare ye both,
On English honour, to betray my flight.
We'll meet again perhaps, or friends, or foes.

            [Exit.

LINCOLN, *and* FITZWALTER.

 Lin. Yes, we shall meet again, but meet in blood.
Surrey may flatter; I am firm to France,
For honour, wealth, and power are her own,

And mine, through her: Fitzwalter! ho! arouse!
Speak! Art thou dreaming?

Fitz. Would to heaven I were!
O my poor country! lost, abandoned isle!
Away, ye needless trappings, ye are toys,
                              [*Throws down his arms.*
There are no hearts to use ye, as of old.
Woe's me! that I should live to see the day,
When England calls, through all her fields, for help,
And have not power to give her ought but groans!

Lin. Whence this despair? when conquest on
              our arms—

Fitz. Away, thou'rt with ambition mad, and mad
With triumph, though thy native land's the prey.
I tell thee, France respects not our great cause.
Are we, at councils; are we, in the field,
Treated as free-born Britons, equals all
With these same upstart foreigners? O shame!
O vengeance for insulted rights! Shall those,
Who once could spurn a tyrant of their own,
Submit thus meanly to their very tool?

Lin. What! hast thou caught the infection of the
              times?
Fly then, and fawn before young Henry's feet,
Before the son of John; fly, beg thy chains.

Fitz. No, no: Thou know'st too well I cannot.
        No:
Cherish the child of him who killed my child,
Cherish the damned murderer's progeny?
The pallid spectre of my daughter dead,
Would thwart my way, and rouse my passions up
To madness, aye, to kill and not caress.
Perish the hated house!—I have no hope.

Lin. Come, come, brave man; thy fears a while
              suspend.
Let us rush forward to the long-sought goal;
And there arrived, we may compose all doubt,

All jealousy, or just or not, 'gainst France,
And fix our cause upon its proper base.
 Fitz. Yes, I must on, through doubt and hate
   must on.
Unhappy man ! I've no alternative.
But when our infant tyrant bites the dust,
We then may turn upon these foreigners,
Teach them to venerate our ancient laws,
To dread our vengeance for those laws attacked,
To own that independence guards our cliffs,
And, through all chances, England must be free.
          [Exeunt.

ACT THE THIRD.

SCENE I.

At SURREY's *Castle. The grand Hall, ornamented
with Trophies of the* SURREYS.

LADY SURREY, *and her Son*, YOUNG PLANTAGENET.

 L. Sur. The evening bell hath tolled, and Surrey
   not
As yet arrived !—Ah me !—Joy, long deferred,
Preys on the heart like very sorrow.
 Boy. Nay,
Why sighest thou so, dear mother ? Art thou now
Unhappy, when my father's coming?
 L. Sur. No,
Best comforter, the time but moves too slow.
I should be happy.
 Boy. O yes ! that thou should'st :
For all the castle seems alive and gay,
To meet Earl Surrey.—On the hill his knights
Are posted, all so bright in arms ! Around
The moat his tenantry are dancing ; while,
Upon the draw-bridge, sits the bard, who chants
Such stories of our ancestors, such deeds—
Is all that truth the minstrel sings?

L. Sur. Yes, boy:
And let the glorious legend warm thy breast
With emulation of thy father's fame.
Look on these walls, with various trophies hung,
The Paynim's scimitar, the Gallic spear,
The shattered standard, and the shield defaced ;
And think the shades of those, who placed them
          there,
Still move, majestic, round this reverend pile ;
Still, in the hollow murmurs of the wind,
At evening's close, from yon dark grove of pines,
Or yonder battlements sublime, they fire
Thy youthful fancy, call thee on to fame,
To swell these records of paternal worth,
And, ripe in glory, e'en surpassing theirs,
Transmit the palm of virtue to thy sons.

Boy. Would I were old enough to be a soldier,
Go with my father, and fight, side by side !

L. Sur. O ! may thy manly prime fulfil the hopes
Thy childhood gives ! Be virtuous for my sake,
And I will bless the bitter pangs I've borne,
My child-bed groans reflect upon with joy,
To think I've given to my native land
A guardian hero, and a faithful son.
O ecstacy of thought ! maternal bliss !
When my own child, by all the world approved,
Comes to my bosom to demand the meed
Of praise parental, to confirm his fame !

Boy. Hark ! the sound of horses—no, 'tis the
          wind,
That howls among the branches of the firs.

L. Sur. My very heart sprung wildly with the
          thought
That Surrey—said he not, that ere the dark
He would arrive ?

      [LADY SURREY *goes towards the great window.*
Boy. The letters said so, mother.

L. Sur. I see no object on yon dusky plain ;
Far as my eye can stretch, 'tis vacant all ;
And night, in dark-blue vapours rolling, sweeps
Along the horizon.   Haste, my Surrey, haste,
And let this poor heart know content once more !
    Boy. I wish my father would arrive.
    L. Sur. He will,
My child : he'll surely come ! he'll come ere long.
Thou'rt like thy father, now ; like what he was,
When youth's soft tints still wantoned o'er his face,
And when he first—O, bless that heavenly time !
Drew from my bosom a congenial flame.
Ye seats of Surrey, witness of our loves,
How oft, within your halls, the midnight lamp
Hath burnt unheeded ; while enwrapt I leaned
To hear the lover's in the soldier's tale :
Or, 'neath your high o'er-arching trees we've sat,
At still of eve, to watch the pale-orb'd moon,
And hear night's songster call, throughout the grove,
The sweetened echo to increase his song,
Till silence was, and we in silence joyed—
Ye seats of Surrey ! your lost lord returns,
Those days of bliss domestic to renew,
And bid, once more, the festive voice of peace,
Through all your haunts, be heard !—Hark, hark !
        I hear—
    Boy. Yes, yes, it is. (*Horn sounds.*) There, there !
        the bugle-horn !
    L. Sur. He comes, he comes ! ye heavens, be
        praised ! he comes !
John, let us meet the hero.   O my heart !
I pant to fly, and yet—my tottering knees—
Give me but fortitude for this sweet trial !
His footstep !—O !—kneel for his blessing, boy.
My Surrey—
        [*As* LADY SURREY *advances, enter a* KNIGHT,
        bloody, and supporting himself upon his

*lance. The Lady screams, and the Boy flies
to his Mother.*

Kni. Dame, forgive—

L. Sur. Who, bloody man,
Who art thou ?

Kni. O, my honoured mistress !

L. Sur. Mercy !
That voice !—

Kni. Thy faithful Eadwald.

L. Sur. Horror ! O !
Horror! he's dead—that sight—he's dead, he's dead!

Boy. My father dead ?

L. Sur. My child, my child, what are we ?

Kni. Softly, sweet lady ; he is still alive.

L. Sur. Ye powers of mercy ! take my thanks
for that !

Kni. But—

L. Sur. " But !"—In pity to my miseries, tell,
O ! tell me all at once.

Kni. Thy noble Surrey,
Suspected of the French, was forced to fly,
Ere yet his plans were ripe : his route was traced :
Our chosen band, assailed on every side,
Fell, man by man, defending their loved lord,
Who, like a madman, dealt destruction round,
Till, fainting—

L. Sur. Fainting ! Ah ! then he did die ?

Kni. No, dearest lady ; faint with toil he fell,
And prisoner but to numbers, bade me fly
To tell thee he was safe : he gave a look
At mention of thy name, that might have moved—
But tis enough—madam, in truth he's safe.

L. Sur. How is he safe, a prey to vengeful foes ?
A prey—O ! we are lost, my child, we're lost
To every joy. This sudden death of hope
Disturbs my judgment. Tell me, sir—alas !
Where can I turn me ?

Kni. Here must thou await
The issue of these wars, and trust in heaven
That Surrey's virtue must ensure his—
   L. Sur. Death !
Triumphant malice never can endure
That he should live, whom, living, it must fear.
Perhaps even now—distraction !—I must go.
   Boy. Nay, mother, wilt thou leave me all alone ?
   L. Sur. My child, my child, O ! do not drive me
      mad.
   Boy. If that I were a man—
   L. Sur. Would unto heaven
Thou wert ! Yet I am strong to think and act.
Woman hath oft her sex's bounds o'erstepped
To fill the measure of unruly passion :
And, when all nature prompts me to the deed,
When virtue calls me, with inspiring voice,
Shall I refuse to show an equal fire,
And, for a husband, rise above my sex ?
No ! I will forth, and seek his prison gloom.
   Kni. Do not give way, sweet mistress, to such
      thoughts.
Thou can'st not travel through a hostile land,
And brave the horrors every step would show.
I scarcely stole my journey through the night ;
For, 'mid the darkness from each hill to hill,
Responsive, blaze the signal fires : along
The roads, the frequent noise of armed troops,
And call of watchword, mark the foe at hand :
While, o'er the neighbouring fields, the doleful
      screams
Of peasants plundered by the greedy French,
Warn of the dangers that await such track.—
Thou'lt sink a victim to these scenes.
   L. Sur. No, no :
The mind, enwrapt with one o'erpowering thought,

Yields not to fears, would harrow it, if void.
I am resolved—wilt thou conduct my steps?

 Kni. I'll bind my wounds, and follow thee—to
   death.

 Boy. O! let me go with you, pray, pray.

 L. Sur. These times
Of blood are not for tender babes to brave.
O heaven! what am I doing?—Doubt, away!
Thy grandsire Pembroke will protect thee, John,
Till I return—till I return? Well—peace.
Come, Eadwald, call thy strength and spirits up;
I'll take the peaceful pilgrim's staff and garb;
Do thou the same, and we shall cheat the foe.
      [*The* KNIGHT *retires.*

 Boy. Then thou wilt bring my father back with
   thee?

 L. Sur. O! O! Good powers, assist me!—So I
   hope.
Unhappy island, prey to civil war!
Such are thy miseries, such thy fearful state!
The helpless infant's robbed of its support,
A parent's tenderness:—the widow sinks,
In silent anguish, to her grave: the wife—
O ye who pant, in expectation high,
To welcome home your hero to your arms,
Beware! he will not come: O ye, more blest,
Who fearless press him, joying, to your heart,
Tremble! to-morrow will pull down your joy.
Most awful period! I can hardly hope.
But come, thou virtuous love, and keep my soul
To that high tone a husband's safety wakes;
And may just heaven these trials bless at last!
        [*Exeunt.*

SCENE II.

A large Gothic Hall at Newark. The LORD PRO-
TECTOR, WINCHESTER, CHESTER, *and* EARL
WILLIAM, *assembled at midnight, previous to the
battle of Lincoln ; attendants bearing torches,
and the back ground heightened by the Barons'
banners, and the spears of the Guards.*

Win. Yes, manly sufferers in the cause of truth,
With pious fortitude await the dawn,
And unto heaven to-morrow's battle trust.
　　Prot. Lords, on to-morrow England's fate de-
　　　　pends.
The siege of Lincoln castle must we raise,
And from possession of the city drive
Yon foe, or here at once the contest yield.
Then think, great spirits, free-born Britons, think
On this terrific crisis, and, inspired
With dauntless energy in such a cause,
Go forth to battle, and the day is ours.
　　Will. I burn, I pant to hail the approaching
　　　　dawn.
　　Win. Though France, with myriads upon myriads,
　　　　come,
And in her strength rejoicing, count us nought,
Yet may her widely scattered powers be turned,
If thus, superior to all fear of death,
And conscious of the smile of heaven, we strike
With one concentred force.
　　Prot. But should we fail,
And mad rebellion triumph, round our prince
We'll throw our swords, and sell king Henry's life
For nothing cheaper than our heart's last drop.

Ches. On terms so glorious we're content to die.
Win. Go then, ye warriors, to the fields of death.
Fight the just fight, your country's rights assert,
Defy the foe, for heaven's on your side.
Prot. O sacred love of our own native land,
Come, with thine energy, inspire our souls!
O sacred love of our own native land,
Send us triumphant o'er each tyrant foe!

    L. Sur. (*Without.*) Admit me to the Lord Protec-
        tor, sirs.
    Ches. Pause; for a female voice breaks on mine
        ear.
    L. Sur. (*Without.*) The Lady Surrey seeks her
        father, Pembroke.

    Enter LADY SURREY *with her Son.*

    Prot. My child, Matilda!—whence this wild de-
        mean?
Why hast thou left thy castle? wherefore, thus,
With my young grandson, at this hour of night,
Seek'st thou——
    L. Sur. O sir, I have a tale of woe—
I am so lost—Thou seest, before thine eyes,
Thy daughter, tumbled from the height of hope,
Of fancied bliss, to—mercy! what? perhaps—
But know, my Surrey in his flight is ta'en,
And now—I know not what hath chanced ere now.
    Prot. Sweet dame, have hope.
After to-morrow's struggle I'll dispatch
An herald with proposals for exchange
Of many noble prisoners of France.
    L. Sur. Send all your French, 'twill not avail. I
        know
They dare not lose my husband. I've no hope,
But to entwine my thread of life with his,
To beg for entrance at his prison-door;

They can't deny me that.   I come to place—
Great Lord ! what am I doomed to bear !
   Will. Matilda,
Alone thou can'st not go.   Disguised, I'll brave
The piercing look suspicion wears, and lead
Thee, sister, spite of death, through this wild land.
   L. Sur. No, by my sufferings, no ! One I have
        lost,
One hero, to my country : She can bear
No second loss in thee.   To battle go,
And victory hang upon thy sword ! I'm fixed.
   Prot. O happy land, whose daughters are so
        fair,
And though fair virtuous, even as my child !
Yet hear, Matilda—
   L. Sur. I'm prepared for all ;
Have weighed events, and cannot now be moved.
All that I ask—there, there's the pang I dread—
All that I ask, is guardianship for him,
Thy best protection for my darling child.
Take him, my father, take him to thy breast ;
Keep him with tenderness as I was kept ;
Let him be such as Surrey's heir should be.
   Prot. Boy, thou'rt mine own.
   Will. To me, even as my son.
   Boy. Yet I would follow my poor mother's steps.
   L. Sur. My child !—O sir !—best brother !—I'll
        away,
Or these wild ecstacies will shake my mind.
God bless thee, boy.   Remember all my words :
I shall return to comfort thee again.
O ! be it so ! teach, sir—I know thou wilt—
Farewell.   Almighty Being, to thy care
Take him ! Farewell, my angel—once—farewell !
                              [*Exit.*
   Prot. Poor dame ! but this sad trial shall not last.

Excuse me, friends, that private griefs have touched
My public state.   But now, my Lords, to arms !
  Ches. And let us bind ourselves by solemn vows,
Ne'er to return, unless with conquering swords.
  Prot. Yes, thus we swear to yield our lives, in
        pledge,
To save our king, our altars, and our laws !
                      [*Flourish—Exeunt.*

ACT THE FOURTH.

SCENE I.

Within the city of Lincoln, after the battle.
Flourish.

Enter the LORD PROTECTOR, WINCHESTER, *and*
EARL WILLIAM, *with soldiers.*

Prot. This is indeed a triumph, this the day,
That gives to freedom promise of success.
  Win. 'Tis strange, the French, with all their nu-
          merous band,
Should yield the city such an easy prey!
  Will. The expiring efforts of a free-born race
Prove more tremendous than yon myriad's threats.
  Prot. Lincoln thus gained, without expense of
          blood,
We may—but where's Earl Chester?
  Will. In the fight,
I saw him, with a troop of cross-bow men,
Forth sally from the castle, where he gained
Admission from our friends, and chase the foe.
  Win. Heaven grant him safe!   [*Shouts.*
  Prot. That shout of victory—
  Will. Yes, see the antient hero comes himself!

Enter CHESTER *hastily.*

Ches. Joy, joy ! my glorious co-mates ! war's the
       word
We've driven the slaves—they darted down the
       hill—
They're scouring o'er the plain, like frighted hares,
E'en trembling at the wind that blows around.
    Prot. Thus, my brave Chester, hast thou proved
       thy words.
    Ches. Armies of prisoners have we ta'en to-day,
But shed no brethren's blood.   O ! 'twould have
       moved
Your hearts, my Lords, to've seen our fiery troops,
When, in the rebels, they beheld their friends,
And gazed upon their kindred's faces, stop,
In pride of victory and the rage of war,
And, touched by pity, weep upon their necks.
    Prot. My glorious countrymen ! thus Britons
       fight,
Disdaining thus the exterminating sword ;
Justice alone can animate their arms.
    Ches. They turned their vengeance solely on the
       foe,
Who, scattered o'er our fields, no quarter find ;
For there the peasantry, with cause enraged
At all their late exactions, take revenge.
    Prot. Alas ! unhappy island ! I could weep
To think o'er all the miseries thou hast borne :
But 'tis my duty now to change the scene.
Dispatch our heralds through the country round,
Proclaiming general pardon to all ranks ;
And that King Henry conquers but for peace,
And to deliver England from its yoke.

Enter a Messenger abruptly.

Whence in such haste ?

Mes. All, all, my Lord, is lost!
A mighty fleet from France was off the coast,
With troops unnumbered, by the Lady Blanch,
Sent to the prince, her husband.   Long ere now
They will have spread wide o'er the Kentish lands,
Though they must grapple with a well nerved race:
But all is vain, so numerous is the fleet!
            [*The* PROTECTOR *turns mournfully aside.*
Win. Alas! alas! when will our troubles cease?
Prot. Softly, but have not the Cinque Ports their
            fleet
In readiness to meet the foe?
    Mes. Their force
Is small—
    Prot. Small let it be; I will not yet
Despair.
    Win. Had the troops landed?
    Mes. No, my Lord,
But nothing could oppose—
    Win. Heaven could oppose!
We're in the hands of one who will not leave
The just.
    Prot. No measure's left to save our cause,
But to attack the tyrant ere this force
(Should it effect a landing on our coast),
Can march to London; for their powers, if joined,
Might baffle all the strength we've just acquired.
To London then, my Lords, to London all:
There to obtain our freedom or our graves.
                    [*Flourish—Exeunt.*

At London.   A Court-yard of the Tower.

Enter the FRENCH PRINCE *and* BEAUMONT, *with attendants.*

Beau. This puissant fleet and army, come from France,
Will soon confirm my prince's empire here.
    Fr. Pr. By holy Denis ! these fair proofs of love,
From Blanch, our royal consort, touch our heart.
We purpose to command her presence soon
In our new kingdom, to receive and share
This well-won crown ; methinks 'tis fairly ours.
    Beau. Ere this I trust all England owns your sway.
Each minute with important news must teem,
Telling how Lincoln falls as London fell.
    Fr. Pr. An angel bearing tidings of great joy—
Look where Nevers approaches !

Enter NEVERS.

Cousin, well ?
    Nev. Dread sire !
    Fr. Pr. On with thy tale, we are prepared
For all.
    Nev. Then let my tongue forego the task
Of telling that which pains to think hath been.
    Fr. Pr. What !—can it be !—Are ye no victors ?
        —speak.
    Nev. Alas ! alas !
    Fr. Pr. Ha ! coward, cease.

Nev. Believe,
My liege, we fought—
  Fr. Pr. Like miscreants as ye are.
Had we been there, ye had not dared to fly.
  Nev. Fitzwalter's rashness 'twas that broke the
    ranks ;
Though Lincoln for his earldom fought, he fled ;
The English, sire, they lost the day to France.

   Enter LINCOLN *and* FITZWALTER.

  Lin. O Prince, your army's ruined !
  Fr. Pr. Traitor, no ;
'Tis false.
  Lin. Sir !
  Fr. Pr. Or, suppose our army's lost ;
Who were the cowards that betrayed it ?
  Fitz. Who?
Ask your Nevers, my Lord ; we know them not.
  Fr. Pr. Nay, 'twas your treachery damped our
    Gallic fire.
  Lin. So far from treacherous, lo ! my troops are
    here,
Firm in the cause, and panting to retrieve
Their laurels lately lost.
  Fr. Pr. Away, away,
We scorn your artifice. Ye love the foe.
Ye're English still.
  Fitz. And such will ever be.
For came you not, my Lord, as England's King,
To rule o'er English ? Where then's the reproach ?
But, that I love the foe—you know full well
I hate young Henry from my very heart,
And while he sends one soldier to the field
Fitzwalter will confront him until death.
  Fr. Pr. Go, go, and vent thy spleen unto the
    winds.
Your cause we here forsake, your aid despise :

For know, false men, officious rebels, know,
That France herself is coming to these shores,
To guard that crown wherewith ye've decked our
    brows.
  Lin. Gracious heaven! do we live?
  Beau. Now, on your coast,
Hundreds of vessels, loaded with fresh troops,
Have safely fixed their prows.
  Nev. Most joyful news!
  Fr. Pr. Another army soon will follow this;
That by a third be strengthened. till this isle
Shall boast no lords but those of Gallic blood.
  Fitz. Now, by St Edward!—Down, my swelling
    heart!
It is not yet the time. (*To himself.*)
  Lin. Yet, prince, reflect—
  Fitz. (*Aside to* Lin.) Cease, Lincoln, cease. The
    die's for ever cast,
And but one way remains.
  Fr. Pr. Ye droop, proud Lords!
But, O beware! for ye are in our power.
  Lin. Sir, for a while, permit us to consult
With our confederates.
  Fr. Pr. Yet remember well,
Suspicion's eye is fixed on all your deeds.
  Fitz. Sir, we shall act as best becomes our state.
    [*Exeunt* Fitz. *and* Lin.
  Fr. Pr. We hate this stubborn race. Each man
    we meet
Seems, from the scowl that knits his angry brows,
To hide revenge and murderous thoughts within.
Give orders, Beaumont, that the Earl of Essex,
And that same subtle Surrey, meet their fate;
They, and the other slaves in Baynard's castle,
We cannot spare them to the foe.—Nevers!
  Nev. My liege!

Fr. Pr. Forget our hastiness.   We now
Perceive thou wert betrayed.

Nev. My gracious lord!

Fr. Pr. Say, know'st thou whither Pembroke
            bends his course?

Nev. A knight o'ertook us, sire, upon the road,
Who said the English were upon their march
To London.

Fr. Pr. Pembroke dare march to London?
Our troops not yet arrived.—We could have wished,
And yet we want them not.   Brave cousins, rouse!
Let us arrange our well-appointed powers,
That those adventurers may rue the day
Whereon they brave the matchless force of France!
                                    [*Exeunt.*

SCENE III.

Dungeon within Baynard's Castle.   Surrey *discovered on a Bench, his Armour lying by him, and
a Lamp burning.*

Sur. Yes, this proud heart at last must be sub-
            dued.
I'm now the wretch whose state I most abhorred.
O! fiends of France, ye've found the only means
To conquer Surrey; for I've fought from morn
Till sun-set, smarting o'er with wounds, wherein]
The wintry wind hath frozen up the blood,
E'en unto agony; and I have marched,
Beneath the noon-tide summer sun, parched, faint,
And with my burning armour scalded o'er,
I've borne each pain to which a soldier's doomed,
And never sent forth one painful groan:

But thus ingloriously, for ever, thus—
Despair, despair ! the future's darker still.
                              [*Takes up his sword.*
The ruffians treat me with contempt, and leave
My arms ; for what ? there's eloquence in this.

   L. Sur. (*At a distance*) Surrey !

   Sur. (*Not attending to the voice.*) My own, adored
           Matilda ! pshaw ! away !
                              [*Throws down the sword.*
Still fond remembrance, 'midst my wildest starts,
Calls thee to soothe the tempest of my soul.
I live not for myself.—For thee I'll bear
What, had I no such angel for my guide,
Might make my horrors—no, no—I must not
Brood thus o'er my cares.

   L. Sur. (*Nearer.*) Surrey !

   Sur. (*Starting.*) Ha ! what ! (*Pauses.*)
These noisome vapours will affect my brain.
O cruel fancy, wherefore thus torment,
Waking so often, on my ravished ear,
The music of her voice, too soon to die
In air, and leave me sickening at the cheat ?

   LADY SURREY *appears at the top of the stage.*
Alas ! I must root feeling from my heart.

   L. Sur. (*Flying to* SURREY.) He's there, he's
           there ! indeed, himself !

   Sur. My wife !

   L. Sur. I have him, hold him, clasp him to my
           heart.

   Sur. Madness of ecstacy ! delirium too
Delicious e'er to cease ! 'tis truth itself !

   L. Sur. They fain would have persuaded me to
           stay,
(*Rapidly.*) And let my dearer life droop all alone.
They all have failed.—I heeded not my friends ;
The monsters too, I've triumphed over thus,

For I have got thee, Surrey, tricked them all,
Thus, thus; ha! ha! ha! oh! oh!
                    [*Bursts into an agony of tears.*
   Sur. Angel mine!
In pity, sink not with thy feelings thus.
   L. Sur. No, no—my spirits have been too much
        tried,
And this last ecstacy—ah me! my heart
Is lighter now.   My Surrey!
   Sur. Is she here?
Matchless Matilda! art thou here indeed?
Yes, it is she; my heart, in feverish fits,
Knocks at my breast, and tells it is no dream—
And our sweet infant, is he well? and where?
   L. Sur. Well, with his grandsire Pembroke.
   Sur. Bless him, bless
The cherub! by my troth, dear wife, mine eye
Runs o'er to think on him.
   L. Sur. Sweet, kindly drops!
   Sur. And thou, blest dame, how did'st thou reach
        these walls?
How brave the journey?   How evade the foe?
   L. Sur. Woman, aroused by pure and virtuous
        love,
Defies all Nature's obstacles combined:
Her soul, exalted even above itself,
Over hill, and precipice, and rocky glen,
Through roaring torrents, and through mountain
        storms;
Yea, all the perils of the ocean's self;
Swift as the winds she'll wing her fearless flight,
Snatch, amidst death, her great inspiring prize;
Then, struck with what she's past, her courage lose,
Her dangers swell, and sinking on herself,
Be all the timid female o'er again.
Thus have I set defiance to my state;
Thus, as a pilgrim through the land—enough:

I have my Surrey.—But this dreary cell!

                   [Looking round.

O! O! how different when we parted last!

  Sur. Forget the past, we'll ne'er part again.

  L. Sur. O never, never.   Said I never? ha!

Where doth my frenzy hurry me? for now,

Even now, they come to tear me from thee.

Hark! hark!

  Sur. What hardy wretch will dare the deed?

I clasp thee now for ever in my arms,

And, like the drowning seaman with his plank,

Will ne'er relinquish thee, e'en as I perish.

  L. Sur. Alas! we must be parted once again:

I've bribed a tender-hearted guard for this,

This little moment of felicity;

For I have stolen hither, not to fix,

But to destroy captivity.   O hear!

  Sur. I stand, all hope and all amazement.   Speak.

  L. Sur. When to her fate bowed England in de-

        spair,

Despairing too, I meant to share thy griefs

Within these walls, all places then the same.

But since old Pembroke, like th' immortal sun,

Though aged, not less powerful, before

Him drives the storm of war, to wreck the French

Who thus up-blew it on our ravaged shores;

Since expectation, elevated, stands

Trembling to see, and calls throughout the realm

All men, to see those French adown our cliffs

Pushed headlong—

  Sur. Madness! I no more can bear

This abject state.   Thy words have driven the

        blood,

That with despair lay curdled at my heart,

To beat again in every pulse to war.

What! when the youth of England, all on fire,

Snatch deathless glory on th' embattled field,

For Freedom conquer, or in Freedom die;
Must I here like a captive tiger rage,
And fall at last by some base ruffian's hand?
By the great God of battles!—

   L. Sur. Thou shalt not.
Loose is this pilgrim's robe o'er all my dress.
Take it, my staff, scrip; wrap thine armour o'er,
And fly.   Ere such mistake can well be known,
Thou wilt have gained the wood that skirts the
               Thames,
Where, with thy favourite courser, waits a squire.
And as for me—

   Sur. Virtue incomparable!

   L. Sur. Here will I rest in silence all the night;
And when the guards discover—

   Sur. Nay, no more.
Thou'rt talking to a rock.   I needed not
This effort to adore thee.   Yet reflect,
My country can command a million souls,
Great and heroic, to defend her rights:
But thou, O! thou can'st boast one, only one;
Should he desert thee in this fearful place,
Who will protect, and soothe, and comfort thee?

   L. Sur. If but for me thou doubt'st, O! doubt no
       more.

    [*A noise and clashing of arms heard, the* LADY
    flies to SURREY.
My husband!—

   Sur. Fear not, there's no harm to thee.

   L. Sur. Me, me! O! would to heaven they meant
      but me!

    [*Noise louder.* SURREY *and the* LADY *pause.*
  (*Voice without.*) Ha! strugglest thou? thus,
      Essex, thus—

   Essex. (*Without.*) Off, slaves,
Not so—

   (*Voice without.*) Down, down—

[*A deep silence.* SURREY *stands in an attitude
of listening, and* LADY SURREY *in that of
agonizing suspense, till a heavy groan, bursting from* ESSEX *as he expires, is heard.*

L. Sur. (*Wildly.*) O save him, save him, save my
  Surrey!

Sur. Silence! O silence! There is no one here.

L. Sur. I heard their weapons ring. I heard the
  cry

Of death.—They shall not kill him.—Help! O help!

 Sur. This clamorous grief confounds—but let
  them come;

They'd better combat, with a single spear,

The wildest ramping lioness of the woods,

Robbed of her whelps, and howling for revenge,

Than face me now.

 L. Sur. Hark! but hark! they come—there!—

Enter the FRENCH GUARD.

[LADY SURREY *snatches up* SURREY'S *sword
(who seizes his battle-axe), and throws herself before him.*

L. Sur. Monsters of hell! here, strike him through
  this heart.

Fr. Gu. Madam, these cries endanger—

L. Sur. Do they not

Come to murder Surrey?

 Fr. Gu. No, no.

 L. Sur. Swear, swear;

Deceive me not, or—

 Fr. Gu. We have now in charge

To watch Earl Surrey's life: the orders that

Gave death to others brought reprieve for him.

But, madam, there are scenes of blood without

For thee unfit.—Fly, fly, while yet thou can'st.

 L. Sur. Fly!—O! whither?—to despair and
  madness?

Sur. Now, now, Matilda, be thyself indeed.
O ! if thou lov'st me—
   L. Sur. Mercy, mercy, heaven !
Sir, sir, canst thou behold us thus, and not
Be moved ?   [*To the* GUARD.
   Fr. Gu. My heart is touched, yet what can I—
   Sur. What ? Thou hast often, in the fields of war,
Stood face to face with death but to discharge
Thy duty. If by pity now thou'rt touched,
Thou'lt surely hazard that, in such a cause,
Which to blind chance—
   Fr. Gu. Show me but how to save—
   Sur. And thou wilt risk thy life ?
   Fr. Gu. If thou can'st prove
Success will likely—
   Sur. Do what now thou say'st,
And I will make the hazard greatly worth :
Thou shalt have lands within my earldom—wealth—
Be taken to my heart—
   L. Sur. These, these in earnest now.
                  [*Giving jewels.*
   Fr. Gu. Too generous English, ye have even my
        life.
   Sur. Then thou must aid my flight this very hour.
I know that thou the access can'st command
To the great western window : thence we may
With safety drop, and from the wall below
'Tis easy to escape.
   Fr. Gu. May death be mine
If I should fail !
   Sur. Come, come, cheer up, my love ;
Till now, I never saw one ray of hope.
Haste, haste.
   L. Sur. Where, where ? I will not leave thee
        now.
   Fr. Gu. Madam, in truth thou must, or we may
        all

Be lost : for if another guard should come
Suspicion would arise—thou must depart :
Say (if thou art stopped), thou cam'st from Hubert
        d'Oisle.
The sign is " Blanch," the countersign " Castile."
Thou may'st in safety pass.

   L. Sur. My Surrey, what?

   Sur. Courage, my heroine, be as thou hast been.
Soon as the bell beats one, within the wood
Expect me.   Nay, no sorrow now—thou must—

   L. Sur. Pardon a few unmeaning drops, that
        thoughts
Which well I cannot justify force from me.
We shall at morning meet.

   Sur. No more farewells.

   L. Sur. No, we shall meet so soon.

     [LADY SURREY *goes to the door, and after ga-*
       zing upon SURREY *returns.*
My only hope !
O if we never meet again ! I'll not,
I cannot leave thee thus.

   Sur. Then we will die
Together.

   L. Sur. Die ? no, no.   Forgive my fears.
'Twas a last effort.   I'm myself again.
I go, I go.   [*Exit with the* GUARD. *Scene closes.*

ACT THE FIFTH.

SCENE I.

The wood near Baynard's Castle.   A Storm.

Enter LADY SURREY *slowly.*

L. Sur. All's silent here ! I surely heard a cry,
Or fancy acts too fearfully upon me.
'Tis strange he doth not come.   'Tis past the time.
Fatal walls ! your bloody scenes still haunt me !
Surrey should be here ere this.   They murdered
Essex—hark ! murder, when once at work—ha !
        [*The bell beats two.*
Soon as the bell beats " one," he said—it beateth
   two.
The night is hideous ; but the night to him
I fear is not ; and yet I cannot bear
This dire suspense, but to the castle walls—
          [*Pauses.*
A footstep ! O, how dismally it sounds !
I dread—

Enter the FRENCH GUARD.

Fr. Gu. The Lady Surrey!

L. Sur. O! 'tis he!

But where's my Surrey? Speak. Where is my
        Lord?

Fr. Gu. Think, madam, think, the proof of faith
        I've given—

L. Sur. But, my chief thought—what? first; all,
        all of him.

Fr. Gu. Earl Surrey, dame—

L. Sur. On, on; this cruel pause—

I have a wild and wandering fancy—on.

Fr. Gu. He made me first descend the rope—

                         [*Hesitating.*

L. Sur. And he,

He never will descend. I see thy look,

I read it there, all, all the dismal tale.

Fr. Gu. A moment, hear!

L. Sur. On. Soften not the truth,

For I can bear it all, familiar grown

With horrors. Thou hast seen me somewhat moved,

And once I trembled, but to hear of chains;

'Twas folly all; for we must hear—of death.

Then say, how he—

Fr. Gu. In safety reached the outer wall,

When the night-watch perceived our armour blaze,

Gave the alarm—and ere he could descend,

Thy husband was arrested; though the clash

Of swords convinced me that he fought—

L. Sur. Ha! what?

Left him arrested in the act of flight,

And madly struggling with a host of foes?

Ah! ha! there's treachery, treachery, man, I say.

Thou had'st not, coward, left him to their swords,

Wert thou not leagued against the wretched pair.

The slave that once hath been bought o'er by
    gold,
Will make a double bargain, and for gold
Sell back his faith to those from whom 'twas
    bought.
We are betrayed, on every side betrayed.

    Fr. Gu. Unjust return for service above price!
For all my perils!   I repel the charge,
And dare before Earl Pembroke prove my faith.

    L. Sur. Ah! there all my wandering thoughts
    must fix!
Good, faithful soldier, true above thy state,
Forget the wildness of a poor mad wretch.

    Fr. Gu. Madam, I own the privilege of grief;
Yet do I trust thy husband is alive.

    L. Sur. Trust!
Thou can'st not know the feelings of a wife,
Or thou would'st never mock me with such comfort.
Poor, poor Matilda! and is this the end,
This the reward for braving fields of war,
The gloom of prisons, and the storms of heaven,
To hear thy very life's spring now perhaps?—
O! O! I must not lose my thoughts that way;
My brain grows feverish, and my heart grows cold;
Yet not so cold, ye midnight murderers, but
It still can rage, and still may spread its rage,
Till yonder English army catch the flame,
And pour down two-fold vengeance on your heads!
                       [*Exeunt.*

SCENE II.

*The English camp near London.   The PROTECTOR'S
Tent.   Flourish.*

Enter the PROTECTOR, WINCHESTER, *and* CHES-
TER.

Win. Hail, London, hail! thou seat of empire,
    hail!
By heaven's mercy! but it joys my heart,
Once more to see thy distant towers arise.
O! may they soon receive their ancient lords!
    Prot. My hopes are strengthened by our late suc-
        cess,
Good Winchester, my very eyes run o'er,
To think how blest we've left the lands behind.
Dear countrymen! till now I never knew
How much I loved ye.   Go, now taste the joys,
Sprung from old freedom and old settled laws;
Go, as old peace and concord reign again,
Till your own lands, their increase now your own;
And 'neath the shade of your accustomed bowers
Pursue the dance, the festive board frequent,
And tribes in union meet to part no more.
    Ches. Till now, great Pembroke, I considered
        war,
Of war productive; but thy loftier soul
Can bend rough Mars to nurse the plant of peace.
Yet still we've work to do at yonder walls.
The French presume to threaten an attack;
Let us anticipate—

Prot. Pause till we hear
The force and number of our friends within.
When for her whelps the tigress prowls the woods,
She softly treads the brakes, and round the prey
Circles slow in many a wily maze,
Till of her aim secure, she pounces down,
And sweeps the unwary victim to her den.
Thus 'gainst the French our wily snares we'll spread,
Till, sure of victory, we may strike at once,
And save, by policy, expense of blood.

Win. Let mercy aim, though justice bid the blow.

Enter EARL WILLIAM.

Will. O father! O my friends! rejoice, rejoice!

Prot. Wherefore, my son, rejoice?

Will. Our fleet—

Prot. Ha! what?

Will. The British navy triumphs still o'er France.

Prot. Speak, speak, my son! have we dispersed
    her fleet?

Will. I've robbed a panting seaman of his news.
Just as the mighty fleet of France began
To land its troops, our ships poured down amain,
And so annoyed its rear, that for revenge
It stood again to sea to crush our barks,
Which, having gained advantage of the wind,
Bore down upon it, boarded sword in hand,
And, though but half its number, took the whole.

Win. Thus all their army at one blow is crushed!

Prot. These wondrous tidings strike e'en to my
    soul,
And bid me glorify, where glory's due!
Now then, my gallant brothers, now's the time,
While all our pulses thus with victory beat,
Come, let us catch the frenzy of the hour,
And, 'mid the storm that shakes the heavens above,
Pour one more dreadful on the astonished foe,

Teaching them all, by land as well as sea,
England will ne'er a foreign master brook.

Ches. On, on, and fix again on London's towers
Old England's standard!

Enter LADY SURREY (*wildly*).

L. Sur. Ho! to arms, to arms!
What! sluggish Britons, rest ye here in ease,
When through yon city roars the sound of war,
When foes in swarms come thundering to your
     camp,
And e'en the heavens are battling o'er your heads?
Wait ye a woman's voice to warn ye forth?

Prot. Matilda, O my child! Whence comest
     thou thus
Wild and distracted? What hath been thy fate?
Where is thy husband Surrey?

L. Sur. Where's my Surrey?
I know not where he is. I'm almost mad.
Arise, my father, brother mine, arise!
Fly, rush at once upon the savage French,
And as ye fight your country's cause, exclaim,
That Surrey bids the torch of vengeance blaze,
That Surrey can o'ercome captivity.
Fly, by one effort save him while ye can.

Prot. They dare not sacrifice thy Surrey's life.
Our ships have beaten their expected fleet,
Their army's lost. They are almost in our power.

L. Sur. Then Surrey may be saved! My hero
     saved!
Come, come, my brother, I am all on fire.
Pembroke, should father, mother, both be lost,
And sure the dart that pierces Surrey's breast
Will not be far from mine, should death be ours,
My child—Thou know'st, thou know'st—peace,
     peace, fond heart.

Earl William, let thy sword from hence be mine;
I'll lead where Surrey, should the day be ours—

Will. Sweetest sister, calm thy troubled bosom!
Here, for the present, in our camp remain,
And trust thy brother to avenge thy wrongs.

L. Sur. Frenzy o'er-rules my reason. Go, go
      bid
The stormy winds lie hushed upon the hills,
The raging billows smoothen to a calm,
The blazing mountains be convulsed no more;
Bid me to rest in peace, when Surrey—No;
Follow me, brother, I can brave the field!

                    [*Exit,* WILL. *following.*

Prot. In truth, I know not how to blame the deed;
'Tis wildly thought, but wild are these our times.
Come, Lords, let's meet yon hasty foe half way.
Brave prelate Winchester and Chester bold,
Ride ye through either wing of right and left,
While I exhort the centre of our host.
Tell them, this day, to finish their great work,
To drive the French from this their last retreat,
And let imperial London own her king!

                    [*Flourish.   Exeunt.*

SCENE III.

The Field of Battle.   Alarum.

Enter the FRENCH PRINCE, NEVERS, *and*
              BEAUMONT.

Fr. Pr. My succours all cut off; my fleet de-
      stroyed!

Beau. Hear me, my liege.   My fears thus veri-
        fied—

Fr. Pr. What though they are, we cannot fly
        the field.

Beau. O sir, defection spreads on every side;
The restless Londoners are up in arms,
They've stormed the castles and the prisons round,
And poured at once the captive rabble forth:
E'en now the insurgents press upon our rear.

Fr. Pr. Perdition on the accursed race! Fly, fly,
Nevers, and turn on them thy chosen corps.

                    [*Exit* NEVERS.

Beau. See, see! our ranks give way! O prince,
        retire !

Fr. Pr. Ho, there !—fly not, ye cowards. Beau-
        mont, haste,
Drive the right wing upon the foe again.

             [*Alarum.   Exeunt.*

SCENE IV.

*Another part of the field of battle.   English and
French troops cross the Stage engaging. Alarum.*

Enter SURREY.

Sur. Oppose my passage! Tell the trembling
        lambs
To stop the indignant lion with their flocks.
Beat down their ranks, brave Londoners.

[EARL WILLIAM *pursues* BEAUMONT *across the Stage*, LADY SURREY *following*.

L. Sur. Victory!

[*Seeing* SURREY, *she flies to him.*

My husband!

Sur. Is it truth? how, wherefore thus,
My blest Matilda, genius of my days?

L. Sur. He lives, he lives!

Sur. My precious, best reward!   [*Alarum.*

L. Sur. But, but—O! O!   [*She sinks.*

Sur. Look up; indeed, all's well.
Softly, Matilda; Surrey's here himself.
Comfort, my own—there, there—

L. Sur. O! art thou saved
From prisons, murders, and from battle saved?

Sur. Awakened to a sense of all their wrongs,
Uprose at once upon their foreign lords
The gallant Londoners; their forces crushed,
Threw open all our prison-gates again,
And called me forth exulting to the field,
Thus to partake the glories of this day,
And thus to win my all in winning thee.

L. Sur. Yet, yet, a thousand fears distract my
mind.
This uproar all abroad—

Sur. O! let us hence.
We soon can gain the English camp.   [*Flourish.*
Joy! joy!
Behold, the royal standard streams around!

Prot. (*Without.*) Let mercy flow to all. Spare,
spare the foe;
And Briton, Briton meet in bands of love.

L. Sur. 'Tis he!

Enter the PROTECTOR, *attended.*

My father and my husband, both,
Both at my breast!   This agony's too keen.

   Prot. My child, my child!   My long lost, glori-
      ous son!

I thank thee, heaven!   It is now complete.
My heart springs upward with unusual warmth,
And age seems running half-way back to youth.

   Sur. My generous sire, be all forgotten thus.

   Prot. Come on, my second hero—Surrey, come.

   Sur. For England ever!

   L. Sur. Surrey, what! again?

Yet, go.   Thou art thy country's, and not mine.

   Sur. Peerless Matilda; but a little while,
And then—

   Prot. To victory—London is our own,
Where we shall meet our countrymen in peace ;
For England's charter Henry shall renew :
And may the troubles that its breach hath caused,
Endear that sacred bulwark of our rights,
To future subjects as to future kings!

               [*Shouts, and flourish of trumpets.*

   Prot. The tyrant yields! my country's free at last!

Flourish.   Enter the FRENCH PRINCE *with his train,
   conducted by* EARL WILLIAM *and the English
   Lords.*

   Will. My Lord Protector, the French Prince sub-
      mits,

Acknowledging young Henry England's king.

   Fr. Pr. Abandoned thus by all our followers,
We bend perforce beneath the fate of war ;
Yet do we trust Earl Pembroke's clemency
Will grant all parties honourable terms,
And let us quit this proud and untamed isle,

seek in safety our paternal realms.

Prot. Go, prince of France; for those who truly
    free
Will ne'er be conquered, can as conquerors spare.
Go then in safety to your own domains,
And tell your countrymen these solemn truths,
That English treachery sacrificed our rights,
But English virtue won them back by force;
Tell them, by your example greatly warned,
Ne'er to assail our sacred isle again,
But know that independence, through all times,
Alike will baffle foreign force or fraud,
And here, in peerless state, for ever reign!

              [*The* PROT. *comes forward.*

O native land! from hence for ever rest
In freedom, union, thus supremely blest!
And should thy genius, Britain, know a time,
When civil Discord flies from clime to clime;
When with the shock each neighb'ring empire
    groans,
And Ruin, menacing an hundred thrones,
Shakes Europe's centre with his giant form—
Calm and collected shalt thou face the storm;
Within thy sea-girt rock securely shrined,
Shalt stand the guardian of oppressed mankind.
Blest in a prince, whose virtue shall deserve,
Whose spirit his important trust preserve,
Shall still thy splendour, in those darksome days,
Break on the world with undiminished blaze,
Survive the fall of each surrounding state,
Nor cease till all creation yield to fate!

        [*The trumpets sound, and the troops show.*

                END OF VOLUME EIGHTH.